A DICTIONARY
OF
THE CLASSICAL NEWARI

A DICTIONARY
OF
THE CLASSICAL NEWARI

HANS JORGENSEN

GYAN

Published by

Gyan Publishing House
5, Ansari Road
Daryaganj, New Delhi-110002
Phone: 011-47034999, 9811692060
E-mail: books@gyanbooks.com

Distribution Network
gyanbooks.com
India, USA, Canada, UK, Australia, France

ISBN : 978-81-212-4285-1 (PB)
First Published, Nordborg, 1935

2nd Impression 2020

Printed at: Gyan Press, Delhi.

A Dictionary of The Classical Newari
Author: Hans Jorgensen

INTRODUCTION

The dictionary I here submit to the public, is a considerable enlargement and improvement of my »Versuch eines Wörterbuches der Nevārī-Sprache« (Wb.).[1] A vast amount of materials has become available and I have embodied in the dictionary a good deal of the very numerous Tatsamas from the MSS. I have endeavoured to define and determine more exactly the meaning of the words, and to give a more detailed description of it. In this way, though fully aware of the insufficiencies of my work, I may hope to have offered an effective help to any one wishing to turn to account the numerous Newārī translations and commentaries of Sanskrit works, or to utilize the Newārī language for the study of Tibeto-Burmese comparative philology.

The language I call classical Newārī, is the language of the MSS. The modern language mainly known from the works of Hodgson, and of which traces are to be found in the MSS, I have taken into consideration only to a very limited extent. The main characteristics of it are considerable phonetic changes in the final consonants, e. g. *mala* < *malak*, *say* < *sas*, *hau* < *hal*.[2]

[1] Acta Orientalia vol. VI (1927), pp. 26—92.

[2] For further information of the Newārs, their language and literature, I refer the reader to Vi (see below p. 6), introduction p. 1 f., and to ZDMG 75, p. 213, and to the references given in these places.

The sources of the dictionary are as follows.

A. Original manuscripts, arranged in chronological order.

H[1] = Hi Wb.; the date is 481 = AD 1360.

V[1] = Add. 1619 Cambridge University Library; 140 foll in Naipālī characters, dated 795 = AD 1674: Vetālapañcaviṃśatikā in Newārī. The contents correspond closely to those of V[2], but the style is more abrupt.

This MS shows some peculiarities of spelling, all of which have not been noted in the dictionary: instead of *a* before nasals we mostly find *aṃ* or *ā*, e. g. *kaṃnaṃ* or *kānaṃ* for *kanaṃ* "he told"; *vo* is often written for *va*, and *ā* for *a* at the end of words, e. g. *salā* "horse"

C[1] = Cā Wb.; dated 811 = AD 1690.

N = Or. 8 British Museum; 53 foll. in Naipālī characters, dated 820 = AD 1699. The title is given in the colophon as Caurapratikheda, but in reality it is the Nepāl-recension of the Nāradasmṛti[1] in Sanskrit with a Newārī commentary. For the interpretation of this rather difficult text Jolly's edition and translation of the Nāradasmṛti[2] has been a most valuable aid to me.

Vd = Add. 1595 Cambr. Un. L., 60 foll.[3] in Naipālī characters, dated 832 = AD 1711: Vaidyāṅga, containing short prescriptions for the cure of various diseases; Newārī, but with a few verses in Sanskrit. To my regret I have not by far been able to overcome all the difficulties of this MS.

H[2] = Or. 4 Br. M., 118 foll. in Naipālī characters, dated 906 = AD 1785; Hitopadeśa, in the beginning Sanskrit and Newārī, from fol. 32 Newārī only, with a few Sanskrit verses

[1] s. SBE xxxiii, p. xix.

[2] Bibliotheca Indica, New Series No. 542 and SBE vol, xxxiii.

[3] Foll. 17, 20, 31, 53 are wanting.

interspersed. Two successive folios are marked 84, I denote them 84 and 84_2.

V² = Ve Wb., dated 921 = AD 1800.

Md = Or. 9 Br. M., 83 foll. in Naipālī characters, dated 951 = AD 1830: Madanavinoda in Sanskrit and Newārī, a work of the same kind as the Lokaprakāśa of Kṣemendra, as may be concluded from the description of the latter work by Winternitz.[1]

C² = Add. 1346 Cambr. Un. L., 76 foll. in Nāgarī characters, dated 965 = AD 1844: Cāṇakyasārasaṃgraha in Sanskrit and Newārī, corresponding closely to C¹.

Bh = Or. 71 Br. M., 166 foll. in Naipālī characters, dated 971 = AD 1850, but apparently much older: Bhāgavatapurāṇa in Newārī. I have used very copious extracts from it. After fol. 15 the pagination starts afresh from 1. The first foll. 1—15 I denote *1—*15.

Ns = Add. 1323 Cambr. Un. L., 40 foll. in Naipālī characters, dated 979 = 1858: Nāmasaṃgīti, a poem in Sanskrit and Newārī, containing a praise of Buddha. From this MS I have taken but a few words and expressions.

The following MSS are not dated.

H³ = Add. 1408, Cambr. Un. L., 62 foll. in Nāgarī characters: Hitopadeśa in Newārī, obviously younger than H² from which it differs a good deal.

B = Or. 10 Br. M., 70 foll. in Nāgarī characters: Batīsaputrikākathā in Newārī, being as far as I am aware a hitherto unknown recension of the Siṃhāsanadvātriṃśatikā.

Ś = Or. 11 Br. M., containing foll. 132—225 of a Newārī recension of the Śukasaptati in Naipālī characters. I have used foll. 142ᵇ.6—170ᵇ.1, giving the stories 47—50.

[1] Indische Literaturgeschichte III, p. 417.

P = Add. 1276 Cambr. Un. L., 65 foll. in Naipālī characters: Pāpaparimocana, being a ritualistic text in Sanskrit with a Newārī commentary. A modern and badly written MS, presenting great difficulties to the understanding.

Pg = Pā Wb.

M = Ma Wb.

B. Other sources.

AH = Hodgson papers vol. 33, India Office Library, containing a Sanskrit-Newārī vocabulary, unorthographically written in Latin characters by a native (Khardar Jit Mohan), being a copious extract from the Amarakośa.

HP 24 = Hodgson papers vol. 24, foll. 99—107, containing a description of Nepal in Sanskrit, Parbatiyā and Newārī.

HP 82 = Hodgson papers vol. 82, containing a Sanskrit, Parbatiyā, and Newārī grammar in Nāgarī characters, with pencil notes in Latin characters (by Hodgson?).

CW = CW Wb.

Wr = Daniel Wright, A History of Nepal, Cambridge 1877, from which a few words have been taken.

Vi = my edition of the Vicitrakarṇikāvadānoddhṛta[1], published with the aid and at the expense of the Royal Asiatic Society, for which I feel impelled in this place to express my most sincere, though I am sorry to say belated, thanks.

From these sources I have — with the said restrictions — taken all pure Newārī words and all loan-words from Indo-Aryan languages, the meaning of which I have been able to ascertain with a satisfactory degree of certainty. On the other hand I have deemed it impossible and un-

[1] Oriental Translation Fund, New Series, vol. xxxi. London 1931.

necessary to pay regard to the whole bulk of Tatsamas, as undoubtedly a good deal of them have been taken over *adhoc* by the translator from the Sanskrit original, especially in religious texts. I have, therefore, principally confined myself to those which from the frequency of their use, esp. in popular tales, may be considered as current in the language; and to all that show peculiarities of form or meaning. But owing to the difficulties of decision in each case it has become unavoidable that my choice of Tatsamas must to a certain extent seem arbitrary.

I have endeavoured to explain all loan-words, as far as possible[1], but have abstained from too hazardous guessing. With our present knowledge it seems impossible to find the exact sources of the loan-words from Indo-Aryan languages. At the outset it would appear most likely that a good deal of them have sprung from that form of Old-Maithilī which before the conquest was used in Nepal[2], but unfortunately this language is unknown. For the present we must resort to modern Maithilī[3] and to Hindī, where especially the forms from Eastern-Hindī and allied dialects, given by Fallon in his Hindustānī dictionary, correspond rather closely to the forms we find in Newārī. Some Arabic and Persian words have found their way into Nepal by means of the said languages. From Parbatiyā we cannot expect to find loan-words till after the conquest, and as most of the works found in the MSS, at all events as regards their origin, date from earlier times, the amount of loan-words from this source is, after all, perhaps not so very great. But, un-

[1] Some words, as *paṃdhān, parihāj* are undoubtedly loan-words, but I have not been able to trace their origin.

[2] Lingu. Survey of India III, 1, p. 181.

[3] Grierson, An Introduction to the Maithilī language of North Bihār Calcutta 1882.

fortunately, I obtained access to this language too late to benefit substantially by it.[1] As for other Indo-Aryan languages, I refer the reader to Wb. p. 28.

In some cases it may seem doubtful whether a word is a loan-word or not. I take e. g. the word *ju* which may be P. *jiu*, but which can be pure Newārī, cf. Tibetan *jo-ba* "lord, master" or *rgyu-ba* "superior quality". Words of that kind I have not treated as loan-words.

I have quite abstained from giving references to the cognate languages, because in the present state of Tibeto-Burmese comparative philology the amount of quite reliable etymologies would prove comparatively small; but I have in not a few cases referred to etymological connexions between different Newārī words.

All etymological references have been placed between square brackets. Form and meaning of the original word have been given only where they differ from tbose used in Newārī; sometimes dashes indicate that I have quoted only a choice of meanings (cf. *daṇḍ*). In Tatsamas the dropping of the final *a* has been ignored, so that *darśan* [S.] means: *darśan* = Sanskrit *darśana*. Sometimes the change from *v* to *b* has been treated in the same way.

The orthography is chiefly the same as I have used in my former works on Newārī.[2] I make no difference between *l* and *r*, as these letters are used indiscriminately in all MSS except before and after consonants in Tatsamas, where we always find *r*.[3] In the main I prefer *l* in pure Newārī words and in loan-words from Indo-Aryan languages,

[1] A few P. words I have picked up from various sources.

[2] ZDMG 75, p. 215; Wb. p. 27, and Vi p. 7.

[3] This *r* seems not to have been pronounced, since it is often omitted, and not seldom a parasitical *r* is found in such places, which I have always ignored (e. g. *bṛrthā*, *prarkhār*, *ryas*).

but where a form with *l* is not found in the MSS, I retain *r*. In the same way I prefer *i*, *u* to *ī*, *ū*, and therefore a word which is found in the MSS as *thil*, *thīl*, *thir*, *thīr*, is spelt *thil* in the dictionary. Where we find *d*, *ḍ* besides *l*, *r*, I give two forms, one with *l* and one with *ḍ* (e. g. *sala*, *saḍa* "horse"). Otherwise I always in Newārī words replace cerebrals by dentals, *ś* by *s*, and *ṣ* by *kh*, and mostly *kṣ* by *khy*. The latter, however, sometimes stands for *ch*. The syllable *li* is in certain words mostly spelt *ḷ*, e. g. *ḷ* "foot" in contradistinction to *li* "back". This peculiarity I have not retained, but have noted it. As for *ĕ* and *wo* I refer to Wb. p. 28. For *wō* I now write *wā*, following the modern notes; cf. Hodgson *wá* »rice«.[1] The letter I formerly transliterated as *ō*[2], and which sometimes is used instead of *vā* in the beginning of words, should rather be read *oā* i. e. *wā*. Final *-a* has always been omitted, except in a few cases where modern notes or V[1] prove it to be pronounced, e. g. *sala*, which in V[1] is generally spelt *salā*. Final *-i* seems to be of two kinds. Some words always have *i*, also in the modern language, e. g. *bhati* "little", some words may drop the *i* and are treated in the modern language like words ending in consonants, e. g. *imuni* and *imun*; *dhalī* is mod. *dhau*.[3] I write *i* and *ī*.

In all other cases I give the various orthographical forms separately, e. g. *seya* : *siya*, *sulĕ* : *swolĕ*, *hṅa-* : *hna-*, *ṅā* : *nyā* ("fish"). Obvious errors have mostly tacitly been corrected; in Tatsamas the original spelling has been restored, except where more radical changes occur, e. g. *jaubhan*.

[1] Essays on the languages of Nepál and Tibet, p. 4.
[2] ZDMG 75, p. 215 f.
[3] HP 24, 105.

Adjoining vowels not forming diphthongs have been separated by an apostrophe, e. g. *na'u*.

As there does not yet exist a complete grammar of Newārī,[1] and as especially the verb hitherto has been treated in no satisfactory way, I feel obliged to give a short description of the structure of the verb, mainly a summing up of what I have previously said.[2]

The verbs may be divided into five classes according to the characteristic consonant of the finite verb: the first has *n*, the second *t*, the third and fourth *l*, which in the third class is dropped in most forms like the *n* and *t* of the first and second, whereas in the fourth class it is kept through all forms (l^1 and l^2). To the fifth class belong all verbs which have a consonant other than *n* or *l* before the *ë* of the fourth form, above all the denominatives in *-lapë* and the causatives. This class inserts an *al* in the finite verb. There are some irregularities and a certain confusion of the classes (cp. *choya, thulë* : *thuya*) which seems to be increasing in the younger MSS, but the great majority of the verbs are regular.

The endings of the simple forms of the verb may be seen from the following table, enlarged and corrected from that in ZDMG 75, p. 214.

As a twelfth form may be added the reduplicated forms: *yā-yā(ṃ)* from *yāya* (*-t*), *na-na(ṃ)* from *naya* ($-l^1$).[3]

The ending *ṅo* of the 2nd form is found only in the oldest MSS, the endings *nnayu* of the 3rd, *ṃja, ca, ja* of the 4th, and *nd* of the 8th form are met with only in N.

[1] I may refer to Conrady's Grammatik in ZDMG 45, p. 1 ff., and to the grammatical sketch in Ling. Survey III, 1.

[2] ZDMG 75, p. 216 ff. and Vi Introd. p. 7 ff., where further information will be found.

[3] All forms in *-ṃ* have alternative forms without *-ṃ*.

	I	II	III	IV	V	= ZDMG
1	*naṃ* *no*	*taṃ* *to*	*laṃ* *lo*	*laṃ* *lo*	*palaṃ* *palo*	1
2	*ṅo, ṅa* *wo*	*wo*	*wo*	?	*piwo*	7
3	*ni, nyu* *nnayu*	*yi* *yu*	*yi* *yu*	*li*	*pi*	6
4	*në* *ṃja*	*ya* *ca*	*ya* *ja*	*lë*	*pë*	3
5	*ṅ*	*k*	*wo*	*l, lwo*	*po, pu*	4
6	*ṅā*	*ṅā*	*yā*	*lā*	*pā*	5
7	*kwo*	*kwo*	*kwo*	*lakwo*	*pakwo*	—
8	*n, nd*	*t*	*l*	*l*	*pal*	2
9	*ṅaṃ*	*ṅaṃ*	—	—	*paṃ*	—
10	*sëṃ* *nasëṃ*	*sëṃ*	*sëṃ*	*sëṃ?* *lasëṃ*	*pā̆sëṃ*	8
11	*le*	*le*	*le*	?	*pale*	—

The causative has the following endings: I *ṇakë*, II *cakë*, *takë*, *kë*, III *yakë*, *kë*, IV *lakë*, V *payakë*, *pëkë*, *pakë*; e. g. *kenakë* from *kenë*, *nakë* from *naya* (-*l*[1]). A few times an enlarged ending -*kākë* is met with.

The most important of the enlarged forms are the converbia[1] in *'āwo, 'sā, 'sanwoṃ, 'sāṃ, 'ṅāwo, 'ṅās, 'ṅāsēṃ*, of which the first is the 6th form + *wo* (*dhāyāwo* from *dhāya* "to say"), the others are formed from the stem of the 1st form, e. g. *bilasāṃ* from *biya* (*-l*[1]) "to give". For the 3rd form is often[2] used an enlarged form, formed by adding *wo* to the simple form, e. g. *coniwo* from *conë*.

Verbs are found in the dictionary in the fourth form; the second and third class which in this form have the same ending, are distinguished by *-t* and *-l*[1]. Where the class is not to be learnt, only the stem is given, e. g. *gu-*; and the forms, actually found, have been added. All irregularities, too, have been given. The grammatical remarks have been placed between round brackets. Some verbal forms which are used as adjectives or substantives, and the causatives have been given separately.[3] The meaning of the causatives has been added only where it is not the ordinary meaning of the causative.

Some derivations, as e. g. the forms in *-hma, -gu, -guli, -gwo* from adjectives, pronouns and numerals are to be found under the simple word; also the derivations of the adjectives in *-u*, see e. g. *hyāṅu*.

Notes and words — among them Sanskrit equivalents —, which may illustrate the meaning of a word more exactly, have been added between round brackets. In some more doubtful cases the exact spelling of the MSS has been added at the end of an article. Compounds are separated by a dash, stem and ending sometimes by a dot. The negative *a-* is separated by a dash in negative compounds, which have not been taken over as a whole from other languages,

[1] ZDMG 75, p. 217.
[2] The simple forms in *-ni, -li, -pi* are seldom used.
[3] Except the causatives from the denominatives in *-lapē*.

but have been formed in Newārī, e. g. *a-jāgart* (but *adṛśy*). The spelling *tha(ṃ)* indicates that the word is found as *tha* and *thaṃ*. An asterisc (*) indicates that a word has been met with only in the passages referred to; it has, however, been omitted in words found only in lexicographic sources (Md, AH, CW). The sign ~ repeats the title-word of the article; in some cases, where a misunderstanding seems impossible, other words too, cf. *thani, thaniyā.*

Other details of arrangement, not mentioned here, will, I hope, be understood without further explanation.

It is my pleasant duty to offer respectful thanks to the Trustees of the Carlsberg Fund for financial aid, by which that institution has rendered possible the collection of the materials for this dictionary and the elaboration of it.

Oksbøl Mark, pr. Nordborg.

September 1935.

LIST OF ABBREVIATIONS

adj. = *adjective*
adv. = *adverb*
B. = *Bengālī*
Bhojp. = *Bhojpurī*
caus. = *causative*
cl-w. = *class-word*
comp. = *compound*
conc. = *concessivus*
cond. = *conditionalis*
conv. = *converbum*
corr. = *corrected, correlative, corrupted*
dem. = *demonstrative*
EH. = *Eastern Hindī*
esp. = *especially*
excl. = *exclusive*
fig. = *figuratively*
gen. = *generally, genitive*
H. = *Hindī*
id. = *idem*
ifc. = *in fine compositi*
incl. = *inclusive*
ind. = *indefinite*
int. = *interrogative*
intens. = *intensivum*
ipr. = *imperative*
irr. = *irregular*
itrs. = *intransitive*
jur. = *juridical*
loc. = *locally*
M. = *Maithilī*
med. = *medicinal*
mod. = *modern*
Mr. = *Marāṭhī*
n. pr. = *nomen proprium*
num. = *numeral*
P. = *Parbatiyā*
part. = *particle*
pl. = *plural*
poss. = *possessive*
p. p. = *participium perfecti passivi (in Sanscrit)*
p. pr. = *participium præsentis activi (in Sanscrit)*
pr. = *pronoun*
prop. = *properly (speaking)*

pr. poss. = *possessive pronoun*
pr. prs. = *personal pronoun*
pr. rel. = *relative pronoun*
prt. = *particle*
ptp. = *participle*
rustH. = *rustic Hindī*
s. = *singular, substantive*
S. = *Sanscrit*
subj. = *subject, casus subjectivus*
syn. comp. = *synonymous compound*
temp. = *temporally*
trs. = *transitive*
v. i. = *verbum intransitivum*
voc. prt. = *vocative particle*
v. t. = *verbum transitivum*

ALPHABETICAL ORDER

a, ā, i (ī), u (ū), e, ai, ë (MSS ya, e, ye), o, au, wā (MSS o̯ā, vā), wo (MSS va, o), k, kh, g, gh, ṇ, hṅ, c, ch, j, jh, ṭ (ṭ), th (ṭh), d (ḍ), dh (ḍh), n (ṇ), hn, p, ph, b, bh, m, hm, y, hy, l (r), hl, v, s (ṣ, ś), h.

a.

a, *pr. dem. that* B 2ª.9; ayā *his* Bh *2ª.2*.

awo, *adv.* = āwo B 8ᵇ.2; ~ hlākwo *aforesaid* N 10ª.8.

aṁś [*S.* aṃsa *shoulder?*], *s. strength* H² 54ª.2. — ~-kha *law*(?) N 46ª.2.

a-kathan, *adv. unjustly* B 33ª.2.

akaraṇ [*S. absence of action*], *adj. invalid* N 8ª.4.

akali [*H.* akaḍ *hard*], ~ yāṅa(ṃ) *harshly* C² 51*.

akalyāṇ [*S. adversity*], ch-hm-yā ~ yāya *to be injurious to…* N 45ᵇ.1*.

akasmātan [*S.* akasmāt], *adv. accidentally* H² 90ª.6. — akasmā-kāraṇ, *id.* H¹ 59ᵇ.1.

a-kāraṇas, *adv. without cause* H³ 38ª.7.

akālas [*S.* akāle], *adv. untimely, out of time* H³ 43ª.6.

akriyā [*S. neglect of duty*], *s. crime* N 15ª.7, *inhonest dealings* 24ᵇ.1.

a-krodh = krodh Vi 57.9.

akṣar [*S.*], *s. a letter of the alphabet* B 64ᵇ.3.

agādhi [*S.* agāḍha], *adj. deep* Bh 11ᵇ.4.

agul [*S.* aguru], *s. aloe* V¹ 111ᵇ.4.

agni [*S.*], *s. fire* H¹ 50ᵇ.5.

agnimand [*S.* agnimāndya], *s. dyspepsia* B 70ª.4.

agnihotr [*S.*], ~ yākwo *an Agnihotrin* N 2ª.8.

agras [*S.* agra *tip*, — *front*], *adv. in front of, before* Ś 162ª.3.

a-ghor [*P.*], *adj. terrible, dreadful* H² 72ª.5.

aṅ, *s. wall of a room* H³ 62ᵇ.6.

aṅk [*S.* - -, *mark, sign*], *s. a mark, criterion* N 8ᵇ.5; ~ ma do *innumerable, not counted* 15ᵇ.3. — ~-kriyā *amount* (*of the debt*) 14ᵇ.7. — ~-dudu *a medicinal plant*(?) Vd 29ª.2.

aṅkalapë [aṅk], *v. t. to count, to fix* (*a sum*)(?) N 15ᵇ.3*.

aṅkulapë [*S.* aṅka *breast, lap*], *v. t. to hug* Bh 10ᵇ.1.

aṅkuś [*S.*], *s. a hook* Ś 148ª.5.

aṁgal, *s.* = aṃgwod Vi 43.31.

aṅgīkār [*S. agreement, promise*], ~ yāya *to promise* H² 45ᵇ.5, *to agree to* (yāyas *doing*) 109ᵇ.3. — aṅgīkāralapë *to agree to* V² 62ª.6.

aṅgīkṛti [*S. agreement, promise*], ~ jāya *to promise* Bh 133ᵇ.1.

aṅgilalapë [*S.* aṅgī(-kṛ)], *v. i. to agree to* V¹ 101ᵇ.5.

aṅgu, *s.* = aṅgulī B 69ᵇ.2; *a span* (vitasti) AH 42ª. — ~-lā = aṅguli-~ CW 8.64.

aṅgulī [*cf. S.* aṅgula *finger*], *s. a* (*finger-*)*ring* B 5ª.1, *a measure of length* (aṅgula) N 43ᵇ.9. — ~-lā *the ringfinger* Vd 7ª.2 (aguii-rā).

aṁgwod [aṅ], *s. a wall* (*of a room*) H³ 32ᵇ.7*.

acittan [*cf. S.* acaitanya *unconsciousness*], ~ yāya *to be unconscious* Vd 7ᵇ.1.

acet [*S.* acetas], *adj. unconscious* Vi 107.11.

aceṣṭā [*S. loss of motion, fainting*],

adj. motionless Bh 10ª.5; *fainted, unconscious* V² 66ᵇ.3.

achal [*H.* achar *letter of the alphabet*], *s. a document*(?) N 6ª.1*.

achin [*S.* achinna *unseparated*], ~ hnithanaṃ *always, incessantly* H² 60ª.4*.

ajamoḍ, °**mor** [*H.* ajmod], *s. the common carroway* Vd 12ª.1.

ajā [*H.* ajā, ājā], *s. a grandfather* (*paternal and maternal*) C² 58. ~-**ju** *id.* Bh 2ª.2; ~-hma *id.* CW 8.32. — ajā-bāp *forefathers* N 2ª.6. — *ifc.* **bāp-**.

a-jāk, *adj. ferocious, unfriendly* B 8ᵇ.7.

a-jāgart, *adj. not awake, not on the alert* Bh 103ª.6.

ajī¹ [*H.* aji, ājī], ~-ju *a grandmother* (*paternal and maternal*) B 69ª2; ~-hma *id.* CW 8.32; ~-mā *id.* B 62ª.2. — *ifc.* **didi-**.

aji² [= ajil?], ~-thwo *an antidote* (*made from linseed?*) Vd 46ª.2.

ajīrṇ [*S.*], *s. indigestion* H² 54ᵇ.4.

ajil-svān, *s. yellow jasmine or Linum usitatissimum* (hemapuṣpikā) CW 6.22.

ajukt [*S.* ayukta], *adj. improper* H² 77ᵇ.8.

ajogy [*S.* ayogya], *adj. improper* (*action*) H² 86ᵇ.3; *worthless, uncapable* (*man*) 24ᵇ.4.

ajñān [*S. s.*], *s. ignorance* H² 78ª.3. *adj. ignorant* Ś 167ᵇ.3. — ajñāni [*S. adj.*], *adj. ignorant* H² 8ᵇ.2.

añjal [*S.* añjana], *s. pigment for the eyes* H² 70ᵇ.1.

at¹, *s. a brick* Vi 93.15.

at², kha **at** chi *a word* Ś 147ª.3.

atamb-si, *s. name of a plant* (kakubha) Md 76ᵇ.6.

ati [*M.*], *adv. very, exceedingly* H¹ 82ᵇ.2, *too much* Vi 148.16; ..sinwoṃ ati jhyātu *far more valuable than*... C¹ 169. — *adj. very great* V¹ 59ᵇ.4. — atin(aṃ) *adv.* = ati H³ 22ᵇ.1.

atik, *adv.* = ati H³ 40ª.5.

atithi [*S.*,] *s. a guest* B 52ª.12. — ~-abhyāgat (*syn. comp.*), *id.* H² 28ª.7.

atithy [*S.* ātithya *hospitality*], ~ yāya *to treat with hospitality* H¹ 32ª.1.

atiyas [*cf. H.* atīs *a root, used in medicine*], *s. name of a medicinal plant* Vd 25ᵇ.6. hāku ~ *a plant* (śuklakanda) Md 15ᵇ.4.

atili-hā, *s. a root used in medicine* Vd 5ᵇ.3.

atiśay [*S. eminence*], ~ yāṅa(ṃ) *excessively* N 46ᵇ.9.

atejh, *s. a plant, the root of which is used in medicine* Vd 38ª.1*.

aṭebaḍ [*cf. Mr.* aṭībād *obstinate, disputing*], *adj. obstinate, refractory* N 16ᵇ.2; ~'an yāya *to act against an order* 21ᵇ.3*.

ateli-hā (*also spelt* °l) ≐ atili-° Vd 15ᵇ.1.

atënt [*S.* atyanta], *adv. very, exceedingly* H¹ 11ᵇ.4.

atti [*cf. S.* asthi], *s. bones* V² 16ᵇ.6*.

at-pā, *s.* = at Vi 93.14.

atha [a?], *adv. then, now* H³ 52ª.8.

athabā [*S.*], *adv. or* N 41ᵇ.3. ~--~, *either*... *or* Ś 161ᵇ.2.

a-thāyas, *adv. at an improper place* N 34ª.1.

athāhā [*M.* athāh *unfathomable*], *adj. deep, bottomless* Bh 1ª.3.

athi-āthi, *s. a joint, articulation* Vd 1ᵇ.5.

athiṁ, *pr. dem. such, like that* H² 81ª.5; ~-gwo *id.* Bh 164ᵇ2; ~-ṅa *id.* M 24ᵇ.1.

athi-tu, *s. a sort of sugar-cane* Md 62ᵇ.8.

athir [*S.* asthira], *adj. transitory* H² 21ª.2.

a-thë(ṁ), *adv. so, thus, in this manner* H¹ 48ª.1, *then, thereon* 35ª.2; athëṅ *id.* 17ª.5; athënaṃ *yet, still, nevertheless* M 16ª.4; athë-ntn julasanwoṃ *id.* H¹ 27ᵇ.4.

adik [*S.* adhika —, *abundant*, —], *adj. very much* Ś 154ª.1, *very great* H³ 99ª.1. *adv. very (much)* H² 74ᵇ.1; adikaṃ *id.* H³ 37ª.8.

adini, ~ cāwo *a kind of disease* Vd 48ª.6.

adṛśy [*S.*], *adj.*, ~ yāya *to become invisible* Bh 8ᵇ.7.

adbhut [*S.*], *adj. wonderful* H² 56ᵇ.8.

adyāpi [*S. even to-day*], thaniyā ~ *to-day* Vi 148.19, thaniyā ~·s *id.* M 34ᵇ.5.

adham [*S.*], *adj. of the lowest kind* N 19ᵇ.1.

adhalapē [*S.* adhara *lower*], *v. t. to neglect* Bh 47ª.5.

adharm [*S.*], *s. unrighteousness* H² 60ª.8; ch-hmyāke ~ yāya *to treat unjustly* Ś 153ᵇ.3. — adharmi [*S.* adharmin] *adj. unrighteous* Ś 145ª.6.

a-dhā-ma-dhā [dhāya²], ~ thanē *to break to pieces* B 45ᵇ.3; ~ danakē *id.* 47ª.1.

adhāy, ch-hm-yāta ch-g-s ~ yāya *to charge somebody with*... H³ 84ᵇ.7.

adhik = adik, *adj.* Vi 89.13; *greater* N 16ª.7, *specially severe* (abhyadhika) 53ª.1. *adv. very much* N 5ᵇ.1; adhikaṃ *not less than* 51ª.5. — ~ yāya *to exaggerate* 18ᵇ.8.

adhikār [*S.*], *s. authority, government* Vi 54.24, *office* H³ 25ª.4, *property* Vi 132.29. — adhikāri [*S.* °kārin] *s. one who possesses authority* H² 60ᵇ.3.

adhīn [*S.*], *adj. depending on* H² 114ᵇ.8.

adhipati [*S.*], *s. 1) a sovereign, master* H² 57ᵇ.1. — 2) *sovereignty* (ādhipatya) H³ 42ª.10.

adhiry [*S.* adhairya], *s. want of self-control* Ś 156ª.6.

ana, *adv. there* V² 48ᵇ.6, *thither* 58ᵇ.6; anaṃ *there* B 18ª.11, *in this manner* H³ 54ª.6. ananaṃ *from there* M 7ª.3; ana-naṃ *even there* B 37ᵇ.5. anayā kha *the story of that* V² 29ª.4.

analekh [*cf. S.* anulakṣya *gerund. conforming to*], ~ ma yāya *to treat with contempt* N 46ᵇ.6*.

anarth [*S. worthless, useless*], *adj. helpless* Ś 161ª.1.

anādar [*S. disrepect*], *v.* ~ yāya *to treat with disrespect* H² 71ᵇ.3.

anā-lā, *s. the ring-finger* AH 42ª (unálá).

ani, *s. distress*; ~ yāya *to be distressed* V² 72ª.3. — ~-kāl *famine* H² 111ª.3.

aniti [*cf. S.* anṛta], *s. a lie* C¹ 80.

anukram [*S.*], *s. order, succession* H² 14ᵇ.6.

anugrah [*S.*], *s. favour, kindness* H² 92ª.2.

anucar [*S.*], *s. a companion, follower* H² 25ᵇ.5.

anumat(t) [*S.* anumata], *s. consent* N 31ª.7. ~ juya *to consent* N 11ᵇ.7; ~ yāya *id.* 31ª.9. thawo anumattan *voluntarily* 6ᵇ.6.

anurakt [*S.*], *adj. attached to, fond of* H² 34ᵇ.1.

anusaran = anusāran N 53ª.5.

anusāran [*S.* anusāra *accordance, consequence*], *adv.* ch-g-yā ~ *conformably to* N 39ª.8; barṇayā ~ *in the order of the* (4) *castes* 20ᵇ.5.

anurūp [*S.*], *adj. corresponding to* H² 57ª.1; thwoyā anurūpan *to suit him* 45ª.5.

anek [*S.*], *adj. many, much* H¹ 13ᵇ.3. — ~-bhati *of more than one mind* (anekadhā) N 53ª.2.

aneg, *adj.* = anek H¹ 21ᵇ.1.

ant¹ [*S.*], *s. an end* B 14ᵇ.11.

ant² [*S.* antra], *s. the skull* CW 8.52.

antar¹ [*S.*], *s. difference* H² 75ᵇ.5. antaras *meanwhile* V² 67ᵇ.2; ch-g-yā ~ *near to*... H² 79ᵇ.5. cha-hnu antar(as) *every other day* V² 69ª.3; ni hnu ~ *every third day* Vd 19ª.5.

antar^2, *s. witness*(?) B 2^a.6.

antardhyān [*S. disappearance*], ~ juya *to disappear* B 49^a.1.

antebaḍ = aṭebaḍ; ~ yāya N 21^b.2*.

aṇḍā [*M. egg*], *s. tha testicles* H^{2}52^a.3.

andol [*S.* andolaya- *to agitate, to swing*], *s. embarassement, perplexity* B 26^a.8. ~ yāya *to be embarassed, to be perplexed* Vi 36.21; ~ ma juyakē *to soothe, to ease* 57.26. — ~-citt *having a perplexed, distracted mind ib.*

andh [*S.*], *adj. blind* H^1 36^a.3.

andhakār [*S.*], *s. darkness* V^1 101^a.1.

ann [*S.*], *s. food* H^1 74^a.4. ~ yāya *to eat* H^3 32^a.2.

anyatras [*S.* anyatra], *adv. elsewhere* H^2 82^b.7.

anyāy [*S. unlawful action*], ~ yāya *to commit a crime* N 52^b.3. — anyāyi *evil-doer ib.*

anyathā [*S.*], *adv. otherwise* H^{2}77^b.6.

anyony [*S.*], *adv. each other* V^1 121^a.3; anyonyan *id.* H^2 35^a.1.

ap, *s.* = amp Vd 46^b.2. — ~-mā *a mango-tree* CW 6.14.

apakār [*S. offence, injury*], ~ yāya *to do harm* H^3 46^b.9.

apaki(r)tti [*S.* apakīrti], *s. infamy, offence* V^2 27^a.2.

apaghāt [*S. s. warding off*], ~ yāya *to ward off* C^2 114.

apac [*S. not able to cook*], *adj. indigestible*(?) Vd 21^b.6.

apajas [*H.* apjas *infamy, calumny*], *s. infamy, disgrace* Bh 43^a.3; ch-hm-yāta ~ biya *to abuse, reproach volubly* B 41^a.4; ~ hlāya *to calumniate* H^2 12^a.4.

a-patyār, ~ juya *not to believe* Vi 168.15.

apabād [*S. s. evil-speaking*], ~ hlāya *to speak evil, to calumniate* H^2 68^b.1. ~-kha hlāya *id.* C^1 260.

apabētr [*S.* apavitra], *adj. impure* C^2 163.

apamān [*S.*], *s. disrespect, humilation* H^2 42^a.6. ~ yāya *to treat with disrespect, to humilate* Bh 143^a.2; ~ lāya *to suffer humilation* H^2 55^b.2.

apalāti = aparādit Vd 7^a.6; toyu ~ 38^a.4.

apalādit [*S.* aparājitā *name of several plants*], ~-svān *a medicinal plant* Vd 13^a.6, toyu ~ *id.* 28^b.6.

aparādh [*S. offence, transgression*], ~ yāya *to commit a crime* N 43^a.5; ~ lāya *to be guilty of an offence* V^1 12^b.1; ch-hm-yāta ~ biya *to charge someone with a crime* Vi 42.18. — aparādhi, *s. an offender, criminal* H^2 72^b.3.

apasan, *adj.* = aprasann V^2 45^a.1.

apasarā [*S.* apsaras], *s. an Apsaras* Vi 143.9.

apasthā, *s.* = abasthā V^1 39^a.7.

apaśrit [*S. retired from*], ~ juya *to retire, to try to manage things alone* H^2 94^a.5.

apā, *s. a king* N 3^b.4.

apāt [*S.* apātra], *s. a worthless person* N 22^a.4.

apāmālak [*S.* apāmārga], *s. a plant* (mayūraka) CW 6.27.

apāy [*S. injury, calamity*], *s. disadvantage* H^2 101^b.1.

apār [*S. endless*], *adj. vast, unlimited* Vi 153.8; *endless, very much, many* H^2 79^a.4. — *ifc.* **sa-, simā-**.

apurb [*S.* apūrva *unprecedented*], *adj. matchless, peerless* V^1 59^a.2. ~·an *adv.* H^1 34^a.1.

apekṣā [*S. regard, consideration*], ~ yāya *to pay regard to* H^2 60^a.5.

aprakāś [*S. not shining, not manifest*], ~ khu *a robber in secret* N 48^b.2.

apramāṇ [*S. s. statement of no importance*], *adj. invalid, incompetent* N 9^b.5.

aprasann [*S.*], *adj. uneasy, anxious* V^1 77^b.1.

abaṁkan, *adv. with due care, in due manner* N 21^a.8.

abadhān [*S.*], *s. attention* V^1 40^a.2.

abay [*cf. S.* avayava], *s. a limb* H^2 88^b.2.

abalā [*S.*], *s. a woman* Vi 133.13; ~-jāti *id.* 107.20.

abaleb [*cf. S.* avalepa *pride?*], *s. carelessness* (?) N 21^b.7*.

abasar [*S.*], *s. occasion* Vi 139.13; *opportunity* H^2 55^a.7.

abasān [*S.* avasāna *cessation*], ~ wonë *to fail* H^3 40^b.7; manas ~ juya *not understand, to give it up* Bh 169^b.3.

abaśeṣ [*S. rest*], ~ juya *to become extinct* N 35^b.1*.

abasthā [*S.*], *s. state, condition* H^2 90^b.7.

abasyan(aṁ) [*S. adv.* avaśyam], *adv. at all events, necessarily* H^1 51^b.3; ~ ma *not in any case* H^2 51^b.5.

abahit [*S.*], *adj. attentive*; ch-g-s ~ juya *to be attentive on* N 53^b.4; ~ ma thwolwo *careless* 11^a.3; ati ~ yāṅaṃ *very impressively* H^2 67^a.4.

abahelā [*S.*], *s. disrespect* H^3 54^b.2; ~ yāya *to treat with disr.* Bh. 8^b.3; ~ ma yāya *to be carefull* N 45^a.3.

abāṭ [*cf. Mr.* abāṭa *unblameworthy*], *s. crime* (*sic*) N 15^b.8. — abāṭi *s. a criminal* 46^b.3.

abāli-si, *s. ichneumon plant* (prācīna Md) Vd 37^b.6 (abāḷ-).

abikṣā [*S.* avekṣā], ~ yāya *to pay attention to* H^2 58^b.4.

abijan, *s. statement, deposition* (*of a witness* (N 6^a.5; ~ yāya *to make a deposition* 9^b.7, ~ haya *id.* 9^a.7.

abibek [*S.* aviveka *non-distinction*], ~-an *without interruption* (?) H^3 33^a.2.

abir-hā, *s.* = abhil-hā Vd 38^a.1.

abu, *s. a father* CW 8.26. — ~-bābā *a paternal uncle* 8.29.

a-belas, *adv. at an improper time* H^1 23^a.5.

a-bëbahāran, *adv. for bad purposes* N 49^b.6.

aboḍ [*S.* abodha *foolish*], ~ yāya *v.i. to act foolishly* M 36^a.7*.

abhay [*S. security*], ~-bācā *safeguard, safe conduct* H^2 59^a.1.

abhāṣ [*S.* ā-bhāṣ —, *to promise*], ~ yāya *to promise, to stipulate* N 21^b.4*.

abhicār, 1) [*S. exorcising*], ~ yāya *to exorcise* N 30^b.7. — 2) [*S.* abhi-car *to act wrongly against*], ch-hm-yāke ~ yāya *to make an attempt on one's life* 36^a.1.

abhiprāy [*S.*], *s. intentions* V^1 41^a.1.

abhimat [*S. longed for; dear*], *adj. dear* (*to each other*) H^2 34^b.6; ~ juya *to be agreed* H^3 12^b.3.

abhil-hā, *s. Asparagus racemosus* CW 6.28.

abhiṣek [*S. inaugurating, consecrating*], ch-hm-yāta ~ biya *to inaugurate, to consecrate* H^2 84_2^b.8.

abhūt, *adj.* = adbhut Ś 161^b.2; ~ cāya *to become astonished* B 9^b.8.

abhyās [*S. exercise, study*], ch-g(-s) ~ yāya *to study something* V^2 6^a.5; ~ juya *to be disposed* (yāya *to do something*) N 11^b.5.

ama, *pr. dem.* = amo Vi 53.19.

amaṅgal [*S.*], [*adj. inauspicious* B 28^a.5. *s. inauspicious sight* H^2 9^a.7.

ama-thiṁ, *pr. dem. such, like that* H^3 9^b.9. ~-gwo *id.* H^2 97^a.4.

ama-thë, *adv. so, thus* H^1 55^b.1.

a-marjāt, *adv. improper* H^3 36^a.10; ch-hm-yāke ~ yāya *to treat someone improperly* H^2 63^a.2.

amā, *pr. dem.* = amo H^1 43^b.1.

amā-ju, *s. used in adressing a woman of inferior rank* B 40^a.8.

amān [*cf. S.* amānana], *s. disgrace, humilation* Vi 129.3. ~ cāya *to feel disgraced or humilated* 133.22. — amāni *id.* H^3 61^a.6.

amāny [*S. adj. not worthy of respect*], ~ yāya *to treat with disrespect* (ch-hm-yāta *someone*) Vi 112.5.

ami, *pr. dem.* = amo B 58^a.11.

amulë [*S.* amūlya], *adj. precious, valuable* V^1 2^a.3.

amṛt [*S.*], *s. Amrita* H^1 52^b.3. — ~-wā *rain of A.* V^1 72^a.6.

amo, *pr. dem. this, that* H^1 64^a.5.

amp [*H.* āmb], *s. mango* C^1 152. — ~-phal *a mango-fruit* V^1 59^b.6. — ~-si *id.* AH 28^a.

amb, *s.* = amp: ~-cikan *mango-oil* Md 59^b.7. — ~-pu *mango-seed* Vd 12^b.1.

ambal, *s. myrobalane* Bh 47^b.3. — ~-ti *the juice of the m°* Vd 28^a.4. — ~-mā = ambal Vd 36^b.5. — ~-mul *the root of the m°* 46^b.5. — ~-si = ambal AH 32^a; *mango* (āmrātaka) 27^b.

ay¹, *s. tax* (bali) N 16^b.6*.

ay² [*S.* ayi], *a vocative particle* B 8^a.8.

ayalā, *s. a kind of spirituous liquor* (kādambarī) AH 61^b (uyalá).

ayās, ~ cāya *to lose courage* B 3^b.12.

ayil, *s. a day of rest* B 62^b.4.

ayuguti [*cf. S.* ayukti], ~-kha *improper words* C^1 198*.

al, *s. a plant* (granthi) CW 6.37.

alagī [*H.* —, *disjoined, at liberty*], ~ misā *harlot* CW 8.10.

arany, *s.* = ārany Vi 75.11.

araguri, *s. business; duty*(?) H^3 25^b.3*.

alaṁkār [*S.*], *s. an ornament* V^1 9^b.4. — ~-tisā *syn. comp. id.* P 9^a.2.

alat [*S.* alakta], *s. red juice or lac* CW 8.87.

araḍ [*cf. S.* eraṇḍa], *s. castor-oil plant, Ricinus communis* Vd 13^b.1. — ~-cekan *castor-oil* 27^b.6.

alaṇḍ [-araḍ], ~-si *Ricinus communis* AH 29^a. ~-cikan *oil of r. c.* Md 58.4.

alapu, *adj. easy* H^2 93^b.3.

alal = araḍ; ~-simā *Ricinus communis* CW 6.17.

alas [*S.* arśa], ~-kaya *hemorrhoids* CW 8.45.

arādhan = ārādhanā; ~ yāya *to pay honour, to worship* V^1 65^a.2.

alāsī [*S.* alasa *adj.*], *adj. lazy, without energy* H^2 93^b.3. *s. idleness, want of energy* C^2 259.

are [*S.*], *a interjection of calling* B 16^a.1.

alë, *s. the intestines, guts*; ~-roy *disease of the intestines* Vd 28^a.4.

arogi [*S.* arogin], *adj. free from disease* H^2 94^a.5.

alon, ~ bilon juya *to be indistinct* N 8^b.4*.

arkaṭi [*S.* arka?], *s. name of a tree* H^1 36^a.2. — ~-simā *id.* H^2 26^b.3.

arguni, ~ yāya *to be untruthful* C^2 81*.

arcalapë [*S.* arc-], *v. t. to praise, to honour* Ns 48^a.8.

arjan [*S.* arjana *s. earning*], ~ yāya *to earn, to obtain* H^2 49^b.8.

arjalapë [*S.* arj], *v. t. to obtain, to earn* H^2 60^a.8.

arth [*S.*], *s. wealth* H^1 28^b.2; *meaning* B 61^b.2, ~ yāya *to explain* 64^a.6. — arthan *adv.*, thwote(yā) ~ *for this reason* V^2 45^a.3; *after 4. form: in order to...* V^1 135^b.2; *after 5. or 6. form: because...* H^1 56^b.4.

al-pe, *s. the spleen* Vd 12^a.4.

al-po, *s. a kind of vessel* B 25^b.8*.

asaṅkhy(ā) [*S.* asaṅkhya], *adj. innumerable* Ś 155^a.7.

asaty [*S.*], *s. falsehood, lie* N 13^a.7; ~ yāya *to tell a lie* H^2 34^b.4.

a-samarth, *adj. unable* H^2 78^b.6.

asal [*M.* asal *true, real from Arab.* aṣal], ~-phiyā (*coin*) *of true value* H^2 89^a.2.

a-sā [a], *adv. then, in this case* V^2 74^b.4; ~ — ~ *either — or* H^1 67^a.2; ~--lā *or perhaps* V^2 79^a.4; asā..lá — asā..lā *whether — or* 15^b.1. asā nikaṃ *or, rather* B 34^a.10.

asār [*S.*], *adj. without strength or value* H^2 90^b.1.

aśuci [*S. impure*], *s.* 1) *faeces* N 30b.3. 2) *an offender (against the law)* 48a.5.

aśuddh [*S. impure; inaccurate*], ~ yāya *not pay the debts* N 44b.7.

asuni-belā, *s.* asurī velā (*"l'heure réservée aux Asuras" Burnouf*) Bh 40b.1.

aśok-bṛkṣ [*S.*], *s. Devadāru-tree* V¹ 15b.1.

asobhalapē [*S.* a + śobhā *splendour*], *v. i. not be splendid* H¹ 7b.2.

aswoy [*cf. H.* asog], ~-svān *Jonesia Asoka* AH 29b.

aṣṭ [*S.* astam], ~ juya *to set (sun)* Vi 109.34.

aṣṭaloh [*S.* aṣṭhaloha *metal*], *s. metal* N 25a.7; *iron* 24b.9.

asti [*S.* asthi], *s. a bone* V² 65a.3.

astr [*S. missile, weapon*], *s.* ~ śastr *weapons for throwing and cutting* H² 78b.3; śastr ~ *id.* 77b.6.

asthi, *s. the 8th day of the lunar fortnight* AH 10b.

aśv [*S.*], *s. a horse* V¹ 47a.4.

aśvawāl [*from S.* aśva *horse*], *s. mounted soldier* H² 88a.7; *a horse-keeper* N 45a.6.

asvast [*S.* asvastha], *adj. not in good health* V² 54b.2.

aśvasth [*S.* aśvattha], *s. the holy fig-tree* Vi 20.2. — ~-mā *id.* Bh 183b.7.

ahaṁkār [*S. s.*], *s. pride, haughtiness* H² 63a.5, ahaṃkāran kāwo *inflated with pride* C² 179. — *adj. proud, haughty* H² 74b.4; ahaṃkārī *id.* H² 109a.1.

ahal [*H.* aheṛ], *s. chase, hunting* V¹ 99b.4; ~ yāya *to hunt* Ś 155b.2. — *i/c.* **calā-**.

ahaliyā [*H.* aheṛiyā], *s. a huntsman* AH 60b. ~ khicā *hound, sporting dog ib.*

ahāli, *adj. proud* C² 86*.

ahit [*S. not good*], ~ yāya *to do evil* H² 53a.7.

aho [*S.*], *a particle implying surprise* H² 90b.7.

ā.

ā¹, *adv. now* H² 74b.1.

ā², *voc. part. oh!* H² 86a.4.

āwo, *adv. now* H¹ 70b.1, ~ belas *id.* Ś 155a.4; āwoyā *id.* H² 87a.1, ~ samayas *id.* 108₂b.5. āwo-hnā *till now* Ś 156a.5; āwon-hnā *id.* Bh 22a.4, *above (in a book)* N 44b.9; āwonaṃ hnā *till now* B 44b.11. āwoṃ-li *from now* H³ 56b.10; āwon-li *id.* V² 72a.4, *below (in books)* N 44b.9; āwonaṃ li-(yā) *from now* B 30a.11. āwo-taleṃ *till now* M 10b.5, āwo-tolē *id.* Vi 177.24. āwo hlākwo *mentioned above, aforesaid* N 49a.8.

ākāś [*S.*], *s. the sky* V¹ 139a.1.

ā-ko, *adv. later on* V¹ 115b.4; ā-kolē *id.* V² 69a.7*.

ākhat [*H.*], *s. whole grain* N 21a.3*.

ākhal [*M.* ākhar], *s. a letter of the alphabet* C² 270, *the art of writing* B 20b.12. thawo ākharan *with his own hand* N 8a.2. ākhal cok-hma *writer* C¹ 224.

āgan-sa, *s. side-locks* (kākapakṣa) CW 8.73; āgam-sa *id.* *P* 15a.1.

āgyā = ājñā B 62a.12.

ācamn [*S.* ācamana *s. sipping water for purification*], ~ yāya *to rinse the mouth* Bh 167b.5.

ācāry [*S.*], *s. a teacher, spirituel guide* H² 51b.6.

ājā [*H.*], *s. a grandfather* C¹ 59.

ājñā [*S.*], *s. an order, word (term of respect)* M 11a.5. ~ biya *to say (term of respect)* H¹ 89b.2; ~ daya *id.* M 8a.6; ~ juya *id.* B 31a.3; ~ dayakē *id.* H¹ 11b.2, *to cause to say* M 21a.5; ~ kāya *to get order* H³ 50b.5, *to get the sanction* N 19a.2, *to greet, salute* Bh 57b.4.

āt [*cf. Mr.* āṭ *obstinacy*], ~ yāya *to be intent upon* H² 95b.8.

ātmā [*S.*], *s. the soul, self* B 47b.4.

ādami [*M.* ādamī *man from Arab.* ādam], *s. a man, man-servant* Ś 149ª.4.

ādar [*S.*], *s. respect* H¹ 57ᵇ.2; (ch-hm) ~ yāya *to pay respect* (*to*...) Ś 167ᵇ.5. — ādaran *adv. full of expectation* H² 67ᵇ.1.

ādas, *s. a plant, used in medicine* Vd 42ᵇ.2.

ādi [*S.*], *after a norm: to begin with, and so on* H² 92ª.5; ādin *id.* H¹ 69ᵇ.1; āditan *id.* 53ᵇ.4; ādipaṃ *id.* V² 80ª.2; ādipaṃyā *id.* N 36ᵇ.6; ādipanaṃ *id.* Vi 41.16. — ādi hṅāpāṃ *adv. at first, in the beginning* Vi 16.1; ādin ant-to *from beginning to end* N 21ª.5. — ādi *adj. the first* H¹ 11ᵇ.3. — byāghrādi *the tiger a. s. o.* H² 85ᵇ.1.

ādin = ādhīn, *adj.*, ch-hm-yā ~ *dependant on* C² 137; thawo ādin *one's own master* N 3ᵇ.6.

ādes [*S.* ādeśa *order*], ~ biya *to give an order* (ch-hm *to*...) V¹ 49ª.5, *to grant permission* 69ª.1, *to say* (*term of respect*) V² 56ª.5; ~ dayakë *id.* 69ᵇ.7.

ādhār [*S.*], *a support* H² 103ᵇ.7.

ādhīn [*S.*], *adj. dependent*; thawo ~ (thwolwo) *independent* N 4ᵇ.3. *s.* mebayā ādhīnas sanë *to be dependent on others* H³ 24ª.6.

ānand [*S. s.*], *s. joy, pleasure* H¹ 26ª.2, *adj. joyful, glad* H² 48ᵇ.3.

āni = anī V¹ 105ª.6*.

āpati [*S.* āpad], *s. distress, misfortune* N 7ª.5.

āpadā [*S.* āpad], *s.* (*time of*) *distress* H¹ 75ª.4; ~ lāya *to get into misfortune or distress* H² 67ª.5, ~ yāya *id.* H¹ 22ª.5.

āpadi, *s.* = āpati N 3ᵇ.2.

āpāl, *adj.* = apār Vi 153.11.

āpyāyamān [*S.* ā-pyāyate *to swell, increase, thrive*], *adj. thrilled with joy* H¹ 30ª.4.

ābā-ju, *s. a paternal uncle* AH 38ª.

ābāhan [*S.* āvāhana], ~ yāya *to bring or lead hither* Ś 164ᵇ.1.

ābhand [*cf. Mr.* ābhaṃḍ *slanderous, mischief-making*], ~ yāya *to slander, make mischief* N 34ª.5*.

ābharaṇ [*S.*], *s. an ornament* H¹ 19ª.4.

ābharāti, *s.* wocu ~ *name of a plant* (nīlaspandā) Md 19ª.4.

ābhāsalapë [*S.* ā-bhāṣ *to promise*], *v. t. to promise, to stipulate* N 6ᵇ.2, kāl ~ *to fix a term* 19ᵇ.7.

ām [*S.* āmaya], *s. disease* Vd 22ᵇ.2.

āma, āmo, *pr. dem. this* V² 58ᵇ.7. — ~-thiṃ-gu *such, like that* B 10ᵇ.7; ~-thiṃ-guli *id.* M 13ª.3; ~-thiṃ-gwo *id.* H² 92ª.3; ~-thiṃ-ṅa *id.* Ś 147ᵇ.3; ~-thiṃ-ṅaṅ *id.* H³ 40ª.4. — ~-thë *adj. such, like that* H² 78ª.1; *adv. so, thus* V¹ 46ª.5. — ~-li *such* H³ 47ª.6; ~-lita *adv. so, thus* Vi 40.34; ~-lito *id.* Ś 165ª.1. — ~-kan *adv. here* Vi 68.7, *hither* H³ 41ᵇ.11.

āmnāy [*S.*], *s. traditionel usage* N 31ᵇ.2; ~ yāya *to conduct life in accordance with tr. us. ib.*

āy [*S. income — profit*], *s. interests* N 26ª.1; ~ ma swosëṃ *regardless of one's interests* H² 60ᵇ.1.

āyat [*S.* āyatti *dependence*], mebayā ~'as conë *to be dependent on others* H² 51ª.7.

āyal-bi, *s. a water-snake* AH 19ª (áyelubi).

āyit = āyat: mebayā ~'an *according to the will of others* H² 51ᵇ.3.

āyimāyi, *s. a wife*(?) B 54ª.4*.

āyu [*S.*], *s. life, duration of life* V¹ 93ᵇ.1.

āyuṣ [*S.* āyus], *s. life, duration of life* C² 51; ~ dayakë *to keep alive* Vi 119.5.

ār [*cf. Mr.* ār *hurrying*], ~ yāya *to rage* (*gale*) Bh *11ª.4.

āraṇy [*S.*], *s. a wood, forest* Ś 166ᵇ.1.

ālamāl, *s. goods and chattels*(?) Ś 144ª.1.

ārambh [*S. s. beginning*], ~ yāya *to begin* H² 95ª.4.

ārādhanā [*S. worship, adoration*], ~ yāya *to pay worship* H² 92ᵇ.7.

āliṅgan(ā) [*S.* āliṅganā, *s. embracing*], ~ yāya *to embrace* Bh 47ᵇ.1.

āliṅgalapë [*S.* ā-liṅg], *v. t. to hug, to embrace* H¹ 32ᵃ.1.

āle, *s. name of several plants* (vāsaka) AH 31ᵃ. ~-har *id.* (vāsovṛkṣa) Md 3ᵃ.1.

ālocalapë [*S.* ā-loc], *v. t. to consider* H³ 57ᵃ.10.

āroni, ~ yāya *to cheer up*(?) B 61ᵃ.5*.

ās [*M.*], *s. hope* C¹ 137. ~ buya (-t) *to lose confidence* B 21ᵃ.7; ~ ma tasë(ṃ) *hopelessly* V² 10ᵇ.6; che āsas coṅāwo *having put their confidence in you* Bh 172ᵃ.4.

āsan [*S.*], *s. a seat* V¹ 113ᵃ.3; ~ yāya *to use as seat* Ś 166ᵇ.1. — *ifc.* **ghāc-**.

āsalapë [ās], *v. t.* ch-g ~ *to hope for..., to wish...* N 2ᵃ.7; ch-hm-yāke ~ *to put confidence in...* Bh 32ᵇ.3.

āśā¹ [*S.* āśā], *s. hope* V¹ 15ᵇ.3. (ch-g) ~ yāya *to hope* (*for something*) Bh 141ᵃ.7; ch-hm-yāke ~ yāya *to pin one's faith to...* H³ 7ᵇ.3; ~ taya *to hope* B 32ᵇ.5.

ā-sā² = a-sā H¹ 38ᵇ.4.

āsi, *s. a fender* AH 58ᵇ.

āśi-khā [*S.* āśis], *s. blessing, benediction, solemn wish* Vi 100.5; ~ yāya *to bless, to wish solemnly* B 22ᵃ.10.

āśir-bād [*S.* āśirvāda], *s. blessing, benediction* Bh 10ᵇ.2.

āsë, *adv. now* B 16ᵃ.6.

āścāry [*S.* āścarya], *s. a wonder, marvel* H² 76ᵇ.1; ~ juya *to wonder* H² 41ᵇ.4; ~ cāya *to become curious* Vi 167.33, *to become surprised* Ś 158ᵇ.6.

āśram [*S.*], *s. an hermitage* V¹ 24ᵇ.2.

āśray [*S.* (*place of*) *refuge*], ch-hm-yāke ~ yāya *to take one's refuge to...* H¹ 30ᵇ.1.

āśrā [*contam. of* āśā *and* āśraya], *s. hope* Vi 118.33, *refuge* 113.7. — ~-bhalosā *hope* 113.14.

āśvās [*S.*], *s. consolation* H³ 28ᵇ.10. — āśvāsalapë *v. t. to console, to reassure* V² 21ᵇ.3.

āhār [*S.*], *s. food* H² 35ᵃ.2; ~ yāya *to eat* 110ᵃ.1, *to earn one's livelihood* Vi 21.8.

i (ī).

i, *adv. there, thither* V² 68ᵇ.7.

ī, *s. a sickle* AH 53ᵇ (ī).

i-kā¹, *adv.*, ~ thi-kā *one another* (yugapad) N 10ᵇ.3*.

ikā², *s.* = ekā AH 54.

iku, *adj.* = yiku Vd 19ᵃ.4.

ich(y)ā [*S.* icchā], *s. wish, desire.* H² 114ᵇ.1; thawo ichān *voluntarily* H³ 18ᵇ.8. ~ yāya *to wish, to desire* Bh 2ᵃ.4.

itar-jan [*S.* itara], *s. the other one's* C² 216*.

i-tā, *adv.* samudr-pāran ~ thëṅāwo *having reached the other side of the ocean* B 39ᵃ.7; ~ thi-tā *on both sides, on either side* 14ᵇ.11; i-tās *on the other side* 16ᵇ.1. Yamunā-pār i-tāwo *having brought* (*it*) *to the other side of the Y.* Bh *12ᵃ.5.

ityādi [*S.*], *and so on* Ś 147ᵇ.4.

inā¹, ~ kāya to divide AH 25ᵃ.

inā², ināyā kha *the story of that* V¹ 44ᵇ.6.

ināp, ~ yāya *to say, to tell* (*mostly with oratio recta* + dhakaṃ) V² 13ᵇ.2.

inālapë, *v. t. to say, to tell* (= ināp yāya) H² 73ᵃ.7.

ināyalapë, *v. t.* = inālapë B 25ᵃ.2*.

inī, *s. a daughter-in-law* V² 50ᵃ.1*.

indrī, *s.* = indriy Vd 10ᵃ.3; *a limb* (aṅga)(?) N 51ᵇ.2.

indriy [*S.*], *s. the senses* H² 50ᵃ.2.

ipā = ihi-pā: ~ yāṅā misā *the first or consecrated wife of a king* AH 37ᵃ.

i-pur, *adv.*, ~ thi-pur *here and there* *H*[3] 56^{b}.3*.

i-bā, *adv.*, thethe ~ thi-bā yāya *to disagree one with another* N 38^{b}.4*.

i-bil, *adv.* (thithi) ~ thi-bil yāya *to give one to another* H[3] 12^{b}.4*.

imā, *s. Falco Cheela* CW 7.9.

imuni, *s. a plant* (yamānikā) Vd 12^{a}.2.

iyikā, *s.* = ekā Md 66^{b}.8.

ilapu, *s. Cassia Tora* AH 32^{b}.

ilān, °**m**, *s. a canopy* Bh 167^{b}.4.

ilipu, *s.* = ilapu Md 14^{b}.5.

irkhyā [*S.* īrṣyā], *s. envy, jealousy* Vi 166.15. — ch-hm-wo nāp ~ taya *to be envious towards...* 166.3; ch-hm-yāta ~ taya *to vie with...* 51.9.

iśān [*cf. S.* aiśāna], *s. the north-east* P 13^{b}.6*.

iṣṭ [*S. beloved*], *s. a friend* Bh 103^{a}.4.

iṣṭamiṣṭ [*corr. from* iṣṭa-mitr], *s. a friend* Ś 149^{b}.7.

iṣṭimiḍi, °**ḍe**, °**r**, *s. name of a medicinal plant* Vd 42^{b}.4.

īśvar [*S.*], *s. a master, lord* V[1] 1^{b}.3.

ihatras [*S.* ihatra], *adv. in this world* Bh 170^{a}.4.

iha-pā = ihi-pā Vi 60.32.

i-hā, *adv.*, ~ thi-hā *hither and thither* N 12^{a}.3*.

ihi-pā [ihi = che], ~ yāya *to marry (of the man)* Ś 160^{a}.3.

u (ū).

u[1], *pr. dem. that* B 2^{b}.10; ~ — ~ *the one — the other* 35^{b}.6. *pr. pers. 3. s. he, she, it* V[2] 44^{b}.3. — u-hma *pr. dem. that* P 17^{b}.2. u-gu *the same* V[2] 35^{b}.1; u-guli *that* M 20^{b}.1. u-pani *pl. those* B 51^{b}.3.

u[2] [= u[1]], ~ lāya *to assemble, to meet* B 59^{a}.9; ~ lāk *adj. alike, similar* 39^{b}.8, ~ lākwo *id.* Ns 27^{b}.4; ~ ma lāk *not alike* Bh 173^{b}.2.

u[3] = uwo (*5th form of* uya *to come*) H[2] 32^{a}.6.

u[4]- (-n *or* -t? *only:* uṅā), *v. i. to bark* C[1] 183.

uṁ, *part.* = wuṃ N 39^{a}.2; ~...~ *be it... be it* H[3] 17^{b}.7.

uṁ-khā, *s. a partridge* AH 35^{a} (won-khá).

u-kul, *adj. of the same family* N 9^{a}.6.

u-khaṁ, *adj. exactly corresponding, of the same tenor* N 6^{a}.6.

Ukhā-debi, *n. pr. name of a goddess* Bh 147^{b}.3.

ukhē, ~ thukhē *hither and thither* M 32^{a}.6.

ugal, *s. a wooden mortar* (ulūkhala) AH 54^{b} (woogala).

ucit [*S. adj. proper, right*], ~ yāya *to help, to assist* (upakāra) C[2] 109.

ucēt, *s.* = ucit C[1] 90. *adj. proper, right* N 7^{b}.3.

uccāraṇ [*S. s. praising*], ~ yāya *to praise, to extoll* Bh 93^{a}.2.

ucce [*S.* ucca], *adj. high, lofty* Bh 83^{b}.7.

uchāl [*cf. Mr.* ucchāl *s. rise, increase*], ~ yāya *to save* Ś 147^{b}.1.

uchāhā [*H.* ucchāo], *s. a festival* C[1] 287.

ujan [*S.* ājñā?], *s. advise* Vi 44.18. ~ daya *to give advice* H[2] 115^{a}.1; ~ dayakē *id.* Ś 148^{b}.1, *to propose* Vi 22.7, *to give an order* 42.12.

u-jāti, *adj. of the same caste* N 31^{b}.1.

uju, *adj. mean, vile* H[2] 53^{b}.2*.

u-jun, *adv.*, ch-hm-wo ~ *in accordance with...* H[2] 58^{a}.2*.

Ujoni, *n. pr.* Ujjayinī B 38^{b}.8.

ujjan, *s.* = ujan H[2] 115^{a}.7*.

Ujjanī, *n. pr.* Ujjayinī V[1] 90^{b}.1.

ujyog [*S.* udyoga], *s. exertion* C[2] 103.

ujhān [*H.* ujjān], *s. a garden, park* V[1] 72^{b}.1.

uṭ [*M.* ūṁt], *s. a camel* N 28^{b}.4. — *ifc.* **mā-**.

utajog [*S.* udyoga *exertion*], ~ yāya *to exert oneself* N 22ª.4*.

utal, *s.* = uttar[1] V[1] 37ᵇ.5.

u-tā, *adv.* ~ hāyakë *to raise to the same hight* H[3] 38ᵇ.6*.

utār [*H. decrease, decline*], ~·an *adv.* (*gradually*) *decreasing* Vd 14ª.4. — ~-bel *time of decline, time destructive* (*of morality*) Ś 155ª.4.

uti, *adj. the same* H[1] 22ª.1 (urtti). *adv. in the same manner* N 40ª.3; ch-g-wo *as, like something* B 3ᵇ.8. ji prāṇawo uti yānaṃ tayā *having been made to be like my life* B 46ᵇ.12. — uti-nań *adj. alike* (ch-g-wo *to something*) 3ª.9. — uti-gëṃ sal *svarita* CW 1.64.

ute = uti N 28ª.5; kāyawo ceḍawo ~ *son and slave are equal* N 3ᵇ.7. ~ biya *to give in equal parts* 38ᵇ.4; ute-han *in the same manner* 10ᵇ.2. gute — ute *as* — *so* 45ª.2.

uttam [*S.*], *adj. utmost, best* H[2] 2ᵇ.1.

uttar[1] [*S.*], *s. an answer*; ~ biya *to give an answer, to answer* V[1] 20ᵇ.2. — ~-bacan =~ H[2] 16ª.6.

uttar[2] [*S.*], *s. the north* B 21ª.12.

uttar[3] [*S.* — —, *following, subsequent*], ~ sākṣī *indirect witness* N 10ª.7.

uttarā, *s.* = uttar[1] H[3] 40ª.5; li ~ biya = ~ biya Vi 35.29. — ~-bacan = ~ H[3] 6ª.8. — *ifc.* li-.

utpat(t)i [*S.* utpatti *arising, origin*], ~ juya *to arise, to come into existence* Bh *3ª.3, *to be formed* H[2] 21ª.1; ~ yāya *to call into existence* 5ᵇ.2.

utpann [*S. arisen, produced*], ~ yāya *to carry into effect, to accomplish* H[2] 64ᵇ.6.

utpal [*S.*], *s. the blue lotus* V[1] 10ᵇ.6.

utpāt [*S.* —, *sudden event*], *s. a trouble, calamity* B 14ª.3.

utphal, *s.* = utpal V[2] 7ᵇ.6.

utrā, *s.* = uttar; ~-phot *reply on reply* H[1] 43ᵇ.1.

utsāh(ā) [*S.* utsâha], *s.* 1) *joy, happiness* C[2] 145. — 2) *effort*; ~ yāya *to exert oneself* H[2] 41ᵇ.7.

uṭh, *s.* = uṭ H[2] 108,ª.7.

uthay [*M.* uṭha *to rise*], ~ yāya *to come into existence, to arise* H[2] 83ᵇ.7.

uṭhalapë [*M.* uṭha *to rise*], *v. i. to increase* N 16ª.6. — uṭhalapayakë *caus. ib.* 5*.

u-thiṁ-gwo, *adj. the same* (ch-g-wo *as*) N 34ª.7*.

u-thëṁ, *adv. thus, like that* B 59ª.5, *in the same manner* N 41ª.9, *alike, the same* H[3] 18ª.8; ch-g-wo ~ *like a thing* C[1] 168; rājāwo misāwo ~ *king and woman are alike* H[3] 27ª.1. uthëṃ uthëṃ *each in the same way* P 7ª.5, *excessively* AH 6ᵇ (woothyan woothyang). -- uthënaṃ *adv. in the same manner* B 17ª.4. uthë-ṅan *id.* 36ᵇ.5. uthë-ṅanakaṃ *id.* 62ª.9. uthë-ṅań *alike, of the same kind* 61ª.2. — uthëṃ-ṅa gwo-hmạ *the same* C[2] 122.

uday [*S. rising* —, *success*], ~ juya *to rise* (*sun*) H[2] 96ᵇ.4, *to succeed* 81ᵇ.1.

udār [*S.* —, *honest, active*?], *s. written receipt* N 7ª.8. — ~-pati *written compact* 14ᵇ.4*.

udālapë, *v. t. to contribute*(?) N 39ᵇ.9*.

udās [*S. apathy*], *adj. common, ordinary*(?) H[2] 53ᵇ.2.

udūgar, *s. a weapon for beating* Bh 35ᵇ.5.

u-dotu-naṁ, °**-noṁ,** *adv. in due manner* N 22ᵇ.2.

udyam [*S.*], *s. effort, exertion* H[2] 89ª.6; ~ yāya *to exert oneself* 49ᵇ.6.

udyān [*S.*], *s. a garden, park* Vi 123.35.

udyog [*S.*], *s. exertion* H[2] 89ª.4.

udhalalapë [*S.* ud-dhar], *v. t. to save* (*from evil*) N 14ª.1.

uddhār [*S. s. rising; taking, pulling out*], ~ yāya *to rescue, to redeem* Ś 152ª.1, āpadās *from distress* H[2] 43ª.6.

ch-hm-yā bhār ~ yāya *to release somebody from obligations* N 2^{a}.3.

u-nugwoḍ, ~ juya *to join hands* N 49^{a}.4*.

unmūl [*S. eradicated*], ~ yāya *to eradicate, to destroy completely* H^2 113^{a}.3.

upakathā [*S. short story*], *s. a happening, adventure* B 35^{a}.7.

upakār [*S. help*], ch-hm-yāke ~ yāya *to help somebody* H^2 53^{a}.2. *med., to attend* Vd 7^{a}.6.

upaṁkaṁ, ~ taya *to confine, to imprison* B 8^{a}.11*.

upacār [*S. treatment*], ~ yāya *to cure (or wound)* Bh 178^{b}.2; ~ yācakë *to let cure (a person)* V^1 73^{a}.4.

upajalapë [*M.* upaj *to come into existence*], *v. i. to grow (seed)* N 33^{b}.6; nyāyan ~ *to live according to* nyāya 1^{b}.8.

upajībinī [*S.* upajīvana *subsistence*], ch-g-n ~ yāya *to live by.., to subsist on...* N 7^{a}.4.

upatan [*cf. S.* udvartana], *s. rubbing (the body) with fragrant unguents* CW 8.85.

upadeś [*S.*], *s. instruction* H^1 89^{a}.4; ch-hm-yāta ~ biya *to instruct* H^2 75^{a}.8.

upabās [*S.*], ~ yāya *to fast* H^1 51^{b}.4.

upamān [*S. comparison; simile*], ātmāyā ~-an *by analogy to oneself* H^3 57^{b}.10.

upalapë [*S.* upara?], *v. i. to escape* Bh 10^{b}.2.

uparalapë [*S.* upara —, *nearer*]. *v. i. to draw near, to approach* H^2 66^{b}.2*,

uparas [*S.* upari —, *with regard to*], ch-hm-yā ~ *for the sake of...* Vi 15.20. ch-hm-yā ~ karuṇā taya *to have pity on...* M 21^{b}.3, ~ ~ tam cāya *to get angry with...* H^2 108^{a}.1. — ch-hm ~ *without, besides...* H^3 42^{b}.2.

uparānt [*H.* uprānt *afterwards*], *adv. then* H^2 86^{b}.7.

upasthambhalapë [*S.* upasthambha *support*], *v. t. to support* N 40^{a}.1.

upahat [*S. damaged, injured*], *adj.*, ch-g-s ~ *injurious to...* N 26^{a}.1.

upahās [*S. jest, mockery*], ~ yāya *to ridicule, to mock* H^2 110^{a}.4.

upāy [*S. way, means*], *s. way, means* H^2 93^{a}.4, *remedy* H^3 50^{a}.6; *cunning, artifice* H^2 58^{a}.6; *advantage* 101^{b}.1. chu ~ yāya *what is to be done?* H^1 88^{b}.1.

upās [*cf. S.* upavāsa], *s. fasting* P 23^{a}.2; upāsan conë *to fast* AH 47^{a}.

upekṣā [*S. negligence*], ~ yāya *to neglect* H^2 94^{a}.2.

upo [= upol?], *adv.* ch-g-yā sinaṃ ~ *more than...* H^3 15^{b}.6*.

upor [*cf. H.* ūpar —, *in addition*], ~ taya *to add(?)* Vi 79.3*.

upoṣadh [*cf. S.* upoṣaṇa], *s. fasting* M 6^{b}.6.

uphal, *s.* = utpal V^1 10^{a}.5. — ~-hā *the root of the blue lotus* Vd 47^{a}.4. — ~-col *pulse made from the bl. l.* 37^{b}.5. — uphol *id.*; ~-svān B 42^{b}.8.

ubār, *s. shelter, safety* C^2 233.

umuni, *s. a measure or weight* N 48^{b}.3*.

u-mul, *adj. of the same price* N 25^{b}.2.

uya[1] (-t), *v. t. to burn (a deceased)* V^1 49^{b}.1; ma uṅā *not burnt i. e. raw (earthenware)* H^1 2^{b}.3.

uya[2] (-l[1]), *v. i. to come* B 51^{b}.5; hṅeḍ ~ *to fall asleep* Bh 67^{b}.5.

uya[3], ch-g-wo ~ juya *to be like a thing* Vi 175.1*.

uyakë, *to (suffer oneself to) be surrounded* Vi 101.12.

uragāban, *s.* = urgāban N 19^{b}.1.

u-li, *pr. dem. that* V^2 14^{a}.6; ulita *id.* M 21^{a}.4. — uli-thë(ṃ) *adv. thereupon* V^2 16^{b}.2.

u-le, *pr.* = u-li; ~-hen ma hlāyā *is no fixed rule* N 25^{b}.1*.

ulë[1], *v. i.* 1) *to be covered with, to*

abound in M 23b.7. 2) *to assemble, to meet* H³ 10a.4. — wā phas ma ulañā-sēṃ *when the storm ceases* H² 75a.6. — gā ulāwo swoya *to look intently at*(?) B 14a.7.

ulë², *v. t. to smear, to rub* Vd 15b.1,3*.

ulok, °**lak** [*S.* ulkā], *s. a meteor* M 32a.4.

urgāban, *s. a servant* (bhṛtya) C¹ 16.

ul-mul, *this or things like that* N 39a2*.

ullol [*S. high wave*], ~ yāya *to raise a cry* N 22b.2; ullolan hālë *to raise a loud cry* H² 27a.2.

ul-si, *s. Ficus indica* P 13b.2. — ul-simā *id.* B 61b.1.

us-tunu(ṁ) [uya²], *adv. soon* Vd 5b.6; ~ — ~ *now — now* 5a.6.

uśra-hā [*S.* uśīra *the root of Andropogon muricatus*?], *s. a root, used in medicine* Vd 22b.6.

u-svāḍ, ~ juya *to become alike* N 47b.4*.

ṛ.

ṛṇ [*S.*], *s. debt* N 2b.1.

ṛṇik [*S.*], *s. a debtor* N 6a.5.

ṛṇīkā, *s. a weight* (aṇḍikā) N 53b.2*.

ṛṇiyā, *s. a debtor* (= raṇiyā) N 7b.2*.

e.

(*See also* ë).

ekacitt [*S. fixedness of thought on one single object*], ~ yāya *to concentrate oneself* H¹ 23b.1; ekacittanaṃ *adv. exclusively* H³ 54b.10.

ekantr [*S.* ekatra *in one place*], *adv. once* H¹ 3b.1.

ekaman [*S.* ekamanas *unanimous*], ~ yāya *to act unanimously* Vi 24.5.

ekaśarīr [*S. with one body*], ~ yāya *to become united, to become one* B 15b.9.

ekā, *s.* (*white*) *mustard* Vd 13b.3.

ekāt = ekānt V² 21b.2. *adv. alone* H³ 4b.2; cha ~ cowo *mind your own business* Vi 112.7; ~ dhāle *separately* Bh 22a.5; ekātan *id.* N 94a.4. ekāt — *s. a single man* N 27a.2, *anybody else* H² 92b.5.

ekānt [*H. adj. secluded, s. seclusion*], *adj. lonely, solitary* M 23a.2, ~ thānas *apart, aside* Vi 90.34. — *s. solitude* V¹ 13b.4; ekāntas *in private* H² 82b.6. *adv.* tham ekānt *alone* Bh 102b.1; ekāntan(aṃ) *id.* Vi 23.9. — ch-hm-wo ekānt yāya *to meet secretly* H³ 43a.10; ~ taya *to bring together* H² 37b.2.

ekāntar = ekānt H² 62a.2.

eya, mikhā ~ kol yāya *to rub the eyes*(?) Vi 36.34.

eyu, *adj. yellow* (= yeyu) Vd 3b.2.

eyukā, *s.* = ekā C¹ 229.

esu, *adj. hoarse, husky*(?) Vd 13b.6. — eso *id.* 21a.2*.

ehe, *s. marriage* N 30a.3. — eho *id.*; ch-hm-wo ~ yāya *to be married to*... (*of a woman*) N 38b.5.

ë.

(*MSS:* e, ya, ye).

ëkaṁ [ëya], ji ma ~ *against my wish* N 4b.4. — ~-guli *adj. in accordance with one's wishes* B 61b.1; *agreeable ib.* 6.

ëkā-guli, *adj.* = ëkaṃ-° Ś 161b.6*.

ëkwo (ëya), *adj. agreeable* C¹ 214. *apt or inclined to* 73.

ëcu, *adj. clear, bright, pure* Vd 42b.4; ëcusëṃ *becoming pure* C¹ 199.

ëja = ëya N 38a.1.

ëṁcu, *adj.* = ëcu CW 2.5 (yeṁcū).

ë-thëṁ [ëya], *adv. as one likes, according to one's wishes* V² 40a.1.

ëya (-l¹), *v. t. to wish, to desire* (*yāya to do a thing*) H¹ 35a.5; *to desire, to covet* (*a woman*) 84b.2. —

jita ma ëwo *it does not please me* Vi 153.10; tam cāya ëwo *irascible* H¹ 21ª.3; ma ëwo *not friendly disposed* H³ 27ª.6. — ëyā *what is in accordance with one's wishes* N 39ᵇ.3; tham ëyā misā *a beloved or coveted wife* H³ 50ª.10; chan ëyā-thë *as you like it* V² 55ª.3.

ëyakë *caus of* ëya; kanyā ëyakaṃ yāya *to have connexion with a willing maiden* N 34ᵇ.1*.

ëyā-pu [ëya], *adj. agreeable* Vi 25.7; ëyā-puk *id.* 81.12; ëyā-pun *adv. in an agreeable way* 92.1.

Ëla, *n. pr. Paṭan* HP 24.99.

ëlā [*S.* elā], *s. a species of cardamom* Vd 11ᵇ.6. — ~-guḍi *a pill made from c.* 50ᵇ.4.

ës, *s. poison* B 82ª.2. — ~-ghar *jar of poison* C¹ 261. — ~-phuli *a cutaneous disease caused by poison* Vd 29ᵇ.5.

o.

(*See also* **wo**).

ogālapë [*H.* ugānā, *caus. of* ugnā *to grow*], sebā ~ *to show honour* N 46ᵇ.9*.

olalaṁ, ~ juya ëwo *unsteady, flickering* P 39ᵇ.3*.

olë, *v. t.* = ulë² Bh 42ª.2*.

olo, *pr. dem. this* (*corr.* gwolo) N 19ª.3; oloto *id.* (*corr.* gwoloto) P 47ᵇ.5.

oṣadhi [*S.* oṣadhī *medicinal herb*], *s. a drug, medicine* H² 47ᵇ.5. — ~-wāsal *id.* H¹ 18ª.1.

au.

auṣadhi, *s.* = oṣadhi H² 12ᵇ.5.

wā.

(*MSS:* **oā, vā**).

wā¹, *s. rain* H² 75ª.3; ~ gāk *it rains* 38ª.1. — *ifc.* **amṛt-, lwoho-, svān-.**

wā², *s. a tooth* H¹ 27ᵇ.1; wā·n ṅāya *to bite* V¹ 37ª.5. ~ kṣaraṃ(?) *cleaning of the teeth* H² 55ᵇ.8 = ~ karaṃ H³ 27ᵇ.9.

wā³, *s. corn, rice* C¹ 9. — *ifc.* **ke-, nāhā-, pu-, bhutu-.**

wā⁴ = wāyo (*esp. after other verbs*) H¹ 18ª.5.

wā'uṁ, *adj.* = wāṅu H² 43ª.1.

wā-wāṁ = wo-woṃ (*redupl. form of* wonë) V¹ 126ᵇ.2*.

wā-kāl, *s. yawning* AH 18ᵇ; ~ tayakë *to cause to yawn*(?) Bh 152ª.1.

wā-kut [wāt], *s. news* H³ 19ª.7.

wā-kul = wā-kāl; ~ chinë *to yawn* M 15ª.4*.

wā-guji, *s. an ear or spike of corn* AH 54ª.

wāṅu, *adj. green* H¹ 78ª.2.

wā-cimi, *s. the awn of grain* AH 54ª.

wā-che, *s. a pod* (simbā) AH 54ᵇ.

wāt [*M.* bāt *news, speech*], *s. news* V² 72ª.2. — *ifc.* **kha-.**

wātu, ~ wālāwo *thoroughly* B 30ᵇ.5; ~ wāṅā *id.* V² 55ᵇ.6; ~ wāṅa(ṃ) *id.* V¹ 90ᵇ.6.

wā-thvāk, *s. a bundle* (*of corn or rice*) (guchha) AH 54ª.

wāṁpī [*S.* vāpī], *s. a pond* CW 2.4.

wāya (-t; wāyāwo CW 8.22), *v. t. to throw* Bh 163ª.5; *to cast off, to leave, to abandon* B 40ª.8; *to let go, to leave hold of* H³ 56ᵇ.6. jāl ~ *to put up a trap* 53ᵇ.1. — wāṅāwo choya *to throw* Ś 161ᵇ.6. — wāṅa(ṃ) taya *to leave, to abandon* V² 56ª.3; ~ tāya *id.* B 44ᵇ.3. — wāṅa(ṃ) tăthë *to throw* V¹ 91ª.3, *to leave, to abandon* B 14ª.3; wāṅāwo ~ *id.* 32ª.6.

wāyo, *come!* V² 58ᵇ.5; *after verbal forms* (*4th and 8th*); wonë ~ *do but come!* H³ 40ª.7, *let us go* 58ᵇ.1.

wāl, ~ juwo *an inhabitant*(?) B 60ª.1*.

wā-lakh [wā], *s. a threshing floor* AH 54ª.

wālë, *v. t.* = bālë Vd 16^b.2.

wāsal, *s. medicine* M 8^b.3; ~ yāya *to treat with medicine, to attend (med.)* H^2 42^a.2, ch-hm-yāke ~ ~ *to poison* B 20^a.5. — *ifc.* **oṣadhi-**.

wāsā, *s. a plough* C^1 186*.

wā-syāk, *s. tooth-ache* Vd 38^b.4.

wā-hān, ~ khāya *to open one's mouth, to show one's teeth (in anger)* Bh 62^a.4; hmutu(n) ~ ~ *id.* H^2 80^a.3.

wuṁ (*spelt* vuṃ, buṃ; *cf.* uṃ). *part. just, even* N 41^b.3, *also, too* 10^a.1. — rājan ~ *it is the king who...* 15^b.6; ch-hm-yā ~ *in regard to...* 30^a.7; yaṅāyā ~ *when... carries away* (= yanasā) 22^b.1.

WO.

(*MSS:* o, va, vo).

wo[1], *pr. dem. s. that* H^1 65^a.5, *adj.* Ś 151^a.7; wo — wo *the one — the other* B 27^b.4,5. — *pr. pers. 3. s. he, she, it* B 2^b.3; wo-pani *3. pl. they* V^2 30^b.1; woyā *poss. his* V^2 44^a.7; wos *id.* Bh 50^b.3; wosayā *id.* V^1 19^b.4. — wo-hma *pr. dem. s. that (of persons only)* H^1 65^b.1, *id. adj.* Ś 160^b.5. — wo-gu *id. s. (of things only)* C^1 155; wo-guli *id.* Vi 74.25, *id. adj.* V^2 71^a.5.

wo[2] = wowo (*5th form of* woya[1]) V^2 34^b.3.

woṁ-kuli, *s. the south-east* CW 1.33.

woṁ-gwo, *s. the Āyurveda* C^2 57.

woṁ-tā, *s. the east* CW 1.32.

wo-ko, *s. jaw-bone* CW 8.70.

wocu, *adj. blue* Md 29^b.7. wocayu *becomes blue* Vd 11^b.3.

woṁco, *adj.* = *wocu* N 11^a.6.

wo-thā, ~ wo-thān sanë *to move from place to place* Bh 62^b.2*.

wo-thëṁ, *adv. like that, in that manner* H^1 38^a.3.

wonaṁ-li, *adv. after that, hereafter* P 21^a.1.

wonakë (*caus. of* wonë), *to cause to come* C^1 67; *to let pass (time)* V^1 15^a.1. *After adj. to make* H^1 20^a.4. — thawo basās wonakaṃ *obediently* H^1 5^a.2.

wonë, *v. i. to go* V^1 113^a.2, *to go away* H^1 92^a.2, *to pass, to elapse (time)* V^2 9^b.1; *to come* H^1 95^a.2. — basās ~ *to get into the power of* H^1 5^a.5; gohārī ~ *to come to one's assistance* N 22^b.2; guli mul wona *what price has it?* Vi 25.4. — *After adj. to become:* bolusëṃ ~ *to bec. muddy* C^1 199; karaṇ ~ *to be or become valid* N 4^b.6, pramāṇ(as) ~ *id.* 5^a.1. — *After 8th form: to start, to begin:* nal ~ *to begin to eat, to start eating* V^2 47^a.6. — *With 9th and 10th form or conv. in* āwo wonë *denotes, that an action has been completed just now (cf. french venir de)*: taṅāwo wonaṃ *has been lost this moment* Vi 103.4.

woṁdasā = wonasā (*cond. of* wonë) N 22^b.2. — woṃdasëṃ = wonasëṃ (*10th form of* wonë) 22^a.5.

wop, ~ danë *v. i. to stand up, to spring up, to rise* H^1 48^b.2.

wopi, *s.* = wāṃpi Md 52^a.5.

wo-phukij, *s. a co-uterine* AH 38^b (wophuki).

woya[1] (-l[1]), *v. i. to come* H^1 56^b.3; *to come into existence, to arise* (ch-g-n *from...*) H^2 71^a.1; *to pass (time)* Bh 130^a.3. — *After adj. to become* M 2^b.4. — wowo yanë = woya V^1 124^a.3. — *In connection with other verbs* = wonë: *inchoativum* H^2 62^b.1; tāsëṃ woyā *I have heard just now* H^1 82^a.4.

woya[2], *adj. furious, insane* C^1 7; ~ cāwo *id.* AH 40^a (woyachá).

woya-kākë, *caus. of* woya[1] V^1 91^b.6.

woyakë (*caus. of* woya[1]) *to cause to come, to procure* V^2 74^a.2; hṅeḍ ~ *to go to sleep* C^1 8.

wolaṁ-li, *adv. after that, hereafter* B 58^b.7.

wolagat, s. *Ficus religiosa* B 68^b.8. — ~-simā *id.* CW 6.12 (waṃlagat-).

wo-la-hnaṁ, *adv. at this time* (*corr.* gwo-la-hnaṃ) N 31^b.5.

woli[1], *pr. dem. adj. that*: gulito — ~ *what — that* P 18^a.2.

woli[2], s. = bali V[2] 62^a.4.

wolito, *pr. dem. that:* gulito — ~ *what — that* Bh 55^a.6.

wole-hma, *pr. dem. s. these:* gwo-hma — ~ *who — these* N 37^b.5.

wosa[1], s. = wosat Bh 173^b.4*.

wosa[2], s. = wosal: wosan kāwo juwo-hma *a poisoner* (garada) C[1] 114*.

wo-sakal, *pr. prs.* 3. *pl. they* Bh 54^a.7.

wosat, s. *a dress, garment* (= bastr) Bh 23^a.2. — ~-kāpal *outer garment* (nicūla) CW 8.33.

wo-sa-pol, *pr. prs. 3. s. he* (*term of respect*) B 20^b.3.

wosal, s. = wāsal; ~ yāya *to treat with medicines* N 31^a.1 (ośar).

wosi, s. *indigo:* ~-guli barṇ *indigo-coloured* H[3] 84^b.6. — ~-**kol** *an indigo-vat* H[3] 45^a.6. ~-kol-thuwāl *the owner of an indigo-vat ib.*

wo-spol, *pr. pers.* = wo-sa-pol Bh 56^a.3.

woho, s. *silver* Bh 184^a.4. — ~-banaj *silver-trade* C[1] 225. — woha = woho H[3] 38^b.1.

wo-hon, *adv. in this case* N 33^a.8; wo-honaṃ *id.* 38^b.7, *in this manner* 33^a.9*.

k.

ka'uli [*H.* kauṛī], s. *a small shell, used as coin, cowrie* B 35^a.11.

kawoḍi, s. = ka'uli N 53^a.7. — ~-mālā *a wreath* (akṣamālā) 44^b.8.

kawosi, s. *an airy room on the top of the house* V[1] 42^b.3. — kawosi-pol *roof of...* M 23^a.4.

kaṁ-ci, s. *salpeter*(?) Vd 25^b.5.

kaṁs = kas H[3] 28^b.7.

kaṁs(ā) [*S.* kaṃsa *bell-metal*], s. *tin* N 25^a.7. — kaṃs-rāṅ *id. ib.*

kakali, s. = kagali Md 76^b.8.

kakā-ju, s. *a paternal uncle* AH 38^a.

kakicā, s. *a comb* B 17^a.12*.

kakhāy [*S.* kaṣāya ... *name of sev. plants*], s. *name of a plant, used medicinally* Vd 47^a.3.

kākhṛ, s. = kagali C[2] 99*.

kagali[1], s. *a cray-fish* H[3] 55^b.4.

kagali[2], s. *stalk, straw* AH 54^a.

kagule, s. *the Numidian crane* (kareṭu) Md 75^a.2.

kaṅkaḍi, s. *i/c.* **cimI-.**

kaṅkaṇ [*S.*], s. *a bracelet* H[1] 15^a.1.

kaṅkayi [*cf. S.* kaṇkatikā], s. *a comb* CW 8.93.

kaṅgāl [*H. poor*], s. *a beggar* Vi 164.12.

kacā, s. *a branch, bough* M 31^b.2; ~-nagal *suburb* AH 24^a. — *i/c.* **mūl-, sisimā-.**

kacaṁ-gal, s. = kaci(ṃ)-°; ~-an lvāya *to quarrel* V[1] 48^b.5.

kacāḍ, s. = kacāl, ~ yāṅaṃ lvāya *to quarrel* B 65^a.11.

kacāl [*H.* kucāl *misconduct*], s. *quarrel* C[1] 259, kacālan lvāya *to quarrel* V[2] 17^b.5; thithi kacāl dayakë *to fall out with one another* H[3] 56^b.5. — *i/c.* **kaḍ-.**

kaci[1] [*H.* kac *raw*], *adj. unripe* CW 6.10; ~ mukhul *bud* (*of a flower*) *ib.*

kaci[2] = kaci(ṃ)gal C[2] 182.

kaci(ṁ)-gal, s. *quarrel, dissension* B 56^a.1, kaci-galan lvāya *to quarrel* V[2] 31^a.6, kaciṃ-gal thaya *to cause qu., diss.* P 39^b.4. kaci-galan hālë *to raise a loud, confused noise* H[3] 9^a.7.

kaci-byāl, s. = kaṃci-° Vd 50^b.5.

kacilan, ~ puya *to scratch, to claw* (*of a cat*) H[2] 98^a.1.

kachi, s. *a woman of the Śūdra-caste* AH 37^b.

kachu [*S.* kacchū *itch, scab, any*

cutaneous disease], s. *a cutaneous disease* Vd 32b.5; ~ thwolwo *who suffers from...* N 32a.8. — *ifc.* **to-**, **biphot-**.

kajjal [*S.*], s. *lead of antimony* Bh 42a.2.

kajhet, s. *jur. the defendant* N 6a.6. — kajhit *id.* 10b.7.

kaṁc-cekan, s. *a sort of oil, used medicinally* Vd 30a.2.

kaṁci-byāl, s. *a sort of Bilva fruit* Vd 21a.6.

kaṁja = kanë[1] N 23b.2.

kañjal, s. = kajjal Bh 44b.1*.

katak [*S.* kaṭaka *an army, camp*], s. *companion, follower* H[1] 27a.4; (*armed*) *attendant* V[2] 24a.4; *army* H[3] 49a.10; *inhabitants, population* B 6a.1. — *ifc.* **nani-**.

katakāy, s. = katak V[2] 69a.1.

kaṭakit [*H.* kuṭakī *a medicinal plant?*], s., *ifc.* **li-**.

kaṭabīr [*cf. Mr.* katabā *from Arab.* katābah *bond of recognizances*], s. *fine* N 28b.7; ~ kāya *to take f.* 28b.1, ~ hluya *to pay f.* 29a.3; ~-an kenë *to fine* 28b.5.

katāmahli-cā, s. *a doll, puppet* B 27a.8, ~-dewo *id.* 27b.3.

kaṭāl [*H.* kaṭārā *a kind of sugar-cane*], ~-tu *id.* Md 63a.1.

katāli [*M.* kaṭār *a knife*], s. *a cudgel* (karapālikā) AH 52a.

katin[1], *adj.* = kaṭhinī C[1] 57.

katin[2], ~ halayā suryy *the sun which have just risen* C[1] 295*.

kati-lā, s. *the month Āśvina* CW 1.50. — ~-kos-lā *the autumn* AH 12b (kaulá koyulá).

kato, *adj. blackish* (śvetakṛṣṇa) CW 1.57.

kator [*S.* kaṭhora], *adj. difficult* M 2a.1.

kaṭṭārak [*S. a weapon. dagger*], s. *a law-officer* Vi.

kathaṁ, °than(aṁ) [*S.* katham *how*], *adv. in due manner* Vi 72.27; thu-gu ~ *in this way* M 24a.5, thu-gu ~ putr *such a son* H[3] 23a.4; brahmayā ~ *in the manner of a Br.* P 7a.5; jyeṣṭ ~ *beginning from the eldest* Vi 120.17; ~-thëṃ *in due order* M 5b.3; duḥkh ma dao-guli ~ *so that they did not suffer misery* Vi 104.18.

kathak [*H.* katthak *a singer*], s., svargayā ~ *a Gandharva* CW 1.24.

kathā [*S.*], s. *a tale, story* H[2] 98b.7; ~-kha hlāya *to carry on a conversation* H[2] 36a.5.

kathi, s. *a stick* H[2] 39b.4.

kathinī [*S.* kaṭhina], *adj. hard, difficult* H[1] 15b.1.

kathu = kaṇṭh H[3] 17a.6.

kaḍamaḍālapë [*cf. Mr.* kaḍama-ḍaṇeṃ *to be feverish*], *v. i.*, °lapaṃ hlāya *to speak with a faltering voice* N 49b.5*.

kadamb[1] [*S. collection, herd*], s. *a family* N 38a.8, *a household* 2b.4.

kadamb[2] [*S.*], s. *Nauclea Cadamba*, ~-se-ke *the stalk of a N° C°* Vd 21a.4 (kaḍab).

kadācit [*S.*], *adv.*, ~ gwo belasaṃ *sometimes, once* H[2] 79b.6.

kaḍ-kac, ~ lvāya *to quarrel* N 42b.8; kaḍ-kacālan ~ *id.* 43a.2.

kanakë, *caus. of* kanë[3] H[2] 37b.1.

kanabir [*cf. Pers.* qanbīla], s. *name of a medicinal plant* Vd 32b.3.

kanas, *adv. to-morrow* H[1] 46a.1; ~ hṅācoṃ *to-morrow morning* H[2] 9a.7, ~ tewolaṃ *id.* 44a.7, ~ sutha (tewo-laṃ) *id.* 92b.8.

kaneṣṭ [*S.* kaniṣṭha], *adj. youngest* Vi 120.3.

kanehar [*cf. Mr.* kaṇer *Nerium Odorum*], ~-svān *a medicinal plant* Vd 14b.3.

kanë[1], *v. t. to tell, to make known, to communicate to, to inform* H[1] 33a.1; je ka-hune *tell me* H[1] 57b.4, rājā kanaṃ *he told the king* V[2] 25a.6, rājāyāke ~ *id.* V² 79ᵇ.1, rāniyāta ~ *he told the queen* B 68ᵇ.4; pheṅayā khaṃ kana *he told about the breaking* H¹ 57ᵇ.1; kaṅa(ṃ) haya *to announce* V² 10ᵇ.1; (ākhal) kanë *to decipher* (*letters*) B 64ᵇ.1.

kanë², *v. t.*, mikhā ~ *to open the eyes* M 37ᵃ.5.

kanë³, *v. i. to melt* H¹ 62ᵃ.4.

kaṇṭ [*S.*], *s. a thorn* CW 6.16.

kaṇṭh¹ [*S.*], *s. the neck, throat* C¹ 198. — *ifc.* **hāl²-**.

kaṇṭh², *s.* = kaṇṭ C¹ 201.

kanthagili, *s. name of a medicinal plant* Vd 42ᵃ.1. — *ifc.* **du-, li-**.

kanthanaṁ, *adv.* = kathanaṃ: janm ~ *according to age* Vi 119.28.

kanthā [*H.* kaṇṭhā], *s. a necklace* B 29ᵃ.12.

kanthu, *s.* = kaṇṭh¹ H² 41ᵇ.3.

kaṇḍ [*B. belonging to the throat, guttural*], *s. the neck, throat* C¹ 275*.

kanyā [*S.*], *s. a girl* V¹ 9ᵇ.6.

kanyādān [*S. giving a girl in marriage*], *s.* ch-hm cha-hm-yāta ~ biya *to give someone to somebody as his wife* V¹ 53ᵇ.4; kanyādān biyakë *to let the marriage be performed* Ś 159ᵇ.3.

kahnas, *adv.* = kanas V² 31ᵇ.3; ~ hnāpāṃ *to-morrow morning* B 49ᵃ.10.

kap, ~ kāya *to take hold of* Bh 82ᵇ.3. — ~ kunë *to contract, to shrink* (*itrs.*) H² 84ᵃ.6. — ~ chinë *to seize* Bh 40ᵃ.1. — ~ tāya *to keep, to retain* B 46ᵇ.6. — ~ tinë *id.* Ś 143ᵃ.5. — ~ tiya (-l¹) *to seize* Bh 35ᵇ.3.

kapat (*seldom* °paṭ) [*S.* kapaṭa], *s. fraud, deception* CW 1.73; ch-hm-yāke ~ yāya *to cheat, to deceive* H² 60ᵇ.8; ~ bacalapë *to speak treacherously* H¹ 47ᵇ.1. — ~-buddhi *cunning* H³ 50ᵃ.6. — ~-juwāl *a sharper* N 44ᵇ.8.

kapati, °**ṭī** [*S.* kapaṭin *deceitful*], *s. a cheat* H³ 61ᵇ.5; *deception* C¹ 239. — ~-juwāl *a sharper* N 44ᵇ.2.

kapan-cā, *s. the rain-bow* B 3ᵃ.4.

kapāl [*S.*], *s. the forehead* C² 270. — ~-kwos *the skull* CW 8.53.

kapās [*H.*], *s. cotton, cotton wool* B 4ᵃ.1. — ~-piri *a strainer made of cotton* Vd 14ᵃ.6.

kapur [*H.* kapūr *the root of a fragrant grass*], *s. name of a plant, used medicinally* Vd 34ᵃ.6.

kaphal, *s. an ingredient of medicine* Vd 28ᵇ.3.

kabat, *s.* = kapat B 52ᵃ.1*.

kabul [*cf. Mr.* kabūl *from Arab., agreeing*], saty ~ yāya *to make an oath* Vi 171.10.

kamān [*H. from Pers.*], *s. a bow* B 9ᵃ.2.

kamāyī [*H.* kamāī *earning, income*], ~ yāya *to earn* H² 105ᵃ.8.

kamālapë [*M.* kamāv *to serve*], *v. t.* ch-hm-yāke ~ *to serve a p.* N 20ᵇ.7.

kampamān [*S. quivering*], ~ juya *to tremble, to quake* (*the earth*) M² 75ᵃ.3.

kaṁbhaṇḍā [*cf. S.* kabandha *a big barrel*], *s. an earthern jar* N 41ᵇ.5*.

kaya¹, (-l¹), *v. t.* (*subj.: a lifeless thing*) *to hit, to strike* (*lightning*) P 46ᵃ.7, (*the wind*) H² 75ᵃ.6, (*a stick*) 33ᵃ.6; *to befall* (*sickness*) H¹ 68ᵇ.5; ch-hm-yāke ~ *to hit some-one* H³ 42ᵇ.10.

kaya², *v. t.* = kāya¹ B 19ᵃ.13; śok ~ *to be stricken by grief* M 13ᵇ.7.

kayakë (*caus. of* kaya¹) = *simpl.* (*subj.: a person*) H³ 56ᵇ.5.

kayaṁ-gal, *s.* = kaci(ṃ)-°; ~ yāya *to quarrel* V¹ 25ᵃ.6; — ~-sal *loud and confused noise* CW 1.63.

kayali, *s. tin* (raṅga) Md 32ᵇ.8.

kay-guli, *s. a sort of pea or pulse* (kalāya) Md 66ᵃ.3.

kay-ṅā, *s. an Iguana* CW 2.8.

kay-hmi, *s. name of a bird* Vi 17.15.

kal [*H.* kar *tax, toll*], *s. tax,* ~ thanë *to pay tax* N 47ᵇ.8; *tribute,* ~ pulë *to pay tribute* B 12ᵇ.10, ~ pulakë *to* *make pay tr.* 56b.10, ~ kāya *to collect tr.* 13a.4; ~ ma māl thāy *where tax is not to be paid* N 17b.6.

kalaṅk [*H. calumny*], ~-lāk *slander, calumny* N 15a.3*.

kalacukul, *s. the loins* CW 8.56. — ~-ca *the hip* 57.

kalache-ṅā, *s. a kind of fish(?)* Md 76b.4.

kalañj [*S.*], ~-pu *seed of Calamus Rotang* Vd 12a.1.

karaṭā [*cf. Mr. id. luckless, ill-starred*], *s. not admitted to Śrāddhas* (aśrāddha) N 11a.3*.

karati, *s. a saw* AH 61b.

karaṇ [*S. making, effecting*], *s. a valid transaction* N 4a.5; ~ woṃ-gwo *adj. valid* 17b.4.

kalaṁtr [*S.* kalāntara], *s. interest* (vṛddhi) N 6b.4; ~ yāya *to bear interest* N 6b.5. — *ifc.* **palik-**.

kalam [*H.* kalmī], *s. Convolvulus repens* AH 33a. — ~-ke *pulse made from* k. 46b.5.

kalalaṁ, ~ hālë *to make a tumultuous noise* H3 9a.8*.

kalaś [*S.*], *s. a vessel* H2 93a.3.

kalah [*S. quarrel*], ~ yāya *to quarrel* H2 8b.2.

kalā1 [*S.*], *s. (fine) art* Ś 153a.6.

kalā2, *s.* = kalāt B 66b.11.

kalāt, *s. wife* V2 21a.6; ~ dasëṃ coṅ .. *was married* Vi 116.29; ch-hm ~ kāya *to make somebody one's wife* H2 36b.6.

kalijug [*S.* kaliyuga], *s. the Kaliyuga* B 51b.4.

kalil [*S.* karīra *name of several plants*], *s. a plantain* Vd 32b.1.

karuṇā [*S.*], *s. compassion*; ~ cāya *to be filled with comp.* H2 80a.1; ~ cāyā-puk *adv. arousing compassion* M 27a.7.

karuṇāband [*S.* karuṇāvat], *adj. compassionate* Ś 164a.4.

karerelen, ~ hālë *to make a tumultuous noise* Ś 143b.7*.

kales [*H.*], *s. distress* Vd 34a.4.

kaleho-svān, *s. Nymphaea Lotus* AH 22a.

karkaṭā [*S.*], ~-si *s. name of a plant* Vd 24b.6.

karti [*cf. Mr.* kartarī], *s. a knife, dagger* M 33a.3.

karṇ [*S.*], *s. the ear* V1 10a.5.

kalpanā [*S. making*, —], ~ yāya *to perform (rites)* P 65b.4.

karm [*S.*], *s. a work, deed* H2 32b.5, *a ceremony* B 47b.6.

karmī [*S.* karmin], *s. a labourer, workman, artisan* B 62a.5. — *ifc.* **na-, lu-, lusi-, lwoho-, si-**.

karṣ [*S.*], *s. a weight of gold or silver* Vd 50b.2.

kas [*S.* kaṣa], *s. a touchstone* H3 57a.4. — kasi-lwoha *id.* P 27b.2.

kasamili, *s.* = kasmili; — *ifc.* **mā-**.

kasāhi [*H. from Arab.* qaṣā'ī], *s. a butcher* M 12b.8.

kasu, *s. name of a plant* (musta) Md 13a.8. — *ifc.* **bude-** — **kasul** *id.* CW 6.36.

kast [*cf. S.* kāyastha], *s. a scribe* N 8a.2*.

kaṣṭ [*S. bad, ill*], *adj. difficult* B 5a.11; kaṣṭanaṃ *adv. with difficulty* H3 37a.10. — *s.*, ~ naya *to suffer want* Vi 21.29. śarīr ~ yāya *to mortify one's flesh* H3 48b.11.

kaṣṭak [kaṣṭ], ~ ma du *indifferent, careless* H2 93b.3. ~ yāya *to undergo religious austerities* 92b.7.

kaṣṭalapë [kaṣṭ], *v. i.* śarīran ~ *to toil and moil, to drudge* H3 51a.5.

kasti, *s. honey* C1 228. — ~-thwo *sweet spirituous liquor* AH 61b. — ~-hā *a bee* CW 7.12.

kastulī [*S.* kastūrī], *s. musk* V1 113b.3.

kasmili, *s. a parrot* Ś 143a.1. — ~-cā *dim. ib.* 5.

kas-lā, *s. the month Āśvina* AH 12a

(kaulá). — ~-koy-lā *the autumn* CW 1.52.

kahan, *s. a coin* (kārṣāpaṇa) N 43b.4.

kā[1], *s. yarn, tissue* N 25b.1.

kā[2], *class-word,* lā-hāth në kā *both hands* H[2] 89a.2.

kā[3], *s. mustard, only ifc.* **e-, pal-.**

kā[4] *prt. of emphasis* H[2] 36a.2.

kā'u [kāya[1]?], ~ ~ *a war-cry* H[3] 51a.1*.

kāwo, *adj. affected with, afflicted by* V[1] 91a.1.

kā-kā[1] [kāya[1]?], *a war-cry* Vi 158.18*.

kā-kā[2] [kāya[1]], ~ yanë *to hand over* Bh 12b.1.

kā-kākë, *v. t. to confiscate* N 44a.8.

kākë, *v. t. to take away* V[1] 37a.5; *to confiscate* N 51b.5.

kāk-jhaṁgal, *s. the plant Leea Hirta* (*sic!*) Vd 26a.4.

kācakë, *caus. of* kāya[2] 1) (?) Ś 157b.3.

kāji [*H.* qāzī *from Arab.* qāḍī], *s. a law-officer, minister* Vi 40.10. — *ifc.* **mal-.**

kātapād, °pāl, ~-lakām *seven-league boots* B 14b.11.

kātar [*S.*], *adj. timid* V[1] 12b.5.

kāth-palë, *s. Nelumbium speciosum* Vd 12b.6.

kāḍhalapë [*H.* kāṛhnā —, *to earn, get*], li ~ *to recover* (*a slave*) N 20b.7*.

kān [*S.* kāṇa *one-eyed*], *adj. one-eyed, blind* H[1] 3b.4, mikhā ~ *id.* H[2] 26b.4.

kānë, *v. t.* = kanë[1] N 8b.1, kāṅa(ṃ) tāthë *to give a statement* 6a.5.

kānd = kan (*8th form of* kanë[1]) N 22a.5.

kāpaḍ, °l [*cf. Mr.* kāpaḍ *cloth*], *s. clothes, wearing apparel* B 34a.2. — ~-che *a tent* CW 8.85. — ~-bastr = kāpaḍ N 41b.6. — *ifc.* **wosat-, hlu-.**

kāpale, *s. a tortoise* H[1] 11a.5. — kāpali *id.* CW 2.7.

kāpālik [*S.*], *s. a Śaiva ascetic* V[1] 59a.5.

kāpoḍ, °ṭ, °l, *s.* = kāpaḍ Ś 145b.1; *a strainer, made from cloth* Vd 27a.2. — kāpol-ku *a "ku" of cloth* Ś 145b.5.

kām [*S.*], *s. love, lust, desire* H[1] 28b.2. — ~-thul *enamoured* CW 8.1. — ~-balā *the arrow of love* H[2] 45a.2.

kāmatul [*S.* kāmātura], ~ yāya *to be sick with love* V[1] 105a.1.

kāmanā [*S.*], *s. wish* M 37b.3; ~ yāya *to wish* Bh 2b.6. — kāmunā *id.* M 31b.5.

kāy, *s. a son, boy* H[1] 20a.4; *a young bird* B 22a.9. ~ macā, mocā, mucā = kāy H[2] 38b.1. — *ifc.* **na(ṁ)p-, bā-, rabat-.**

kāya[1] (-l[1]), *v. t. to take* (*in order to keep*) H[1] 18a.5, *to fetch* 41b.4; *to accept* (*a gift*) Vi 166.26; *to take as one's wife* H[1] 60a.4; ch-hm-yāke ~ *to take away from* N 22b.4. — balan ~ *to rape* 41a.6; jaṃ ~ *to get wages* 21b.8; ghel ~ *to produce ghee* Md 57b.4; janm ~ *to come into existence* V[2] 71b.4; abatār ~ *to make an Avatāra* Bh 3b.7; duḥkh ~ *to suffer distress* M 29b.8; saṃdeh ~ *to be in doubt* 14b.1.

kāya[2] (-t), *v. t.* 1) *to grasp, to hold firmly* H[2] 101a.7. — 2) *to crush* 52a.3.

kāyakë, *caus. of* kāya[1] B 57b.11.

kāl[1] [*S.*], *s. time* V[1] 122a.6. — *ifc.* **ani-.**

kār[2] [*cf. H.* kār-ḫāna *from Pers.*] *s. a workshop*(?) Vi 151.7.

kāraṇ [*S.*], *s. cause, reason* H[2] 99a.4; thwoyā kāraṇas *therefore* Vi 38.25, yāya(yā) ~ *in order to* H[3] 25a.6, pë-tyākayā ~ *because (he) was hungry* H[2] 108₂b.6, bhayayā ~ *on account of the danger* H[2] 50b.8; cho kāraṇas *why* H[2] 36a.1; kāraṇan = kāraṇas Vi 106.14.

kārabās, *s. a kind of medicinal plant* Vd 16a.6.

kālālā, *s. a kind of pepper(?)* Vd 47b.2.

kālijili, *s. name of several plants* Md 23a.7.

-kāle, *added to verbal stems, expressing the idea of "if", "when":* si-kāle *when... dies* N 22a.3; khaṃ-kāle *when... sees* 23a.2; ma lusëṃ jowa-kāle *if... is not found* 21b.6; ju-kāle... ju-kāle *be it... be it* 2a.5; gu-gu thāsa-ṃ juwo-kāle *wherever it may be* B 15b.9; ma dvā-kālen hṅā *before there is...* N 38a.6.

kālë, *v. t. to mix up(?)* Vd 38a.3.

kārj, *s.* = kāry V[2] 34a.5; chu kārjan *for what reason* M 69a.5; je prāṇan ~ datasā *if (you) care for my life* V[2] 73a.2.

kāry [*S.*], *s. a work, affair* B 13b.9; ~ ma du *it is meaningless* H[3] 5a.5; ch-hm-wo ~ dawo *to have to do with* C[1] 83; ~ yāya *to make preparations* V[2] 12b.3.

kāl-sā [*S.* kāla *black*], *s. the spotted antelope* CW 7.4.

Kās(a)mīr [*S.* Kāśmīra], *n. pr. Kashmir* H[3] 23b.1.

kāṣṭ [*S.* kāṣṭha], *s. wood* H[3] 33b.7.

kāṣṭapād = kātapād B 14a.5.

kāhāl [*cf. Mr.* kāhāḷa *an ancient instrument of music*], *s. a kettle-drum* CW 1.65.

ki-, *v. t. to cut* V[2] 70a.7. kisëm he *to prevent(?)* N 27b.1.

ki-ki, *look, look or show, show (a war-cry)* Vi 100.19*.

kikë, *v. t.* 1) *to cover* C[1] 148. — 2) *to smear, to defile* P 25a.5.

kīkhatu, *s.* ca ~, tawo ~ *name of two plants* (indravāruṇī *and* indrāhvā) Md 8a.1.

kicakë, [= kecakë] *v. t.* 1) *to cover* B 25b.6. — 2) *to smear, to defile* H[3] 61a.2.

ki-cot [kikë], *s. a shadow* H[2] 80a.2.

kijā, *s. a younger brother* V[1] 82b.5. — ~-ju *id.* B 53b.8. — ~-phupa *id.* N 38a.4. — *ifc.* **dadā-**, **phupa-**.

kiṃj(ā), *s.* = kijā N 38a.6.

kiṭapaṅg, *s.* = kil-pataṅg H[1] 31a.3*.

kinë, *v. t.* = kenë[2] 1) *to hide (from view)* Vi 61.26. — 2) *to smear, to defile* H[2] 114a.1; *to taint (with sin)* Vi 48.9.

kinnar [*S.*], *s. a Kinnara* Ś 158a.4.

kipā, *s. a reflected image* H[3] 35b.4.

kimi [*S.* krimi], *s. a worm* Vd 13a.5; — ~-roy *a disease, caused by worms* 25b.3.

kiyal [*cf. S.* keyūra], *s. a bracelet, worn on the upper arm* CW 8.79.

kil[1], *s. a worm* CW 7.6.

kīl[2] [*S.*], *s. a column, pillar* H[1] 22b.1.

kilakilāyamān [*S.* kilakilāya — *to crie*], *adj. screaming* Vi 46.28.*

kiraṇ [*S.*], *s. a ray of light* V[1] 74b.6.

kili [= kīl?], *s. a sort of boundary mark* N 5b.1*.

kīrtti, *s. a house(?)* Vi 22.18*.

kil-pataṅg [*S.* pataga *bird*], *s. a kind of bird* H[3] 8a.2*.

kisi, *s. an elephant* H[1] 76a.3. — ~-ku *a post, to which an e° is secured* AH 50a. — ~-ṅatā *smell of an e° (? gandha)* AH 50a. — ~-cā *a young elephant* AH 50a. — ~-bathān *a herd of elephants* H[2] 77a.2. — ~-mā'ut *an elephant-driver* HP 24.100. — ~-māga *id.* AH 70a. — *ifc.* **rājā-**.

ku[1], *s. a burden* N 21b.7; *adv.* ~ buya *to carry* H[3] 43a.8, ~ buyakë biṣay *animals of burden* N 20b.8.

ku[2], *s. a hand* C[1] 233; *a handfull* Vi 27.3; *a measure of length* B 4a.4. — *ifc.* **kāpol-**.

ku[3], *s. dust* M 36b.1. — ~-ḍani *dust-coloured* CW 1.56.

ku[4] [= kwo], ~ woya *to go down, to go along* B 43b.6. — ~ hṅyāya *to start (on a journey)* N 21b.6. — ~ cinë *to prepare (food)* B 54a.7. — ~ chinë, mi-sa ~ *to knit the brows* Vi 56.28;

wā ~ *to set the teeth* M 33b.7. — ~ tinë *to fall out, to come out* Vd 16a.5, *to fall down* H² 50a.6. ~ tinakë *to throw down, to throw out* B 49b.1. ~ **tikal** choya *to throw down* Vi 151.21. — ~ phayakë *to let subside, to let settle* Vd 33a.2.

kukull-sa, *s. a lock (of hair)* CW 8.73.

kuṅkum [*S.*], *s. saffron* V¹ 15a.5.

kucalapë [*S.* kuc], *v. to utter a shrill cry* Bh 83a.1*.

kucilā, *s. name of several plants* ("jyotiṣmatī") Md 12a.3. — ~-cikan *a sort of oil* 59a.3*.

ku-chand [*S.* chanda *pleasant*], ~ yāya *to treat roughly* N 49a.7.

ku-jaṁ [ku¹], *s. wages for transporting* N 21b.6.

kuñcit [*S.*], *adj. crooked* N 43b.4.

kut¹, *s. Costus speciosus* AH 32a.

kuṭ², ~ ~ tāya (-t) *to cut to pieces* M 14b.6; ~ ~ dhyāya (-t) *id.* 12b.3.

kutani, *s.* = kuṭini Ś 147a.2.

ku-tal, *s. care, attention:* thwoyāke ~ dayu *there will be taken care of it* H² 60a.6. — ~ ma yāya *not be attentive or careful* Vi 36.1, ~ ma dayakë *id.* P 58b.3. (kutol); rānīyāke ~ ma du *the queen did not mind it* B 69a.4. — ~-dhali *bad (coagulated) milk* Md 56b.7; — ~-byabahār *special rules* N 6b.7. — ~-misā *a procuress* CW 8.12.

ku-tā, *s.* = kul-tvāt AH 25.

kuṭini [*H.* kuṭnī], *s. a procuress* B 58a.1.

kutumā [*H.* kuṭum *kindred*], ~-**hma** *a householder's wife* CW 8.6.

kuṭunī, *s.* = kuṭini H¹ 86a.1.

kuṭumb [*S.*], *s. family, household* H² 55b.2. — *ifc.* **mūl-.**

kuṭ-bij, *s. the seed of Costus speciosus* Vd 22b.2.

kuthi [*H.* kuṭī], *s. a secluded place* B 60b.2. — *ifc.* **thwo-, laṁkha-, lākha-.**

kuthi-ṅā, *s. a kind of fish* (śakula) AH 21a.

kuḍ¹ [*cf. S.* kuṇḍa *a particular measure*], *s. a measure* Vd 16a.1.

kuḍ² [*H.* kūṛā?], *s. sweepings, rubbish*(?) N 35b.8.

kun [*H.* kon], *s. a corner, angle* Vi 59.27.

kunakë, *caus. of* kunë¹ Ś 145b.6.

kunar [*S.* kunaṭa, kunalin?], *s. name of a plant;* ~-hā *the root of it* Vd 2a.6.

kuni, *s. dust*(?) N 27a.3*.

kunu(ṁ), *adv.* = kuhnu(ṃ) H² 31b.6.

kunë¹, *v. t. to lock up, to confine, to imprison* Bh 2a.6, *to dam* N 27b.2. — kunë thās *a prison* AH 52b (kanethása).

kunë², *v. t. to blow, to stir (the fire)* B 45b.8.

kūnt, *s. a weapon*(?) Bh 160a.3*.

kundhār, *s. a student's waterpot* (kuṇḍikā) P 4a.1.

kuhnalī (*cf. S.* kunalin], *s. name of several plants* Md 20b.1. — ~-bu *Bauhinia variegata* 10a.6. — ~-si *id.* AH 27b*.

ku-hnu, *s. a day* V² 43a.1; thwo ku-hnu(s) *on this day* P 62a.5.

kuhnu(ṁ), *adv. at least* Vi 119.5; thwo kuhnuyā pālis *on each foot* Bh 77a.4.

kūp [*S.*], *s. a well* V¹ 32a.3.

ku-biṣay [*S.* ku + viṣaya — —, *concern*], *s. want of care* N 16b.1*.

ku-bëharan, *adj. misbehaved* C² 171*.

kumbh-kwos [*S.* kumbha], *s. the bone from the frontal globe of an elephant* Vd 12b.5.

kuhmar, *s. name of several medicinal plants* Vd 48a.5.

kuhmār [*M.*], *s. a potter* H³ 56b.2.

kuya (-l¹), *v. t. to shade, to over-*

shadow Md 80b.1. — kuyakë *caus. to (suffer oneself) to be shaded* H[2] 28b.6.

kuyi-svān, *s. name of a plant* ("kukṛka") Md 30b.3*.

kul[1] [*cf. S.* kūṭa *fraud, trick*], ~ yākwo *a forger* N 48b.3; ~ yāṅ sākṣī *a false witness* 12a.2, ~ sākṣī *id.* 12a.5, kulan sākṣī *id.* 12a.4; ~ kapat yāya *to act fraudulently* B 29a.5.

kul[2] [*cf. S.* kuḍava], *s. a measure of grain etc.* AH 57b.

kul[3] [*S.*], *s. family* H[2] 49b.5. — ~-kha *family quarrel* N 9a.6. — ~-strī *a decent woman* H[2] 87a.4. — *ifc.* **u-, lāy-.**

kul[4] [= kul[3]?], ch-hm-wo ~ yāya *to know carnally (a woman)* N 34b.5*.

kul[5] = kol[2]: ~ chinë *to shut firmly (the mouth)* M 15a.4.

kulā, *s. intermediate point of the compass* CW 1.38.

kulām, *s.* = kwolāṅ H[3] 34b.7.

kulāh [kul], *s. a quack, cheat* N 11a.6. — ~-mi *id.* 11b.5.

kuli, *s. an intermediate point of the compass; only ifc.* **woṁ-, yaṁ-, yai-, yau-.**

kuli-kuli-sa, *s. curls on the fore-head* AH 42b.

kule, *s. a spade* B 34a.7, kuli *id.* Bh 166b.2.

kule-svān, *s. name of several plants* Md 19a.5.

kurkuṭ [*cf. S.* kukkuṭa], *s. a cock* H[2] 98a.3.

kul-tvāt, *s. a ladder* CW 4.12.

kūrm [*S.*], *s. a tortoise* V[1] 48a.6.

kuśal [*S. well, healthy*], chi ~ juwo lā *are you doing well* B 24a.9.

kusal-hā, *s. a medicinal root* Vd 51b.6.

ku-sā [kuyakë], *s. an umbrella* Md 8b.1.

ku-si, *s. Cordia Myxa* (śelu) Vd 18a.2. — ~-mā *Calamus Rotang* Md 37a.6.

kusiyāl, *s. a sort of sugar-cane* N 47a.6. — °yā *id.* Vd 49b.2.

kuṣṭ [*S.* kuṣṭhā], *s. leprosy* Vd 26b.5. — ~-roy *id.* 32b.7.

kusyāl = kusiyāl, ~-tu *id.* Vd 33a.5. kusyā-tu *id* Md 62b.6.

kṛttam [*S.* kṛtrima *artificial, falsified*], ~ yāya *to act fraudulently* N 16a.1.

kṛḍā, *s.* = krīḍā V[2] 50a.2.

kṛpaṇ [*S. miserable, poor, wretched*], (*and* ~-hma) *adj. poor* H[3] 39a.1, *miserly* 72b.4.

kṛpā [*S. mercy*], *s. favour, mercy* H[3] 60a.10; ~ yā-hune *be as good as to...* (-·sëm) H[1] 86b.5; chi ~ datasā *if you permit, with your permission* B 52b.8.

kṛśān [*S.* kṛṣāṇa *ploughing*], ~ bāhalapë *to perform agricultural work* N 19a.3, ~ yācakā *an agricultural servant* 21a.7. — kṛśānī *s. who lives by tillage of the fields* 26b.3*.

ke, *s. broth, decoction* H[2] 88a.8. — *ifc.* **palak-, biḍe-, lalik-.**

ke-wā, *s. a sort of rice* Bh 18b.2*.

kecakë, *v. t. to smear;* mukhas ~ *to smear the face* V[1] 14a.4.

ketu, *s.* kelë.

kenakë (*caus. of* kenë[1]), *to have a thing pointed out* H[2] 42a.6.

kenë[1] (keo *ipr.* V[2] 81a.1), *v. t. to show* H[1] 16a.1, rājā *to the king* V[1] 88a.4; *to manifest, to display (strength)* H[2] 75b.3, *to point out* N 22a.6, *to decipher* B 64a.5. — *v. i. to appear, to be seen* H[3] 54a.6, svapnas ~ *to have a dream* B 22a.11.

kenë[2], *v. t.* = kanë[1] B 52b.3.

kenë[3], *v. t.* 1) *to cover* Vi 81.9. — 2) *to taint (with sin)* Bh 13b.4. — kaṭabīran ~ *to fine* N 28b.5.

kend — ken (*from* kenë[1]) N 23b.1.

kepā, *s.* = kipā H[2] 42b.5.

ke-ba, *s. a shadowy place* C[3] 296, *a garden* Vi 16.30. — *ifc.* **che-.**

kebaly [*cf.* S. kevala], *adv. only* B 16b.9. — kebal *id.* H² 53a.4.

kel, *s.* = kil; *only ifc.* **pul-pulu-**, **yaṁ-**.

kelā [*M.*: *a plantain*], *s.* ~-mā *a banana-tree* AH 31b.

kererehen, mikhā ~ kanë *to cast amorous glances, to ogle* Ś 152b.5*.

kelë, *v. t. to grind, to press*; ketu ~ *intens.* Bh 81b.5.

kel-pataṅg, *s.* = kil-° H² 22a.2*.

kehe, *s. a (younger) sister* V² 33b.3. — ~-cā *little sister (term of endearment)* Vi 26.30. — ~-tatā *a sister generally* P 59a.2. — *ifc.* **tvāc-**.

kaitak [*M.*], *s. curiosity* CW 1.70.

këṁ, *s. a couch* (khaṭvā) N 41b.5*.

kënakë, *caus. of* kënë V¹ 119a.5.

kënë, *v. t. to catch (game)* H¹ 21b.3; pāśas, pāśan ~ *to be caught in a trap* 26a.5.

këhë, *s.* = kehe N 37b.7.

kokāli, *adj. younger* AH 68b; ~-hma *s. a younger brother* AH 39a.

kokhato, *s. a plant, the root of which is used medicinally* Vd 29b.4.

kocakë, *v. t. to destroy*(?) N 26a.5 (kocako)*.

koṭ [*H. a city wall?*], ~-khā *the outer door* (bahirdvāra) CW 4.11.

koṭān-koṭi [*S.* koṭi], *s. ten thousands of* Bh 144b.6.

koṭi [*S.*], *s. ten thousand* H² 81b.8.

koḍ-se, *s. a medicinal plant* Vd 16b.5.

kopalapë [*S.* kopa *anger*], *v. i. to become angry, excited* M 14a.3; *med. to be incensed* Vd 3a.5.

koput, *s. a chair* (pīṭha) AH 45a.

komal [*S.*], *adj. soft, bland, charming* V¹ 9b.2.

koya, *v. t.* = kuya CW 5.6. — koyakë *caus.* = kuyakë C¹ 296.

koyār, *adj.* ~ karm *a dirty work* N 19b.5*.

koyil [*M.* koil *the Indian cuckoo*], *s.*, ~-svān *name of several plants with dark flowers* (kokilākṣa) Md 31a.

koy-lā, *s. the month Kārtika* CW 1.51.

kol¹, *s. a species of grain, eaten by the poor* (kodrava) AH 54a.

kol², ~ chiya *v. t. to settle (a quarrel)* Ś 149b.3; ~ jiya *v. i. to perish* Vi 122.21; ~ thaya *v. t. to fell (a tree)* H¹ 110b.2. — ~ ma jik *unutterable* AH 16b.

kolapë, *v. t. to encourage* H³ 44b.7.

kolāhal [*S.*], *s. a great and indistinct noise* H² 96b.7.

koli, *s. a measure of length*(?) Ś 145b.2*.

kolë, *v. t. to irrigate* N 27b.3; laṃ kolë bandh *a dike for irrigation* 27b.2.

koloṭ-khā, *s. a kind of curlew* (krauñca) CW 7.10.

kol-tok, *s. a skull* CW 8.54.

kol-bus, *s. a grass-hopper* CW 7.13.

kol-se, *s.* = koḍ-~ Vd 41b.4.

koś [*S.* krośa], *s. a measure of length* Bh 35b.7. — *ifc.* **bā-**.

kos, ~ ma dale *secretly*(?) H² 31a.6*.

kautuk [*S.* — *curiosity, anything creating c°*], *s. wonder, marvel* B 30a.3; ~ cāya *to wonder* H¹ 32a.5, *to become curious* H³ 59b.7; ~ juya *id.* B 10b.2. — ~ ma dayakaṃ *carelessly* P 26a.3.

kausi, *s.* = kawosi Bh 78b.6.

kaustuk, *s.* = kautuk, kaustukan *from curiosity* V² 38b.6. ~ yāya *to cause curiosity, to attract one's attention* V¹ 49b.5.

kwo¹, *adv.*, ch-g-n ~ *down from...* H³ 22b.6, *from... downwards* Vd 48a.2; simā ~ woya *to come to the spot below a tree* H¹ 95a.5; simā ~ twol-lë *to leave the spot beneath a tree.*

kwo² [= kwo¹], ~ kāya *to take down* (ch-g-n *from...*) V¹ 96b.5, *to waste, to squander* H² 49b.8, *to prepare (food, medicine)* Vd 46a.2; ch-hm-yā nāmas ~ ~ *to take one's name from...* B 21a.4.

~ kākë *to waste, to squander* H³ 23ᵃ.5. — ~ khāy (-l¹) *v. i.*, gal-potas ~ *to hang round the neck (ornaments)* Vi 160.16. ~ khāyakë *caus.* C¹ 26. — ~ cuya *to wash down, to swill down (food)* Vd 49ᵃ.3; ~ cuyakë *caus.* 29ᵃ.5 — ~ chuya (-t) *v. i. to bend down* Vi 43.18; *v. t.* moḍ ~ *to bend down one's head* H² 51ᵇ.4. ~ chukë *caus.* = *simpl. trs.* 86ᵃ.1. — ~ tanë *to fall down* V¹ 2ᵃ.3; ~ tanaṃ choya *to throw down* 31ᵇ.5. ~ tanakë *caus. to throw down* V² 4ᵇ.6; ~ taṃkë *id.* 2ᵃ.5. — ~ tānë *v. i. to fall down* V¹ 6ᵇ.3; *v. t. to throw down* N 14ᵃ.2, *to put down (the foot)* P 19ᵇ.6. — ~ tinë *to fall down* H¹ 24ᵃ.5; ~ tinakë *caus. to throw down* P 51ᵇ.4, *to throw out* (ch-g-s *into…*) Bh 166ᵇ.1; ~ tiṃkë *id.* P 51ᵇ.4. — ~ telë *to put down (the foot)* Bh 57ᵃ.4; ch-hm-yāta ~ *to defeat, to subdue…* Vi 153.29. — ~ tonakë *to let fall, to let drop* V² 20ᵇ.4. — ~ thaya *to make come out (worms etc.)* Vd 48ᵃ.2; ~ thë : mocā ~ ~ *to produce abortion* N 36ᵃ.1. — ~daya : ~ dawo *there is diarrhoea* Vd 23ᵇ.6; cā kwo dawo *there happens an abortion* Bh 59ᵃ.7, garbhasaṃ ~ ~ *id.* H³ 23ᵃ.4. ~ dayakë *caus. to make come out (worms)* Vd 47ᵇ.6, *to make flow (blood)* 39ᵃ.2. — ~ dhāya (-t) *to throw oneself down* M 15ᵇ.8. — ~ puya *to wrap up*(?) Vd 48ᵃ.5. — ~ poya = *foreg.* 50ᵃ.2. — ~ phiya *to throw* (jalas *into the water*) Bh 40ᵃ.1. — ~ phvāya *to drive out* H² 105ᵇ.4. — ~ bvāya *to leap down* Bh 185ᵃ.2. — ~ lāya *to perish* H¹ 66ᵇ.5; *to set (the sun)* P 45ᵃ.2; ch-hm-yāke ~ *to bend down before…* H³ 54ᵇ.4; ~ lākwo *s. an apostate* N 11ᵃ.7. — ~hlāya (-t) *to perish* C¹ 176, *to suffer a loss, to be diminished in value* N 25ᵇ.2. — ~ sālë *to drag or pull down* H¹ 59ᵇ.2. — ~ swoya *to look down* (ch-g-n *from…*) Ś 161ᵇ.7; ~ swokë *caus.* H² 66ᵇ.4. — ~ hāya *to go down* Bh 69ᵃ.3.

kwo-wonë, *adv. farther down (the river)* H² 22ᵃ.2.

kwo-kā, *see* **tha-kā.**

kwo-kwo-byāṅ, *s. a frog* H² 112ᵇ.3.

kwokha, *s. a crow* H¹ 11ᵃ.5. — kwokhā *id.* C¹ 121. — *ifc.* **ba-, mā-, sa-.**

kwoc, *s.* = kwos H² 31ᵇ.6, kwocan hṅā *to the bones* N 51ᵇ.1.

kwo-ta, ~ yanë *to lead down* B 58ᵇ.5. — ~ haya *to bring down* Vi 177.29.

kwoṭawāl, °ṭu° [*M.* kotavāl *a watchman*], *s. an armed guard, police* V¹ 20ᵃ.4.

kwo-tal = ku-tal H³ 11ᵇ.2; kwotol *bad*(?) N 22ᵃ.2.

kwo-ti, ~ wonë *to go down* H³ 26ᵃ.4.

kwo-tu, *adv.*, kwo-tu-tu yanan *according to the order* (anukramāt) N 38ᵇ.2*.

kwothā¹ [*H.* koṭhā], *s. a room, apartment* V² 23ᵃ.4, *house* H² 96ᵇ.6; *the female apartments* C¹ 244.

kwothā², *s. a mule*(?) H² 68ᵇ.8 = H³ 37ᵃ.3*.

kwothu, *adj. low, lower:* ~ phal *a verandah, balcony* (vitardi) CW 4.11; ~ hmutu-si *the lower lip* AH 42ᵃ.

kwo-thyāk, *adj. deep, low* AH 20ᵇ (kothyá).

kwo-du, *adv. below* Bh 33ᵃ.4*.

kwon, ~ daya *to suffer from diarrhoea* Vd 22ᵇ.1. — ~ puya (-l¹) *to be depressed*(?) 39ᵃ.3; ~ poya *id.* N 17ᵇ.6. — ~ wol phas *one of the vital airs* (apāna) CW 1.26.

kwonë¹, *v. t. to clasp, to cling to*(?) B 55ᵇ.9*.

kwonë², *adv. below, downstairs* B 17ᵃ.7*.

kwo-pipi [= °-pepe], ~ wonë *to go down to* Bh 21ᵇ.6*.

kwo-pu, *see* **thwo-pu.**

kwo-pepe, ~ yanë *to let down, to lower* Bh 4a.6*.

kwo-bah, *adj. next or lower in rank* N 40b.6*.

kwo-bi, *s. the middle region* (madhyadeśa) CW 3.2.

kwo-bvāj, *s. a low caste, low-casteman* N 45a.8; ~-jāti *id.* 45a.7.

kwolāṅ, *s. a granary* H[2] 65b.2. — °lām *id.* H[3] 34b.2.

kwolot, *s., see* **ëyu, hyāṅu.**

kwo-loy, *s. diarrhoea*(?) Vd 42b.3.

kwos[1], *s. a bone* H[1] 29b.2. — *ifc.* **kumbh-, dugu-, bëko-, hāl-.**

kwos[2], *adv.*, ch-g(-yā) ~ *below* H[1] 94b.3; *among* N 26a.3.

kwoṣṭ [*S.* koṣṭha], *s. the intestines* Vd 4a.5*.

kwohaṁ, ~ ~ hālë *to scream violently* M 26a.5*.

kwo-hā(ṁ), ~ woya *to go or step or climb down* (ch-g-n *from*...; ch-g-s *into*...) V[1] 11b.3; ~ wonë *id.* M 5b.3; ~ bt-jyāya *id.* 26a.1.

kwo-hāwo, *adj. deep* C[2] 32*.

kyātu, *adj. tender* H[1] 27b.1; kyātuyāo *becoming tender* Ś 157b.2; kyātu la'uni *fresh butter* Md 57b.7.

kyāya, *v. t.* = khyāya N 8a.4.

krīḍā [*S. sport, play, amorous sport*], ~ yāya *to play* (*as children*) Bh 12b.2, *to have sensual intercourse* 54b.1.

krīḍālāpë [*s.* krīḍā], *v. i. to have sensual intercourse* V[2] 45b.3.

kripann = kṛpaṇ (*miserly*) V[1] 50b.2.

kriyā [*S. act, action*], *s. a lawsuit, case* N 13b.1, *title, right* 5b.7, *a* (*righteous*) *act* 41a.1; ~ yāya *to begin a lawsuit* 6a.2, *to be entitled* 5b.5; ch-hm-yā ~'s juya *to become the property of* ... *ib.* 4. — *ifc.* **aṅk-.**

krodh [*S.*], *s. anger, wrath* V[1] 18a.2. — krodhalapë *v. i. to get angry* Bh 124a.3.

kvadhi, *s. a bodily defect*(?) Bh 43b.4*.

kvā-[1] (-t *or* -l?), *v. t. to peck* (*of birds*) H[1] 94a.3. kvātu ~ *id. intens.* H[2] 76a.8.

kvā[2], ~ ~ yāya = kvā-[1] H[3] 21b.9.

kvāk [kvāya], *adj. hot, warm* H[1] 50b.5.

kvāṅu, *adj. hot, warm* Vd 32a.3.

kvācakë (*caus. of* kvāya), *to make hot or warm* H[2] 33b.5.

kvācu, *adj. hard* M 33b.8. kvācayu *becomes hard* Vd 6a.6.

kvātu, *s. excess* (atiśaya) CW 1.29. — kvātukaṃ (*also* °ta°, °ti°), *adv. firmly, tightly* H[2] 32a.3.

kvāth[1] [*S. a decoct*], *s.* ~ dāya *to decoct* Vd 2a.2; ~ cāyā ti *extracted juice* AH 73a. — ~-ti *an infusion, extract.* 71b.

kvāth[2], *s. an array of troops* (vyūha) AH 51b.

kvāya (-t), *v. i. to become hot or warm* Vd 9b.5.

kvāsë, *s. the scrotum, testicles* H[3] 25a.2. — ~-maṃgwo *an abscess of the testicles* Vd 27b.3. — kvāsi = kvāsë AH 41.

kṣa = khë[1] V[2] 23b.5.

kṣatrapalapë [*cf. S.* kṣetra], bījā ~ *to sow seed* N 31a.5*.

kṣatrī [*S.* kṣatrin], *s. a man of the Kṣatriya-caste* V[2] 79a.4.

kṣaṇ [*S. a moment*], cha-hnuyā ~'s *some day* V[1] 13a.6. — kṣaṇamātraṃ.. ma *not even a moment* 117a.6.

kṣamā [*S. patience, forbearance*], ~ yāya *to forgive, to bear with* H[2] 78a.3; ch-hm-yāke ~ taya *to be lenient or indulgent to*... H[2] 72b.3; ~ yācakë *to ask for forgiveness* V[1] 125a.3.

kṣamābant [*S. adj. indulgent*], *s. forbearance* H[2] 11b.4.

kṣamālapë [kṣamā], *v. i. to agree to* V[2] 62a.6.

kṣay [*S. loss, decay*], *s. loss* (*by using or wearing*) N 25a.3; ~ juya *to* *perish* Bh 103ª.3. — ~-log *consumption* CW 8.42.

kṣale = **khële.**

kṣi, *incorr. spelling for* chi B 51ᵇ.4.

kṣikṣiri, *s. the bowl of a bhikṣu* Vi 95.3*.

kṣudhā [*S.* kṣudh], *s. hunger* H² 93ᵇ.6, ch-hm-s ~ julo... *has become hungry* V¹ 13ª.1.

kṣepalapë [*S.* kṣip], *v. t. to throw* Bh 114ª.5, bij ~ *to produce seed, to beget* N 31ª.5.

kh.

kha¹, *s. a word, tale, story* H¹ 57ᵇ.1, *a message* V¹ 63ª.4, *an affair* Ś 149ª.5, *a lawsuit* B 33ª.1. — gupt ~ *a secret* H¹ 53ª.2; ~ ṅenë *to ask a question* Ś 151ª.7; ~ hlāya *to converse* 159ᵇ.2; ~ saya *to be able to speak* (*of a parrot*) 143ª.5; ~ sawo *eloquent* V² 33ᵇ.2; ~ ṅanë sawo-hma *a Śrotriya* H³ 13ª.1. — *ifc.* **aṁś-, kul-, guṇ-, cho-, jāsu-, phas-, bu-, bṛttānt-, bṛthā-, bo-, mi-, lu-, samācār-, sā-, spaṣṭ-.**

kha² [khaya¹], *used after the verb. fin. concludind the sentence* (*lit.:* "*so it is*") H¹ 72ª.4. ~ jak *indeed, it is true* V² 76ª.7; ~ jukwo *id.* V¹ 129ᵇ.5 (khā).

kha-wā, *adj. garrulous* C¹ 142*.

kha-wāt, *s. news* B 8ᵇ.5.

khawo¹ [khaya¹], *adj. right, correct* B 18ª.3; ~ yākwo *virtuous* N 45ᵇ.7.

khawo², *adj. left* (*opp.: right*) M 19ᵇ.8; khawos *on the left side* Vd 14ª.2.

khaṁs, *s.* = kha¹ V¹ 108ª.4.

kha(ṁ)-khaṇḍalapë, *v. i.* = kha-ṇḍalapë (*intens.*) H¹ 22ᵇ.3.

khaṅg [*cf. S.* khaḍga], *s. a sword* B 11ª.9.

khaṁ-gwo [khanë¹], *s. a witness* N 15ª.1.

khacalapë [*cf. Mr.* khacaṇeṃ], *v.t. to set* (*with gold, jewels*...) Bh 173ᵇ.3*.

kha-ci, *adv. sometime, a moment* H¹92ᵇ.2; ~ khācā *id.* Bh 92ᵇ.7; kha-cinaṃ... khacinaṃ *now...now* Vd 5ᵇ.5; khacin-li *after a moment* V² 22ᵇ.3.

kha-chi, *adv.* = kha-ci V¹ 118ª.2.

khajānā [*H. from Arab.* ḫazānah], *s. a treasury* H² 97ᵇ.6, *provisions* 84ª.3.

khajur-se [*S.* kharjūra], *s. Phoenix dactylifera* Vd 52ᵇ.1.

khajhāl [*cf. Mr.* khajāḷ *libidinous*], *adj. soft* H² 72ᵇ.7*.

khañjan, *s.* = kajjal Bh 44ᵇ.1*.

khat, *s., ifc.* **bimān-.**

kha-taṅā, *s. a piece of wood projecting like a nose over a door* (nāsā) CW 4.9.

khataras [*S.* ṣaḍrasa], *adj. having the six flavours* H³ 44ᵇ.11.

khati [*H.* khaṭiyānā *to live as friends*], ch-hm ~ yāya *to be associated with*..., *to be married to*... C² 252.

khaḍagwol, *s. a bolt* (*of a door*) CW 4.12.

khadu, *s. a threshold* CW 4.8. — *ifc.* **lukhā-.**

khaḍg [*S.*], *s. a sword* V¹ 42ª.6.

khanakë (*caus. of* khanë¹) *to make visible, to show*; hi ~ "*to show blood*" *i. e. to get a bleeding wound* N 44ª.6; ma khanakāwo *without being seen* V¹ 44ᵇ.5.

khanati [*M.* khanati], *s. a hoe* H¹ 34ª.2.

khanë¹, *v. t. to see, to become aware of* H¹ 12ᵇ.3, wowo khaṅāwo *on seeing* (*him*) *come* 63ª.2; *to regard, to look upon* (*as*) H³ 11ᵇ.8. mikhānaṃ ma khaṅ-hma *quite blind* 9ª.5. khiṅu khanë *to look dark* Vd 9ᵇ.1. khanë daya *to be or become visible* Vd 9ᵇ.1, ~ dayakë *to make visible* Ś 152ᵇ.5; khanë ma du *has become invisible, has disappeared* H² 99ª.4.

khanë², *v. t. to open* (*a door*) B 48ª.7.

khanti, *s.* = khanati H² 38ª.3.

khaṇḍ[1] [*S.*], *s. a piece, fragment* Bh 13a.7; ~ ~ juya *to go to pieces* 62a.1.

khaṇḍ[2] [*H.*], *s. a tract, region* H[2] 86b.7.

khaṇḍ[3] [*S.* khaḍga?], *s. a weapon* (vāhana) N 12a.8*.

khaṇḍalapë [*cf. S.* khaṇḍita *disappointed, betrayed*], *v. i. to become dismayed, to lose one's senses* H[2] 41b.6.

khahn, *s. sword* H[3] 47a.5.

khaparā [*H. tile*], *s. a pot-sherd* N 26b.4.

khapali [*cf. Mr.* khaparī *a pointed bit of stone*], ~-bhu *stony soil* (śarkarā) CW 3.3.

khabal [*H.* ḫabar *from Arab.*], *s. news* Vi 166.33; ~ choya *to send word* Ś 169b.1.

khabij-se, *s. a kind of medicinal plant* Vd 28b.2.

kha-bu, °**-bo,** *s. (confidential) conversation* H[3] 44a.11.

kha-ma, *part.* V[2] 13a.6; āwo ~ = āwo H[2] 40a.5; kha-ma-ne = kha-ma Ś 149a.1.

khaya[1] (*1st form:* khata, khato, khate; *5th form:* khawo, khu, kha; *6th form:* khayā; *cond.:* khatasā, kha(ṃ)sā), *v. i. to be (somehow)* V[2] 32a.4; *to be right, to be proper* H[3] 47b.3. — kha(wo) ma khu *whether it is so or not* V[1] 21b.4, *what is right and what is wrong* V[2] 33b.4.

khaya[2] (-l[1]), *v. i. to shine, to radiate* H[1] 39b.5, ch-g-s *upon...* V[1] 73a.2; *to become apparent* H[2] 95b.2; ma du khaya *to disappear* V[2] 32b.6.

khaya[3] (-l[1]), *v. t. to open (a door)* B 31b.1.

khayakë (*caus. of* khaya[2]), *to make bright* M 4a.2, *to make shine* H[2] 62a.3; kha~ *to make out or to unravel an affair* B 26b.2; ghāl ~ *to inflict a wound* N 42b.6; khayakaṃ, *adv. openly* 48b.3, *plainly* B 17a.3.

khayamugal, *s.* = khāya° Md 18a.5.

khayal [*cf. Mr.* khayar], *s. Acacia Catechu* Vd 13a.3. — ~-sì *id.* Md 37b.5. — *ifc.* **khor-, cet-.**

khayi(l), *s. phlegm* M 12a.6.

khal, *s. the thigh, femur* V[1] 19a.3.

khalak [*Mr.* khaṛak *a pound for cattle*], *s. a flock, troop* CW 7.17.

khalac, *s.* = kharc V[1] 42a.5.

khalam, *s. a harrow* AH 53b.

khalu, *s.* = khadu AH 24. — *ifc.* **kwo-, tha-.**

kharos, ~ ma cāyā (*we*) *don't succeed* (?) N 49a.4*.

kharg [*H.* khaṛag], *s. a sword* V[2] 27b.4.

kharc [*H. from Pers.* ḫărč], *s. money, provisions* V[2] 68b.7, *wages, hire* H[2] 89a.4.

khal-pāy, *s.* = khal B 43b.9.

kha-hlāsal, *s. telling tales; conversation* B 28b.1*.

khas[1], *s.* = kha[1] V[2] 32b.2.

khas[2] [khaya[1]] = kha[2] H[1] 90a.3.

kha-su, *s. hoar-frost* CW 1.42.

khā[1], *a cock* C[1] 121. — *ifc.* **uṁ-, koṭ-, koloṭ-, guṁ-, che-**[2]**, thas-, pi-, pipili-, hmas-, hmus-, hmos-.**

khā[2], *s. a door.* — *ifc.* **che-**[1].

khā[3], *s.* = kha[1] V[1] 108b.4.

khā[4] [= khā[2]], *cl.-w. (of a house)* Vi 43.26.

khā-kākë, *v. t. to cut off* N 51b.1.

khākë (*caus. of* khāya[1]), *to let cut* N 41b.1.

khā-khā, sal ~ tukë *to stutter, to stammer* M 8b.8, tucakë *id.* Vi 55.8, tutakë *id.* Bh 4b.6, twocakë *id.* N 49b.5.

khācakë, *v. t. to produce (milk)* Vd 40b.2*.

khācā, *see* **kha-ci.**

khāco-svān, *s. Anethum Sowa* Md 15a.5.

khātā [*M.* khāṭ *a bed*], *s. bed, a bed-*

stead V² 75ª.7; ~-talas *under the bed* H² 80ᵇ.7. — ~-khol *the leg of a bed-stead* B 39ᵇ.9.

khādo, *s. a plant, the root of which is used medicinally* Vd 3ᵇ.2.

khān [*H.* khānā *to eat*], khān pān yāya *to eat and drink* P 55ᵇ.2*.

khāṇi [*S.*], *s. a mine* H¹ 9ᵇ.3, *fig. source* Vi 89.30. — *ifc.* **hel-**.

khā-pā, *s. a leaf of a door, door* Bh 12ª.7; *a gate* 73ᵇ.4.

khāpur, *s. an ingredient of medicine* Vd 16ª.4.

khāya¹ (-t; khāyāwo N 13ª.7), *v.t. to cut* V² 73ᵇ.1.

khāya² (-t), *v. t. to perform (a ceremony)* N 32ᵇ.5.

khāya³ (-t), *v. t. to keep off* (nivāraya) N 28ᵇ.1.

khāya⁴ (-l¹), *v. t. to hang, to suspend* H² 36ª.4.

khāya⁵ [-t], *v. i.* je bhāgyan khānā *I am favoured by luck* H² 18ª.7, ji ~ khāyā *id.* B 5ª.11; ch-hm-yāta parigati khāta *the authority rests with...* N 39ᵇ.9.

khāyakē, *caus. of* khāya⁴; *see* **kwo**.

khāyamugal, *s. Abrus precatorius* (guñjā) CW 6.28.

khāyu, *adj. bitter, pungent* Vd 45ᵇ.2. khāyuwo *id.* 46ª.5. khāyu laglā *cucumber* CW 6.35; ~-bastu-si *mountain ebony* P 30ᵇ.5.

khāl¹ [*H. a rivulet, creek*], *s. a ditch* Vi 51.6; *a moat, trench* H² 84ᵇ.2; *the coast (of the sea)* B 11ª.6.

khāl² [*H.* khār *alkali*] *s. crystal, quartz* H¹ 9ᵇ.3. — ~-ci *rock salt* Md 24ᵇ.4.

khāl³, *s.*; *only ifc. (in plant-names):* **yamas-**, **sit-**, **set-**.

khā-lā, *s. meat of a cock* Vd 45ᵇ.6.

khāsā¹, *s. an article of dress* B 51ᵇ.12*.

khāsā², *s. the felly of a wheel* AH 50ᵇ.

khi¹, *s. excrements* H¹ 29ᵇ.2. — *ifc.* **bal-khunī-**, **sa-¹**, **sā-**, **hi-**.

khi-² (-t *or* -n), *v. t. to dig out(?)* C¹ 109 (khiṅāwo)*.

khi'u¹, *adj.* = khiṅu; *dark, gloomy* Vi 56.20, ~ milā *the dark fortnight* AH 11ᵇ. — khi'ukē *to make dark or gloomy* Vi 111.28.

khi'u², *adj. empty* Ś 156ª.3; khi'uro *is empty* 6.

khiṁ, *s. a sort of drum* CW 1.65. — *ifc.* **daṁgo-**, **nay-**.

khi-khā, *s. the buttocks* N 44ª.4.

khi-gu, *s. name of a plant* (prasāriṇī) CW 6.34.

khiṅu, *adj. dark* C¹ 150; *s. darkness* C² 151. khiṅasē(ṃ) wonē *to become dark* 17.

khicā, *s. a dog* V² 12ª.6. — ~-khvāc *a mark of a dog's foot, branded on the body* N 41ᵇ.1. — *ifc.* **gu-**, **mā-**.

khiti, *s. secretion, excretion* AH 40ᵇ.

khin [*cf. S.* kṣīṇa], *adj. weakened, feeble* Vd 44ᵇ.3.

khinukē, *v. t.*, khvāl ~ *to show a gloomy face* Vi 50.4*.

khinwoṁ, °**naṁ**, °**nuṁ**, *adv. at least* H¹ 45ª.1; cho ~ *what ever* 59ª.5.

khipot, *s. a rope* V¹ 15ª.6. °pat *id.* H² 63ª.3, *the string of a musical instrument* AH 17ª.

khu-¹ (*1st form:* khuta, khuto, khute, khure; *5th form:* khu), *v. i.* = khaya¹ (*used only after* ma); ma khu *is not* H² 52ª.2; *is not proper* B 18ª.3; *after a verb. fin.: not, not at all* 58ᵇ.4; ma-khu hanwoṃ — lā... ma-khu hanwoṃ — lā *shall it be so... or shall it be so* Ś 164ª.7.

khu², *num. six* H¹ 9ᵇ.5.

khu³, *s.* = khwo¹ B 68ᵇ.8. — ~-si *the bank of a river* C² 249.

khu-⁴ (-t *or* -n?), *v. t. to tear asunder* B 55ᵇ.9 (khuṅā-).

khu(ṁ), *s. a thief, robber* V¹ 19ᵇ.6; ~-hma *id.* C² 80. — *ifc.* **dohi-**.

khukhul-cā, *s. name of a bird* Md 74ᵃ.6.

khu-tā, *num.* = khu² C¹ 121.

khu-nu(ṁ), *adv.* = °-hnu(ṃ) Vi 113.13.

khunë, *v. t. to boil, to roast* Vd 55ᵃ.6.

khuṇṭ [*H.* khũṃṭā *a (tent-) peg*], *s. a peg (used as boundary-mark)* N 27ᵃ.4.

khu-hnu, *s. a day* M 3ᵇ.8.

khu-hnu(ṁ), *adv. only, at least* Vi 113.9.

khuya¹ (-l¹), *v. t. to steal, to rob* H¹ 17ᵃ.3. khuyāwo *secretly* V² 53ᵃ.1, khusëṃ *id.* V¹ 85ᵇ.4; khusëṃ yanë *to cary off secretly* N 22ᵇ.1.

khuya², *num. sixty* Ś 145ᵇ.2, ~-tā *id.* C¹ 238.

khuya³, yal ~ *to bend* C¹ 48.

khul¹ [*cf. S.* kṣura], *s. a razor.* — ~-hmicā *s. a razor-case* H² 63ᵇ.1.

khul² [*H.* ḫol *a cover, case*], *s. the outer coverings of a thing; only ifc.* **bi-, mut-, saṁ-, si-.**

khul³, *adj.* = khol¹ Vi 94.22.

khul⁴, *s.* = khwoḍ C¹ 238*.

khusi¹, *s. a river* C¹ 176. — ~-ṅā *a fish, living in rivers* Md 76ᵃ.3. — ~-dhik *the bank of a river* B 58ᵃ.2. — ~-si *id.* B 45ᵃ.5.

khusi² [*M.* khusī *delighted, glad from Pers.* ḫūšī], *s.*, ch-hm-yā ~ juya *to be at one's disposal* Vi 40.25; thawo ~·naṃ *of one's own accord* HP 24.104; wosapolayā ~ *it is you to decide it* B 34ᵇ.10; thawo ~ yāya *to do as one likes* Vi 41.3; ~ yāya *to enjoy* B 46ᵇ.2; ~ juya *to become pleased* 58ᵇ.6; ~ juyakë *to please* H³ 44ᵃ.4; mebuyā ~ *dependent* AH 63ᵃ; thawo ~ du *independent ib.*

khewā [*M.*], *s. ferry hire* Vi 92.33.

khewo, *adj. strongly made* (sthūla) N 30ᵇ.2*.

khet = khë¹ H³ 31ᵇ.11.

khe(ṁ)-ja, *s. an egg* H³ 58ᵇ.4, ~ choya, chaya *to lay eggs* B 64ᵃ.9. — *ifc.* **ṅā-.**

kheḍ [= khel¹?], *s. an island* Bh 46ᵇ.3*.

kheyā [khaya¹?], ~ liwonë *particularly* (viśeṣataḥ) N 46ᵇ.6*.

khel¹ [*S.* khila], *s. a desert, uncultivated land* N 28ᵃ.1. — ~-lalik *a medicinal plant* (jīvantī) Md 5ᵇ.5. — *ifc.* **bā-.**

khel² [*H. play, game*], *s. (sensual) pleasure* Vi 43.11; — ~-bacan *playful words* Bh 142ᵃ.6.

khelati-si, *s. a kind of medicinal plant* Vd 34ᵇ.2.

khelalapë [khel²], *v. i. to play, to enjoy oneself* Bh 46ᵇ.6.

khes = khë¹ V² 74ᵇ.2.

khë¹ = kha² V¹ 123ᵇ.5.

khë-² (-t *or* -n?), *v. t.*, cal ~ *to unfold* B 4ᵃ.11 (khëṅā)*.

khëṁ, *a class-word*(?) M 32ᵇ.8.

khën [*S.* kṣaṇa], *s. a moment* H¹ 63ᵃ.1.

khële (*also spelt* kṣale), ~ ma du *is useless, is of no account* C¹ 157; chus ~ *what is to be done?* C² 206.

khokhar-mā, *s. a plant used in medicine* Vd 22ᵃ.4.

khoj [s. khojalapë], ~-khabal *hue-and-cry* Ś 155ᵇ.5*.

khojalapë [*M.* khojab], *v. t. to seek, to search for* V¹ 20ᵃ.5.

khoṭ [*cf. M.* khuṭā *a peg, post*], *s. a trunk, stem; only ifc.* **si-.**

khotāki, *s. a small well* (kūpaka) AH 20ᵃ.

khotopā, *s. a medicinal plant* Vd 12ᵇ.5.

khoḍ, *adj.* = khol¹ N 43ᵇ.3*.

khon, ~ yāya *to rebuke severely* N 49ᵇ.1.

khopar [*Hi.* khoprā *kernel of a cocoa-nut?*], *s. a plant, used in medicine* Vd 34ᵃ.5*.

khopas, *s. tin or lead* (vaṅga) AH 58ᵇ.

khoya (-l^1), *v. i. to become clarified* (*milk, butter*) Md 55^b.4.

khol^1 [*S.*], *adj. lame, halting* CW 8.41.

khol^2, *s.* = khul^1 H^2 63^b.1.

khol^3, *s. a leg of a bedstead* B 39^b.11. — *ifc.* **khātā-**.

khor^4 [*S.* khura], *s. a hoof* Bh 62^a.1*.

kholalapē [*M.* khor *a heap of grain*], *v. t. to heap up*(?) V^2 18^a.1*.

khorā^1, *s. a cup* (*measure of capacity*?) Vd 23^a.4. — *ifc.* **sijal-**.

kholā^2, *s. bark*; *only ifc.* **simā-**.

khol-khayal-si, *s. name of a plant* (arimeda) Md 37^b.2.

khol-si, *s. a walnut* Md 43^b.4.

khwo^1, *s. a river* H^1 56^a.1. — ~-si *the bank of a river* C^1 249. — ~-ho *the confluence of two rivers* N 33^b.9.

khwo^2, *adv. at least, only* N 29^b.5.

khwo^3 [= khu^1?], ma ~ tānē *to kill*(?) N 36^a.1*.

khwoṁs, *s.*, ~ kāwo *a receiver of bribes* (utkocaka) N 48^b.3*.

khwokan, *s. a medicinal plant* (parpaṭa) Vd 41^b.3.

khwoṅaṁ, *adv. only* H^1 64^b.5.

khwoḍ, *s. an eunuch* C^2 238*.

Khwopa, *n.pr. Bhatgaon* HP 24.102*.

khwo-bi [khwoya^1], *s. a tear* V^1 130^b.5; ~ hāyakē *to shed tears* Bh 131^b.2; mikhās ~ taya *to get the eyes filled with tears* M 27^b.4, ~ ~ huya *id.* Bh 54^a.1. — ~-dhāl *streams of tears* Vi 56.3. — khwo-bhi = khwo-bi Ś 156^a.2.

khwoya^1 (-l^1), *v. i. to weep, to lament* V^2 78^b.5.

khwoya^2 (-l^1), *v. t. to catch*; ṅā ~ *to fish* Wr.V, 31.

khwoyakē^1, *caus. of* khwoya^1 Vi 46.29.

khwoyakē^2, *caus. of* khwoya^2 (?) B 54^b.10*.

khwolay [*cf. Mr.* khoḍaṇeṃ *to acquire evil habits*?], bharam ~ yāya *to perplex, to embarass* B 44^a.10.

khwosi, *s.* = khusi^1 Bh 12^a.4.

khyāk [khyāya], *s. a Piśāca* AH 4^a.

khyāti [*S. renown, fame*], *s.*, ~ juya *to be well known* N 6^b.7*.

khyāya (-t), *v. t. to frighten, to terrify* H^1 80^a.2.

khyāl, *s. joke, pleasantry* B 2^b.8; khyālan(aṃ) *in jest* Ś 157^a.4, *easily* H^2 76^a.6; khyāl yāya *to joke, to sport* Bh 22^a.6; ch-hm-yāta khyāl juya *to ridicule* M 11^b.8. — *adj. jocose* Bh 164^a.1.

khvā'uṁ, *adj.* = khvāṅu H^3 40^a.11.

khvāk, *adj. crooked*(?) M 36^b.1*.

khvāṅu, *adj. cold, cool* Vd 9^a.1; khvāṅayu... *becomes cold* 8^b.5; khvāṅakē *to make cold* H^1 66^b.5.

khvāc^1, *s. a foot-print, track* V^2 80^a.4. — *ifc.* **khicā-, li-**.

khvāc^2, *adj. deaf* N 43^b.4*.

khvāy, *adj.* = khvāc^2 Ns 38^b.3.

khvāl, *s. the face* V^2 47^a.7. ch-hm-yā ~ swoya *to look into the face of...* N 12^a.3. ~ jyāya *to make faces* Bh 162^b.3. ~ sēnakaṃ saṃ-gwo *looking suspicious* N 49^b.5. — *ifc.* **sala-**.

khvāhusā, *s. an upper garment* AH 44^a.

g.

gaṁ, ~ bikwo *who has lost his caste, an outcast* N 43^b.7.

gaṁ-gwo, *adj. dry* Vd 38^b.5.

gaṁ-labhā, *s. one of the ten palāṇḍus* P 58^a.1*.

gaṁsi-hma, *adj. feeble, thin* (amāṃsa) AH 39^a.

gaṅ, *adj. dry* C^1 48.

gaji, *s.* = gañji? Vd 23^a.1.

gajuli [*H.* gajrā *silken cloth*?], *s. a* (*silk*) *curtain*(?) B 25^b.6*.

gaṁjakē, *v. t. to make dry* N 12^a.3.

gañjalapē [*S.* gañja *disrespect*], *v. t. to treat with disrespect* N 43^b.9.

gañji, *s. hemp* Md 20^b.2.

gat [*cf. S.* ghaṇṭa], *s. a bell* C^{2} 26*.

gati [*S. moving*, —, *state, condition*], *fate* Vi 21.21, *state, condition* H^{3} 55^{b}.1. ~ dhalalapë *to beat, to throb* (*pulse*) Vd 3^{b}.5.

ga-to-thëṁ = gw(? H^{2}108,^{a}.5.

gath, *s. a savage, mountaineer*(?) B 59^{b}.8.

gathali [*EH.* gaṭhrī], *s. a bag, sack* Ś 145^{a}.2*.

gathi [*H.* gaṭṭhī *a small bundle*], *s. only ifc.* **bastr-**.

gathi(ṁ), *pr. int. how, of what kind, what a* V^{2} 1^{b}.4; *adv. how* (*before adj.*) B 5^{a}.2. — ~-hma = ~ (*of persons only*) M 3^{b}.6; ~-gwo *id.* (*of things and persons*) V^{2} 28^{b}.6, *adv.* H^{1} 54^{b}.4; ~-ṅa *id.* M 15^{b}.6, *adv.* Vi 29.1; ~-ṅa-hma = ~-hma M 6^{a}.7; ~-gu = ~-gwo B 19^{b}.5.

ga-thë, *adv. int. how, in what manner* H^{1} 46^{a}.1; *why* V^{2} 57^{b}.5; *rel.* (*corr.* athë) N 19^{a}.4; ~ dhālasā *for so it is said* (tathā coktam) H^{1} 15^{b}.2; ~-two(ṃ) = ~ H^{3} 30^{a}.3. gathën = gathë Ś 150^{b}.1; gathënaṃ *still, yet* B 8^{b}.3, *in some way or another* V^{2} 33^{b}.2.

gaḍ, *s.* = gadh Bh 14^{a}.2.

gaḍā [*H.* gadā *a club*], *s. a stick, club* Bh 136^{b}.2.

gaḍe-must, *s. a medicinal plant* Vd 39^{b}.5.

gaḍh [*H.*], *s. a fort, citadel* Bh 101^{b}.3. — ~-palakhāl *the wall of a fort* H^{2} 84^{b}.3.

gana, *adv. interr. where* V^{2} 22^{b}.6, *whither* M 15^{b}.7, *wherefrom* C^{1} 271. — ganan(aṃ) *wherefrom* (*starting-point*) H^{2} 25^{b}.1; ganaṃ *id.* Vi 17.24. — ganayā *id.* (*origin*) B 51^{b}.4. — ganata *where* Vi 152.26. — *rel.* gana *where* V^{2} 48^{b}.3. — *indef.* ganaṃ *wherever* H^{2} 94^{a}.2, ~... ma *nowhere* 79^{b}.2; gana wolasanwoṃ *whereever he goes* C^{1} 45.

ganakë[1] (*caus. of* ganë[1]), *to make stop* B 56^{a}.2.

ganakë[2], *caus. of* ganë[2] C^{1} 188.

gananā [*S.* gaṇana *reckoning*], ~ ma yāya *to disregard, to overlook* Bh 8^{b}.1.

ganā, *adv.* = gana; ~ julasanwoṃ *whereever it may be* V^{2} 30^{b}.4*.

ganë[1], *v. t. to stop, to hinder*; ch-hm-yāta *somebody* B 48^{b}.8, ch-g-s *to prevent from* M 33^{b}.3; *to warn, to dissuade*; ch-hm *somebody* V^{1} 76^{a}.6.

ganë[2], *v. i. to become dry* C^{1} 188.

gantā, *s.* = gantāy Bh 33^{b}.3.

gantāy [*cf. H.* gintī —, *estimation*], ~ ma yāya *to disregard, not care for* M 34^{b}.7.

gantās = gantāy Vi 37.10, ~ ma dayakë = ~ ma yāya Vi 39.33.

ganḍe-must, *s.* = gaḍe-~ Vd 32^{b}.5.

gam [*S. intercourse with a woman*], ~ yāya *to have intercourse* (*with a woman*) N 34^{b}.7.

gaman [*S. going, moving*], ~ yāya *to make a journey* B 16^{a}.7; ch-g-wo ~ yāya *to use as a means of conveyance* H^{2} 88^{a}.1.

gambhāli [*cf. M.* gaṃbhaṛī *early kind of winter rice*], *s. Gmelina arborea* AH 28^{a}. — ~-si *id.* CW 6.14.

gambhīr [*S.*], *adj. deep* H^{2} 69^{a}.6.

gamy [*S.*], *adj. accessible* B 10^{b}.8.

gaya (-l[1]), *v. t. to mount* (*a horse*) V^{2} 6^{b}.1, *to ascend* (*a tree*) 4^{b}.5. — gayakë *caus.* Ś 167^{b}.1.

gal[1] [*M.* ghar?], *s. a house* B 6^{a}.8. — ~-bujār (*slave*) *born at* (*his master's*) *house* N 20^{a}.1. — *ifc.* **sala-**.

gal[2] [*H.*], *s. the throat, neck* V^{1} 117^{b}.4.

garaḍ [*cf. S.* galagaṇḍa], *s. goitre* Vd 18^{a}.2.

galal, *s.* = garaḍ Vi 46.5.

galiwo, *adj. poor* AH 64^{b} (gariba).

gark(?), *s. interior* Vi 93.5.

garjay [*S.* garj... *to roar, thunder*], ~ yāya *to thunder* H^{2} 113^{a}.5. —

garjamān yāya *id.* Vi 159.2. — garjalapë *id.* Bh 178^{a}.5.

gal-pot [gal^{2}], *s. the throat, neck* Bh 15^{b}.2. ~-pat *id.* CW 8.68.

garbh [*S.*], *s. the womb* H^{2} 49^{b}.6; ~'as daya *to become or be pregnant* M 2^{a}.7; garbhasëṃ nisëṃ *from his birth* H^{2} 5^{b}.2. — garbhapatn [*cf. S.* garbhapāta], *s. miscarriage* Bh 179^{b}.7.

gal-mes [*cf. S.* gaṇḍa(ka)], *s. a rhinoceros* CW 7.2.

gal-sa [gal], *s. a beard* N 44^{a}.5.

gah, *s. a sort of silk* N 41^{b}.6.

gahani [= grahani], ~ cāya *to suffer from diarrhoea* Vd 24^{a}.2.

gahilī, *adj. lean, meagre* M 14^{b}.8; *weak, powerless* H^{2} 37^{a}.8.

gā^{1}, *s. a cloak, dress* V^{1} 12^{a}.4, *the dress of a monk* P 13^{b}.6. — *ifc.* **saṁ-**.

gā^{2} = gāk (*5th form of* gāya^{1}) B 44^{a}.5.

gāwo [*H.* gāṃv *a village?*], *s. a palace, tower* V^{2} 22^{b}.2. — ~-jhyāl *a window of a palace* B 56^{a}.1. — ~-lok *people from a village(?)* N 19^{a}.2.

gācakë (*caus. of* gāya^{2}); wā ~ *to make it rain* Bh 30^{b}.4.

gā-cot, *s. the hem of a garment* H^{2} 61^{b}.8.

gā-che, *s. a veil* AH 44^{a}. — ~-gā *a screen of cloth* (yavanikā) CW 1.68. — ~-duwone *a place behind the stage ib.*

gād = gāl^{1}; *only ifc.* **bo-**.

gāḍh [*S.*], *adj. deep* C^{1} 32; ~-hma *skilled* H^{1} 23^{a}.2.

gādhā [*B.*], *s. an ass* N 24^{b}.8.

gāḍhu [*cf. Mr.* gāḍhava], *s. an ass* C^{1} 121. — *ifc.* **mā-**.

gām, *s.* = grām V^{2} 16^{a}.3.

gāmāl-gowāl [*cf. Mr.* gāmāḷ-gubāḷ *refuse, dregs*], *s. anybody, this or that* N 9^{b}.3*.

gā-hma = gayā-hma *from* gaya V^{2} 8^{a}.5*.

gāya^{1} (-t), *v. i. to suffice* H^{1} 74^{a}.4; *to do a thing or to become something in a sufficient degree (with 4th form of the verb)* M 14^{b}.4. — gāk *it is sufficient, it will do* (yāyan, yāṅānaṃ, yāsëṃ *to do...*) V^{1} 18^{b}.2; ma yā ma gāk *it won't do not to do it* B 7^{b}.9; cha-polanaṃ gāk *at once* Vi 119.32; dhanan gākwo-hma *who has plenty of wealth* C^{2} 191; meb gāyā *the surplus* N 17^{b}.2; thwo padārth ja (= je) ma gāyā *I don't like this, it doesn't suit me* 24^{b}.2.

gāya^{2} (-t), *v. i. to pour down (rain)* H^{3} 40^{a}.11; wā ma gāwo *it does not rain* H^{3} 41^{a}.9.

gāya^{3}, *v. t. to cross, to transgress(?)* P 56^{a}.2*.

gāya^{4}, *v. t.* = gaya N 28^{b}.4*.

gāyakë (*irr. caus. of* gālë) = *simpl.* M 4^{b}.1.

gāl^{1}, *s. depth* (nimna) AH 20^{b}, *a hole, pit* Bh 185^{a}.6; *class-word* Vi 154.26. — *ifc.* **bu-, mi-**.

gāl^{2}, ~ biya *to reproach* Bh 114^{b}.6*.

gāl^{3}, *s.* = gāwo (*palace*) B 69^{b}.2*.

gālakë (*caus. of* gālë) = *simpl.* H^{2} 51^{b}.8.

gālë, *v. t. to fan* B 14^{a}.7.

gāl-sā, *s. a fan* H^{2} 71^{a}.1.

gi, *adv. whereto, whither?* Bh 42^{a}.4.

gik, *adj. rotten* Vd 21^{b}.6, *decayed* 50^{b}.1.

gi-khā, *s. a sky-lark* AH 34^{b}.

gīt [*S.*], *s. song, singing* Bh 12^{a}.3.

gin, *adv. whither?* V^{2} 44^{a}.2*.

ginār-si, *s. name of a plant* (agnimantha) Md 3^{a}.9.

gu^{1}, *pr. int. what, which* Pg 23^{b}.3; *pr. rel. who, which* B 10^{a}.7. — ~-hma *pr. rel.* P 17^{b}.2. ~-gu *id.* Vi 132.10; *pr. int.* B 5^{b}.2. ~-guli *id.* Vi 16.4; *pr. rel.* B 29^{b}.2.

gu^{2}, *s. a rope* H^{1} 23^{b}.4. — *ifc.* **sa-**.

gu-^{3} (*only* guk), *v. t. to tear asunder* B 53^{a}.9.

gu^{4}, *num. nine* Vi 147.23; ~-hma *id.* Ś 151^{b}.6.

gu(ṁ), *s. a wood, forest* H^{2} 52^{a}.4.

gurh, *s. a mountain* CW 5.1. — *ifc.* **cvā-porh-.**

gurh-khā, *s. a kind of partridge* (kṛkaṇa) Md 74ª.6.

gurh-cwo, *s. the top of a mountain* CW 5.2.

gurh-si, *s. a creeper* AH 27ª (gunshi).

gukhi, *s. a creeper* (latā) C¹ 177.

gu-khicā, *s. a jackal* M 24ª.5; *a wolf* AH 34ª.

guguli [*cf. S.* guggulu], *s. Bdellium* Md 28ª.2.

gu-ciyānarh, *adv.*, mele ~ *somewhere else* C¹ 279*.

gu-chinarh, *pr. indef. s. some* Bh 55ª.1.

guji, *s. an ear (of corn)*; *ifc.* **wā-.**

gu-jhamar-se, *s. a kind of medicinal plant* Vd 36ª.2.

gu-tā, *num.* = gu⁴ N 17ᵇ.1.

gutu, *s. Dūrvā grass* AH 33ª, tuyu ~ *white... ib.*

gute, *adv. as* (— ute — *so*) N 45ª.2.

guthi, *s. an ancle bone* CW 8.55. — ~-cā *id.* AH 41.

guḍagu, *s. a medicinal plant (a sort of grass?)* Vd 42ᵇ.3.

guḍālapë, *v. i. to become angry(?)* H² 66ᵇ.5*.

guḍi [*S.* guḍa], *s. a pill* Vd 12ᵇ.6. — *ifc.* **ëlā-.**

guṇ¹ [*S.*], *s. a thread, cord* B 57ᵇ.3; *virtue* H¹ 51ª.2, *skill* B 50ᵇ.7. — ~guṇ(an) *ifc. with regard to* N 24ª.8. — *ifc.* **bā-, li-.**

gun², *prt.*, bosë wonë gun *they may fly* H¹ 23ᵇ.2.

guṇabant [*S.*], *adj. endowed with good qualities* H² 5ª.6.

guṇik [guṇ], *adj. excellent, virtuous* H² 55ᵇ.2.

guṇ-kha [guṇ¹], *s. praise* H² 27ᵇ.2.

gun-lā, *s. the month Śrāvaṇa* CW 1.50. — **gun-lā yaṃ-lā** *the rainy season* 1.52.

gupt [*S. hidden, secret*], ~ yāya *to keep secret* H² 71ᵇ.4, *to act with discretion* 83ª.7; kāryas ~ yāya *to take into the secret* 83ª.7. — ~ kha *s. a secret* 56ᵇ.7. — guptan(aṃ) *adv. secretly* H¹ 90ª.4; guptasaṃ *id.* H² 83ª.8.

gu-phā, *s. a boar* Vi 35.20.

gubāhāl, *s. a sub-division of the highest buddhistic caste among the Newārs* B 27ᵇ.1.

gumān [*H. from Pers., pride, haughtiness*], *s. courage* Bh 9ª.4. *adj. haughty* H² 107ᵇ.8.

guya, *num., ninety*, ~ dol *90 000* Bh 134ª.2.

gu-lambhā, *s. a kind of medicinal plant* (ṛddhi) Md 5ª.4.

gulāp [*H.* gulāb *from Pers.*], ~-svān *a rose* Md 30ᵇ.4.

guli, *pr. int. how many, how much* Bh *3ª.2, *which, what* Vi 43.12. *pr. rel. which, what* P 18ª.2; ~ bastuk julasā-ṃ *how many things ever* H³ 34ª.9. *pr. ind.* ~ mi-janana-ṃ *through ever so many men* H² 65ª.1. — gulita *pr. int. which, what* H² 86ᵇ.2, *what a...* Vi 48.26; (*before adj.*) *how* 67.24. *pr. rel. which, what* 40.29. — gulito *pr. int. how much* H² 89ª.5, *which (of them)* B 58ª.2. *pr. rel.* P 18ª.3. — guli-chiṃ *pr. ind. some* H³ 52ᵇ.2; ~-chinaṃ *id.* V² 73ᵇ.3; ~-chiyāṃ *id.* B 43ª.2.

gulini, *s.* (*subj.* gulininaṃ) *the wife of a cow-herd* H² 63ª.5.

guru [*S.*], *s. a spiritual teacher* H² 95ª.2, *the master (of an apprentice)* N 19ª.5. — ~-bhalaḍi *a spiritual teacher's wife* 34ᵇ.4. — ~-mām *id.* B 38ᵇ.6.

gurutalp [*S. bed of a spiritual teacher*], ~ yāya *to violate the bed of a sp° t°, to commit incest* N 34ᵇ.5.

gule = guli; ~-chinaṃ *some* V¹ 57ª.1.

gulë, *v. t.* = gwolë; *see* **pet.**

gurgulu, *s. name of a plant* (guḍhūcī) Md 3ª.4.

gurbinī [*S.* gurviṇī], *adj. gravid* Bh 179ᵇ.7.

gu-lvāḍ, *s. Symplocos racemosa* Vd 21ᵇ.2. gu-lvāl-simā *id.* CW 6.15.

gusāhī [*M.* gosāī *a hermit*], *s. your lordship, your honour* B 17ᵃ.6.

guhā [*S.*], *s. a cave* V¹ 130ᵇ.1.

guhāli [*H.* guhār *fighting with clubs or sticks*], **guhālin kaya** *to fight or beat with a club* Bh 63ᵃ.1*.

guhy [*S.*], *adj. hidden, secret* H² 68ᵇ.5. *s. the privy parts* B 62ᵃ.10.

gṛdh(r) [*S.* gṛdhra], *s. a vulture* H³ 26ᵇ.4.

gṛh (*loc. not seldom:* gṛhes) [*S.*], *s. a house* V¹ 9ᵇ.3.

gewo, *adj. weakened, decayed (body)* Vd 6ᵃ.3*.

gewonasanworh, ~ ma *never* N 7ᵃ.7*.

gena, *adv. where?* H² 60ᵃ.2, *wherefrom?* V¹ 30ᵃ.4; **genaṃ** *wherefrom?* H² 74ᵃ.6, *indef.* 77ᵇ.4.

geya (-t *or* -l¹?), *v. t. to risk (one's life)* N 16ᵇ.3.

gelu [*H.* gerū], *s. red chalk* CW 5.6.

gē, *adv. where?* V¹ 20ᵇ.4; *whither?* H² 70ᵃ.2; gēgē (*corr.* e e) *whereever (...there)* N 24ᵃ.9.

gē-chi, *adv. corresponding to*; **thawo hma ~ lu** *the weight of his body in gold* V¹ 133ᵇ.4.

gēnakē [gē-chi?], *v. t. to make correspond*(?) Ś 151ᵇ.6*.

gēnenarh, *adv. everywhere*(?) N 47ᵇ.3*.

gēl-bo, *s. Gloriosa superba* CW 6.29.

gowāl [*cf. Mr.* govārī], *s. a cow-herd* N 26ᵇ.3.

gokhāl [*H.* gokhrū], *s. name of a creeper, which is used in medicine* Vd 39ᵇ.4. — gokhvāl *id.* AH 30ᵇ.

gocar [*S.* (*being within the*) *range*], 1) ch-hm-yāke ~ yāya *v. t. to bring before...* V¹ 86ᵇ.5, *v. i. to appeal to...* Bh 22ᵇ.5. 2) ~ yāya *to controle* H² 31ᵃ.6.

gotr [*S.*], *s. kinsmen, relations* N 7ᵃ.7. — *ifc.* **babā-, babī-**.

godhu [*S.* godhūli *the time of the day where the sun is half risen*], ~-samay *dawn* Bh 11ᵃ.7*.

gopalapē [*S.* gopa *a herdsman*], *v. t. to protect* C² 107.

gopāl [*S.*], *s. a cowherd* Bh 11ᵃ.3.

gopinī [*S.* gopī], *s. a cowherdess* Bh 21ᵇ.5. — gopikanyā *id.* 157ᵇ.4.

gophaki, *s. rice or grain flattened* (pṛthuka) AH 55ᵇ.

goma-ti [gomay?], *s. an ingredient of medicine* Vd 32ᵇ.2.

gomay [*S.*], *s. cow-dung* H² 84₁ᵃ.5.

gomātā [*S. cow of plenty*], *s. a cow* N 48ᵃ.8.

gomun, *s. Phaseolus trilobus* AH 31ᵇ.

goṣṭi, °**sti** [*S.* goṣṭhī —— *family connections*], *s. relatives* B 28ᵇ.3.

goṣṭhi, *s.* = goṣṭi H² 37ᵃ.5.

gwo¹, *pr. int. who, which, what* N 2ᵃ.1; *where* H¹ 46ᵇ.4. — *pr. rel. who, which* V² 43ᵃ.1. — ~ belasa-ṃ *at any time, at whichever time* M 2ᵃ.3; ~ belasa-ṃ ... ma *never* H³ 23ᵃ.3. — ~-hma *pr. int.* (*of persons*) Ś 149ᵇ.3; *pr. rel.* H¹ 78ᵃ.1; *pr. dem. this* P 7ᵃ.1. gwo-hma...gwo-hma *some...some* M 36ᵇ.1. — ~-gu *pr. rel.* H³ 4ᵃ.6; *pr. indef. some* 40ᵃ.9. — ~-gul *pr. int.* (*of things*) Vi 33.3; *pr. rel.* H³ 12ᵇ.7.

gwo² = gwol: ~ tulē B 38ᵃ.1*.

gwo-kuhnurh, *pr. ind.:* ~ gwo belasaṃ *at whichever time it may be* Ś 150ᵃ.4.

gwo-gwo, *pr. ind.:* ~ prakāran *each one in (her) own way or attitude* Bh 169ᵃ.2.

gwoc, *s.* = gwoy(?) Vd 48ᵃ.5*.

gwo-chi-nworh, °-**narh**, *pr. ind. some, any* H¹ 54ᵇ.3. gwo-chin *id.* H³ 55ᵃ.4.

gwoto-thērh, *adv. how, in what*

manner, only: ~ dhālasā *so it is said* (tathā coktam, *litt. "if you say: how?"*) H¹ 18ª.1.

gwoḍā [*H.* golā *a large ball*], *s. a piece, lump* Vd 48ª.1; ~ ~ hilë *to clot (faeces)* Vd 11ª.4. — *ifc.* **cā-, maṇik-, lā-**.

gwoḍ [*M.* gola *a heap, mass*], *s.* 1) *a ball (of medicine)* Vd 24ᵇ.5, *a funeral ball* (piṇḍa) P 35ª.3; si cha gwoḍ *a piece of wood.* — 2) *cl.-w.* (*Caitya*) Vi 93.3, (*stone*) V² 76ᵇ.5, (*fruit*) 37ª.2, (*beauty-spot*) Ś 148ᵇ.4. — *ifc.* **mikhā-**.

gwoḍ-sohon, *s. Coriandrum sativum* Vd 50ᵇ.5.

gwon, *pr. int. who-, which-, whatever* N 2ª.1. *pr. rel. which-, whatever* 42ᵇ.8. *pr. ind. any* C¹ 68. — ~-hmaṃ *pr. rel. which-, whatever* V¹ 1ª.3. — ~-khu *id.* C¹ 17. *pr. ind. any* C² 104. ~-khu-hma = ~-khu *rel.* V² 46ª.4. — ~-kho-hma *pr. int. who after all* V¹ 28ª.5.

gwo-phas, *s. a gale (of wind)* (?) M 36ª.3.

gwoy, *s. a betel-nut* H² 105ª.8. — *ifc.* **lā-**.

gwol¹ [= gwoḍ?], ~ tulë *to fall down, to tumble down* Bh 14ᵇ.2, ~ tolë *id.* 119ª.1. — gwol munë *v. t. to gather, to collect* Vi 111.26, *v. i. to gather, to meet* H¹ 80ᵇ.3.

gwol² = gwoḍ V¹ 111ᵇ.5.

gwola, *pr. rel. who, which* V¹ 98ª.2, ~-pane *pl.* N 46ᵇ.2; ~-hmaṃ julasanwoṃ *however many it may be* N 2ª.2; ~-chin *ind. some* 22ᵇ.8. — gwolanaṃ *pr. ind. at any time, always* H¹ 61ª.2; ~ — ma *never* H² 49ᵇ.5. — gwolanu(ṃ) = °naṁ Bh 33ᵇ.5.

gwoli, *pr. rel. which* Vi 163.14; ~-to *id.* P 52ᵇ.5; gwoliṃ — guli *some — some* Vi 159.15; gwoli — ~-to *id.* H² 91ᵇ.5. — gwoli-chiṃ *pr. ind. any* H³ 18ª.5, *some* H² 103ª.3. — gwoli-ma-chi *so much* H³ 31ª.4. — gwole-chinoṃ — ~ *some — some* N 23ᵇ.7.

gwolë, *v. t.*; *see* **pet**.

gwolo, *pr. rel.* = gwola Ś 148ᵇ.7; ~-ta *id. which, how many* Bh 1ᵇ.6. ~-pane *adv. one time or another*(?) N 46ª.9. — gwolono = gwolonaṃ Ś 150ª.2. — gwolohnaṃ *rel. at which time* N 31ᵇ.5.

gwosār [*H.* guzārnā *to bring to pass, — — to lay before*], ~ yāya *to propose* (yāyata *to do*) B 15ᵇ.8*.

gwohāli, *s.* = gvāhāli, ~ yāya *to help* N 15ᵇ.6; ~ wonë *to go to one's assistance* 42ª.1; ch-hm-yāta ~ tanë *to bring assistance* Bh 111ª.3.

gyāṅā-pu [gyāya], *adj. dreadful, terrible* C¹ 235; ~-së(ṃ) wola(ṃ) *has become very timid (sic)* Vi.

gyān [*S.* jñāna], *s. wisdom* H³ 17ᵇ.4.

gyāni [*S.* jñānin], ~-hma *adj. reasonable, sensible* H³ 17ᵇ.1.

gyānibant [*S.* jñānavant], *adj. wise, prudent* H¹ 67ᵇ.1.

gyā-phal [gyāya], *adj. timid, cowardly* H² 93ᵇ.3.

gyā-bhal [gyāya], *adj. timid, cowardly* H³ 6ª.9.

gyāya (-t), *v. i. to be afraid* H¹ 91ᵇ.2, ch-g-n *of a thing* 25ᵇ.3; ~ jogy *frightful, dreadful* C¹ 265.

gyālā-bo, *s. name of various plants* (lāṅgalī AH) Vd 35ª.2.

grahani [*S.* grahaṇī], ~-roy *diarrhoea* Vd 23ᵇ.3.

grām [*S.*], *s. a village* V¹ 74ᵇ.1.

grās [*S. swallowing*], ~ yāya *to devour, to swallow* H² 22ª.3. ~ grāsalapë *v. t. id.* Bh 62ª.5.

grībā [*S.*], *s. the neck* Bh 162ª.7.

gvāk-bhu, *s. salt and barren soil* AH 23ª. — gvākh-~ *id.* 70ª.

gvāc, *s.* = gvāy¹ AH 43ª.

gvācak-palak, *s. one of the ten palāṇḍus* P 58ª.1.

gvāth [*cf. Mr.* goṭhā], *s. a cow-pen, pasture ground* N 26b.3. — *ifc.* **sā-**.

gvāṭh-palak, *s. a plant, the root of which is used medicinally* Vd 31b.3.

gvāy¹, *s. a beard* CW 8.74; ~ buwo-hma misā *a hermaphrodite* 8.12.

gvāy², ~ ëwo bu *salt and barren soil* C¹ 242.

gvāy-pal, *s. name of a plant* (gojihvā) AH 31b.

gvāl¹ [*M.* goār], *s. cow-herd* H² 81b.4.

gvāl², *s. the betel plant* H³ 47a.9.

gvāl³, *s.* = gvāy¹ H³ 49a.1.

gvālatopā, *s. a coffin* B 49a.4.

gvā-li (*mostly spelt* -ḷ), *s. a heel* CW 8.55. ~-cā *id.* AH 41a. — ~-jyāk *an ulcer on the foot* CW 8.43.

gvāhāli [*Bhojp.* gohārī *a call or cry for help*], *s. help* H² 107a.3; ~phonë *to ask for help* V¹ 129b.2.

gh.

ghaghalā [*S.* gharghara *an ornament*], *s. an ornament of the feet* (nūpura) AH 43b.

ghaghali [*H.* ghāgrī *dim. of* ghāghrā *a skirt*], *s. an article of dress* B 27b.1.

ghatay [*H.* ghaṭānā *to lessen, degrade*], ~ yāya *to destroy* Vi 174.28.

ghaṭit [*S. planned, devised*], ~ juya, lāya *to be proved* N 49a.4*.

ghaḍ [*H.* ghaṛā], *s. a (water) pot* C² 261.

ghaṇṭh¹ [*S.* ghaṇṭā], *s. a bell* H² 59b.4.

ghaṇṭh² [*S.* ghaṭa], *s. a pot, vessel* H³ 56b.3*.

ghal¹, *s.* = ghaḍ. — *ifc.* **ghel-**, **yas-**.

ghalas, *s. a kind of antelope* (vātamṛga) CW 7.3.

ghalasāl [*cf. Mr.* gharasaṃsār], *s. household and other affairs* H² 67b.2.

ghali [*H.* ghaṛī], *s. a space of 24 minutes* Bh 56b.3. — ~-belā *id.* B 10a.2. — *ifc.* **bā-**.

ghali, *adj. disgusting* V² 31a.7.

ghal-cāk, *s. the nave of a wheel* AH 58b; *a wheel* H² 6a.1.

ghas, ~ puya (-t) *to embrace, to hug* H¹ 63a.2; galpotas ~ ~ *to throw oneself about one's neck* Vi 136.2. ghas poya (-l¹) *id.* Bh 42a.7.

ghasiyā [*H.* ghasiyārā], *s. a grass-cutter* Vi 20.28.

ghā¹, *s.* = ghāl M 13a.5.

ghā-², *v. t. to fasten* B 36b.2 (ghāṅā).

ghāṁs, *s.* = ghās B 61a.8. — ~-dwo *a heap of grass* AH 33b.

ghāṅ, *s. a bridge* CW 3.6.

ghāc, *s.* = ghās H¹ 23b.4. — ~-āsan *a seat made of grass* P 13b.5.

ghāṭ¹ [*H.*], *s. a bathing place on the bank of a river* B 13a.9. — ghāṭ wāle *an ordeal* B 17b.6.

ghāt² [*H.* ghāṭī *a custom-house*], *s. ifc.* **dan-**.

ghāṭalapë [*S.* ghaṭ *to effect, accomplish*], *v. t. to establish* N 39b.4.

ghāl [*M.* ghāo], *s. a wound, sore*; ~ kaya *to inflict a wound* (ch-hm-yāke *on...*) P 51b.2, ~ lācakë *id.* 51a.7, ~ lāya *to receive a wound* H³ 41a.6, ~ juya *to be wounded or hurt* Vi 159.32; ~ juyakë *to suffer oneself to be* w°., h°. Vi.

ghālalapë, *v. t.*, du ~ *to make responsible* (?) N 16b.1*.

ghāli, *ifc.* **si-**.

ghās, *s. grass* V² 32a.1. — ~-ban *a reed-bed* (naḍyā) CW 6.38, *grass-land* H² 76a.2. — *ifc.* **pasuli-**.

ghiwo-svān, *s. name of a plant* (jhiṇṭī) AH 30a.

ghilay [*H.* ghirnā *to gather* (*as clouds*)], ~ yāya *v. i. to gather* (*subj.* bairi·n) H² 96a.6.

ghucā, ch-g-s ~ yāya *to revile a thing* N 41a.3,5*.

ghel [*cf. rust. H.* gheo], *s. clarified butter* H¹ 62ª.4. — ~-ghal *a pot with cl° b°* 62ª.4. — *ifc.* **sā-**.

gho-ti, *s. buttermilk mixed with water* (takra) AH 56ª.

ghor [*H.* ghorā], *s. a horse* B 33ᵇ.7.

ghol-churh, *s. a small mouse* (girikā) CW 7.5.

ghaur, *s.* = ghalí Vi 43.7*.

ghwok-sal, *s. rattling* (*of a carriage*) CW 1.64.

ghwokh-śabd, *s.* = ghwok-sal Bh 98ª.6*.

ghvāya (-t), *v. t. to push* Bh 69ª.12.

ṅ.

ṅa¹, *s. a horn* Bh 69ᵇ.6; ~ du *horned* C¹ 248.

ṅa², *num.* = ṅā³ N 25ᵇ.1; ~ sal *five hundred* V² 72ᵇ.5.

ṅa-³, *v. t.*, calati ṅaṃsëṃ *wiping off the sweat* Bh 169ª.7*.

ṅa-⁴, *v. t.*, ṅasëṃ tā *loans for use* (yācita) N 6ª.1.

ṅaka, *s. a horn* C² 233*.

ṅakwo [ṅaya²?], samudran ~ *bounded by the ocean* C¹ 293*.

ṅatāl, *s. a cheek* Bh 163ᵇ.2.

ṅanakë¹ (*caus. of* ṅanë¹), 1) *to make alike*; ratn thëṃ ṅanakaṃ *making (it) like a jewel* B 2ᵇ.6. 2) *to make oneself alike i.e. to look like* V² 43ª.5, *to behave like* H³ 38ª.6; ma khaṅā-thë ṅanakāwo *pretending not to have seen* Ś 157ᵇ.6.

ṅanakë² = ṅenakë; ma ṅanakwosëṃ *without being asked* N 37ᵇ.8*.

ṅanë¹, *v. i. to be alike, to resemble*; ratnawo uti ṅaṅ *resembling a jewel* B 3ª.9, gathë ṅana *what is it like?* 3ª.6, biya-thë ṅana *it is as if... had given* 46ᵇ.11, thawo-thëṃ ṅaṃ-gwo *suitable to her* N 31ᵇ.11.

ṅanë², *v. i. to wither* H¹ 67ª.3*.

ṅanë³, *v. t.* = ṅenë² B 48ᵇ.9.

ṅaya¹ (-l¹), *v. i. to be finished, to be done for* B 32ª.4; *to be cured (a disease)* H³ 17ᵇ.2.

ṅaya², *v. i.* = ṅeya¹ V¹ 12ª.5*.

ṅaya³, *num. fifty* Bh 99ª.5.

ṅayakë (*caus. of* ṅaya¹) *to conquer (an enemy)* H³ 51ᵇ.12; *to cure (a disease)* 17ᵇ.3.

ṅalā-pu, *s.* = ṅālā-pu Bh 23ª.5*.

ṅā¹, *s. a fish* H² 99ᵇ.4; ~ wāya *to fish* Bh 116ᵇ.1. — *ifc.* **kuthi-**, **khusi-**, **bhusā-**, **loh-**, **sisu-**, **soh-**.

ṅā², *num. five*, ṅā-hma M 30ª.6. ṅā-hma-hma *the fifth* M 8ᵇ.6.

ṅā³ (ṅāya¹), ~ ~ woya *to bite violently* Bh 9ª.6.

ṅā-khej, *s. spawn* B 76ᵇ.5.

ṅā-khoyaṁ, *s. a fish-basket* AH 20ᵇ (gnákhoyan).

ṅācakë (*caus. of* ṅāya¹), *to make bite* N 44ᵇ.1.

ṅā-tā, *num.* = ṅā² H¹ 56ª.1.

ṅān, *forming imperativs* = hṅān: bi-ṅān *give* V¹ 92ª.5.

ṅānakë = ṅanakë¹ V² 68ª.2.

ṅāya¹ (*mostly* -t, *but not seldom* -l¹), *v. t. to bite* H¹ 88ᵇ.5, *to lacerate* Vi 76.6, *to devour* B 6ª.4, *to seize (with the teeth)* H² 101ª.7.

ṅāya² (-t), *v. t. to buy* H² 105ª.7.

ṅāya³ (-l¹), *v. i. to move* Bh 58ª.2.

ṅāya⁴, *num.* = ṅaya³ N 43ᵇ.1*.

ṅāyakë (*caus. of* ṅāya³), sambandh(an) ~ *to accomplish a marriage by uniting husband and wife* N 31ª.1.

ṅālā-pu, *adj. ashamed* B 44ª.7. *s. shame* CW 1.72.

ṅi- (-n, -t?), *v. t. to count* N 23ᵇ.7.

ṅiṅ, *s. healthy food* C¹ 146.

ṅiya (-t, -l¹?), *v. t.* moḍ mos niyāwo *beating with fists* Bh 58ª.5*.

-ṅun, *forming impr.*: bi-ṅun *give* V¹ 24ᵇ.5*.

ṅuya (-l[1]), *v. i. to assemble, to meet*(?) Bh 161^a.4*.

ṅuyakë (*caus. of* ṅuya), 1) *v. t. to encircle, to enclose* H[2] 74^a.1. 2) *to gather, to assemble* V[1] 131^b.2.

ṅeṅā, *adj. dark* C[1] 17*.

ṅetāl, *s.* = ṅatāl, Vi 163.21.

ṅenakë[1] (*caus. of* ṅenë[2]), *to cause to be questioned* N 6^a.8.

ṅenakë[2] = ṅanakë[1] H[3] 37^b.5.

ṅenë[1], *v. t. to hear, to listen* H[1] 51^b.3.

ṅenë[2], *v. t. to ask* H[2] 75^a.8; ch-hm-yāke ~ *to ask, to question somebody* V[2] 57^b.5, ch-hm-yāba *id.* H[3] 32^b.4.

ṅenë[3], *v. i.* = ṅanë[1] H[3] 46^a.5.

ṅeya[1] (-l[1]), *v. i. to be covered* H[2] 76^a.3.

ṅeya[2], *v. i.* = ṅaya[1] H[2] 42^a.3.

ṅeyakë (*caus. of* ṅeya[1]), 1) *to cover* H[3] 41^a.1. 2) *to surround* H[2] 62^a.6.

ṅoya[1] (-l[1]), *v. i. to be surrounded* C[2] 175; *to be protected* N 28^b.4; *fig. to derive one's superiority from* C[2] 175.

ṅoya[2], *adj. insane* C[2] 7; ~ cāwo *id.* CW 8.49, *furious (elephant)* H[2] 105^b.6.

ṅoyakë (*caus. of* ṅoya[1]), *to surround* Bh 54^a.2. deś ṅoyakaṃ *everywhere through the town* N 49^a.7.

ṅolë, gā-ghar ṅolāwo swoya *to look intently at*(?) Bh 112^a.7*.

ṅyā, ~ ~ sā *a milch-cow* C[2] 236.

ṅyāk, began ~ *moving rapidly* C[2] 281*.

ṅyāya (-t), *v. t.* = ṅāya[2] H[1] 68^b.2.

hṅ.

hṅa[1], *adv. first* N 47^a.5. — ~ bvāya: ~ bvāṅaṃ woya *to rush forward against* Bh 151^b.5. — ~ luya *to agree* N 2^b.7. — ~hāya *to go in advance* H[1] 10^a.1; ~ hāsëṃ *first, as the first* H[2] 24^a.4, ~ hāsëṃ woya = ~ woya Bh 72^a.6.

hṅa-[2] [hṅa[1]?), thithiṃ ma hṅa-sëṃ *equally* ("*not forestalling one another*"?) N 43^a.3*.

hṅawo, *adj. the first comer* C[1] 51; ~ kālas *in former times* H[3] 52^b.9. *adv.* prātan në ghari ~ *two gharis before dawn* Bh 56^b.3; hṅawo hṅawo *at the head* Vi 164.3. — ~ taya *to make room to pass by* N 47^a.2; *to place before; to hand over, to consign* V[1] 88^b.6. — hṅawoyā *adj. former* H[1] 96^a.1; ~-thëṃ *as before* H[2] 38^b.2.

hṅa-wonë, *adv. first* H[1] 13^a.4; ch-hm-yā ~ *before, in the presence of* .. M 7^a.4; ch-hm *or* ch-g ~ *before, in front of...* V[2] 38^a.2.

hṅa-wos(aṁ), *adv. first, before* H[2] 53^b.1; hṅawosëṃ *id.* C[1] 3.

hṅa-co, *adv.*, ch-g pënoṃ ~ *before.., ere...* N 18^b.4; hṅacoyā *mentioned above* V[1] 26^b.3.

hṅathu, *adj. former, previous* H[1] 5^a.2.

hṅa-thë(ṁ), *adv. previously* Bh 127^b.4.

hṅathwo, *adj.* = hṅathu V[1] 121^b.3; *the former wife* N 31^a.2.

hṅa-thyākaṁ, *adv. early* C[1] 124.

hṅa-pa, ~ cyāya *to place before* P 62^b.6; *to prefer* H[2] 106^a.2. ~ cyātakë *to let place before* Bh 64^a.5.

hṅa-pā, *adv. first* H[1] 74^a.4; ~ nisëṃ *before, previously* H[2] 102^a.8; ~ ku-hnu *on the first day* P 61^b.5; hṅapāyā *mentioned above* V[2] 17^b.1 (hna°), ~-thëṃ *as before* Bh 12^b.1. — ~ wonë *to go in advance of, to go at the head of* H[1] 22^a.1. — ~ lāya *to come as the first* B 8^a.2.

hṅa-pe, *see* **li-pe**.

hṅā, *adv. first* N 21^b.1; ~ nisëṃ *from the beginning* B 41^a.7; hṅā-hṅā *previously* N 49^b.6. — ch-g-n ~ (*temp.*) *before* 49^b.4; swo lān ~ *within three months* H[2] 33^a.7; āwonaṃ ~ *till now* Bh 142^a.4; ma juwola(ṃ) ~ *before becoming* N 31^b.6, ma juwo(ṃ) ~ *id.* H[2] 96^b.4; mocā ma don ~ *before* *a child is born* N 39a.5. ch-g-n ~ (*loc.*) *to..., as far as...* N 51b.1. — ~ bvāṅaṃ wonë *to rush forward against* Bh 83a.2; ~ ma do thāy *a place where it has not been before* N 27b.5.

hṅā-wonë = hṅa-° M 14a.8.

hṅākë = hṅācakë B 54b.8.

hṅācakë (*caus. of* hṅāya[1]), *to put in motion* (*a car, ship etc.*) H[2] 6a.2.

hṅā-co, *adv. previously, before* N 35b.3; kanas ~ *early to-morrow morning* H[1] 46a.1; ~ sutha tewolaṃ *id.* H[2] 106a.3. — hṅā-ca = °-co Vi 98.14.

hṅā-toṁ, cyā dan ~ *till after the lapse of eight years* N 10a.6*.

hṅān, *forming imperatives,* bi-hṅān *give* V[1] 123a.2.

hṅā-pā, *adv. first* N 31a.4; *formerly, previously* 27a.3; ādi ~ *first* Vi 16.1; kahnas ~ *early to-morrow* H[3] 32b.2. hṅāpāyā-thëṃ *as before* 39b.7.

hṅāya[1] (-t), *v. i. to move* B 11b.8, *to run* (*water*) H[2] 111b.3. — *v. t.* hatāl ~ *to wage war* Vi 158.2; balā ~ *to shoot an arrow* H[3] 42b.10; balān ~ *to hit with an arrow* H[2] 41a.4. — dudu ~ du-hma sā *a milch cow* C[1] 186; ~ du sā *id.* 236.

hṅāya[2] (*irreg.* hṅāk, hṅāwo, hṅāyā), uti ~ *to become alike* Vi 99.14; ch-hm-(-wo) uti ~ *to be or to become like someone* H[2] 49b.1. — conë hṅāyā-pu *flat, even* (*as to be fit*) *for sitting upon* Vi 116.22.

hṅāyakë, khipotan ma hṅāyaku *the rope wouldn't suffice* Bh 35b.4.

hṅā-hā, ~ wonë *to go in advance* H[3] 50b.7; ~ woya *id.* 49a.10. ~ wosëṃ *prematurely* 12a.4.

hṅinakë, *see* **jhwok.**

hṅilë, *v. i.* = hṅelë H[1] 33a.1.

hṅewo, *adv. previously* B 4b.11; ~ bigrahayā *before the battle* H[3] 40b.6. — ~tayakë *to cause to place before* 56a.9.

hṅe-wonë = hṅa- H[2] 3b.4; ~ taya *to place before, to hand over, to consign* Ś 162b.2.

hṅe-hṅā, *adv.,* ma juwon ~ *before having...* V[2] 29a.2*.

hṅethu, *adj.* = hṅathu V[2] 71a.5. *s. an elder sister* B 51b.7, *a first wife* 17b.2; hṅethu-hma kalāt *id.* 18a.1.

hṅe-thyākaṁ, *adv.* = hṅa-~.

hṅeḍ, *s. sleep* C[1] 126; ~ woya *to go to sleep* B 16a.4; ~ woyakë *id.* H[3].42b.9; ch-hm-yā ~ woyakë *to cause somebody to go to sleep* V[2] 56b.1.

hṅe-pa = hṅa-pa: ~ cyāya *to place before, to introduce to* B 50a.6. cyācakë B 43b.8 *and:* ~ cyākë 15a.10 = hṅa-pa cyātakë.

hṅe-pi, *see* **li-pi.**

hṅeya[1] (-l[1]), *v. t.* ch-hm-wo ~ *to be superior to...* H[3] 50a.1*.

hṅeya[2] (-l[1]), *v. t. to gnaw or bite through* H[1] 74b.1.

hṅel, *s.* = hṅeḍ V[1] 91b.6.

hṅelakë, *caus. of* hṅelë H[2] 49b.6.

hṅelë, *v. i. to laugh* Ś 146b.6; musuhun ~ *to smile* Vi 62.18.

hṅyācākë (*caus. of* hṅyāya[1]) = hṅācakë H[1] 6b.1.

hṅyātakë = hṅyācakë Bh *12a.3.

hṅyāya[1] (-t), *v. i.* = hṅāya[1] N 27b.2.

hṅyāya[2] (-t) [= hṅyāya[1]], dudu ~ *to milk* Bh 63b.5; ~ du sā *a milch cow* 93a.6; dudu ~ dayāwo coṅ-pani sā *id.* Vi 83.21.

hṅyāya[3] (-t[1]), *v. t. to fine, to punish* N 44a.6.

hṅyāya[4] (-t), *v. t.* = ṅāya[2] N 40b.4.

hṅyāya[5] (-t), *v. t.* = ṅāya[1] V[1] 33a.2.

hṅyāyakë[1] [= hṅyācakë?), khyālanaṃ ~ *to enjoy oneself* Ś 160a.4; yāya ~ *to make someone do a thing* Ns 35b.8*.

hṅyāyakë[2], *v. t. to cause to smile* Ś 160a.4*.

hṅyā-sā [hṅyāya[2]], *s. a milch cow* N 21b.9.

C.

ca[1], *adj. little;* ~ sal *Anudātta* CW 1.63.

ca[2], *s.* = câ[2]; *only before* chi Vi 85.19. *cl.-w.* cā ca chi *one night* B 30^{b}.12.

cawo, ~ kanë = cat ~ B 60^{b}.7.

cawo-svān, *s. name of several flowers* M 36^{a}.8.

cawol-svān, *s. Nelumbium speciosum* Md 29^{b}.2.

cak, *s. the pole of a carriage, to which the yoke is fixed* (kûvara) AH 50^{b} (chuka).

cakanā-kha, *s. a contradictory statement* N 9^{b}.6; cakanān-kha *id.* 49^{a}.3*.

caku(?), *s. a father* V[2] 80^{a}.7*.

cakr [*S.*], *s. a wheel* H[1] 76^{b}.3.

cakrabā(k) [*S.* cakravāka], *s. the cakra bird* H[2] 82^{b}.4. — **cak(r)abāki** *id. m. and f.* V[1] 119^{a}.1.

cakvā [*H.*], *s. the cakra bird* CW 7.90.

cakṣ [*H.* cakṣu], *s. an eye* Vi 61.34.

cakhabā, *s.* = cakvā V[2] 71^{a}.1.

ca-khuṁ, *s. mod.* = cal-khunī AH 35^{a}.

caṁgu-lā, *s. the month Caitra* CW 1.49. — ~-baṃcholā *the spring* AH 12^{a}.

ca-ca, sa ~ puya *to tear one's hair* Vi 43.30*.

cacalapē [*S.* cañcala *movable*], *v. t. to remove*(?) N 22^{b}.7.

ca-cikan, *s. light* (āloka) AH 65^{a}.

cañcal [*S.*], *adj. unsafe, unsteady* H[2] 73^{b}.7.

cat, ~ kanë *to blossom out, to bloom; to be bright, to beam (the face)* B 12^{b}.9; *to come untied (a turban)* N 18^{b}.7. — ~ kanakë *to unfold (wings)* H[2] 80^{a}.2; *itrs. to brighten (the face)* Vi 62.17, *to blossom out (a flower)* Ś 152^{a}.5. ~ kaṃkë *id.* Vi 112.17. — ~ phanë *to tear asunder* 160.16. — ~ phunë *id. (usual form)* 118^{a}.4. ~ phunakë *caus.* Vd 14^{b}, 3. — ~ bu- (-n *or* -t?) *to go to pieces* H[3] 17^{a}.6.

cataṁ, *s. a ladle* AH 55. — *ifc.* **si-.**

catāk[1], *s. a whip* C[1] 234. — *ifc.* **lu-.**

catāk[2] [*H.* caṭāk *from* cak *smack, snap*], ~ wāya *to throw or knock down* Bh 81^{b}.4.

cati, ~ ṅoya *to cover* Bh 55^{a}.3*.

catur [*S.*], *adj. skilled* H[2] 34^{b}.1.

caturdig [*S.*], *s. the four quarters of the sky* V[1] 1^{b}.3.

caḍhāy [*rust. H.* caḍhānā], ~ yāya *v. t. to dedicate, to devote, to sacrifice* Vi 71.27.

canā [*H.*], *s. a chick-pea* Md 69^{a}.1.

cantā, *adv.,* ~ ma *not at all*(?) N 17^{b}.7*.

caṇḍāl [*S.*], *s. a Caṇḍāla* H[2] 28^{b}.7.

candr [*S.*], *s. the moon* V[1] 74^{b}.6.

candramā [*S.* candramas], *s. the moon* H[1] 39^{b}.4.

capal [*S.*], *adj. unsteadily, unreliable* H[2] 33^{b}.6. *s. unsteadiness* C[1] 209.

capāl, *s. a hut* B 54^{a}.7.

cabakan, *s. Amaranthus polygonoides* Vd 40^{a}.6. — *ifc.* **mal-.**

cabadas, *s. the 14th day in the lunar fortnight* H[3] 32^{b}.1.

cab-haṭ, *s. a public market* N 23^{a}.3.

camā, *s. a mother's sister* N 34^{b}.3, *a father's sister* 34^{b}.4; *the second wife of the father* B 11^{a}.8. — ~-ju *the second wife of the father* Vi 55.21.

camār [*H.*], *s. a shoemaker* Ś 147^{b}.6.

ca-me, *s. the tongue of a serpent* CW 2.2.

camp(ak) [*S.* campaka], ~-svān *Michelia Campaka* H[2] 24^{a}.7.

caya, *num. eighty* Vi 126.1. ~-tā *id.* C[1] 238.

cay-pvāth, *s. the abdomen* Ś 151^{a}.1. — cay-pvāl *id.* AH 41^{b}.

cal, ~ khënë *to unfold*(?) B 4^{a}.10. — ~ ~ phāya (-l[1]) *to tear to pieces* Bh 162^{b}.6.

calaṁ, *see* **calati.**

calati [*M.* calatī *increase in reputation*], *s. celebrity, power* M 7ª.1. — calaṃ ~ yāya *to sway, to rule* B 50ª.11. — bhog ~ yāya *to enjoy the rule* H² 114ᵇ.8.

caraṇ [*S.*], *s. the foot* (*term of respect*) Bh 177ª.5.

calay [*H.* calnā *to move*], ~ yāya *to go, to move* H² 89ª.3; *to blow* (*the wind*) M 38ª.1; *to live* (*somewhere*) Vi 138.5. — pāpas ~ ~ *to lead a sinful live* Vi 146.17; sukhan ~ ~ *to live happily* H² 75ᵇ.7. — *v. t. to be occupied in* H² 118ª.5; puṇy ~ ~ *to acquire merit* Vi 90.3.

calalapë [*see* calay], *v. i. and t. to go, to move* Vi 93.8, *to be abroad* H³ 33ᵇ.9; *to conduct oneself* C² 177; *to live* (dharmas *in righteousness*) Vi 169.5; *to practise* H¹ 46ª.1; ājñā ~ *to carry into effect* (*an order*) N 46ᵇ.6, gīt ~ *to sing* Bh 69ª.2. — calalapayakë *caus.*: caryas ~ *to bring back to his duty* N 45ª.8.

calas, *s.* = colas N 22ª.7.

calā, *s. a gazelle* H¹ 11ᵇ.5; calāta *pl.* Vi 122.32; calānī *fem.* 37.11. — ~-ahal *gazelle-hunting* H² 94ª.7. — ~-cheṃgu *a hide of a gazelle* AH 34ª. — ~-bathān *a herd of gazelles* M 25ᵇ.8.

caritr [*S.*], *s. behaviour, conduct* H¹ 38ª.4.

cal-khu (*only gen.* ·yā), *s.* = cal-khunī; *ifc.* **mā-**.

cal-khunī, *s. a sparrow* P 53ª.5. — *ifc.* **che-**, **bā-**, **bu-**, **mā-**.

carcā [*S. repetition*], *adv. repeatedly*(?) Bh 148ᵇ.3*.

cal-ti, *s. sweat* Bh 44ª.5. — ~-kaya *a blister* AH 39ᵇ.

cary [*S. behaviour, acting*], *s.* (*good*) *behaviour, duty* N 45ª.8.

ca-sa(ṁ), *s. the hair* (*of the head*) H¹ 59ᵇ.2; ~ jwonë *to seize by the hair* V² 29ª.1.

casa-pol, *s. the crown of the head, a head* H³ 43ª.1.

casal-kan, *s. a species of Soma grass* Md 17ᵇ.8.

cā¹, *s. earth, clay* B 59ᵇ.5; cāyā *earthen* H³ 12ª.6.

cā², *s. a night* B 30ᵇ.12; swo cā pë hnu *three days and nights* (trirātra) P 47ª.1; swo cā *id.* 57ª.7; cānaṃ hninaṃ *day and night* Bh 172ª.1, cāwoṃ hniwoṃ *id.* Ś 138ᵇ.4. — *ifc.* **no-**, **bā-**.

cā³, *s. a young one* (*of animals*), *a child*; ~ thwol *pregnant* N 28ᵇ.7; śaḍayā(ṃ) ~ thuro *the horse became with young* B 33ª.9. — *ifc. forming deminutives, e.g.* che-cā *a small house,* nagal-cā *a small town.*

cā⁴, ~ buya (-t) *to stop, to pause:* cā cā buṅāwo *interruptedly* Vd 8ª.1.

cāk [*M.*], *s. a wheel* C¹ 147, *a potter's wheel* H³ 2ᵇ.7, *a circle* H¹ 6ᵇ.1; swo ~ ulë = ~ cākal ~ M 3ᵇ.1. toyuwo cāk *small-pox* CW 8.44, hyāṅu ~ *another sort of cutaneous eruption* (maṇḍala) *ib.* — ~-lāk *the sensible horizon* AH 8ª.

cākakë, °**ku**°, *v. t. to encourage* H³ 33ᵇ.5; cākakaṃ bodhalapë *id.* H² 64ª.2; cākakaṃ taya *to make love to* H² 65ª.3; cākakāwo conë *id.*(?) CW 8.18.

cākanakë, *v. t. to sharpen*(?) M 33ª.3*.

cākal¹ [*cf. S.* cakra], *s. a wheel; circle* H² 84ᵇ.6; swo ~ ulë *to circumambulate thrice* Ś 146ª.2, swo ~ pradakṣiṇā yāya *id. from left to right* Vi 48.5; cākal cikal swoya *to look around* V² 61ª.6, cākr cikran swoya *id.* Ś 157ᵇ.4. — cākal-bṛddhi *interest upon interest* N 6ᵇ.6.

cākal² [*M.* cā̆kar *a paid servant*], *s. a servant* M 19ª.8, *a maid-servant* H² 115ª.4; ch-hm-yā ~ yāya *to be a servant to* Vi 118.22.

cāku, *adj. sweet* H² 13ᵇ.3, ~ bacan *sweet, bland words* C¹ 111; hmutu cāku, nugalas kapat dawo *the month sweet, treachery in the heart* Bh 54ᵇ.3. — *s. (raw) sugar* Bh 31ᵇ.1. — *ifc.* **chvālu-**.

cāti, *s. a night; only ifc.* **bā-**.

cāto (*pl. of* cā³), *s. young ones* H¹ 36ᵇ.1.

cā-do, *s. a heap (of earth?)* (kūṭa) CW 4.11.

cā-dhal-pwo, *s. an earthen jar* H¹ 52ᵃ.1.

cānas, *adv.* = cāhnas N 22ᵇ.1.

cāṇḍāl [*S.*], *s. a Caṇḍāla* Ś 154ᵃ.2.

cāhnas, *adv. at night* B 45ᵇ.2. *s. a night* Vi 106.11.

cāhnus, *adv. during the night* Pg 6ᵃ.5*.

cāp, *s. a spot* Vd 32ᵇ.6.

cā-pāy, *s. a lump of earth* AH 53ᵇ.

cāputi, *s. a whip* AH 61ᵇ.

cāmar [*S. coming from the Yak*], *s. the tail of a Yak, used as fan* V¹ 111ᵇ.4.

cāhmal, *s.* = cāmar H² 51ᵇ.8. — ~-sā *Yak* CW 7.4.

cāya¹ (-t), *v. t. to tear or break asunder* H¹ 95ᵃ.2; hā cāṅāwo biyā simā *a tree which has been uprooted* Vi 106.34.

cāya² (-l¹), *v. i. to awake* (hṅelan *from sleep*) C¹ 8.

cāya³ (-l¹), *v. t. to wash (the feet, mouth)* P 15ᵃ.2, *to shampoo* N 18ᵃ.8

cāya⁴, ~ ëwo *garrulous, foul-mouthed* (mukhara) C² 74*.

cāya⁵ [= cāya²?] (-l¹), *v. i. forms in connexion with Sa. nouns periphrastic verbs with the meaning of an inchoativum:* bismay ~ *to become astonished* H¹ 26ᵇ.1 *a. s. o.* — *seldom used in other connexions:* khwoyān chu cāwo *why do (you) weep?* H² 101ᵇ.5; ṅoya cāwo-hma *wild, furious* CW 8.49.

cāyakë¹, *v. t. to open (a door)* M 10ᵃ.2.

cāyakë² (*caus. of* cāya²) *to awaken* C¹ 126.

cāyakë³ *caus. of* cāya³ V¹ 113ᵃ.3.

cāyakë⁴ (*caus. of* cāya⁵), āścāry ~ *to astonish* M 35ᵃ.7.

cāyā-pu [cāya⁵], ghali ~ *disgust* CW 1.70; karuṇā cāyā-puk *adv. pitifully, pitiably* H² 89ᵇ.1.

cār¹ [*S. a spy*], ~-citt kāyakë *to send as spy* H³ 54ᵇ.1.

cār² [*S.* cāraka], *s. a keeper* N 29ᵃ.1.

cālakë *caus. of* cālë B 57ᵇ.3.

cālalapë [*S.* cāraka *a companion*], *v. t. to wait on(?)* C² 125*.

cā-lā, *s. the little finger* Vd 44ᵃ.6. — ~-kuchi *an elbow* CW 8.67.

cālë¹, *v. t. to open (a door)* Bh 11ᵇ.7.

cālë², *v. i. to become thick (blood)(?)* Vd 42ᵃ.5.

cāsu, *s. itching* C¹ 259; hnas-potas ~ wotaṃ *the ear is itching* H² 58ᵇ.8. — ~-kaya = cāsu CW 8.43. — ~-kachu *a cutaneous disease* Vd 32ᵇ.3.

cāhālapë [*M.* cāh *to wish for, to desire*], *v. t. to search for* N 42ᵃ.7; *to desire* 24ᵃ.8; *to keep company with* C¹ 125. — cāhālapayakë *caus. to cause to be searched for* N 50ᵃ.7.

ci, *s. salt* N 11ᵃ.7. — *ifc.* **kaṁ-**, **jir-**, **pāgā-**, **beḍ-**, **saṁ-**, **saṁbhuri-**, **subhūri-**, **sedhu-**.

ciwā, ~ kāya *to watch, to explore* B 30ᵃ.4, ~ yāya *id.* 43ᵃ.10; ~ kāyakë *to let explore, to use as spy* H³ 102ᵃ.7, ~ yācakë *id.* 83ᵃ.4.

cikan [*S.* cikkaṇa *smooth, slippery*], *s. oil* B 17ᵇ.1. ~ lāk *smooth, unctuous* AH 55ᵇ. — ~-madhi *a cake made from oil* Md 69ᵇ.1. — cikan wāle *an ordeal* B 17ᵇ.6. — *ifc.* **amb-**, **alaṇḍ-**, **kucilā-tisi-**, **nip-**, **pal-kā-**.

cikay-si, *s. name of several plants* (somavalka) Md 29ᵃ.

cikal, *see* **cākal**.

ciki(t)sā [*S.* cikitsā], *s. medical attendance* Vd 42ᵃ.6.

ciki-dhaṅ, *adj.* = ciku-° Ś 148b.4. ~-dhan *id.* H³ 42a.9. — ciki-dhaṅāo *being insignificant* Vi 26.7.

ciki-dhik, *adj. young* H³ 41a.8. ~-dhikal *id.* Vi 60.5.

cikil, *ifc.* **mi-**.

ciku¹, *adj. cold* Bh 22b.2. *s. cold, frost* H² 51a.5, *med. ague* Vd 19a.5; ~-roy *id.* 19a.3. — cikuyāwo *becoming cold or chilled* H² 75a.3; cikayu *becomes cold* Vd 11b.2. cikuwo *s. cold, frost* Bh 34a.3.

ciku², *adj. small, unimportant* H¹ 23b.4; ~ dhāya *to speak but little* Vd 9b.4.

cikuti, *adj.* 1) = **ciku²** H¹ 59a.4. 2) *the other people* C¹ 222. — **~-dhaṅ** = ~ 1) Bh 115a.2. — cikuti-cikuti-dhanakaṃ *in a much lesser degree* B 55b.10.

ciku-dhaṅ, *adj.* = ciku² C² 240, *a little* Vd 7b.1; ~ deś *a suburb* CW 4.1. ciku-dhan = °-dhaṅ C¹ 132.

ciku-dhik, *adj. short* CW 8.41.

cicakë, *caus. of* ciya B 55b.5.

cicā, *adj.* 1) *small, unimportant* H² 58a.6, *a little* H³ 41a.10. 2) *the other people* (itare) C¹ 216.

cici, ~ tyāya *to unmask* (*fig.*) H² 55b.1*.

cicili, *s. rippling* (*of the waves*) Bh 11b.4*.

cicun, *s. a kind of drug* (*opposed to* mvāc) Vd 46a.4.

ci-chu, *s. a musk-rat* Vd 18a.1.

ci-jak(aṁ), *adv. quiet* B 40b.8.

ciṁci, ~ ḍikë *to order to be poured in* N 44a.1*.

cit(t) [*S.* citta], *s. mind, disposition* Bh 21b.4 (cirtt); ~ taya *to make up one's mind* H² 70a.7, ~ yāya *id.* V² 62b.5; ch-hm-yāke ~ taya *to take fancy to* 23b.3, ~ ~ yāya *id.* 77b.2, ~ ~ wonë *id.* 67a. 2.

citakār [*S.* citrakāra], *s. a painter* B 27a.5.

citakë, *caus. of* ciya H³ 33a.3.

citali [*cf. Mr.* citaḷ]; *s. the spotted antelope* Md 72b.8.

citā = cintā; ch-g-s ~ yāya *to take care of...* M 9a.8; ~ yākë *to cause to care about* B 45b.4.

citu, *see* **cinë**.

cit-phol, *s. a kind of ornament of the forehead* CW 8.76.

cit-hma, *adj.* nugal ~ *poor, wretched, miserly* (kṛpaṇa) AH 64b.

citrakār [*S.*], *s. a painter* B 62a.5.

cit-hā [*H.* citā], *s. a creeper, used medicinally* (citraka) Md 22b.1.

cin [*H.*], *s.* = cihn V² 14b.5; ~ chyāya *to examine* Ś 145b.5.

cinā, ~ tayā uṭh *a young camel* AH 56b.

cinālapë, *v. t.* = cihnālapë V¹ 130b.5*.

cinë, *v. t. to increase* M 10a.7.

cintanā [*S. thinking*], *s. consciousness* Vd 11a.1. jatn ~ yāya *to take care of eagerly* Ś 148a.1; ch-g-s ~ yāya *to take care of...* H³ 25a.4.

cintalapë [*S.* cint- *to think about, to care for*], *v. i. to think, to reflect* Bh 12a.5, *to think about, to consider* H¹ 4a.4, *to think out, to devise* 22b.4, *to resolve, to decide* 24a.1. — cintalapekë *caus. to make think about* Bh 71b.4.

cintā [*S. care, thought*], *s. care, anxiety* Vd 44b.3; ch-g(-s) ~ yāya *to take care or charge of* H² 53a.2; ch-hm-n ch-g-s ~ yācakë *to cause someone to take care of...* Bh 184a.1.

cihn [*S. a mark, spot, sign*], *s. a mark, sign* Ś 148b.3; ~ yāya *to make a mark* N 5b.2, ~ biya *id.* V¹ 21b.4; ~ chuya *to know by a mark* B 61a.7.

cihnālapë [*M.* cihn], *v. t. to know, to recognize* V² 76b.7; *to trace out* B 68a. 3*.

cipa(ṁ) [*cf. H.* cipcipā *adhesive, glutinous*], *s. remnants of food in the mouth* P. 25a.4.

ci-bhāy, *adj. some, a little* V¹ 70ᵃ.2.

ci-bhās, *adj.* = ci-bhāy Ś 155ᵃ.5.

ci-bhin, *adv. a little*(?) Bh 34ᵃ.2*.

cimī, ~-kaṅkāḍi *bristling of the hair of the body* Vd 4ᵃ.2; cimī-sa *the hair* (*of the body*) H² 81ᵇ.7, cimī-sa-pvāl *a circle of hairs* Vi 16.22. — *ifc.* **wā-**.

cimilī = cimī; ~-sa *the hair* (*of body*) H³ 44ᵃ.2.

ciya (-t), *v. t.* = ceya¹ H³ 33ᵃ.1; simān ~ *to tie to a tree* B 47ᵇ.5.

cilakāl [*S.* cirakāla], *s. a long time* V¹ 59ᵃ.5.

cilakë (*caus. of* cilë), *to let turn round* Bh 137ᵇ.5.

cili¹, *s. a daughter-in-law* (= yili(ṃ)) V² 36ᵃ.4.

cili², ~ ~ phāya *to tear to pieces* B 55ᵇ.5.

cili-pal, *s. a straw mat* (kaṭa) AH 59ᵇ (chilingpulu).

ci-luk, *adj. salt, briny* Md 83ᵃ.2.

cilë, *v. t. to roll away* (*a stone*) V¹ 131ᵃ.3; *to withdraw* V² 3ᵃ.4. — *v. i. to turn away from* P 16ᵃ.4.

cirtt, *s.* = **cit(t)**.

ci-sawāl, *s. briny taste* H¹ 84₂ᵃ.5.

ci-sal, *s. Anudātta* AH 15ᵇ.

cis-ma-ciṁ, *s. the bristling of the hairs of the body* CW 1.74.

cihin, *s. fever*; ~ woṅ *fever arises* Vd 19ᵃ.2.

cu, ~ dhënë *to cut off* B 34ᵇ.6. — ~ ~ pyā-(-n *or* -t?) *to lick* H³ 14ᵃ.4.

cuṁ, *s. a* (*fragrant*) *powder* AH 66ᵇ.

cuk¹ [H. cauk], *s. an* (*inner*) *court-yard* Bh 163ᵇ.7.

cuk² [*cf. Mr.* cauk *the small of the back*], *s. the groin* AH 41ᵃ.

cuk³, *s. the tamarind-tree* AH 55ᵃ.

cuk⁴ [*M.* cuk *to make a mistake*], ~ ma dayakaṃ *without a fault* N 46ᵇ.1*.

cukuti, *adj.* = cikuti V² 80ᵃ.6.

cukuri [*cf. Mr.* cukūr *bewildered, confused*], ch-hm-yāke ~ yāya *to make mischief between* H² 71ᵃ.2*.

cu-cekan-tu, *s. Jussioea repens* Md 18ᵃ.1.

cutaṁ, *s. a wooden trough* (droṇī) AH 20ᵇ.

cutu, *see* **culë.**

cūḍā [*S.*], *s. a tuft of hair, left on the top of the head* H² 56ᵃ.7.

cupā, *s. a kiss,* ~ naya *to kiss* H¹ 59ᵇ.2.

cupi, *s.* = copi B 40ᵇ.3; ~-cā *id.* AH 61ᵇ.

cupwo-svān, *s. name of a plant* (kecuka) Md 50ᵇ.6.

cumakë, *v. t. to make tepid or lukewarm*(?) Vd 38ᵇ.2*.

cumbalapë [*S.* cumb-], *v. t. to kiss* Bh 42ᵃ.7.

cuya¹ (-l¹), *v. i. to be carried off* (*by water*) V¹ 78ᵃ.5. *v. t. to carry away, to wash away* H³ 37ᵃ.7.

cuya² (-l¹), *v. t.* = culë; pulin pṛthis ~ *to scratch the ground with the knee i. e. to touch* — — Vi 81.31.

cuyakë (*caus. of* cuya¹), 1) = *simpl. trs.* H² 84ᵇ.1. — 2) *to let be carried away* (*by water*) Vi 140.11.

cul, ~ lāya *v. i. to meet* ('wo... 'wo) B 12ᵇ.6. *v. t. to obtain* Vi 101.25, ~ lātakë *id.* 109.18.

culi, ~ woya *to sprout forth, to grow out* B 40ᵇ.10, ~ woyakë *caus.* 9ᵇ.11. ~ jāwo *s. a sprout, shoot* CW 6.3.

culi, *adv.*; me ~'n pi kāya *to throw one's tongue far out* M 10ᵃ.8; jihvā ~ ~'n pheya *id.* Bh 3ᵇ.4*.

culë, *v. t. to rub* (ch-g-s *on...*, *against...*) H³ 28ᵇ.7; *to grind* (*to powder*) Vi 26.22; *med.*: *to imbrocate* Vd 14ᵃ.6. tuti bas ~ *to put the foot to the ground* ("*to rub the* f° *against the* gr°") Vi 107.2.

curṇ [*S.* cūrṇa], *s. powder* Vd 47ᵇ.3; ~ yāya *to pulverize, to grind* Vd 2ᵃ.7.

culyā, *s.* 1) *an elbow* AH 41ᵇ. 2) *a bracelet, armlet* B 5ᵃ.1. — *ifc.* **lu-**.

cusabu-ke, *s. decoction of a plant* Vd 46b.6.

cu-sā, *s.* 1) *tce porcupine* CW 7.2; 2) *a quill of the porcupine* 7.3.

cusi, *s. a sort of silk* N 41b.6*.

ce, *s. a house* (? = che?) CW 8.15.

cekan, *s.* = cikan N 50b.4. — *ifc.* **araḍ-**, **hāmal-1**.

cecakë, *caus. of* ceya1 H2 63a.3.

cet(t), *s.* = cit(t) H1 84b.1; ch-g-s ∼ taya *to set one's mind upon* H1 60a.3; ∼ ma dayakë *to become disheartened* V2 42b.3; ∼ dayā(wo) wolaṃ (*she*) *regained consciousness* Vi 99.5.

cetakë, *caus. of* ceya1 Bh 24a.6; *to let confine or imprison* N 19a.5.

cetan1 [*S.*], *c. the soul, mind* H2 64b.6; ∼ yāya *to restore to consciousness* V2 66b.4.

cetan2, ∼-kane *unguent laid on* CW 8.82. —∼teyā *a mark on the forehead ib.*

cetanā [*S. consciousness, understanding*], ∼ daya *to regain consciousness* V1 56a.5; ∼ yāya *to understand* Vi 140.24.

cetannë [*S.* caitanya], *s. consciousness* Vd 7b.1.

ceṭik [*S.* ceṭikā], *s. a maid-servant* Vi 44.26.

cet-khayar, *s. a medicinal plant* Vd 33a.1.

cet-lā, *s. the month Phālguna* CW 1.49.

ceḍ, *s.* = cel; ∼ conë *to be a slave,* N 20b.3. — ceḍi *s. a female slave* N 34b.8; ∼-misā *id.* 51b.1.

cen, *s.* = cin; *a mark, sign* N 22b.3; *a brand* 52a.7.

cen-mud, *s. building materials* N 22b.8.

cehn, *s.* = cihn; *a symptom* Vd 5b.1.

cep, ∼ ithimithi juya *to be blamable* P 20a.5*.

cemo, ∼ jawo *a symptom of tumors* Vd 29a.2; cemasëṃ *id.* 32a.6.

ceya1 (-t *and* -l1), *v. t. to bind, to tie, to fetter* H1 91b.5; *to confine, to imprison* N 53a.4.

ceya2, *see* **pol.**

cel [*M.* celā *a disciple*], *s. a servant, slave* B 38b.10. — ∼-to *pl.* B 35b.12.

celu, *adj. salt, briny* Vd 46a.5.

celë1, *v. t. to consider as* N 8b.7.

celë2, *v. t.* = cilë V1 3b.1*.

ċertt = **cet(t)** Bh 147b.3.

certtannë = cetannë Vd 7b.4.

ceṣṭ(ā) [*corr. from* cet?], ∼ daya *to recover one's senses* Bh 163a.1, ∼ juya *id.* 62a.7.

ceṣṭā [*S. a gesture, action*], *s. actions* H2 53b.7.

ceṣṭhā, *s.* = ceṣṭā H3 26a.7.

co1, *s. the outmost part of a thing; top* (*of a mountain*) H3 41b.6, *ends* (*of hair*) H2 58a.5, *the mouth* (*of a well*) B 5b.8. ∼ jāwo *adj. high, tall* P 9a.1. — *ifc.* **hnās-**, **parbat-**, **me-**.

co2, *s. urine* H1 29b.2. — *ifc.* **colas-**.

co3, *s. a dog*(?) H1 61a.5*.

cokaṁ, *adv.* = cokwo B 34a.3.

cokā, *s. the tip* (*of an ear*) B 9a.12. — *ifc.* **dudu-**, **hnas-**, **pot-**, **me-**.

cokë, *caus. of* coya1 M 39a.5.

cokë2, *s. rice* H1 13a.5. coki *id.* H3 4a.6; *the eye of corn* (kaṇa) AH 69a.

cokwo, *adv. completely, entirely* B 16b.12.

cocakë, *caus. of* coya1 B 33b.11.

co-co, ∼ yāya *to lacerate* H1 22a.2*.

co-jyā, *s. painting work* Vi 145.20.

cot1 [co1], *s. a hem, corner* (*of a garment*) B 17b.8. — *ifc.* **gā-**.

cot2, ∼ kāya *to seize, to grasp* Bh 84a.1; ∼ kāyakë *to cause to accept*(?) H3 57b.1.

coda [*M.* caudaha *fourteen*], *s. the 14th day of the lunar fortnight* AH 10b.

conakë (*caus. of* conë), khwoyāwo ∼ *to cause to weep* Vi 86a.2; hṅāpāyāthēm̥ ~ *to restore to it's former state* 78.28; chal-pol-thēm ~ *to make like you* B 19^{b}.2.

conē, *v. i. to be (somewhere)* H^{2} 10^{a}.7, *to sit, to stand* M 37^{b}.4, *to stay* H^{1} 80^{a}.3, *to live* (ch-hm-yāke *with...*) V^{2} 20^{a}.5, *to remain* V^{1} 112^{a}.3, *to last* P 51^{a}.3, ch-hm-yāke ~ *to be found with...*, *to be in the possession of...* N 20^{a}.2; disā ~ *to sit down* P 13^{b}.6; ch-hm-wo saṅgan ~ *to keep company with...* H^{1} 12^{a}.4; sukhan ~ *to be at peace* V^{1} 24^{a}.1; guptan ~ *to be hidden* H^{1} 90^{a}.4. ma cosēm̥ wonē *to disappear* V^{2} 9^{a}.1. com̥-gwo *what is said (in a book)* N 5^{b}.3, co(m̥)kwo *id.* 5^{b}.1. — conē *with other verbs forms a sort of durativum:* basalapam̥ ~ *to be living or staying (for a longer space of time)* H^{1} 12^{a}.5; swosēm̥ ~ *to be watching* 12^{b}.3; khwoyāwo ~ *to be weeping* V^{2} 20^{b}.6.

cond = con (*s. form of* conē) N 20^{b}.7.

copi, °pe, *s. a knife* H^{1} 94^{b}.5.

coya^{1} (-t: cotam̥, cok, *caus., and* -l^{1}: *the other forms*), *v. t.* 1) *to write* V^{2} 71^{a}.4; cosēm̥ taya *to subscribe* N 10^{a}.5; cosēm̥ tā *s. a document* 8^{a}.8; coyā *id. ib*; coya byabahār *id.* 8^{a}.2. — 2) *to paint* Vi 71.21.

coya^{2} (-l^{1}) = cuya^{1} H^{2} 69.8^{a}.

coya^{3} (-l^{1}), *v. t.* = cuya^{2} N 12^{a}.3.

coyakē^{1}, *v. t. to announce, to proclaim* Vi 157.32.

coyakē^{2} = cuyakē P 33^{a}.6.

col^{1}, *s. pulse, vegetables* Vd 41^{b}.5. *ifc.* **uphar-**, **nālu-**, **nip-**.

col^{2}, me ~ jowo *an incendiary* N 10^{b}.3; me ~ juwo-hma *id.* C^{1} 114.

colawāl [*cf. M.* cor *a thief*], *s. a rogue, knave* H^{2} 110^{a}.5. ~-mantrī *the rogue of a minister* Ś 166^{a}.1.

colakē (*caus. of* colē) Vd 7^{b}.4.

colas, *s. a goat* V^{1} 49^{b}.6. — ~-co *urine of a goat* Md 61^{b}.8. — ~-jhawāl *a goat-herd* AH 60^{a}. — ~-dudu *milk of a goat* V^{1} 50^{a}.3. — ~-dhali *coagulated goat-milk* Md 56^{a}.8. — ~-nā *smell of a goat* V^{1} 50^{a}.2. — ~-bathān *a herd of goats* AH 56^{b}. — *ifc.* **dhwom-**, **mā-**.

co-lā, *s. the fore-finger* C^{1} 290; swo colān *with three fingers* V^{1} 15^{a}.5.

colē, *v. t.* = culē Vd 7^{b}.3. hmutu ~ *to rinse one's mouth* P 20^{b}.4.

-cos [co^{1}], *on the top of, upon, on*; simā-~ *on the tree* H^{1} 80^{b}.1.

caur [*S.*], *s. a thief* V^{1} 37^{b}.6.

causathi [*M.* cauṁsaṭhi], *num. sixty-four* B 65^{b}.12*.

cwo, *s. the privy parts of a man* N 34^{b}.5.

cwok, *s. the female parts* N 42^{b}.5. — ~-bān *a brand shaped like the* f° p° 52^{a}.7*.

cwotaṁ, *s. a watch-tower* (aṭṭa) CW 4.7 (cvataṁ).

cyā, *num. eight* C^{1} 297; cyā da du *eight years old* CW 8.8. cyā-gu *the Vasavaḥ* CW 1.2.

cyāk, *s. a mole (on the body)* Ś 148^{b}.4.

cyāk-cik, *adj. variegated* CW 1.57.

cyā-tā, *num.* = cyā N 48^{a}.8.

cyāya (-t), *v. t. to light* (mat *a candle*) M 80^{a}.4.

cyu, *mod. ipr. of* ciya (= ciwo) Vi 158.19*.

cvāk, *adj. diligent, skilful* AH 66^{b}.

cvā-pwo, *s. snow* CW 1.43. — ~-gum̥ *Himālaya* 5.1.

cvāmukē, *v. t. to blow up, to inflate* M 32^{b}.8*.

ch.

cha^{1}, *num. one*: cāk cha cākan *with one wheel* H^{1} 6^{b}.1. *indef. some, a*: simā cha mā *a tree* 12^{a}.3; **cha thāyas** *somewhere* Vi 130.4, **cha kṣaṇas** *at one time* H^{2} 66^{b}.1. — **cha-hma** = **cha** (*of living beings only*) *one* **Vi 170.21**, *a, some* H¹ 36ª.3; *standing alone: one (of them), the one* V² 31ª.5. ji chahma *I alone* Vi 38.32. cha-hma cha-hma *each separately* Bh 22ª.5. — cha-guli = cha (*of things only*) *some, a* Ś 162ᵇ.1. cha-gulis *somewhere* V¹ 119ᵇ.4.

cha² (chan, chanata, chanake, chawo), *pr. prs. 2. s. you (used mostly in adressing inferiors or equals)* H¹ 17ᵇ.3. cha-pani *pl. you* Ś 150ª.4, *poss. your* M 20ª.6.

cha³, *pr. int.* = chu¹ V² 59ᵇ.6. — cha-nuṃ = chu-° Vi 51.30.

cha-ṁ = cha-nuṃ Vi 133.31.

chak, *adj.* = chāk C¹ 209.

cha-khē, *adv. separately* B 59ᵇ.2.

cha-je, *pr. prs.* = che-je V² 29ª.4.

chat, ~ bēnē *v. i. to burst* H¹ 74ᵇ.2*.

cha-ta, *num.* = cha-tā H¹ 24ª.1; chataṃ...ma *nothing* 4ᵇ.2.

cha-tā, *num. one* C¹ 189. *indef. some, a* M 8ᵇ.1; chatā(ṃ)... ma *nothing* H¹ 26ª.1; chatān(aṃ)... ma *id.* V² 8ᵇ.6; chatāṅ... ma *id.* V¹ 125ᵇ.2; chatārinaṃ *at once, together* H² 58ᵇ.4.

chatiwo, *s. Mimosa pudica* AH 27ᵇ (chhatiwang).

chatr [*S.*], *s. a parasole (ensign of royal power)* H² 51ᵇ.8.

chan (*gen. of* cha¹), *pr. poss. 2. s. your* H¹ 17ª.1; ~-guli *id.* Vi 23.18.

cha-naṁ = cha-nuṃ V² 27ᵇ.4.

cha-nuṁ, *pr. ind.*: ~...ma *nothing* Vi 51.30.

cha-hnaṁ, *adv. once, once only* N 31ᵇ.7.

chapan [*M.*], *num. fifty-six* Ś 169ᵇ.6*.

cha-bāl, *adv. once* P 24ª.4.

cha-bhinā, *adv. separately* V¹ 130ª.2.

chay¹, *s. a grand-child* B 60ª.3. — ~-cā *id.* Vi 72.29. — ~-cyā *id.* B 60ª.3. *ifc.* **kāy-**.

chay², *adj. hard, harsh* C² 208.

chaya¹ (-l¹), *v. t.* kheṃ-ja ~ *to lay eggs* H² 69ª.7.

chaya² (-t), *v. t.* = chuya¹ B 19ᵇ.2 (chanyā)*.

chayakē, *caus. of* chaya¹ H² 75ª.1.

chal¹ [*S.*], *s. fraud, deceit* H² 109ᵇ.4.

chal², ~ phāya *to stroke, to caress* (?) Bh 95ª.3*.

charaṁ, *s. a continued abode* (sthāna) N 6ᵇ.2*.

cha-la-pani, *pr. prs. 2. pl. you* Vi 118.16*.

chalay [*H.* chalnā *to impose upon*], ~ yāya *v. t. to cheat, to impose upon* Vi 95.27.

chaliṅā-si, *s. name of a plant* (kunduru) AH 32ª.

chale, *want of right, liberty (to do a thing)*(?) B 5ᵇ.8.

cha-lapol, *pr. prs. 2. s. you, your honour (used in adressing persons of high rank)* V² 52ª.6.

chal-laṁ-hāwo, *s. a road, row* (vīthī) CW 6.3.

chasipol-dhuṁ, *s. a leopard* Md 71ᵇ.7.

cha-siṁ-bu, *s. name of several plants* (punnāga) Md 31ª.4.

chāk, *adj. hard* C¹ 240, *rough, harsh (word)* Vi 115.7, *sharp* (tīkṣṇa) AH 69ᵇ, *violent* (karkaśa) 72ᵇ.

chāku-tu, *s. a kind of sugar-cane* (tāpasa) Md 63ª.1.

chāṅ¹, *adj. sharp, fiery* Vd 45ª.1.

chāṅ² = chān H¹ 17ª.2.

chāṅā = chān V² 4ᵇ.5; chāṅān *id.* V¹ 32ª.1.

chātakē [chāṅ], *v. t. to make sharp or fiery* Vd 45ª.1.

chāḍ [*M.*], ~ yācakē *to expel, to repudiate* N 16ᵇ.2*.

chāḍalapē [*M.* chāḍ *to leave, desert*], *v. t. to leave, to abandon (a husband, wife)* N 33ª.1, *to give up (an occupation)* 45ᵇ.5, *to break (the law)* 35ᵇ.8.

chān, *adv. int. why?* V² 61ᵇ.4; ~ dhālasā (*lit. "if you say: why?"*) *for (it is as follows)* H² 74ᵇ.1.

chāp, *s. an onion* CW 7.33.

chāy[1], *adv. int. why?* V[2] 63[a].4; nvāṅāwo ~ *why this quarrelling?* H[2] 31[a].1; kaṅān ṅeṅān ~ *let alone those stories* 112[b].5.

chāy[2], *s. a dress, attire* B 36[a].5. — ~-pāgu *id.* AH 43[a].

chāya (-l[1]), *v. t. to carry* Vi 89.11; (ch-hm-yāta) *to offer, to sacrifice* V[1] 117[a].2.

chāyalapē [chāy], *v. t. to trim, to adorn* Bh 174[a].6*.

chāyā [*S.*], *s. a shadow* H[2] 79[b].7.

chāyu, *adj. pointed* CW 8.39.

chālā [*M.* chāl], *s. a skin, hide* H[2] 75[b].8. — *ifc.* **bāgh-**[1].

chālā-pu [chālē], *adj. bold, daring (of persons)* V[1] 30[a].6.

chālē (5. *form* chāwo B 6[a].2), *v. t. to like* (yāya *to do a thing*) H[1] 66[b].5; *generally:* ma ~ *not dare* V[1] 125[b].6. thathiṃṅawo gathē biśvās ma chārā *why not dare to place confidence in somebody like that* H[1] 16[a].3.

chi[1], *num. one* C[1] 142; ji bos chi bo *a tenth part* N 21[a].7. — chi chi-hmaṃ lesēṃ *one by one* N 26[b].7; chi chi-guḍi rāṣṭras *in each principality* N 50[a].2; chi chitā maṃs *one* maṃs *of each* Vd 41[b].2. — kāl chiṃ *at one time* V[2] 63[b].7; hni hni chiyā *every day* M 5[b].3. chi-yanakaṃ *one only* H[1] 74[a].4.

chi[2] (chin, chita, chike, chiwo), *pr. prs. 2. s.* = che[2] Vi 21.15. *poss. your* H[2] 22[a].1.

chi[3], *s. salt* (= ci) H[2] 44[b].9*.

chikay = chekay: ~ yāya H[2] 97[a].2.

chi-kal, *pr. prs.* = che-kal *2. s.* H[2] 8[b].7; ~-pani *2. pl.* B 32[b].9; ~-piṃ *id.* 6[a].5.

chikē, *v. t.* = chicakē H[2] 52[a].5*.

chicakē, *v. t. to saw* H[2] 25[a].1*.

chi-ji, *pr. prs. 1. pl. incl.* H[2] 45[b].3. *poss. our* B 4[a].4.

chi-to, *num.* = chi[1]: lā la chitoyā *one month* Vi 52.26.

chidr[1] [*S.*], *s. a hole, slit* H[2] 32[b].7.

chidr[2] [*S.* chidura], *adj. hostile (word)* M 12[b].5.

chinakē (*caus. of* chinē) *to strengthen* Vd 43[b].4; la ~ *to force one's way* M 7[a].7*.

chinārī [*H.* chinār *a loose woman*], *adj. desirous, lustful* H[2] 109[a].2.

chinē, *v. i. to be strong or vigorous*; *only:* ma ~ *to become feeble, to lose one's strength* B 20[a].10. nugal ma chiṅ *he has lost his courage, has become depressed* Vd 4[b].1.

chinn [*S.*], ~ juya *to be opened* Bh 11[b].6.

chipā, *s. a dyer, washerman* C[1] 205. chipāni *id.* H[2] 84[b].6.

chi-pi, *pr. prs. 2. pl. you* B 32[a].3.

chi-mi, *pr. prs. 2. pl. you* B 17[b].4.

chiya (-t), *v. t.*, khusi ~ *to cross a river* B 45[b].11; gathi ~ *to form a bundle* Bh 58[a].3.

chili, *s. price, value*; dviguṇ ~ *twice its value* N 24[a].3.

chi-sakal, *pr. prs.* = che-sakal B 5[b].6.

chi-sak-pani [chi-sakal], *pr. prs. 2. pl. you* B 60[a].10.

chi-skal, *pr. prs.* = chi-sakal H[2] 10[a].9; *2. s.* Vi 22.7, ~-pani *id.* Vi 22.22.

chu[1], *pr. int.* (*of things only*) *what, which, s.* H[1] 91[a].3, *adj.* 88[b].1. *pr. ind. some* V[2] 74[b].2. *pr. rel.* (*corr.* u-guli) *which, what* B 29[a].11. — chu dhakaṃ *why* B 2[b].1; chu chu dhālasā *which are they* C[1] 171; chu chu sāmāgri *whatever may be necessary* M 8[a].5. chuyā *how, why* Bh 67[a].3. chuyāta *for what purpose* C[1] 169.

chu[2], *s. a mouse* H[1] 59[a].4. — *ifc.* ci-.

chu[3] [chuya[3]], ~ yāya *to pretend* (sik *to be dead*) H[2] 48[a].2.

chu-[4] (chusëṃ *only*) = chonë(?): tham chusëṃ *of one's own accord* N 3ᵇ.6*.

chu-ṁ, *pr. ind.* = chu-naṃ M 14ᵇ.6.

chuk, *s. an apartment* (? koṣṭha) AH 68ᵇ (chhuku).

chu-khunu, *pr. ind. something* H[3] 58ᵇ.5.

chuṅā-pu, *adj. agreeable, delightful*; ches conë ma~ *the house is not agreeable to dwell in* Ś 155ᵃ.5; ma chuṅā-puyāo *when it had become tedious* B 27ᵃ.9.

chucakë (*caus. of* chuya[1]), svānan ~ *to cause to be adorned with flowers* Bh 49ᵇ.1; ch-hm-yāta svān ~ *id.* B 10ᵇ.10.

chu-cā, *s. the young of a mouse* H[2] 103ᵃ.8; chu-cā-ca *id.* H[3] 55ᵃ.5; chu-cā-cā *id.* H[2] 103ᵃ.4.

chu-chu, ~ yanë *to attach to, to fasten* V[1] 78ᵃ.6.

chu-naṁ, *pr. ind. any, anything*: ~...ma *no, nothing* Vi 21.7.

chu-nu(ṁ), *pr. ind.* = chu-naṃ H[1] 80ᵃ.6. chu-nu *pr. int. what* B 60ᵇ.7. je chu-nuṃ ma khu *I am none of these* Ś 158ᵃ.7. — chu-nuṅ *pr. ind.* Ś 164ᵇ.6.

chu-hnas, *s. name of a plant* (mūṣikaparṇī) CW 7.26.

chupiri-svān, *s. a plant, used in medicine* Vd 55ᵃ.6.

chu-pvāl, *s. a mouse-hole* H[1] 32ᵃ.3

chuya[1] (-t *and* -l[1]), *v. t. to fasten, to attach* (ch-g-s *to*...) B 27ᵃ.1; pās ~ *to set up a trap* H[1] 44ᵃ.3; svān ~ *to fasten flowers* B 19ᵇ.3, svānan ~ *to adorn with flowers* Bh 12ᵃ.2; nām ~ *to give a name* (ch-hm *to*...) B 43ᵃ.7; ch-hm cihn ~ *to point out, to indicate* 61ᵃ.7.

chuya[2] (-l[1], *but a few times* chuṅ, chuṅāwo), *v. t. to warm, to make hot* V[2] 13ᵃ.3; *to roast* H[3] 54ᵃ.9; *to bake* V[2] 12ᵃ.5.

chuya[3] (-l[1]), *v. i. to pretend* (sik *to be dead*) H[1] 48ᵇ.2.

chuya[4] (-t), *v. i. to fall (in war)* Bh 137ᵃ.2.

chuya[5], *v. t.* = choya[3] C[2] 21.

chuya[6] (-t), *v. t.* = choya[1] B 9ᵇ.7.

chul = chu[3] Ś 144ᵃ.5.

churān, *s. a plant, the root of which is used medicinally* Vd 38ᵇ.2.

chulu, pët churu cvārāwo woṃ-go *dysentery* Vd 3ᵃ.6.

chu-si[1], *s. name of several plants* (puṃnāga) AH 27ᵇ.

chu-si[2], *s. fuel* H[2] 110ᵇ.1.

che[1], *s. a house, home* H[1] 90ᵇ.1; *the nest (of a bird)* B 22ᵇ.8. bairiyā ches conë *to side with the enemy* H[2] 73ᵇ.3. — *ifc.* **kāpaḍ-, bal-khunī-, bhita-khā-.**

che[2] (chen, cheta, cheke, chewo, ches), *pr. prs. 2. s. you (used mostly in adressing superiors or equals)* H[1] 50ᵃ.4. *poss. your* 51ᵇ.4. — ~-thiṅ *one like you* V[2] 68ᵃ.5.

che-[3] (-n *or* -t?), *v. t.* sa cheṅāwo *having dressed the hair* B 17ᵇ.10*.

che'uli, *s.* = cheguli CW 8.50.

chewoḍi, *s. leather* N 50ᵇ.4*.

cheṁ, hnaspot ~ ~ taya *to prick up one's ears* H[2] 71ᵇ.1*.

chekay [*H.* cheknā], ~ yāya *v. t. to stop on the road* Vi 143.26.

che-kal [= °-sakal], *pr. prs. 2. s.* H[2] 105ᵇ.7; ~-pani *2. pl.* 75ᵃ.3.

che-keba, *s. a pleasure grove near a house* (niṣkuṭa) CW 6.1.

che-khā[1], *s.* 1) *a house-door* Vi 168.28. 2) *household utensils* N 41ᵃ.4.

che-khā[2], *s. the common cock* Md 74ᵃ.6.

cheguli, *s. a skin* H[3] 41ᵃ.4. — ~-lāsā *the hide used by a student* (ajina) AH 17ᵇ (chhengulásá).

cheṁgu, *s. mod.* = chegulī AH 14ᵃ. — *ifc.* **calā-.**

checalapē, *v. t. to remove (doubts)* H[1] 21b.1*.

che-cal-khuni, *s. a kind of sparrow* Md 73b.3.

che-cā, *s. a small house, hut* CW 4.7.

che-che, *s. the shank* (jaṅghā) CW 8.56. — ~-pā-li *id.* AH 41a.

che-je, *pr. prs. 1. pl. incl. we* V[1] 107b.1.

chedan [*S. s. cutting*], ~ yāya *to cut off* Bh 100a.1; *to fell (a tree)* H[2] 28b.6.

chedalapākē, *caus. of* chedalapē N 51b.2.

chedalapē [*S.* chid-], *v. t. to cut off* V[1] 44b.1; *to bite in two* V[2] 7b.2.

che-ḍi, *s.* = che-li N 35b.7*.

chen[1] (*gen. of* che[2]), *pr. poss. 2. s. your* V[2] 9b.2.

chen[2], *s. fire, heat*(?) M 10a.7*.

chen[3], *s.* = kṣaṇ Bh 40b.6*.

chenē, *v. t.* pyās cāwo chenaṃ *quenched his thirst* H[3] 17b.9*.

che-pal, *pr. prs.* = che-lapol V[1] 4b.4*.

che-phā, *s. the village hog* AH 61a.

che-boḍ, *s. stores* (bhāṇḍa) N 16a.8.

che-bhu, *s. a building ground* AH 25a.

cheya[1], *v. i. to become thin (blood)* (?) Vd 42a.6.

cheya[2], *v. t.* = chiya N 47a.5.

cheyā-pani, *s. housemates* P 60b.1*.

che-lapol, *pr. prs. 2. s. you, your honour (used in adressing persons of high rank)* Bh 10b.7.

chel, *s. a head* H[2] 91a.4.

che-li [che], *s. the hindmost part of a house* B 17a.8.

chelē (?, *only* chelasā), *v. i. to move*(?) C[1] 34*.

ches (*gen. of* che[2]), *pr. poss. 2. s. your* Bh 40a.2.

che-sakal [che + *S.* sakala *all*], *pr. prs. 2. pl. you* H[2] 8b.3.

che-skal = che-sakal H[1] 81a.2.

che-hajar, *s. a threshold* H[2] 34a.6*.

cho[1], *s. wheat* C[1] 9; tawo-gwol ~, ciki gwol ~ *two sorts of wheat* Md 65a.6.

cho[2], *pr.* = chu[1] H[2] 51a.3. cho bala-ṃ ma *no strength* H[2] 49b.5.

cho[3], *s.* = co[2] P 63a.6.

cho-[4] (-n *or* -t? *only* choṅāwo), *v. t. to make mischief* ('wo — 'wo *between*) H[2] 49a.2; *to instigate* B 53b.2, ch-hm-yāke *to prejudice* 20a.5.

cho-[5] (-n *or* -t? *only* choṅāwo), *v. t. to hand over, to deliver* N 38a.4; choṅāwo biya *id.* B 51a.6.

cho-kha, ~ bo-kha yāya *to slander, to calumniate* C[1] 243.

cho-khinuṁ, -khinwoṁ, *pr. ind. something* H[1] 59a.5.

cho-chinwoṁ, *pr. ind. some* H[2] 37b.7.

cho-thwo, *s. a beverage made from wheat* Md 61a.4.

choḍalapē [*cf. H.* choṛnā *to omit*], *v. t. to induce, to instigate* N 44b.1.

cho-naṁ, °-**noṁ**, *pr. ind. something, anything* H[2] 65a.4.

cho-ba, *s. a wheat-field* H[1] 44a.1. ~-bo *id.* H[3] 10b.1.

cho-madhi, *s. a cake made from wheat* Md 69a.1.

choya[1] (-l[1], *but mostly* chota-), *v. t. to send, to dispatch (a messenger)* H[1] 90b.1, *to send away* 63b.2, *to destine (fate)* H[3] 6a.4; *to throw* H[1] 49a.4; *to leave alone*(?) V[2] 62b.4. — jyā ~ *to execute a commission* C[1] 71, banaj ~ *to carry on trade* V[1] 94b.6; chosēṃ haya = choya, *to send out* V[2] 39a.5. — *After other verbs* choya *has a meaning much like that of* tāthē Vi 18.32.

choya[2] (-l[1], *but* choṅaṃ Vd 37b.5), *v. t.* = chuya[2] Vd 21b.5. — *v. i. to burn* H[3] 28a.10.

choya[3] (-l[1]), *v. t. to enjoy, to experience* H[3] 18b.3.

choya[4], *v. t.* = chaya[1] H[3] 37a.5.

choyakë, *caus. of* choya²; *to kindle* C² 211, *to set on fire* H² 33ᵇ.5.

cholawāl [choya¹?], *s. a messenger* AH 48ᵇ, *a groom* Vi 16.31.

cholalapë, *v. t.* = choḍalapë C¹ 291.

cho-lā, *s. the autumn* Ns 27ᵇ.4.

chohalā, *s. a chick-pea* Md 66ᵃ.4.

chyā, ~ ~ yāya *to take measures*(?) H³ 19ᵃ.8*.

chyāṅu, *adj. stiff, rigid* Vd 4ᵃ.1.

chyāt = chyātā; ch-hm-wo chyātan juya *to ask advice of* H² 51ᵃ.2.

chyātā, ~ yāya *to consult together* H² 47ᵇ.1, ~ biya *to give advice* 55ᵃ.8.

chyātyā = chyātā H³ 27ᵇ.1; ch-hm-wo ~ juya *to ask advice of* H³ 24ᵃ.3.

chyān, ~ yāya *to accomplish*(?) Bh 155ᵇ.2*.

chyāya (-t), *v. t.* 1) *to prepare (medicine)* Vd 45ᵃ.2; *to till, to cultivate* N 28ᵃ.1. — 2) = tawo ~ B 55ᵃ.8.

chvāk, *adj.*, wā ~ *having terrible tusks* (daṃṣṭrākarāla) Ns 15ᵇ.3*.

chvālu-cāku, *s. the inspissated juice of the sugar cane* Md 63ᵇ.4.

j.

ja (jan, jata, jawo), *pr. prs. 1. s. I* (= je¹) H¹ 55ᵃ.2. *poss. my* H³ 41ᵇ.3; jan *id.* N 33ᵃ.6; ja-guli *id.* Vi 52.29. ja-pani *pl. excl. we* B 30ᵇ.9.

jawāl [jaya], *s. a herdsman* N 22ᵃ.6. — *ifc.* **phayi-**, **sa-**, **sā-**.

jawo¹, *adj. right (not left)* V² 13ᵃ.3; thawo jawos *at his right hand* B 36ᵇ.7. jawo khawo *on both sides* Vi 177.11, jawo khawos *id.* H² 87ᵇ.6, jawo khawo swoya *to look around* Bh 74ᵃ.6.

jawo² [jaya], *s. interest* N 6ᵇ.6.

jawo-si, *s. a pumpkin* B 30ᵃ.6. māku ~ *a kind of pumpkin* Md 46ᵇ.4.

jaṁ¹, *s. wages*, ~ kāya *to get as wages* N 21ᵇ.8; *(ferry) hire* N 47ᵃ.5. — *ifc.* **ku-**, **jyā-**.

jaṁ², *adj. middle* CW 8.50.

jak, *prt. only* B 58ᵃ.6; *however* Vi 53.26.

jake, *s. rice* V¹ 106ᵇ.6.

jagalapë, *v. i.* = jāgalapë V² 23ᵃ.1.

jaṅgam [*S. movable*], *s. movables* N 8ᵃ.6.

jaṅgal [*M.*], *s. a wood, forest* Ś 158ᵃ.3.

jajñ [*S.* yajna], *s. a sacrifice* V¹ 48ᵃ.6.

jaṭ [*S.* jaṭā], *s. the hair, as worn by ascetics* CW 8.74; *the mane (of a lion)* H² 58ᵃ.5.

jaṭā-mā-si, *s. a medicinal plant* Vd 35ᵇ.2.

jaṭi-dhap [*S.* jaṭin *ascetic*], *s. the bowl of an ascetic* B 45ᵃ.7.

jatti, *emphasiz. prt. after pr.* Vi 122.22.

jatn [*S.* yatna], *s. exertion* H² 2ᵇ.5; ~ yāya *to exert oneself* Vi 55.15; ~ chuṃ ma data *there is nothing to be done* Vi 129.17.

jathājogy [*S.* yathāyogya], *adj. proper* H² 114ᵇ.7.

jathārth [*S.* yathārtha], *adj. proper, suitable* H² 115ᵃ.3.

jathāśaky [*S.* yathāśakya], ~-thë *to the utmost of one's power* H² 82ᵇ.2.

jaṭhu [*S.* jatru], *s. the collar-bone* N 30ᵇ.2.

jan [*S.*], *s. a man* H² 61ᵇ.6; ~-lok *men* B 24ᵇ.5. — *forming plurals* M 21ᵇ.6. — *ifc.* [*H. from Pers.* zän *a woman*?] **misā-**, **strī-**.

janik, *s. the vow of fasting* P 8ᵃ.1.

jantal [*H.* jantar *a machine, instrument*], *s. a (musical) instrument* CW 1.62.

jantu [*S.*], *s. a living being* Bh 154ᵃ.3.

jandhu, *s.* = jal-dhu H³ 11ᵃ.8*.

janm [*S.* janman *birth, origin*], *s. origin* Ś 158ᵃ.3; ~ juya *to be born* (misā *as a woman*) V¹ 45ᵃ.5; ~ yāya *to revive* B 14ᵇ.7, *to suffer oneself to* *be born* (manuṣy *as a man*) B 33ª.3, ~ kāya *id.* P 2ª.2.

japalapē [*S.* jap *to mutter (prayers)*], *v. t.* hāth ~ *to clasp the hands* C¹ 223.

japu-se, *s. Eugenia Jambolana* CW 6.12.

jabāp [*H.* javāb *answer — reward — dismissal, from Arab.*]; ~ **biya** *to give an answer* Ś 154ª.5; ch-hm-wo nāp ~ ~ *to return, to retaliate* B 33ª.3; ~ yāya *to dismiss* 60ª.5.

jabhil, *s. a woman's girdle* (mekhalā) AH 43ᵇ.

Jam [*S.* Yama], *n. pr. Yama* H² 9ª.4.

jamadar, °**mu**°, *s. a kind of weapon* B 45ª.1.

jambūk [*S.*], *s. a jackal* H¹ 33ᵇ.5.

jaya (-l¹), *v. t.* 1) *to tend (cows)* N 21ᵇ.8. 2) (kalantr) ~ *to bear interest* N 6ᵇ.8.

jayakē (*caus. of* jaya) *to make tend* N 20ᵇ.2; sā jayakā *a cow-herd* 21ª.7.

jayalapē [*S.* ji-], *v. t. to conquer, to defeat* V¹ 113ª.4.

jayāwo, *adj. sharp, pointed* M 14ᵇ.5; ~ coṅ *id.* Vi 154.7.

jal [*S.*], *s. water* H¹ 95ª.2.

jalakrīḍā [*S.*], *s. frolicking in water* H² 77ª.3.

jari [*H.* zarī *from Pers. anything woven with gold thread*], *s. gold thread* Vi 71.19*.

jalijabāp, *s. a towerlet, blanket* M 3ª.8. — jalijalābāp *id.* Bh 167ᵇ.4; °pāp *id.* 173ᵇ.4.

jale, *s. a kidney* (?) Vd 21ª.3.

jal-dhārā, *s. a shower of water* Vi 19.18.

jal-dhu, *s. the back of the body* H¹ 48ᵇ.1.

jal-dhuni, *s. a water-course, river, lake*(?) B 57ª.10*.

jarm, *s.* = *janm* H¹ 29ᵇ.5.

jal-si, *s.* = jawo-si B 30ª.9.

jas [*M.*], *s. praise, reputation* H² 113ᵇ.8, *glory, fame* 97ᵇ.3.

Jahorāj, *n. pr.* B 55ᵇ.1.

jā¹, *s. food* B 11ᵇ.12; ~ nakē *to give food* N 42ª.2.

jā², *prt. denoting, that a fact ought to be known, "after all", "you know"* Vi 35.6.

jā-³ (-n *or* -t? *only* jāñānaṃ), *v. t. to smell (at)* H² 41ᵇ.5*.

jāk, *adj. friendly, attached to* H² 49ª.2; ma ~ *hostile* H² 54ª.3.

jāke, °**ki,** *s. rice (out of the ear)* V² 64ᵇ.3.

jāgat = jāgart B 30ᵇ.4.

jāganā = jāgarnā Bh 39ᵇ.7.

jāgalapē [*M.* jāg *to awake*], *v. i. to be awake* C² 202, *to awake* Bh 147ᵇ.1, *to keep watch* (ch-hm-yāke *on* . . .) H² 70ᵇ.1.

jāgart [*S.* jāgrat *adj. waking*], ~ yāya *to keep watch* (ch-hm-yāke *on*...) H² 38ª.5, (nidrā) ~ yācakē *to arouse (from sleep)* Bh 104ᵇ.4; ~ juyā *to awake* Bh 10ᵇ.6; ~ dayakē *to awaken, to restore to consciousness* B 66ᵇ.6.

jāgartanā [= jāgart] ~ yāya *to keep guard* Vi 149.4, *to keep attention* 157.4.

jāgarnā [*S.* jāgaraṇa *s. awaking*], ~ yāya *to be awake* Ś 156ᵇ.6.

jācak [*H.*], *s. a beggar, mendicant* M 2ᵇ.1; ~-phogi *syn. comp. id.* Vi 67.28.

jā-ceḍ, *s. one who has become a slave in order to get a maintenance* (bhaktadāsa) N 20ᵇ.2.

jājwoly [*S.* jājvalyate *intens. of* jval-]; jājwolyan *vehemently* Bh 97ᵇ.4. — jājwolyamān *adj. shining, splendid* M 7ᵇ.4; krodhan ~ yāya *to burn with rage* Ś 148ª.2.

jāt¹ [*S. born*], ~ juya *to be born* Bh 10ª.6.

jāt², *s.* = jātrā V² 48ᵇ.1*.

jāti [*M.* jāt, *a race, caste, kin*], *s.*

descent B 65ᵃ.5, *a caste* N 38ᵃ.5, *a kind (of flower)* B 11ᵇ.1. — *ifc.* **abalā-, paṁksi-, misā-, strī-.**

jātrā [*S.* yātrā], *s. a festival* V¹ 56ᵃ.2.

jānalaṁ, mantriyāke ~ *(he) said to the minister* H³ 61ᵇ.9*.

jānu [*S.*], *s. the knee* Bh 81ᵇ.4.

jāp [*S. muttering*], ~ yāya *to mutter (prayers)* V¹ 91ᵇ.5.

jā-bast, *s. food, living* N 21ᵇ.9.

jāya¹ (-l¹), *v. i.* 1) *to rise, to ascend;* co jāwo *high, tall* C¹ 144; co **jāsēṃ** wonē *to ascend to heaven* H³ 15ᵇ.1; 2) *to rise, to come into existence* N 8ᵇ.4, *(the parts of the day)* B 62ᵇ.9. — *v. t. to climb (a mountain)* Vi 25.23.

jāya² (-t¹), *v. i. to unite, to gather* N 32ᵇ.6. — thithiṃ jāṅāwo *jointly* C¹ 133; thethe jāsēṃ *from mutual love* N 32ᵇ.6; ma jāsēṃ *if impossible* 79ᵇ.8.

jāyakē, *caus. of* jāya¹: nīk jāyakaṃ *so that nothing can climb over(?)* N 28ᵇ.4; bohaṃ bohaṃ ~ *to make (the hair) bristle* M 36ᵇ.7.

jāyalapē [*S.* jāyate], *v. i. to be born* H¹ 4ᵇ.3, *to arise (misery)* H³ 17ᵇ.10, *to grow* (deh *the body*) H¹ 74ᵃ.2; *to be carried through (a work)* H³ 44ᵃ.10; sakrodh ~ *to grow angry* H³ 40ᵃ.7. — jāyalapayakē *caus. to bear, to bring forth* H¹ 85ᵃ.1.

jāl¹ [*S.* jāra], *s. a paramour of a married woman* B 48ᵃ.8.

jāl² [*S.*], *s. a net (for catching birds, fishes)* H³ 52ᵇ.4.

jālalapē [*H.* jārī karnā... *to circulate, propagate*], *v. t.* kha jālalapāwo haya *to send word* Ś 147ᵃ.6*.

jāsi, *s. a small earthern water-jar* (aliñjara) AH 54ᵇ.

jāsu-kha, *s. brevity* (? pulāka) AH 65ᵇ.

jāhān, ~ thvaya *to light up, to illuminate* Bh 53ᵇ.4*.

ji¹ (jin, jita, jike, jiwo), *pr. prs. 1. s. I* (= je¹) V² 50ᵃ.4. *poss. my* B 2ᵃ.1; ji-gu *id.* M 32ᵇ.6; ji-guli *id.* Vi 20.13. ji-pani *pl. excl.* M 7ᵃ.5. — jitayā sinaṃ *more than I* H³ 13ᵃ.5.

ji², *num. ten* C¹ 21; ~-hma *id.* 186.

ji³, *s.* = je² H³ 28ᵃ.3.

jiwo [*S.* jīva], *s. life* Ś 166ᵃ.2. *adj.* = jiwoy Vi 159.15. — ~ tayāwo mvākē *to restore to life* B 57ᵃ.4.

jiwoy [*S.* jīva *life*], *adj. alive* Vi 132.12.

jik¹, *adj. fragrant, odorous(?)* Bh 48ᵃ.4.

jik² [jiya¹], kol ma ~ *unfit to be uttered* AH 16ᵇ.

jik³, *adj.* = jek C¹ 232.

jicakē, *caus. of* jiya² Vd 16ᵇ.2.

ji-cā [<jil-°], *s. a son-in-law* AH 38ᵇ.

ji-chi, *pr. prs.* = je-che B 18ᵃ.8.

jitay [*M.* jīti *victory*], ~ yāya *to conquer, to defeat* Vi 130.33. ~ yātakē *to (suffer oneself to) be conquered* Vi 129.8.

ji-tā, *num.* = ji² P 9ᵃ.2.

jit-phol, *s. nutmeg* Vd 54ᵃ.2. — ~-svān *Hibiscus Rosa sinensis* CW 6.24.

jithi, *adj. old (of female beings only, cf.* jyāth) V² 9ᵃ.1. *s. the old one* B 58ᵃ.4; ~-cā *s. the old (wife)* 58ᵇ.2.

jithi-svān, *s. name of a plant* (jayantī) AH 29ᵇ.

ji-de, *tenfold* N 50ᵇ.6.

jinu, *s.* = jyonu M 32ᵇ.4*.

jibani [*S.* jīvana *manner of living*], *s. living, maintenance* V¹ 42ᵃ.1; ch-hm-yā ~ taya *to get one's living from...* C² 266; ~ kāwo *a soldier* N 19ᵇ.2.

jībant [*S. life*], *s. maintenance, allowance* N 41ᵃ.1.

jim-, *num. ten (in the numbers 11—19)*; ~-cha *eleven* Bh 107ᵃ.1, ~-chiṅ *id.* B 32ᵃ.1; ~-ni *twelve* V² 72ᵇ.6, ~-ne *id.* V¹ 122ᵇ.2.

ji-mi, *pr. prs. our* H³ 43ᵇ.3, ji-mis *id.* Vi 48.8; ji-mita *me* 26.28.

ji-hma, *s. a rogue* N 23ᵃ.4*.

jiya[1] (-l[1]), *v. t. to be able* H[1] 23[b].5, *to succeed* H[3] 17[b].5, *to thrive* Vi 25.34; ma jiwo *is impossible* H[1] 87[a].2; jiwo khe *may it be so, all right* V[1] 68[a].6.

jiya[2] (-t[1]), *v. i. to cease (vomition)* Vd 16[b].2.

jiyakākë (*caus. of* jiya[1]) = jiyakë V[1] 30[b].6.

jiyakë (*caus. of* jiya[1]), *to make able* V[2] 20[a].2, *to prepare, to put in order* Ś 165[a].7.

jilalapë [*S.* jīryati], *v. i. to grow old* C[1] 196.

jilā-jan, *s.* = jilī B 48[a].4.

jilī[1], *s. a son-in-law* V[1] 32[b].1; ~ kāya *to make somebody one's s°-in-l°* N 40[b].3, ~ yāya *id.* 30[b].1.

jilī[2], *s. Jasminum grandiflorum* Vd 19[a].1. — ~-svān *id.* H[3] 7[b].7; guṃyā *Jasminum Zambac* Md 30[a].8. — *ifc.* **hak-**.

jir-ci, *s. a kind of salt* Vd 46[a].6.

jirn [*S. digested, worn out*], ~ wonakë *to digest* H[1] 20[a].4; ~ woṅ *worn out* C[1] 245.

ji-hlāk, *adj.* = je-° M 33[b].5.

ju[1], *s. a term of respect, placed after a noun*; rāni-ju B 58[a].6.

ju[2], ~ polakë *to make false statements* N 26[b].7*.

ju[3], ~ seya ma du *strongly made* (?) N 30[b].2*.

juwāl[1] (*H.* juārī], *s. a gambler* V[1] 29[b].6.

juwāl[2], *s.* = jawāl B 62[a].9.

juṁluṁ-kwos, *s. the spine, backbone* CW 8.54.

juku-hun, *adv.* ~ conë *to be tired* H[3] 6[a].9.

jukwo[1] [juya[1]], *s. fortune, luck* H[1] 6[b].1.

jukwo[2] [juya[1]], *adv.* 1) *only* Bh 82[b].2, thwoyā jukwoyā lā *only his flesh* H[2] 24[a].2. — 2) *however* N 2[b].1.

jukt [*S.* yukta], *adj. suitable, approbriate* H[2] 56[b].3.

jugi, *s. a Newāri caste of tailors and musicians* B 43[b].6.

juguti [*M. device, dexterity*], *s.* 1) *a device* Ś 160[b].6. — 2) (*cf. S.* yukti) *the right or correct conduct* N 31[a].1.

juju [ju], *s. a king* B 34[a].4.

juddh [*S.* yuddha *a war, battle*], ch-hm-wo ~ yāya *to wage war upon* H[2] 71[a].5.

juni, *impr. go!* Bh 39[a].2*.

june, *forming imperatives:* kā-june *take!* Ś 147[b].1*.

juya[1] (-l[1]), *v. i. to become* H[1] 12[b].5; *to come into existence, to arise* Bh 155[a].4; *to happen, to be done* H[3] 22[a].4; *to be* H[3] 87[b].3. ch-hm-yā ~ *to belong to...* B 7[b].10; ch-hm-yāta ~ *id.* N 2[a].8. — gathë ji juyuwo *what is to become of me* Vi 43.20; thathë jule *meanwhile* V[2] 47[a].3; amathë julasā *under these circumstances* H[1] 37[b].2. — *A number of forms of this verb may be used as emphasizing particles ("as for"):* julaṃ N 12[a].4; julo Ś 152[b].4; ju-kāle N 24[a].1; julasā B 19[a].4; ju-sāṃ M 16[a].7; julasāṃ (*very common*) Vi 70.1. — julasāṃ... julasāṃ *whether ... or* Vi 21.21; julasanwoṃ *even* C[1] 5, su ~ *whosoever* H[1] 38[a].2. — juya *forms compound verbal forms apparently without any change of meaning:* wowo julo = wolaṃ ("*he came*") B 4[b].2. — *The forms* jula(ṃ) *and* julo *may be added to nearly all predicative forms of the verb without changing its meaning:* yāya julaṃ = yāya ("*I shall do*") Vi 41.1.

juya[2] (-*t*) *v. i. to fall* (ch-g-s *on, into a thing*) V[1] 72[b].3. *to get into a thing* H[1] 21[b].4; *to sit on (of birds)* Bh 11[b].7.

juyakë (*caus. of* juya[1]), *to make* Vi 29.28, *to cause; to bring about* Bh 3[b].4; ma ~ *to make undone* H[3] 2[b].3, *to remove* Vi 57.26. — juyakāwo yanë *to lead to* Ś 156[b].4.

jul [*H. cheat, trick*], *s. a play, game*

V^1 32^b.5; ~ lvāya *to play, to gamble* B 43^a.9; julan buya *to lose at play* V^2 55^b.5, ~ tyāya *to win* — B 43^a.9.

julu, *s. exhaustion* H^2 16^b.1. — julu-hun conë *to be exhausted* H^1 23^a.5.

je^1 (jen, jeyā, jeta, jeke, jewo), *pr. prs. 1. s. I* H^1 37^b.1; *poss. my* 15^a.3; **je-gu** *id.* V^2 9^b.4; **je-guli** *id.* B 109^b.6. — **je-pani** *1. pl. excl.* H^1 26^b.3; **je-panis** *poss. our* 50^b.3.

je^2, *s. a sort, kind* N 42^b.3; *difference* H^2 56^a.4.

jek, *adj. cruel* C^1 32.

jekwo, *s. a criminal* N 10^a.2*.

je-che, *pr. prs. 1. pl. incl.* H^2 70^a.5.

je-jhe, *pr. prs. 1. pl. incl.* H^2 71^b.5.

jeḍ, *adj. soiled, dirty* N 25^a.1; *stupid, foolish* 5^a.7.

jeya (-t), *v. i.* = jiya^2 Vd 43^a.4.

jel, *adj.* = jeḍ AH 64^b; *cruel* C^1 50; ~ kāpal *old cloth* AH 43^b.

je-hlāk [je^1 + hlāya], *adj. proud, arrogant* H^2 79^a.3*.

jaisi, *s. an astrologer* (*one of the Vaiśya castes*) H^2 87^a.7.

jëṣṭ [*S.* jyeṣṭha], *adj. eldest* V^2 66^b.3.

jokwo, *adv.* = jukwo, 1) *only* Vd 9^a.4. — 2) *however* H^1 7^b.4.

jokhalapë [*H.* jokh *weight, measurement*], *v. t. to examine* H^3 56^b.11.

jog [*S.* yoga], *s. Yoga* M 5^a.4.

jogālapë [*S.* yoga — *performance*], *v. t.*, sebā ~ *to yield obedience* N 18^b.3*.

jogi [*S.* yogin], *s. a Yogin* V^1 19^a.2.

jogy [*S.* yogya], *adj. proper, suitable* H^1 66^a.3, ch-hm-yāta *for...* M 5^b.6; mocakë ~ juya *to deserve to be killed* H^2 27^b.5.

jochi, ~ ma jochiṃ *adv. denoting celerity or eagerness* Bh 79^b.5*.

jojan [*S.* yojana], *s. a measure of distance* H^2 22^a.2.

jojalapë [*S.* yojaya-], *v. t. to appoint, to install* (ch-g-s *to...*) H^3 28^a.4; *to make versed in* C^1 24; *to furnish* (ch-g-n *with...*) H^3 33^b.8; *to honour* (pūj-) H^1 87^a.5. — hāth ~ *to clasp the hands* Vi 109.5.

joti [*H.*], *s. light, brilliancy* Vi 159.3.

jotik [*M.* jotiṣ *astronomy*], *s. an astrologer* B 20^b.8.

jod, ~ yāṅā-lapë = joḍalapë V^2 65^a.3*.

joḍalapë [*M.* joḍ, jor *to unite*], *v. t. to unite* V^1 107^b.5, hāth ~ *to clasp the hands* C^2 223; dhanukas bān ~ *to put an arrow to the bow* Bh 99^a.4.

jodhā [*H.*], *s. a warrior* Bh 114^a.2*.

jonā [*H.* jūnā *a rope of grass*], *s. the sacred thread* (upavīta AH) V^1 135^a.2.

joni [*S.* yoni], *s. the privy parts of a woman* Ś 148^b.4.

joya (-l^1), *v. i.* = juya^1 Bh 12^a.7.

jol [*H.* joṛ], *s. a pair* C^1 186.

jolan, *s. equipment, outfit* V^2 68^b.6; pūjā-~ *utensils for pūjā* H^2 114^b.5.

jolay [*M.* jor *to unite*(?)], ~ yāya bairiwo *to engage the enemy* H^2 104^b.5*.

jolalapë [*S.* jval-], *v. i. to burn* (*brightly*) B 51^b.1.

jolī [*H.* joṛā, joṛī], *s. a counterpart, match* B 22^a.1; *an equal, peer* (ch-hm-wo) Ś 164^a.5; wowo jiwo joliṃ ma khu *he and I are not equals* 147^b.4. — ~ phāya *to compare* B 36^b.4.

jolo-hon = julu-hun Vd 5^a.1.

josi, *s. an astrologer* AH 48^b.

johali, *s. name of a plant* (yavanāla) Md 67^a.4.

jauban [*S.* yauvana], *s. youth* V^1 68^b.4; *a young one* H^3 47^b.4.

jaubhan [= jauban], *s. youth* H^2 89^b.6; *a young one, young people* Vi 108.13.

jau-se, *s. a kind of pumpkin* (tumbī) CW 6.35.

jwonakë (*caus. of* jwonë), *to let take away* V^1 15^a.3, *to let hold* H^2 90^a.3.

jwonë, *v. t. to take, to catch, to seize, to grasp* V^1 109^b.6; bhutan jwoṅā *possessed by a Bhut* Vd 7^a.4; **kha jwonë** *to hit upon a word* Ś 147^b.3.

jwopalapë [*cf. Mr.* joppeṃ *to feed, nourish?*], *v. i. to increase (fever)* Vd 44ᵇ.2.

jwopë, *v. t. to salute* N 47ᵃ.2.

jwoya (-l¹), *v. i. to go, to walk* N 47ᵃ.6. ch-hm-s ~ *to have intercourse with (a man)* C¹ 180; ch-hm-yāke ~ *id. (with a woman)* N 10ᵇ.4.

jwol¹ [*S.* jvala], *s. fever* Vd 42ᵃ.4. — *ifc.* **bāt-¹**.

jwol², *s. a cave* M 5ᵃ.5. — *ifc.* **par-bat-**.

jwolapë, *v. t.* = jwopë N 47ᵃ.2*.

jñān [*S.*], *s. knowledge, wisdom* Ś 164ᵃ.4.

jñānabant, °**ni**° [*S.* jñānavant], *adj. wise, prudent* H¹ 62ᵃ.5.

jñāni [*S.* jñānin], *adj. wise, prudent* H² 2ᵇ.1.

jyā¹, *s. a work, craft, art* V² 41ᵃ.7, *an affair* Vi 45.13; ~ choya *to settle an affair, to do an errand* C¹ 71; ~ jhāya *to go to work* H³ 43ᵇ.4; ~ yāya *to do a work, to practise an art* N 16ᵃ.3. — mvāṅāyā ~ ma du *it is useless, to no purpose to live* H³ 48ᵃ.11; ~ yāk mi *a servant* N 21ᵃ.5; ~ yācakwo *an employer* 21ᵇ.9. — *ifc.* **co-**, **thā-**, **bu-**, **hmu-**, **hmo-**.

jyā², *adj.* = jyāth H³ 35ᵃ.11*.

jyāk [jyāya²], *adj. broken, torn, split* H² 34ᵃ.7. — *s. ifc.* **gvā-li-**.

jyācakë, *caus. of* jyāya¹ B 49ᵃ.4.

jyā-ja(ṁ), *s. wages, hire* N 21ᵃ.4.

jyāth [*H.* jeṭhā *oldest*], *adj. old (of male beings only)* H¹ 60ᵇ.1. ~ jithi *father and mother* Vi 111.9, ~ juya *to grow old* H² 36ᵇ.5.

jyā-payakë, *caus. of* jyā-pë N 21ᵃ.4.

jyā-pë, *v. t. to perform a work* N 21ᵇ.1; bu ~ *to cultivate a field* 29ᵇ.3.

jyāpo, *s. an agricultural labourer* N 21ᵃ.7.

jyā-mi, *s. a hired labourer* AH 60ᵃ.

jyāya¹ (-t), *v. t. to make, to produce, to manufacture* V² 34ᵇ.6; banaj ~ *to carry on trade* Vi 74.4; lun jyāṅā *made of gold* H² 34ᵃ.7.

jyāya² (-t), *see* **tawo**, **tap**.

jyālā, *s. ferry-money, freight* AH 20ᵇ.

jyā-lāk, *s. wages, hire* AH 61ᵇ (jyálá).

jyā-sāl, *s. a workshop* CW 4.4.

jyu = jiyu (*3. form of* jiya¹) M 32ᵃ.7*.

jyoti [*S.* jyotis], *s. splendour* N 24ᵃ.8.

jyonā, *s. porridge* (odana) AH 55ᵇ.

jyonu, *s. a part of a head-gear(?)* M 32ᵇ.8*.

jvālā [*S. a flame*], *s. flame (fig.)* H³ 19ᵇ.5; *a jet (of water)* Bh 1ᵇ.2. — *ifc.* **mi-**.

jh.

jha, ~ tānakë *verbal phrase, denoting some criminal or dishonest action* N 43ᵇ.8*.

jhawāl [jhaya¹], *s. a herdsman* B 33ᵃ.10. — *ifc.* **colas-**, **pasu-**, **sa-**, **sala-**, **sā-**.

jhawo-svān-si, *s. Tamarix indica* AH 28ᵇ.

jhagal, *s.* = jhaṅg(a)l H³ 40ᵇ.5. — ~-tvāth *the bill of a bird* AH 36ᵃ. — ~-paputi *the feathers of a bird* 36ᵃ (jhagapapoo).

jhaṅkāl, *s. a bird* V¹ 9ᵃ.4*.

jhaṅg(a)l, *s. a bird* H¹ 41ᵇ.4. — ~-cāto *young birds* H² 27ᵃ.2. — ~-paṃchi = ~ M 32ᵃ.5. — ~-swo *the nest of a bird* H³ 40ᵇ.4. — *ifc.* **tupun-**, **duy-**, **bhuglu-**, **mā-**, **salāṁ-**, **siṁ-tvāk-**.

jha-je, *pr. prs. 1. pl. incl. we* H¹ 19ᵇ.5. jha-jes *poss.* 25ᵃ.3.

jhatu-se, *s. a medicinal plant* Vd 45ᵃ.3. — **jhatu-ti** *juice from this plant ib.*

jhadhī, *s. a water-melon* Md 46ᵇ.

jhan, *s. name of a plant, the seed of which is used medicinally* Vd 48ᵇ.6.

jhaṁti, ati ~ *chronic (disease)(?)* N 32ª.8*.

jhamar-se, *s. the citron-tree* Vd 12ª.5.

jhama-si, *s.* 1) = jhamar-se AH 27ᵇ. — 2) *the Jambu-tree ib.*

jhaya¹, *v. i. to graze* Bh 26ᵇ.7.

jhaya², *v. i.* = jhāya¹ H¹ 57ᵇ.3*.

jhalukit, *s. a bat (the animal;* ja-tukā) AH 35ᵇ.

jhaleṁ, *s.* hāku ~ *the apple or pupil of the eye* CW 8.72.

jhali, *s. lac, gum* CW 8.87.

jhari-svān, *s. name of a medical plant* Vd 39ª.6.

jhale-cāhmal-si, *s. Aegle Marmelos* Vd 35ª.5.

jhasan, *s. a radish* Md 49ᵇ.2.

jhāwo, *adj. fatigued, tired* N 11ª.5. *s. fatigue* H³ 39ª.2.

jhāmikaṁ, *adv.*, ~ jwonë *to seize vehemently*(?) Bh 94ᵇ.3. — jhāmina-kaṃ *id.* M 26ᵇ.8.

jhāya¹ (-l¹), *v. i. to come* H¹ 80ᵇ.4; jyā ~ *to go to work* H³ 43ᵇ.4; *ipr.* jhā-sane B 60ª.10; wāyo jhās *come!* Vi 41.13.

jhāya², *only:* jhāyāwo *having become tired* H¹ 94ᵇ.2.

jhāyakë (*caus. of* jhāya¹), *to exercise, to practise* Md 79ª.8.

jhāl [*H.* jhāṛ *bushwood*], *s. grass* (tṛṇa) C¹ 151.

jhāli [*M.* jhārī], *s. a vase, drinking vessel* M 19ᵇ.8*.

jhās, *see* **jhāya¹**.

jhā-sane, *see* **jhāya¹**.

jhāsu = jhāswo; ~-kāl taya *to sigh* H³ 70ª.3.

jhāswo, ~ taya *to sigh* V² 68ª.4.

jhāsvā = jhāswo H¹ 47ª.2.

jhi, *num. ten* (= ji²) Vi 49.33; jhi-guli *id.* N 11ª.4.

jhikasalapayakë [*cf. H.* jhiknā *to whine, to cry*], *v. t. to make cry (from horror)*(?) N 49ª.7*.

jhiji, *pr. prs. 1. pl. incl. we* H² 77ª.2.

jhijhi = jhiji B 12ª.11.

jhi-tā, *num.* = jhi Ns 11ª.8.

jhim-, *num. ten (in the numbers 11—19:* = jim-); jhim-khu *sixteen* Ns 40ᵇ.3.

jheje = jhiji H³ 16ᵇ.2.

jhejhe = jhijhi V¹ 42ª.2.

jhoḍ [*cf. Mr.* jhoḍ *heavy rain*], ~ yāya *to cause inundation* N 27ᵇ.4*.

jhol, *s. a row, line* H² 101ᵇ.6. — *ifc.* **simā-**.

jhwok, ~ hninakë *verbal phrase, denoting some criminal or dishonest action* N 42ᵇ.4, 43ᵇ.8*.

jhyā, *mod.* = jhyāl. — ~-phal *a window-sill* Vi 144.21. — *ifc.* **mikhā-**.

jhyātaṁ [jhyātu], (*it*) *is important* H² 37ª.2; jhyātayu (*it*) *becomes heavy* Vd 6ª.4.

jhyātakë [jhyāta], *v. t. to be important* C¹ 197; jhyātaka(ṃ) *adv. vigorously* H² 59ᵇ.6.

jhyātu, °to, *adj. heavy* B 63ª.1, *fig. (sin) ib.* 2; *important* H³ 37ª.1, *dear* H¹ 61ª.2. — jhyātusë(ṃ) woya *to become pregnant* M 2ᵇ.4; jhyātuyāwo conaṃ (*it*) *is the (most) important* H² 116ᵇ.6.

jhyātukë [jhyātu], *v. i. to be heavy* Bh 13ª.4. jhyātukaṃ taya *to honour, to appreciate* H³ 36ª.10, ~ yāya *id.* H² 53ᵇ.3.

jhyāl [*P.*], *s. a window* Bh 73ᵇ.4. — *ifc.* **gāwo-**, **mikhā-**.

jhval, *s.* = jhaleṃ Ns 13ª.4*.

jhvāpakë, *verb, denoting some criminal or dishonest action* N 42ᵇ.4*.

t (ṭ).

ta¹, *adj. tall* B 35ᵇ.8; ~ salan *aloud* AH 16ª; ~ tuyakë *to make last* C¹250.

ta², ~ chyāya *to break in pieces* B 2ᵇ.9*.

tawo[1], *adj. great, important* C[1] 222; *large* V[3] 80ª.4, *tall* H[2] 75ª.1; *a good deal of* C[1] 241; *loud* H[1] 48ᵇ.2. — *adv. very* V[1] 51ª.1. — tawo sal *Udātta* CW 1.63; ~ mi *hell-fire* 1.24; ~ cā *a series of nights* (gaṇarātra) AH 11ª.

tawo[2] = tap; ~ chyāya B 55ª.8. — ~ jyāya H[3] 12ª.6. — ~ dāya *to tear off* Bh 59ᵇ.6.

tawo-cokaṁ, *adv. very much* Pg 27ᵇ.5. ~-cokan *adj. great* M 32ª.7, *adv. very* P 59ª.5. ~-cok-gu *adj. heavy (sin) ib.*

tawo-cotaṁ, *adj. great* Vi 108.34. ~-cotan *id.* Vi 25.15; *adv. very much* Vi 37.2. ~-cotanaṃ *id.* M 16ᵇ.4.

tawo-chā, *adv. very much* H[3] 61ª.2. ~-chān(aṃ) *id.* V[1] 117ª.5.

tawo-ji, *adj. excellent* Vi 103.27. tawo-tawo-ji *adj. manifold* M 38ª.3.

tawo-dhaṁ, *adj. great, excellent* V[2] 30ᵇ.5, ~-hma *id.* H[2] 84ª.8.

tawo-dhaṅ, *adj. great, important* H[1] 36ª.1; ~-hma *id.* H[2] 113ª.6.

tawo-dhan, *adv. very* P 7ᵇ.2, *adj. great, important* H[3] 5ª.5; ~-hma *id.* H[3] 24ª.5. ~-dhanaṃ *adj. rich* H[3] 18ª.9. ~-dhanakë *v. i. to become great* H[3] 6ᵇ.2. ~-dhani *adj. rich* V[1] 34ª.4. ~-dhany *adj. great* P 59ᵇ.3, *large* B 22ª.9.

tawo-dhānā, *adj. abundant* Bh 18ᵇ.2*.

tawo-dhāy, *adj. rich* H[1] 31ᵇ.1.

tawo-dhi, *adj. great, big* B 6ª.5.

tawo-dhik, *adj. great, big* Ś 155ᵇ.3; ~ juya *to grow up* B 33ª.6; ~-hma *adj. great, big* Bh 116ᵇ.2. ~-dhikal juya *to grow up* Vi 72.28.

tawo-puyā, *adj. big, thick* Vi 20.30.

tawo-mi, *adj. rich* Bh 18ᵇ.2.

tawo-se, *s. Citrus medica* Vd 24ᵇ.2.

taṁ, *a short form of* taya *with the meaning of the 10. form* N 34ᵇ.8.

taṁ-bu, *s. a camp* (śivira) AH 49ᵇ (tangbu).

takarāy, *s. a plant, the root of which is used medicinally* Vd 37ª.1.

takë (*caus. of* taya); yāṅaṃ ~ = yācakë V[1] 80ᵇ.6.

takṣaṇanaṁ [*S.* tatkṣaṇam], *adv. at once* Vd 7ᵇ.2.

ṭaṅkā [*S.*], *s. a weight, a coin* H[3] 47ª.5.

taṅgāy, *s. name of a plant* (tagara) Md 28ᵇ.8.

ta-cho, *s. barley* Bh 31ᵇ.1; tawo-gol ~, ciki-gol ~ *two kinds of barley* Md 65ª.8. — ~-bo *a field sown with barley* AH 53ᵇ. — ~-lā *the month Jyeṣṭha* CW 1.40. — ~-lā-dit-lā *summer* 1.52.

ta-ta-ji, *adj. manifold* M 38ª.3*.

tatā, *s. an elder sister* AH 17ᵇ. ~-ju *id.* B 37ᵇ.3. — ~-kehem *sister (generally)* CW 8.27.

tati, ~ pënakë *to lift, to raise (the tail)* B 71ᵇ.1. — ~ yāya *to censure, to control* N 39ᵇ.3.

tati-pë, *v. t. to censure, to control* N 26ᵇ.1, *to blame, to reproach* C[2] 260.

tatkālan(aṁ) [*S.* tatkāla *adj. immediately*], *adv. immediately, at once* H[2] 99ª.1; ~-saṃ *id.* 102ª.8.

tatkṣaṇanaṁ [*S.* tatkṣaṇam], *adv. at once* Bh 62ᵇ.1.

tatpar [*S.*], *devoted to, intent upon* (yāyas *doing*) Vi 172.17.

tathë, *v. t.* = tāthë V[2] 52ª.5.

taḍawāl, °ḍu° [*H.* talvār], *s. a sword* B 51ᵇ.12.

tanakë (*caus. of* tanë[1]), *to make vanish* B 58ᵇ.4.

tanë[1], *v. i. to vanish, to be lost* H[1] 19ª.1.

tanë[2], *v. i.* = tenë V[1] 69ᵇ.6.

tap[1] [*M.*], *s. penance, austerities* Bh 56ᵇ.7.

tap[2], ~ ciya (-t *or* -l[2]; *only* cisëṃ) *to chew, to masticate* Md 63ª.3. — ~ chyāya (-t), *v. t. to break asunder, to shatter* H[2] 34ᵇ.1. — ~ jyāya (-t) *v. i. to be broken* H[1] 52ª.1. — ~ svāya

(-t), hma ~ *to bend up one's body* M 32b.7; tap svāk gum̥-*an abyss, precipice* CW 5.2.

tapam̐, °**n**, *adv. completely* N 38a.9; *after a subst. which takes the ending* ·m̥ *or* ·n: *the whole of*...; banam̥ ~ *the whole wood* C¹ 190, bayan ~ *the whole expense* N 19a.3; hman ~ *on the whole body* Vd 9a.2.

tapas(i)yā [*S.* tapasyā], *s. asceticism, austerities* H² 4b.4.

ta-pĕn̐ [*mod.* = tal-pĕn̐?], *adj. straight* CW 1.41.

tabadhi [*S.* stabdha], *adj. proud, haughty* C¹ 298*.

ta-bu, *s. a tent* AH 44a.

tabdhi, *adj.* = tabadhi C² 298*.

tam [*M.* tamas *to be enraged*], *s. anger, rage* V² 14b.3; ~ cāya *to become angry or enraged* H¹ 42b.5, ~ cāyakë *to make angry, to provoke* H² 115b.7; taman danë *to be irritable* Vd 19b.2.

tam-kāli, *s. wrath, anger* H³ 6a.9. — *adj. angry* 5b.8.

tambā [*S.*], *s. copper* N 25a.7.

taya (-l¹), *v. t. to act* H¹ 62a.5; *to put, to place* (ch-g-s *on or in something,* ch-hm-yāke *on someone*) Bh 139b.5; *to appoint* (ch-g-s *for*...) H³ 32a.2. — mi taya *to set fire to* (ch-g-s) V² 75a.7; cākal ~ *to make a servant* H² 89a.1; guptan ~ *to keep secret* H³ 38b.7; manas pāp ~ *to be evil-minded* Vi 60.32. — *With other verbs (mostly in the 9. or 10. form or the conv. in* ·āwo) taya *forms compound verbal forms, the meaning of which by preference is that of a completed action (in* N *short forms of* taya *are usually used in this case:* tā = tayā, tāwo = tayāwo *a. s. on*): cesëm̥ tayā *bound, fettered* H¹ 95a.2; hān̐am̥ talam̥ (*she*) *said* (*and was done with it*) B 5a.4.

tayakë¹, *caus. of* taya P 8a.2.

tayakë² = teyakë¹ V² 30b.5.

tayāl [*H.* taiyār], *adj. ready*, ~ yāya *to make ready, to prepare* M 3a.3, mocakë ~ juya *to be ready to kill* H² 75b.3. janm ~ juo *life is done for* Vi 119.29.

tal¹, *adj.* ~ biya *to give more or a greater share* N 38b.4; ~-hma *many* N 16a.4; putrādi tal-hmam̥ datam̥ (*she*) *bore him many sons and daughters* V¹ 93a.3.

tal², ~ pënakë *to bend, to bow* H³ 36b.2.

tarawāl, *s.* = taḍawāl Ś 162b.1. — ~-hma *the hilt of a sword* AH 51b.

tarak [*H. beam, rafter*], *s. a kind of weapon* B 9a.2.

talay [*S.* tarati], ~ yāya *to subdue, to conquer (distress)* H² 100a.5; ~ ma jura(m̥) *is of no use* 93a.7.

talalapë [*S.* tarati *to cross, surpass, subdue*], *v. t. to cross* C¹ 10, *to subdue, to conquer (distress)* H² 64b.7; ch-hm āpadis ~ *to save from distress* N 2b.2.

talas [*S.* tala *the lower part, bottom*], *adv. under:* lāsāyā ~ *under the couch* B 46a.5; lāsā-~ *id.* V² 32a.6.

talasīm, *s. an owner of a field* (kṣetrika) N 33b.1*.

talāju [*cf. S.* tulā?], *s. a scale, balance* N 48b.3.

taruṇi [*S.* taruṇī *fem. of* taruṇa], *adj. young* H² 46b.7; jim-ni dayā ~ *twelve years old* B 10b.1.

tale [*cf. S.* tala *surface, level*], *s. the upper or the best part of a house* B 40b.6.

tarkāri [*H.* tarkārī], *s. an esculent vegetable* M 11a.2*.

tal-gulasam̐, *adv. vehemently* H² 40b.3.

tal-dhār, *adv. repeatedly* N 14b.7.

tal-hnam̐(?), *adv. severely*(?) N 18b.7*.

tal-hnu, *adj. exhausted* H³ 59a.4*.

tarpaṇ [*S. satisfying, refreshing (of a god or deceased)*], ch-hm-yāta ~ yāya *to refresh, to satisfy* P 16a.1.

tar-bar, nugal ~ juya *to be impatient(?)* Bh 74ª.7*.

tal-bhinaṁ, *adv. vehemently* H³ 16ᵇ.3*.

tal-hanaṁ, *adv.*, nānā ~ *in different ways* B 46ᵇ.7.

tasa, *s.* = tasal N 25ᵇ.1 (tasa·yā)*.

tasal [*M.* tasar *silk, tisser*], *s. a silk garment* CW 8.81.

tastan, *adv. to and fro* H³ 39ᵇ.7*.

tas-mocā, *s. a woman* C² 216*.

tā¹, *adv.* 1) *a long time* Vi 119.10; ~ conë *to last long* C¹ 249; ~ nuyakë *to make last* C² 250; ~ ma lasëṃ *from the beginning* ("*without waiting long*") H³ 46ᵇ.11; ~ dato *a long time* V¹ 57ª.2; adik ~ tu tān *far too long* H² 42ᵇ.3. — 2) *far off*; ~ ma pāsëṃ coṃgwo *the nearest* N 42ª.6.

tā², *s. a bridge* Wr 304.

tā³, = tayā (*6th form of* taya) N 23ª.1.

tā⁴, *s. a quarter of the sky*; *only ifc.* **woṁ-**, **yaṁ-**, **yal-**, **yau-**.

tā'u, *adv.* ~ taya *to protract, to prolong* B 45ª.2.

tā'u-jālo, *adv. a long time* B 44ᵇ.9*.

tā'uti(ṁ), *adv. a long time, for a long time* Bh 40ª.1; tā'utin *id.* H³ 26ᵇ.6, tā'utinim *id.* M 28ᵇ.2.

tāwo = tayāwo (*conv. of* taya) N 21ª.6.

tāk¹ [*M.* tāk *to look at, to watch*], ~ yāya *to keep watch* Vi 128.27.

tāk², ~ juya *to be betrayed* H² 75ᵇ.8.

tā-kan, *adv. from afar* H³ 33ª.10*.

tā-kāl, *s. a long time* V² 51ª.6; tā-kāl(aṃ) *adv. long, a long time* H¹ 33ᵇ.3; tā-kāl(aṃ) dato *id.* H² 89ᵇ.8, *for a long time past* H² 46ᵇ.7; tā-kāl-toṃ *a long time* 75ᵇ.7; tā-kālan li *after a considerable lapse of time* V¹ 137ª.6; ji tā-kālayā mitr *my friend for many years* H¹ 55ª.2.

tāku, *adj. large* (vyūḍha) AH 69ª.

tā-khon, *adv. for a long distance* Bh 19ª.3*.

tāṁ-gwo [tānë¹], *ptp. lost* N 22ª.4.

tā-tāyine, *adv. very far off* H²36ᵇ.1.

tāthë, *v. t. to leave (behind)* Bh 102ᵇ.1. — *After the 6th, 9th, 10th form or the conv. in* ·āwo *of another verb* tāthë *denotes, that an action is carried through completely* H³ 52ª.4.

tāḍ¹ [*cf. H.* tār *string (of a musical instr.)*], *s. a musical instrument* Vi 151.2.

tāḍ² = tāl¹ Bh 133ᵇ.4.

tāḍanā [*S.* tāḍana *s. beating*], ~ yāya *to beat* H² 93ª.2.

tāḍalapë [*S.* tāḍayati], *v. t. to beat* C¹ 21.

tādasi [*cf. S.* tādṛśa], *pr. such, like that* H¹ 48ᵇ.8*.

tānë¹, *v. i.* = tanë¹ N 26ª.1.

tānë², *v. i.* = tanë² V¹ 103ᵇ.6.

tāp [*S.*], *s. heat* Bh 162ᵇ.1, tāpan kāya *to suffer from heat* H³ 42ᵇ.9. tāp noyāwo *as the heat increased* V¹ 78ª.3.

tā-pā, *adj.* ~ laṃ *a long, desolate road* (prāntāra) AH 24ª; ~ ajā-ju *a great grandfather* 38ᵇ.

tā-pāk [tā-pāya], *adj. far, distant* B 49ᵇ.3; *different from* H² 21ª.3.

tā-pācakë (*caus. of* tā-pāya) *to remove* H² 85ª.5, tā-pācakaṃ *adv. far away, in a distance* H³ 59ª.4; ~ twol-të *to avoid completely* C² 244.

tā-pāya (-t), *v. i. to be far away* M 33ᵇ.2, *to withdraw* Bh 103ª.1.

tā-pāle, *adv. far off, far away* C¹ 156; ~ bhuṃ wonë *to cover a long distance* Bh 26ᵇ.2. tā-pālen(aṃ) *from afar* H³ 55ᵇ.5.

tā-pu, *s. a bridge* AH 23ᵇ.

tābatā [*S.* tāvat], *so much* B 41ᵇ.10.

tā-bhin, *adv. far*; *a long time(?)* Bh 170ᵇ.1*.

tāmbūl [*S.*], *s. betel* V¹ 13ᵇ.1.

tāya¹ (-l¹), *v. t. to perceive* (**na** *a*

smell) V^2 32^a.1; *to perceive* (*a sound*), *to hear, to overhear* H^1 4^a.3; hnasan tāya *to* (*be able to*) *hear with the ear* Vd 36^a.6.

tāya^2 (-l^1), *v. i. to perish* N 45^b.4, *to be injured* 24^a.2 (tāliwo!).

tāya^3 (-t, *but* tāyā(wo) H^2), *v. t. to divide, to distribute* B 68^a.5; ·kūt ~ *to cut to pieces* M 14^b.6; phahaṃ ~ *to split, to cleave* (*with a wedge*) H^2 52^a.5.

tāya^4, *see* **duḥkh, las.**

tāya^5 (-l^1), *v. t. to place, to set up* (= taya) B 25^a.6.

tāya^6, *s. mcd.* = tāyal Vi 70.14.

tāyago-simā, *s. the palmyra-tree* AH 33^b.

tāyal, *s. fried or parched grain* Ś 170^a.3. — ~-baji *id.* AH 55^b.

tā-yākwo, *adj.* ~ lib *a high seat* N 18^b.3*.

tā-yine, *adv. far, far off* H^1 59^a.4; tā-yinen(aṃ) *from afar* H^2 55^a.1.

tāyune, *adv.* = tāyine V^2 80^a.3*.

tāl^1, swo ~ *three times* B 41^b.8.

tāl^2 [= tayāl?], ~ lāya *to be ready* B 49^a.3, ~ lācakë *to make ready, to prepare* H^2 114^b.6.

tālan^1 [*H.* tālā *lock*], ~ daya *to shut up* B 51^a.9.

tāraṇ^2 [*S. s. crossing, safe passage*], ~ yāya *to save, to rescue* M 27^b.3.

tālapatr(ak) [*cf. S.* tārapattaka], *s. a sword* B 9^a.5.

tālamul [*cf. S.* tālamūlikā], *s. name of a medicinal plant* (musalī AH) Vd 9^a.6.

tāray [*S.* tāraya- (*caus. of* tṝ) *to carry across*], ~ yāya *to manage* (*an affair*) Ś 163^a.5.

tālāju, *s.* = talāju H^2 116^b.6.

tālis [*S.* tālāśa], *s. a plant, the leaves of which are used medicinally* Vd 40^b.2.

tās [*H.* tāš, tās], *s. brocade* Vi 71.19.

tā-hāwo, *adj. high, tall* B 21^b.3, *long* C^1 247.

tā-hāk, *adj. high, tall* H^1 12^a.3, *deep* H^3 53^a.3; hni tā-hākala(ṃ) *the day hangs heavily* Ś 155^a.5.

tā-hācakë, *v. t. to make high* N 28^b.4.

tāhā-po [*cf.* dhal-pwo], *s. an auspicious jar* Ś 162^b.5.

tā-hāya (-t^1), *v. i. to be long* Vi 120.15.

tā-hāyakë (*caus. of* tā-hāya), tuti ~ *to lash out with the feet* H^3 38^b.6*.

ti^1, *s. sap, juice* Vd 14^b.6. — *ifc.* **ambal-, kvāth-, gho-, dhali-, bhu-**^{1}**, lā-, sa-khi-**^{1}**, su-. seb-.**

ti^2, mikhā ~ siya *to shut the eyes* Bh 14^b.2.

ti^3, *prt.* B 10^b.9*.

ti^4 = tiwo B 4^a.4.

tiwā, ~ hlāya *to praise, to extoll* B 45^a.12; ~ hlāk *s. a bard, herald* (vandin) AH 52^a. — ~ hlākë *caus.* H^2 98^a.6.

tiwo, *ipr. of* taya H^3 38^b.7.

ṭiṁ, *s. cane* (kāṇḍa) N 50^b.3*.

tiki = teke, ~ naṅāwo *incessantly* H^3 23^a.8*.

tiko, *s. a basin of water round the food of a tree* (ālabāla) AH 21^b.

ticakaṁ, *adv. carefully, thoroughly* Ś 144^a.2.

tī-jak, *adv. quiet* B 5^a.11 (= ci-jak).

titan [= titiṃ?], *adv. cautiously*(?) V^2 73^a.1 = titin V^2 122^b.5*.

tital [*H.* tītar *partridge*], *s. a quail* H^3 42^b.7; *a partridge* (tittiri, Md 73^a.7.

titi^1 [ti^2], hmutu ~ yāya *to shut the mouth* Ś 152^a.3.

titi^2, *s.* = °-huli. *ifc.* **bā-, mā-.**

titiṁ [= titi^1?], *adv. gently, cautiously* Bh 168^b.7.

titi-juli, *s.* = °-huli H^3 37^a.5*.

titi-huli, *s. name of a bird* (*a sandpiper, partridge*?) H^3 37^a.1. ~-hudi *id. ifc.* **mā-.**

ti-tu, *s. a sort of sugar-cane* Md 62^b.8.

titul-se, *s. the tamarind-tree* Vd 13ª.2.

tithi [*S. lunar day*], *s. a day, term* N 8ª.3. — ~-bār *a day, date* B 3ᵇ.5.

ti-dhu(ṁ), *s. a wolf* Md 71ᵇ.8, *a hyena* CW 7.1.

tini [ti³], *prt. emphasizing* Vi 110.1; āwo ~ *just now* M 35ª.2.

tinë, *v. t.*, lāhā hnaspanas ~ *to put the hand to the ear* Vi 53.14, hnaspan ~ *to touch the ear* H³ 9ᵇ.8; khāpā ~ *to shut the door* B 53ª.10; jāl ~ *to set up a trap* H² 101ª.3.

tiṁti(ṁ), ~ hnuya *to stamp the ground* M 10ᵇ.6.

ti-pāyal, *s. an ornament of the feet* (nūpura) CW 8.80.

tiya¹ (-l¹), *v. i. to adorn oneself* V² 7ª.4. — tiyakë *caus. to adorn* B 17ᵇ.1.

tiya² (-l¹), *v. t. to stab* H² 104ᵇ.7.

tiya³ (-l¹, *only* tiyāwo), *v. t. to lock (a door)*? V¹ 127ᵇ.6*.

tiya⁴, = teya³ H³ 50ª.3.

tiyakë (*caus. of* tiya¹), *to adorn* B 17ᵇ.1.

til¹ [*S.* tīra], *s. a bank, coast* V¹ 48ᵇ.2.

til² [*H.*], *s. a mole of beauty* B 62ª.10.

tilagāl, *s.* ~ cāyā lākh *water from a tank* (pālvala) Md 52ᵇ.1.

tilā, *s. the third day of the lunar fortnight* AH 10ᵇ.

tiri [*M.* tiriā *a woman*], *s. a woman* C¹ 287; *a wife* H³ 10ᵇ.9; ~ dayakë *to get a wife* H² 46ª.4; ~-puruṣ juya *to become man and wife* B 12ᵇ.8. — ~-jan *womankind* H² 100ᵇ.6. — *ifc.* **baniyā-**.

tīrth [*S.*], *s. a bathing-place* H² 9ª.2.

til-si, *s. Symplocos racemosa* AH 28ᵇ.

til-hil, *s. ornaments* H¹ 90ᵇ.3.

tisā [tiya¹], *s. an ornament* M 18ª.2. — *ifc.* **alaṁkār-**, **hnas-**, **hnas-pot-**, **siṁh-**.

tisi, *s. flax* Md 66ᵇ.5. — ~-cikan *linseed-oil* 59ª.1.

ti-suk, *adj. compact* (vyūḍha) AH 69ª.

tisëṃ = tasëṃ (*10th form of* taya) N 40ª.8.

ti-sok, *adj.* = ti-suk; ~ yaṅ *fat (milk)* Md 56ᵇ.5.

tibi(ṁ), ~ nuya *to spring, to leap, to start up* Bh 82ᵇ.5; ~ nwoya *id.* H² 48ª.7. ~ svāyakë *to raise, to erect* (hnas-pot *the ears*) H³ 38ᵇ.6.

tu¹, *s. a worm* (svedaja) AH 65ª.

tu², *s.* = tuti Md 79ª.1.

tu³, *s. sugar-cane* Md 62ᵇ.3. — *ifc.* **athi-**, **kusyāl-**, **ti-**, **tesu-**.

tu⁴, *part. the meaning may be something like: just, even* V² 54ª.2.

tu⁵, *s. tetanus*(?) Vd 30ª.6.

tuk-svān, *s. name of a plant* (buka) Md 31ª.6.

tu-kha, *part.* = tu⁴ N 20ᵇ.5.

tucakë¹ (*caus. of* tuya⁴), *to make agree, to make tally* V¹ 41ª.6; *to tan, to dress (a skin)* Ś 147ᵇ.6; *fig.: to thrash, to break (the skin)* N 44ª.6.

tucakë² = twocakë H³ 20ª.3.

tujan, ~ dayakë *to explain* Ś 153ª.4*.

tutān, °m, *s. a stick, staff* H² 93ª.1.

tuti, *s. a leg* V¹ 44ª.6. — tute *id.* H² 50ª.6.

tutu-mā, *s. a nurse, midwife* P 59ª.3.

tuthī, *s.* = tuṃthī N 76ᵇ.3.

tudu-hma, *s. a mark on the forehead* (tilaka) AH 39ᵇ.

tunāth, *s. a ridge of a roof* (gopānasī) CW 4.10.

tunāl, *s.* = tunāth AH 25ª.

tuni, *prt.* = tini H² 97ª.6.

tunuṁ, *adv. immediately after* B 48ᵇ.7; *mostly after verb forms:* khanas-~ Ś 148ᵇ.6, jus-~ H² 5ᵇ.7, thīyās-~ B 29ᵇ.9, wā-~ B 35ᵇ.8, *a. o.*

tunthī, *s. a well, water-reservoir* H² 88ª.8. — ~-dhāle *a kind of jasmine* (vaṭapatra) Md 16ᵇ.6.

tupun-jhaṅgal, *s. the wild cock* AH 36ª.

tupuli [*cf. H.* topī *cap*], *s. a sort of head-gear* P 15ª.1*.

tuphe, °**phi**, *s. a broom* CW 4.13.

tuya¹ (-l¹; *only:* tuyā), *v. t. to draw water* Vi 24.17.

tuya² (-t), *v. i.* = toya¹ Vd 39ª.3.

tuya³ (-t), *v. i.* = twoya H³ 4ª.10.

tuya⁴ (-t), *v. t. to reach* M 38ª.4; *to suffice, to answer* H³ 26ª.10. — ma tuk *insufficient*(?) Ś 167ª.6.

tuyikë, *v. i. to be bright* Ś 156ª.5*.

tuyu, *adj.* = toyu AH 33ª.

tuliwo, *s. a sprout, shoot* AH 26ᵇ.

turuk [*H.* turk], *s. a Mahomedan* Ś 147ᵇ.5. — **turukh** *s. id.* Ś 147ª.2.

tulululuṁ, hi ~ woyakāwo *while streams of blood are flowing* B 23ª.1*.

tulë, *v. i. see* **ģwol**.

tuly [*S.*], *adj.*, ch-g-wo ~ *like, alike* H¹ 70ᵇ.2; ~ yāya *to treat alike* H² 56ª.4.

tur-se, *s.* = tu-se(?) Vd 26ª.4.

tu-se, *s. Cucumis utilissimus* CW 7.35.

tuṣṇi [*S.* tuṣṇīm], ~ yāya *to keep silence* Bh 90ª.2.

tṛkhā [*S.* tṛṣā], *s. thirst* V¹ 99ᵇ.5; ~ juya *to be thirsty* V¹ 59ᵇ.4.

tṛgār, *s.* = **tilagāl**; *a vessel, jug*(?) Bh 94ª.6*.

tṛpt [*S.*], *adj. satisfied* H² 39ᵇ.6. — tṛpti [*S. satisfaction*], *adj. id.* 71ᵇ.7; ~ yāya *to satisfy* Bh 46ᵇ.5.

te¹, 1) = taya N 36ª.2. — 2) *5th form of* teya³ H² 51ª.6.

te², në te *twice* Vd 36ª.5.

te-wā¹, *s. a kind of rice*(?) Vd 48ª.6.

tewā² = tiwā B 45ª.9*.

tewo 1) = tiwo Vd 12ª.3. — 2) *5th form of* teya³.

tewolaṁ, *adv. in the morning, at dawn* B 28ᵇ.1;

te-kākë, *v. t.*, cen ~ *to make a brand* N 41ᵇ.1*.

teke, ~ yāṅa(ṃ) *incessantly* H² 50ª.3*.

te-ģuli, *see* **teya**³.

tecakë, *v. t. to provide with* Bh 49ᵇ.1, cen ~ *to make a brand* N 52ª.7.

tej [*S.* tejas], *s. light, splendour (prop. and fig.)* H¹ 10ª.4.

tej-mul, *s. name or a plant* (maṇḍūkaparṇa) AH 29ª (tejamoo).

tetul-se, *s.* = ti° Vd 28ª.6.

tenu, *s. name of an animal* Vd 54ª.6.

tenë, *v. i. to be about to…, to be in the act of…* (*with 4th form*) V 29ᵇ.6; *to be willing to…* Vi 37.27. — twoḍ-të ma teṅ *he cannot leave* H¹ 61ª.4 (tyaṅ).

tephu, *s. the navel* Vd 24ᵇ.4.

temāl, *s. Ficus heterophylla* Md 15ª.8. — ~-ke *name of a plant, used medicinally* Vd 46ᵇ.5. — ~-khe *name of a plant the root of which is used medicinally* 41ᵇ.4.

teya¹ (-l¹), *v. t. to bar, to block up* Bh 162ª.3.

teya² (-t *or* -l¹; *only* teyāwo), *v. t. to powder* Bh 173ᵇ.5*.

teya³ (-l¹; *1st form:* telaṃ, telo, tele; *5th form:* tewo, te), *v. i. to be allowed* V¹ 18ᵇ.1, *to be proper* H¹ 66ª.3; *usually used with the 4th form of a verb in the sense of: may* H³ 27ª.10, *must, shall* B 12ª.1, *will* (*subj. 1. pers.*) Vi 171.1 — *With* ma *this verb* (*mostly the 5th form*) *forms neg. imperatives:* twol-të ma tewo *don't leave* H¹ 76ª.1, chunu dhāya ma te *don't say any thing* B 20ᵇ.3. — ma te-guli *improper* H³ 44ª.8.

teyakë¹, *v. i. to be about to, to start to* (yāya) V¹ 10ª.4.

teyakë², *caus. of* teya¹ V² 76ᵇ.5.

teyakë³ = tayakë¹ V¹ 29ᵇ.4.

tel, ~ taya *to kick* (*with the foot*) C² 278*.

telakë, *v. i.* = teyakë¹ V² 17ª.4*.

telë, *v. t. to conquer* H³ 87ᵇ.2*.

tesu-tu, *s. a sort of sugar-cane* Md 62^b.8.

tel-svān, *s. Ipomoea Turpethum* AH 31^a (telaswang).

tëbhulī, *s. Tamarix indica* Vd 18^b.4; ~-se *id.* CW 7.15.

tëya (-t), *v. i. to be gained or earned* Bh 177^a.6*.

tëlakë, *caus. of* tëlë N 41^b.1.

tëlë^1, *v. t. to anoint* N 35^a.5.

tok, ~ thenë *to cut off* H^2 63^a.5. — ~ daya *to fall out (teeth)* H^1 27^b.3. — ~ ḍe-kāke *to cut off* N 34^b.5. — ~ dhulë *to be broken, to be fractured* H^3 23^b.2. — ~ dhënë *to cut off* H^2 63^a.7; hān-tapaṃ ~ *to uproot, to destroy completely* C^2 247. ~ dhënakë *to let break asunder* Bh *13^b.3. — ~ puya (-l^1) *to cover, to veil* C^2 149, *to block up* Bh 62^b.6; *fig.: to protect* H^3 51^b.4; *to get the better of* V^1 117^b.2. ~ puyakë *to cover* Bh 68^b.7; *to get the better of* M 10^a.7. — ~ pulë *to break asunder* Ś 144^a.2. — ~ pwoya = ~ puya C^2 151. — ~ phiyakë *to scatter* Vi 78.19. — ~ pheya (-l^1) *to lose* C^1 110. — ~ byācakë *to blot out(?)* C^2 59. — ~ hlāya *to cut to pieces* C^1 70, *to gnaw through* H^3 29^b.5.

to-kachu, *s. a kind of cutaneous disease* Vd 34^b.6.

tokan [toya^4], *adv.* ch-g-wo ~ *in accordance with…* N 46^b.7.

tok-pusā, *s. a covering* AH 8^a.

tocakë^1 [= tucakë^1?], *v. t. to keep well, to treat well* N 17^a.2*.

tocakë^2 (*caus. of* toya^1), *v. t. to shake* N 12^a.3.

toti, °**te**, *s. a leg* H^1 48^a.1.

to-to, ~ yanë *to drink frequently* Vd 52^b.6.

totr [*S.* stotra], *s. a song of praise* Vi 77.21.

toḍ = tol; ~ pheya *to lose* N 23^a.1*.

tomar [*S.*], *s. a lance* Bh 150^a.3.

toya^1 (-t), *v. i. to shake, to tremble* Vd 19^a.6.

toya^2, *v. t. to take off (a garment)* V^1 12^a.4.

toya^3 (-l^1), *v. i. to shine (sun)* C^1 148, *to flash (lightning)* Vi 17.25.

toya^4 (-l^1), *v. i.* ch-g-wo *to be in accordance with…:* dharmawo towo *lawful* N 32^b.8; lokawo tok *good-mannered, popular* C^1 56.

toyakë^1, *caus. of* toya^4; ch-g-wo ma toyakaṃ *disagreeing, incongruous* N 33^a.7.

toyakë^2, *caus. of* toya^3 P 17^b.7.

toyi, *adj.* = toyu; toyiwo CW 7.11; toyisëṃ *becoming white* B 16^b.11; toyiyāwo *shining* H^3 4^a.2.

toyu, *adj. white* H^2 43^a.1, *light, lucid* C^2 257. — toyuwo *light, lucid* C^1 257. — toyu belā *moonshine* V^1 73^a.1; toyu belā yāya *to shine (moon)* H^1 12^b.2. — toyu ṃilā *id.* AH 8. — toyu uphol-svān *a water-lily* (kuvalaya) Md 29^b.7. — toyuwo cāk *small-pox* (gulī) CW 8.44.

tol, ~ pheya (-l^1), *v. t. to lose, to drop* B 11^b.7.

tolā [*H. a weight of 12 mashās*], *s.* cha tolā *a weight* (= karṣa AH) Ś 151^b.6.

tolo-kān, *adj.* = tol-~ H^2 4^a.5*.

tol-kān, *adj. blind* H^3 2^a.6; tol-kānā *id.* H^1 4^b.1*.

tol-hma, bhūmi ma ~ *who does not leave his country* H^2 49^b.3*.

tosan, *adj. poor, not rich* B 50^b.8; ~ yāṅa jāyalapë *to be born poor* N 13^b.8.

to-se, *s. a plant used medicinally* Vd 46^a.6.

two(ṃ)^1, *adv. unto:* gal-pot ~ *unto the neck* Bh 22^a.6; *untill* N 5^a.8; *before the lapse of* 36^b.5. thaṃ… twoṃ *from… to* 53^a.3.

two(ṃ)^2, *part. as for…* Bh 57^a.3; *just, even* (= tu^4) V^1 129^a.5.

twoṁkë, *caus. of* twonë B 20ª.4.

twocakë (*caus. of* twoya), *to plunge, to immerse* H¹ 85ᵇ.8.

two-të, *v. t.* = twol-të H³ 26ª.2.

twoḍ-takë (*caus. of* twoḍ-të), *to cause to give up* Bh 155ᵇ.2.

twoḍ-të, *v. t.* = twol-të H¹ 20ª.4; twoḍ-taṃ choya *to let go, to release* N 49ᵇ.1.

twonakë, *caus. of* twonë V² 32ª.4.

twonë, *v. t. to drink* H¹ 94ᵇ.3; *s. a drink, beverage* N 41ª.4.

twoya (-t), *v. i. to dive, to sink* H¹ 18ᵇ.2.

twol-tayakë (*caus. of* twol-të), *to cause to leave* P 30ª.7.

twol-të (*5th form:* -tawo, -tu. *Irreg. forms:* -tuṅāwo = -tāwo; -tayuwo, -talayiwo = -tiwo. *Neg.* ma twol-të *or* twol ma të), *v. t. to leave, to quit* H¹ 94ª.4, *to give up, to resign* H² 54ᵇ.4, *to abandon, to forsake* N 19ª.5, *to neglect* H² 94ª.2, *to shun, to avoid* H¹ 23ª.4, *to omit* Vd 18ª.3, *to dismiss* H³ 36ª.7, *to release* (ch-hm(-n) *someone*) Bh 57ª.3; *to surrender* Vi 117.10, ch-hm-yāta ~ *to leave to...* 167.25; — prāṇ ~ *to die* V² 8ª.3; saṃkhān ma twol-tu-hma *sorrow-stricken* H² 14ᵇ.5; lajyān ma twol-tu-hma *bashful, timorous ib.*

twoha, °**ho**, *s. a pretext;* ~ ciṅāwo *pretending* H³ 43ª.11; wonë twohon *under pretext of going* V¹ 127ª.1; bi-lbaphal-twohon *in the disguise of a Bilva-fruit* 3ª.3; bëthā-~ *pretending pain* V² 4ᵇ.6.

tyajalapë [*S.* tyaj], *v. t. to repudiate* (*a wife*) N 32ª.7. thethe wuṃ ~ *to dissolve a mutual agreement* 32ª.3.

tyā, *s. half;* la-tyās *in one month and a half* H¹ 49ᵇ.1; la-tyā·n-thi *id.* H¹ 33ª.7; la-tyāta *id.*(?) P 48ᵇ.3.

tyāg [*S. s. leaving, abandoning*], ~ yāya *to abandon, to give up* H² 92ª.4; dhanas ~ ma dataṅāwo *when there is no munificence connected with riches* H² 40ᵇ.5.

tyāgi [*S.* tyāgin], *adj. liberal, munificient* H² 40ᵇ.7.

tyā chiya (-t), *v. t. to decide* (kha *a lawsuit*) B 17ª.3.

tyājalapë, *v. t.* = tya°, *to disown* (*a daughter*) B 8ᵇ.6.

tyāya¹ (-t), *v. t. to win* (kha *a lawsuit*) N 14ª.2; *to win in playing* B 17ᵇ.5, julanaṃ ~ *id.* 43ª.4.

tyāya² (-t), *v. t. to borrow* N 6ᵇ.8, *to take upon trust* V¹ 95ª.1, dānāgān ~ *to get into debt* N 3ª.2; tyāk dayakë *to lend*(?) B 51ª.5; tyāya biyā-hma *a creditor* V¹ 94ᵇ.6; tyāṅā kāyā *a debtor* AH 53ª; tyāya-tu biyā tawo-mi *an usurer* 53ᵇ.

tyo = tewo H³ 33ª.5*.

trās [*S. fear*], ~ yāya *to make afraid of* N 49ᵇ.2; ~ cāya *to tremble with fear* Bh 98ª.2.

trāhi [*S. ipr. of* trai *to protect*], ~ trāhin gyāya *to be very much frightened* Bh 12ª.6; ~ trāhimānanaṃ juya *id.* M 36ª.5.

tri, *s.* = tiri V² 27ᵇ.6.

tvā, ~ ~ hlāya *to break to pieces* Bh 151ᵇ.7*.

tvāk¹, *s. a bundle* B 4ª.10; *log* 23ª.8. — ~-dibā *a ball to play with* Bh 94ª.5. — ~-svān *a wreath* (*of flowers*) C² 152. — *ifc.* **svān-**.

tvāk² = tok: ~ thaya *to lacerate* H² 113ᵇ.7. — ~ dhënë *to cut or to break asunder* P 27ᵇ.2. — ~ hlāya *to pierce* Bh 152ª.7.

tvāk³, *only ifc.* **hnas-**, **la-**, **siṁ-**.

tvākā-tikā, *s. a seller* (vikrayika) AH 56ᵇ.

tvāc, *s. a friend* B 24ª.3. — ~-ju *id.* 24ª.6. — ~-kehe *a friend's sister* N 34ᵇ.4. — ~-bhari *a friend's wife* 34ᵇ.4. — ~-bhot *id.* B 28ª.7.

tvāt, *s.* = tvāth CW 7.15.

tvāti, *s. a kind of muscle shell* AH21ᵇ.

tvāth, *s. a bill* (*of a bird*) H[2] 98[a].3.

tvāpal, *s. a peak, top of a mountain* H[2] 49[a].3. — *ifc.* **datho-.**

tvāy[1], *s.* = tvāc B 27[b].10. — ~-bhot *a friend's wife* 28[a].6.

tvāy[2], ~ cinē *to form a great crowd* C[1] 132*.

tvāl, *s. a principal road* N 42[a].1.

th (ṭh).

tha[1], *pr. dem. this* V[2] 12[a].1. ~-gu *id.* B 4[b].11.

tha[2], *adv.* = than V[2] 67[b].2; mokasāṃ, tha mole *if it perishes, then it may perish* Ś 152[b].1.

tha[3] = tha(ṃ): ~ jula (*sometimes* jule) *though it is, even if it is* H[3] 27[a].9, *after 5th form also: though, even if* (= *conv. in* ·asāṃ) H[1] 7[b].4; sunānaṃ ~ jule *whoever it may be* 23[a].5; tha jula... tha jula *be it... or be it* C[1] 20. — ~ khet = ~ jula C[2] 76.

tha(ṁ), ~ woya *to vomit* CW 8.46. — ~ kāya *to take out of* (*a well etc.*) B 56[a].12, *to raise* H[3] 45[a].7; *to elevate, to exalt* 55[a].2; *to ascend* (parbatas *a mountain* H[2] 53[b].3. — ~ choyakē *to direct, to guide* N 25[b].6. — ~ jāya *to ascend* Bh 74[a].2. — ~ tinē *to throw up to* Bh 179[a].6, *to lift, to raise* Ns 2[a].4. — ~ thēnakē *to ascend* (ch-g-s *something*) Bh 83[b].7. — ~ dinē *to elevate* 81[a].5. — ~ pakē *to embezzle* B 1[b].8. — ~ panē *to stem, to stop* Vd 26[b].2. — ~ biya (-t) *to run away* B 62[b].7. — ~boyakē *to cause to fly upwards* M 30[a].3. — ~ bvāya *to leap up* H[2] 36[a].4. — ~ hlanē *to put out* (hast, hastan *a hand*) H[1] 16[a].1. — ~ hlāya (-t) *id.* H[3] 11[a].7. — ~ sālē *to draw, to pull out of* H[2] 13[a].5. — ~ suya *to tuck up* (*one's dress*) Bh 184[b].5. — ~ swoya *to look upward* M 23[a].3. — ~ svācakē *to raise, to cock* (*the tail*) H[3] 38[b].6. — ~ hāya *to go out* (ch-g-n *out of...*) Bh 69[a].7; *to ascend* (ch-g-s *something*) H[2] 77[b].3; ... tha hāsēṃ *in a distance of...* H[1] 31[a].2.

thawo, *pr. refl. for all perss.* H[1] 34[a].3. *id. poss.* 4[a].3; ji ~ lā-hāt *my own hand* H[3] 5[a].1. — thawo thawon (*subj.*) *every one for himself* N 40[a].5; thawo thawos *each in his own place* V[2] 6[a].2; thawo thawoyā byabahār *the respective ceremonies* P 3[a].7; thawo thawo juya *to be kept separately* N 44[a].6. thawo yāya *to take possession of* C[1] 232, ~ juya *to become the property of* (*gen.*) N 23[b].4. thawo sukh *independence* H[1] 62[b].2; ~ sukhi *independent* H[3] 40[b].3, ~-hma *id.* N 20[b].3. thawo thithi *kinsmen* Ś 150[a].1. thawota thamanaṃ *of one's own accord* M 13[a].6; thawo-thē thamanaṃ *id.* B 19[a].6.

thaṁ, *adv.* pēnoṃ ~ *more than* N 43[b].9; dāyen ~ syāya toṃ *from beating to killing* 53[a].4.

thaṁ-ko, *s. the palate* CW 8.70.

thaṁ-bvāj, *s. a high-caste man* N 20[b].5. — ~-jāti *id.* 44[a].3.

thaṁlabāḍ, *s. food* (piṇḍa) N 16[a].8*.

thaṁ-sā, *s. eructation* Vd 9[b].1.

thaṁ-si, *s. Pinus longifolia* Md 12[a].7.

ṭhak [*M.*], *s. a robber, assassin* N 10[a].2.

thakalapē [*s.* ṭhak], *v. t. to rob* N 48[b].3.

tha-kā, ~ kwo-kā ma yāya *to make no distinction between people of higher and lower rank* H[2] 60[b].8*.

thakāḍi, *s.* = thaṃ° N 35[a].3.

tha-kāli, *adj. eldest* AH 68[b].

thaku[1], *s. a man of the Vaiśya-caste* AH 53[a].

thaku[2], *s. a casket* (samudgaka) AH 45[a].

thakudā, *s. name of a medicinal plant* Vd 54ᵇ.2*.

thakuni [thaku[1]], *s. a woman of the Vaiśya-caste* B 8ᵇ.9.

thakul, *s.* = thākul N 20ᵇ.7. — thakuli *a mistress* Ś 159ᵇ.1.

thakë (*caus. of* thanë[1]), *to let pour* (ch-g-s *in...*) Vd 7ᵃ.6.

tha-gu, *pr.* = thu-gu B 4ᵃ.9.

thaṁkāḍi, *s. a householder, head of the family* N 4ᵃ.1; *the relations of a woman, being her spirituel guides* 35ᵃ.7. — ~-babi *an elder brother (as head of the family)* 4ᵃ.7.

thaṁjāti, *s. cream* Vd 46ᵇ.1.

tha-ta, ~ kāya *to take out of* (ch-g-n) Vi 72.2; *to save* 15.7. — ~ choya *to raise (a hand)* 109.4. — ~ boṅaṃ (boṅāwo) yanë *to lead or conduct up into* B 57ᵇ.1. — ~ yanë *id.* Vi 73.4. — ~ haya *to take out of* Vi 150.31, *to raise, to stretch out of* Bh 12ᵇ.1.

thaten, *adv. therefore* V² 23ᵇ.1.

tha-tha [thanë[1]], ~ yanë *to pour* (ch-g-s *in*) Vd 29ᵃ.1.

thathi(ṁ), *pr. dem. such a...* C¹ 137; *adv. (before adj.) so, as* V² 44ᵃ.5; ~ belas *at this time* M 2ᵇ.5; ~-pani *these* P 49ᵃ.6. — ~-hma (*of persons only*) *such a...* V² 41ᵃ.4. — ~-gwo (*of things and persons*) *id.* V¹ 100ᵇ.6; ~-gwo-hma (*of persons*) *id.* C¹ 53, *adv. (before adj.) so, as* V² 46ᵇ.7. — ~-gu *such a...* V² 35ᵇ.3; ~-gu-hma *id.* C¹ 126. — ~-ṅa *id.* H¹ 163ᵃ.3; *adv. (before adj.)* V¹ 130ᵃ.5; ~-ṅa-hma *id.* Ś 164ᵃ.3; ~-ṅa-gu *id.* P 6ᵇ.7. — tha-thiwo *such a...* V² 43ᵇ.6. thathiwole *under these circumstances* H³ 28ᵃ.3. thathiṅāle *id.* Bh 44ᵇ.4. thathinaṃ-li *after that* C¹ 126.

tha-thë(ṁ), *adv. so, thus, in this manner* V¹ 10ᵇ.4, *then, thereon* V² 68ᵃ.3, *there* Ś 143ᵃ.6, *hither* Bh 61ᵇ.6. *pr. dem. this* Ś 153ᵃ.5; *such a...* N 52ᵃ.1. — thathën *adv. so, thus* V² 20ᵃ.2. thathënaṃ *still, yet, nevertheless* H³ 23ᵇ.4, *therefore* B 54ᵃ.6; thathëna-ntu *even so* C¹ 116; thathë-ṅanakaṃ *so, like that* H² 49ᵇ.7; thathë-ṅale *under such circumstances* H² 57ᵃ.3, ~-ṅele *id.* 28ᵃ.7. — thathë(ṃ)-gwo *adv. (before adj.) so, as* V² 56ᵃ.2; ~-gwo-hma *pr. dem. such a ...* C¹ 52.

tha-thwo, *pr. dem. this* V² 78ᵇ.6. — *adv. thereon* H¹ 88ᵃ.5.

tha-thyāk, *adj. high, elevated* AH 20ᵇ (thathyá).

tha-duṁ, *adv.,* ~ kwo-duṃ *above and below* Bh 33ᵃ.4*.

than[1], *adv. here* H¹ 70ᵃ.5, *hither* Ś 162ᵃ.1; *then, thereon* H¹ 94ᵃ.5. — thanayā kha *the tale about this* Vi 94.2, ~ ācār *the customs of this country* Vi 132.31.

than[2] [= tha(ṃ)], ~ woyakë *to take away (a disease)* Vd 42ᵇ.6. — ~ kāya *id.* 43ᵃ.1.

thanaṁ, *adv. thereafter* B 1ᵇ.5. — thana(ṃ)-li *id.* 41ᵃ.1, ~-li-thë *id.* H¹ 17ᵇ.2.

thani, *adv. to-day* V² 31ᵇ.2; ~ din *id.* B 13ᵃ.9; thaniyā adyāpi(s) *id.* M 34ᵇ.5; ~ abasaras *id.* Vi 154.3; ~ dinas *id.* M 7ᵇ.6, *some day* Vi 24.6; ~ rātris *this night* V² 12ᵇ.6. thaniyāta *for this day* Vi 112.25; thani-tolen *till this day* H² 111ᵃ.5; thanin *from this day* V² 34ᵃ.1. — thane = thani Ś 161ᵇ.6.

thanë[1], *v. t.* 1) ch-g ~ *to fill* H¹ 68ᵃ.3. 2) ch-g ch-g-s ~ *to put or pour something in...* H³ 32ᵃ.2, *to place* V² 34ᵇ.5. — nugalas ~ *to keep to oneself* H³ 15ᵃ.9; nugalas thaṅāwo palapë *to read by heart* Ns 38ᵃ.4; kaciṃgal ~ *to cause dissension* B 41ᵃ.2; dān ~ *to pay tax* N 47ᵃ.5; dhup ~ *to burn incense* Vi 18.31; nām ~ *to refer to a name* N 43ᵇ.8; mokwoyā ~ *to make good a loss* N 22ᵃ.3; thaṅa(ṃ) yanë *to seize hold of* N 29a.5; yas thaṅā ghaḍ *a pitcher, filled with poison* C² 261.

thanë², *v. t. to arouse (from sleep)* B 27a.9.

thanë³, *v. i.* ch-g-s ~ *to arrive at...* H¹ 82a.4.

thap, *s. the shed (of a potter)* H³ 56b.2. — *ifc.* **mi-**.

tha-bah, *adj. superior in rank* N 40b.6.

tham, *pr. self, himself* V² 22b.1; ~ ~ ëyā *everyone according to his own wish* H¹ 32a.2; ~-thëṃ *of one's own accord* N 20b.3, ~-thëṃ-thama(na)ṃ *id.* M 13a.7; ~ khasëṃ *id.* N 9b.7. — tham ekānt *alone* Ś 166a.2.

tha-hma = thawo Vi 160.15.

thaya (-l¹), *v. t. to place*; manas ~ *to take into one's mind, to set one's mind upon* M 19b.7; piṇḍ ~ *to offer funeral balls* B 62a.2; kalah ~ *to cause dissension* C² 287; beg ~ *to spur (a horse)* B 61a.8.

thayakë, *caus. of* thaya C¹ 173.

thal, *s.* = thāl H¹ 21b.4; *a measure of capacity*(?) B 4b.6. — *ifc.* **laṁkha-**.

tha-la-, thalaṃ-li *thereafter* B 58b.8; thalanaṃ nisëṃ *from this time* H¹ 64a.5; thalas *at the time of*(?) Vi 161.10.

thalalaṁ, ~ nuwo *s. trembling* CW 1.74; ~ khāk *adj. agitated, perturbed* AH 64b.

thalā-thiṁlā, *adv. here and there, everywhere* Bh 147b.2*.

thalāyamānanaṁ [*see* thar-tharāyamān], *adv. trembling* M 27a.1.

thalī [*H.*], *s. firm or dry ground* P 30a.6.

thalu, *s. a shoulder* CW 8.91.

thar-tharāyamān [*H.* thartharānā *to tremble*], *adv. trembling* Vi 130.29.

tha-si, *s.* = thaṃ-si Vd 35b.1.

thas-khā, *s. name of a bird* Md 74a.6.

thahal, ~ juya *to hide oneself* H² 93a.1*.

tha-hā, *adv.* = thā-hā Bh 1a.2.

thā, *s. a place, abode* V² 35a.6; rājāyā thās *to the king* M 9a.8; thugu thās *at this time or junctur*- B 2b.5. — o thā o thān sanë *to move from place to place* Bh 62b.2.

thāk- [thāku], phasan thāk *flatulence*(?) Vd 54a.2; ~ thākwo *id. ib.* 4.

thāku, *adj. difficult* H² 35a.2.

thākul [*H.* ṭhākur], *s. a lord, master* B 42a.3, *the master (of a slave)* N 20a.2.

thākë¹ (*caus. of* thānë), *to hit* Vi 37.12.

thākë² (*caus. of* thāya²), ghaṇṭh ~ *to let sound a bell* H² 59b.2.

thākwo, *adj.* = thāku H¹ 54a.4.

thācakë¹, *caus. of* thāya² B 10a.2.

thācākë² (*caus. of* thāya¹?), man ~ *to be ready (to do a thing:* yāya) N 7b.2*.

thā-jyā, *s. weaving* AH 61a.

thātakë, *caus. of* thāya² M 25b.2.

thā-thā, ~ yāya *to knock (at a window* jhyālas) B 48a.7*.

thān¹ [*H. locality, seat*], *s. a place, abode* H² 102b.8.

thān², *adv. now, then*(?) Bh 168a.5*.

thānakë (*caus. of* thānë), *v. i. to arrive* Vi 46.30.

thānā, *s. a camp* H³ 49b.1.

thānāntar [*cf. S.* sthānāntara], *s. another place* H² 92a.6.

thānë, *v. t. to place or put into* (ch-g-s) Vd 4a.4; *to produce, to build* Vi 140.11. — *v. i. to arrive* V² 9b.5.

thāpalapë [*cf. S.* sthāpaya- *to cause to stand*], *v. t.*, agni ~ *to kindle the sacrificial flame* N 32b.6*.

thābar [*S.* sthāvara], *s. immovables* N 5a.3.

thām [*cf. S.* stambha], *s. a post, pillar* H³ 33a.1.

thāy [*cf. Mr.* thāya], *s. a place, abode, seat* H¹ 33b.2; samast pāpayā ~ *an abode of every sin* V² 26a.1; samast thāyas *everywhere* H¹ 42a.4; tha-gu thāyas *then* B 4ª.9. pi hāya **thāy** *an exit* H¹ 25ᵇ.5. — *ifc.* **pāk-**.

thāya¹ (-t), *v. t.* sākṣi ~ *to call to witness* N 11ᵇ.3.

thāya² (-t), *v. t. to play, to let sound (a musical instrument)* M 4ª.7; bādy ~ *to make music* B 70ª.8; lā-hāt ~ *to clap the hands* AH 60ª.

thāl [*M.* thār *a plate for eating from*], *s. a plate* Vi 83.19.

thālapā, *s. a priest*(?) P 43ª.5.

thālā, *s.* = thāl; ~-bhālā *plates and vessels for eating from* B 43ᵇ.8; *fig.* prītiyā thālā *an abode of love* H² 47ᵇ.5.

thās, *s. a place, abode, seat* V² 38ᵇ.2.

thā-hā, ~ uya = ~ woya. — ~ wonë *to go upward* Vi 64.5. — ~ **woya** *to get out of, to come out of* B 56ª.12; *to escape* H¹ 18ᵇ.1. — ~ kāva *to take out of* Ns 40ª.6. — ~ ma du *is not to be eluded* H³ 42ª.9; ~ ma siya *not know the way out (of a difficulty* 29ª.4; ~-hma *being more than that* Vi 15.5.

thi, *adv. here, there* V¹ 127ᴰ.1, *hither* 32ᵇ.2; thiyā mantri *the minister of this place* V² 8ᵇ.5.

-thi(ṁ), *adj. like:* je-pani-thi *people like us* V² 29ª.5; cal-khuniyā-thiṃ mati *a mind like that of a sparrow* B 10ᵇ.9. — ~-gwo *id.*: kisi-~ *an animal like an elephant* H¹ 31ᵇ.1; chalopo-layā-~ *one like you* 9ª.2. — ~-gu *id.*: je-~ svabhāb *a character like mine* H³ 7ᵇ.3. — ~-hma *id.* H³ 7ª.3.

thik, *adj. shining* M 5ᵇ.1*.

thikay [*cf. H.* thaknā *to be fatigued*?] ~ juya *to be consumed or spent*(?) B 50ᵇ.10.

thikā¹, ~ thikānaṃ sanë *to be excited* Bh 62ᵇ.1*.

thi-kā², *adv. see* **i-kā**.

-thiṅa = thi(ṃ) C¹ 123. ëyā-~ tawo-dhaṅ *as great as one might wish* H² 56ª.4. — ~-hma *id.* Vi 36.11.

thiṅā, *adj. authorized*(?) N 23ª.4; ma ~-pu *dishonest*(?) 7ᵇ.2.

thichi, ~ ma thichiṃ *adv. denoting celerity or eagerness* Bh 79ᵇ.5.

thi-tā, *adv. on or to this side (of a river)* B 56ᵇ.1.

thiṭhi, *adv.* = thëthë B 1ᵇ.5; thithisënaṃ *id.* Bh 155ª.4, thithi anyonyan *id.* H² 71ᵇ.5, thithi para-spar *id.* 72ª.3. — *adj. mutual* H³ 1ᵇ.10; ~ iṣṭ(-mitr) *a friend* Vi 170.28.

thithi-thāhā, *s. sexual capacity* N 30ᵇ.8*.

thi-dā, *adv. see* **yi-dā**.

thi-pul, *adv. see* **i-pul**.

thi-bā, *adv. see* **i-bā**.

ṭhi-bi(l), *adv. see* **i-bil, yi-bi**.

thiya (-l¹), *v. t. to touch* H¹ 40ª.3, bhūmis ~ *to touch the soil* H³ 9ᵇ.8, hnās ~ *to touch the nose* V² 74ª.2. byādhin thiya *to be infected with a disease* Vi 88.30.

thiyakë, *caus. of* thiya; *only* ma thiyakaṃ *without touching* Vd 49ª.2.

thil [*M.* thīr], *adj. firm, quiet, tranquil* Vd 19ᵇ.1; cit ~ yāya *to compose oneself* H³ 38ª.3; prān ~ yāya *to live in peace* Ś 163ᵇ.7; ~ yāya *itrs. to keep quiet* Bh 179ª.7.

thilālapë [*cf. Mr.* thirāvaṇeṃ *to stop, settle*], *v. t. to decide, to arbitrate upon...* N 27ª.6.

thi-sār, *adv. see* **yi-sār**.

this-lā, *s. the month Mārgasirṣa* CW 1.48. — ~-poslā *the winter* 1.51.

thi-hā, *adv. see* **i-hā**.

thi-huni, *ipr. of* thaya Vi 44.14*.

thu¹, *s. an arrow* Bh 99ª.5; *used as class-word:* pë thu balā *four arrows* Bh 114ª.4. — *ifc.* **balā-**.

thu², *pr. dem. this* B 8ª.5; ~-gu *id.* 5ª.3; -guli *id.* M 23ᵇ.2.

thu-³ (-t *or* -l¹? *only:* thuṅaṃ, thuṅāwo, thusëṃ), *v. t. to place* B 18ᵇ.11, *to fix* Vi 74.30. ratn thuṅāwo tayā *studded with jewels* H³ 14ᵇ.3.

thuwāl [thulë], *s. an owner; only ifc.* **bāli-**[1], **bu-**.

thukā, *part. the meaning of which may be defined as: "as it is known", "as you see"* H³ 58ᵃ.5.

thucā, *s.* = thwocā. — *ifc.* **muti-**.

thuco, *s.* = thwocā. — *ifc.* **moti-**.

thutakë, *caus. of* thuya²(?) Vd 24ᵃ.4*.

thuti, *pr. dem. this, that* V² 29ᵃ.2; thutin *therefore* H¹ 9ᵇ.5, thutis *thereby* C¹ 9.

thuthā [*B.* ṭhōṭā *mained, stump*], *adj. crippled, maimed* B 8ᵇ.3.

thu-mi, *pron. dem. this* H³ 49ᵃ.11.

thu-mes, *s. a buffalo bull* Wr p. 301 (thumē).

thuya[1] (-l¹), *v. t.* = thulë Vi 16.12, *to master, to understand* Ś 162ᵇ.6, *to obtain* N 40ᵇ.4; *to find, to detect* 23ᵇ.1.

thuya[2] (-l¹), *v. t. to cook* B 11ᵇ.12.

thul (*5th form of* thulë) = thwol C¹ 249.

thu-li, *pr. dem. this* Vi 63.32; ~ ma-chi *so much* M 31ᵃ.5. — thulita = thuli Vi 92.21.

thulë, *v. t.* = thwolë B 47ᵃ.4; saḍayā cā thulo *the horse became pregnant* B 33ᵃ.9.

thu-sā, *s.* = thwo-sā H³ 22ᵇ.1.

the[1], *adv.* = thi V¹ 130ᵇ.2.

the[2] = thaya N 38ᵇ.9.

thetu, *adv. here* V¹ 18ᵃ.6.

thenakë, *caus. of* thenë; lā-toṃ thenakaṃ *cutting to the flesh* N 44ᵃ.5*.

thenë, *v. t. see* **tok**.

thes, *adv. in this case* N 29ᵃ.5, *then* H² 74ᵃ.3, *there* Bh 123ᵃ.3.

thëṁ[1], ~ ma dvāyu *a slope* (nimna) N 26ᵇ.4; thëṃn dvāyu *a hill* (unnata) *ib.* *

thëṁ[2], *prt as, like:* bohol ~ *as a crane* H¹ 7ᵇ.3, palëwo ~ *like a lotus* C¹ 184, Paraśurāmayā ~ *like P°* V¹ 110ᵇ.5. sik coṅā ~ *as if (he) were dead* H¹ 34ᵇ.2. chan dhāyā ~ *as you have said* H 3ᵇ.2.

thëkānā [*M.* ṭhekānā *fixture, appointment*], *s. obligation* Bh 8ᵇ.2; ~ dayakë *to enter into an engagement* 8ᵃ.7*.

thëṅg [*H.* ṭheṃgā], *s. a club, cudgel* H¹ 48ᵃ.5. — *ifc.* **na-**.

thëthë, *adv. each other, one another* H¹ 54ᵃ.1, *mutually* N 40ᵃ.6; ~ jāsëṃ *from mutual love* 32ᵇ.6.

thënakë (*caus. of* thënë), *v. i. to reach, to arrive at* V² 54ᵇ.2; thënakal woya *id.* M 7ᵃ.1, ~ yanë *to lead to* 26ᵇ.6.

thënë, *v. t. to place, to put* B 17ᵇ.10; mocā ~ *to bear a child* H³ 60ᵇ.8. — *v. i.* ch-g(-s) *to reach, to arrive at* V² 20ᵇ.3; puruṣayāke ~ chotaṃ *(he) send to the man* 23ᵃ.5.

thokā, *s.* = thvākā; *only ifc.* **svān-**.

thwo, *pr. dem. adj. this* H¹ 64ᵇ.3, *id. s.* 72ᵇ.3; thwo thwo *each of these* Vd 18ᵃ.2; thwo-pani *s. these* V² 67ᵇ.1. — thwo-hma (*of persons only*) *this s.* H¹ 87ᵃ.5, *adj.* V² 52ᵇ.2. thwo-guli (*of things only*) *id. s.* H² 49ᵃ.5, *adj.* Ś 149ᵃ.3.

thwo(ṁ), *s. an (intoxicating) drink* C¹ 149; thwon kā- *to be drunk* N 11ᵃ.3. — ~-kuthī *a tavern* (gañjā) CW 4.5. — *ifc.* **aji-**[2], **mit-se-**.

thwowo[1], *pr.* = thawo H² 49ᵇ.6.

thwowo[2] = thwol C¹ 47.

thwoṁ-gwo, *s. a drunkard*(?) N 48ᵇ.4*.

thwok[1], *s. an association* (varga) N 9ᵇ.3; thwokas coṃ-gwo *a member of an association ib.* — thwok thwok jāya *to form an association* 26ᵃ.3; ~ ~ munë *to assemble, to form an assembly* Bh 15ᵇ.5. — ~ lāya *to increase (moon)* C² 185. — thwokaṃ thwokaṃ *adv. repeatedly*(?) M 27ᵃ.2.

thwok[2], ~ dhënë = tok ~ H³ 48ᵃ.9*.

thwok-sal [thwok^1], *s. echo, resonance* H^2 82^b.6.

thwogusi, *s. a musical instrument* Bh 58^a.1*.

thwomňa, ~ tasëm̧ tā *deposited* N 23^a.8*.

thwocakë [thwok(-sval)], *v. t. to make a noise* H^3 13^b.4, kha ~ *id.* H^2 36^a.6.

thwocā, *s. a garland*(?) Bh 167^b.4.

thwo-chi-naṁ, *pr. ind.* ~ belas *once upon a time* H^1 3^a.2*.

thwota, *pr. dem.* = thwote V^2 56^b.6.

thwoti = °te C^1 120; °titā = °tetā H^1 66^a.5.

thwote, *pr. dem. this* H^1 52^b.1, *these* N 38^a.2; ~-gwo *id.* (*of things only*) C^1 290. ~-tā *these* H^2 60^a.7, *this* N 41^b.8. ~-to *this* H^2 73^a.5. — thwoten *adv. therefore* H^1 56^a.2, *in this manner* N 52^a.3. thwotetān *adv. therefore* H^2 78^a.7.

thwo-to, *pr. dem. this* H^2 5^a.4. — ~-thëm̧ *adv. so, thus* H^1 50^a.1; ~-sëm̧ *id.* 19^a.2.

thwo-thiṁ- = tha-thim̧: ~-gwo *such a*... Bh 177^a.7; ~-gwo-hma *id.* Vd 10^a.6; ~-ňa *id.* Vi 159.17.

thwo-thëṁ, *adv. thus, in this manner* H^3 30^b.10; biyāyām̧ ~ *as if (he) has given* N 38^a.3.

thwona(ṁ)-li, *adv. after that, thereupon* V^1 82^b.2; ~ -lis *id.* N 24^b.7; ~-liwo *id.* V^2 15^a.3; ~-li-thëm̧ *id.* 15^a.3.

thwoni, *adv.* = thani; thwoniyā dinas *to-day* Vi 90.21.

thwo-pu, ~ kwo-pu juya *to turn topsy turvy* Bh 166^b.2*.

thwopo-nād, *s. a plant, the root of which is used medicinally* Vd 49^b.2.

thwoṁ = tham V^1 113^a.3.

thwoya, *v. t. to gather (flowers)* Vi 114.28; sval ~ *to catch the sound, to hear* H^2 85^b.2.

thwoyānaṁ, *adv. thereon* B 11^b.9. — thwoyām̧-liwo *id.* H^2 3^a.3.

thwol (*5th form of* thwolë), *possessing, endowed with* C^2 166, ~-hma *id.* H^3 16^b.6. (bu) ~ *the owner (of the field)* H^1 44^a.3; kāy ~ *a mother of male issue* N 36^a.4; puruṣ ~ *married* 33^b.7.

thwola-, *pr.*, ~-tā *the following* N 45^a.5; thwolas *in this case* V^1 80^a.4*.

thwoli, *pr. this, that* Ś 164^b.7; thwolita *id.* P 23^b.7; thwoliwom̧ *thereafter* C^1 23; thwolis *to this extent* H^2 89^a.4, *in this case* 19^b.2; thwolitetes *to this extent* H^1 59^a.4, *in this case* 27^b.1.

thwole-, *pr.*, ~-ma-chi *so much* H^2 60^a.4; ~-titi *this* V^1 45^a.1; ~-teti *id.* 41^a.6.

thwolë, *v. t. to possess (esp. bodily and mental qualities)* C^1 43; kāy ~ *to have a son* N 13^b.4.

thwolo, *pr. dem. this* N 22^b.6; ~-to(m̧) *these* 30^a.8, *adv. here* Ś 166^b.3.

thwolwo = thwol; abahit ma ~ *careless* N 11^a.3.

thwos, 1) *pr. dem. this (used reverently)* H^2 74^a.5. — 2) *adv. there* V^1 40^a.5.

thwo-sapol, *pr. dem. s. this (only of persons of high rank)* N 2^b.8.

thwo-sā, *s. a bull* H^2 49^a.2.

thyāk^1, *adj. entitled* N 38^b.6, ḍah kāya ~ *entitled to inherit* 40^b.6; thyāk kāya *a lawfully begotten son* 38^b.2, ~ (kalāt) *a lawfully married (wife)* B 20^a.4, ~ (dah) *legitimate (property)* N 35^a.7; ...māyāta ma thyāk ...*don't belong to the mother, the mother cannot lay claim to*... B 32^b.10.

thyāk^2, *see* **kwo-**, **hňa-**, **hňe-**, **tha-**.

thyākā, *s. a vessel* H^3 43^a.1. — *ifc.* **dhali-**.

thyākwo, *adj.* = thyāk^1 N 17^b.7.

thyācakaṁ, gurus pënom̧ kwo ~ conë *to sit on a lower seat than the teacher* N 18^b.4*.

thyātu, *adj. slimy, slippery* V^1 48^b.3.

thvā- (-n *or* -t? *only:* thvāṅāwo), *v. t. to beat* Bh 118a.7.

thvākā, *s. a cluster of blossoms* AH 27a. — *ifc.* **wā-, svān-**.

thvācā, *s.* = thwocā Vi 20.4*.

thvānā, *s.* = thānā, ~ taya *to pitch a camp* M 22a.4.

thvuti, *pr. dem.* = thuti P 28a.3*.

d (ḍ).

da, *s. a year* H[1] 49b.1; da da chi *one year* Vi 123.10.

daṁśalapē [*S.* daṃś], *v. t. to bite* H[2] 50b.4; *to devour* Bh 10b.2.

dakwo, *adj.* 1) *all*; nadi dakwo's *of all rivers* C[1] 167; samastaṃ dakwo dikwo *everything whatever* V[2] 68a.7; dakwonaṃ (*subj.*) *everyone* H[3] 18a.8. 2) *whole*; ~ rājy *the whole empire* M 21a.4.

dakṣiṇ [*S.*], *adj. southern* B 14b.1.

dagdh [*S. burnt*], ~ yācakē *to cause to be burnt* Bh 161b.4.

dagdhalapē[1] [dagdh], *v. t. to burn* Bh 10b.7.

dagdhalapē[2], *v. t.* = digdhalapē H[2] 67b.5*.

daṅ, *s. a stalk* (*of a flower*) B 42b.9*.

daṅā, *adj.* = dayā B 28a.9*.

daṁgo-khiṁ, *s. a large military drum* (ānaka) AH 17a.

dachin [*M. the south*], ~-deś *the south, the Dekhan* N 53a.7 (daṃchin).

dato, *pl. of* da C[1] 21; data *id.* H[2] 64a.4.

dathu, *s. middle*; ch-g-yā ~ *into the middle of* H[1] 82b.2, ~ dathus *in the middle of* Ś 158a.3, ~ dathun *from the middle of out of* M 10b.1. — ~-aṅgal *a Buddhistic shrine* (*containing relics*) (eḍūka) AH 24a. — ~-kwothā *the midmost room* B 56b.1. — ~-ji *of a middling quality* H[3] 28a.4. — ~-lā *the middle-finger* Vd 44a.5.

ḍathwo, *s.* = dathu H[2] 56a.6. — ~-ṭvāpal *the side of a mountain, a valley* (kaṭaka) CW 5.2. — ~-lā-kwo-lā *the palm of the hand* 8.65.

dadā, *s. an elder brother* V[1] 51b.6. — ~-kijā *brothers* H[3] 39a.4.

danakē (*caus. of* danē), *to let perform* P 62b.6.

ḍani, *see* **kuṁ-, lā-**.

danē, *v. i. to rise, to arise* M 16a.4; ratha(s) ~ *to get into a carriage* 37a.3; lasan ~ *to live in joy* Vi 81.19; *to grow up* (*a plant*) B 34b.6. — *v. t. to build, to erect* B 34a.6, *to appoint* N 26b.1; brat ~ *to perform a vow* Vi 170.35; kāryas ~ *to employ for a work* H[2] 56a.5. — che danē bhu *a building ground* CW 4.15.

dant [*S.*], *s. a tooth* V[1] 10a.5.

daṇḍ [*S. a staff* — —, *punishment*], *s. punishment* N 29a.2, ~ yāya *to punish* H[3] 14b.5. — ~ taya *to make a king* H[3] 56a.9. — *ifc.* **sāhu-**.

dandabā, *s. a kind of drum* (ḍiṇḍima) CW 1.65.

daṇḍalapē [daṇḍ], *v. t. to punish* N 32a.4.

dandhā, *s.* = dhandā Vi 161.8*.

dabu dabu, *s. a small drum* (ḍamaru) CW 1.65.

dabul, *s. a dancing place* CW 1.68.

dam-dam [*cf. H.* damādam *incessantly, continually, from Pers.*], *adv.* ~ dhāsēṃ *always* Vd 8b.3.

dambh [*M. pride*], ~ yāṅanaṃ *from vanity* N 34a.5*.

daya (*1st form:* data(ṃ), dato; *5th form:* dawo, do, du; *6th form:* dayā; datasā *a. so on*), *v. i. to be, to exist* V[1] 42b.5, *to happen* H[3] 23a.9; *to pass, to elapse* (*time*) Ś 168a.3; *to be possible* B 52a.6, yāya ~ *can* ... H[2] 17a.6, *may*... B 56b.11, *to have or to be to*... Vi 36.16. ch-hm-yā ~ *to have, to possess* H[1] 65a.5, ch-hm-yāta ~ *id.* C[1] 67; ma ~ *to be gone, to be lost* H[1]

64ᵇ.1, ma dayāwo conë *id.* H[3] 22ᵃ.4. dasëm̩ conë *to be, to exist (permanently)* H[2] 3ᵃ.6, dayāwo conë *id.* H[3] 26ᵃ.5. — dayiwo ma khu *it won't do* Vi 102.3, *it will cease* 104.11. — khanë daya *to become visible* Vd 6ᵃ.3. — daya *after 6th form denotes a completed action:* mocakā dawo *has killed* H[1] 85ᵇ.5.

dayakë (*caus. of* daya), *to cause to be or to exist: to make, to produce* N 41ᵇ.5, *to build, to erect* H[2] 75ᵃ.4; *to beget* H[3] 19ᵇ.8; *to procure* H[1] 7ᵃ.4; *to arrange* V[2] 78ᵇ.3; *to make possible* M 8ᵃ.5. — kalāt ~ *to take a wife* H[2] 105ᵇ.1, śilok ~ *to compose a verse* Ś 157ᵃ.5; wonë ~ *to permit to enter* M 10ᵃ.2. ma ~ *to lose* B 21ᵇ.8, *to make impossible* H[1] 67ᵇ.1; cet ma ~ *to lose heart* V[2] 42ᵇ.2, khanë ma ~ *to prevent being seen* Vi 117.26; ch-g ma dayakam̩ *without...* H[1] 87ᵃ.2, ~ ma dayakāwo *id.* V[2] 70ᵃ.4.

dayā[1] [*S. sympathy, compassion*], ~ yāya *to treat with gentleness* H[1] 39ᵇ.4; ~ cāya *id.* Ś 164ᵃ.4.

dayā[2], *adj. all:* ~ samastam̩ H[1] 51ᵇ.2.

dal[1] [*S. a small shoot or blade*], *s. a stalk* (nāla) C[1] 164*.

dal[2], *num.* = dwol H[1] 57ᵃ.5.

dalam̐ = datam̩ (*1st form of* daya) Bh 185ᵃ.6.

dalapati [*S.* dala *a body of troops*], *s. a commander of troops* V[1] 87ᵇ.5.

daridr [*S.*], *adj. poor, indigent* V[1] 130ᵃ.4. *s. poverty* H[1] 45ᵇ.1.

darth, jepanis darthan *at our expense*(?) V[2] 9ᵃ.4*.

dal-bi, *s. an earth-worm* (mahīlatā) CW 2.7.

darśan [*S. s. looking*], ~ yāya *to see, to behold (gen. term of respect)* H[1] 26ᵃ.4, *to visit* Vi 156.31; *to obtain* H[2] 18ᵇ.1. ~ lāya *to see, to behold* Bh 22ᵇ.2. ~ yācakë *to show* P 10ᵃ.3, yākë *id.* H[1] 3ᵇ.3; ~ biya *id.* Ś 165ᵃ.1, biyakë *to cause to be shown* (ch-hm-yāke *to...*) *ib.* 5. ~ dayu *there will be a rendez-vous* V[1] 35ᵃ.4.

daśā [*S.*], *s. want, distress* H[2] 99ᵃ.7.

daśu, *s. the stalk of a flower*(?) Vi 17.13.

dastul [*H.* dastūr *from Pers*], *s. custom, fashion* M 18ᵇ.1.

dah[1], *s. the property, left at a person's death* N 37ᵇ.5; ~ kāya *to inherit* 19ᵇ.7; ~ kāwo *an heir* 31ᵃ.8; dah-dāyad *id. ib.*

dah[2] [*S.* dah *to burn*], ~ yāya *v. t. to burn* Bh 51ᵇ.1; ~ ~ dhāsëm̩ *burning (from fever)* Vd 9ᵃ.1*.

daha(m̐) [*H.* dah *a river*], *s. a lake, pond* H[2] 77ᵃ.4. — dahan *id.* B 59ᵇ.7.

dahalapë [dah[2]], *v. t. to burn* V[2] 70ᵇ.7. *fig.* C[1] 289.

dām̐, *s.* = dām, *used as cl.-w.* M 8ᵇ.2*.

dāk, *s. fat* M 14ᵇ.5.

dākwo, *adj.* = dakwo H[1] 66ᵃ.2.

dācakë (*caus. of* dāya[5]) = dayakë N 14ᵇ.7. — dācakiwo (*ipr.*) *in regard to* 14ᵇ.2.

dā-ju [da-dā], *s. an elder brother* B 11ᵃ.8.

dātaby [*S. to be given*], ~ yāya *to give, to bestow* M 3ᵇ.5*.

dāti-hma, *s. a younger brother* V[2] 65ᵃ.4.

dān [*S. gift*], 1) ~ yāya *to give (term of respect)* N 47ᵇ.7; ~ biya *id.* M 5ᵇ.8, *to teach* N 19ᵃ.3; ~ kāya *to receive as gift* H[1] 17ᵃ.3. — 2) *toll* (śulka) N 16ᵇ.6; ~ thanë *to pay the toll, the duty* 47ᵃ.5.

dānapan [*S.* dāna *gift* + paṇa *compact*], *s. any sum of money, one is obliged to pay* N 16ᵇ.7.

dānāgān, *s. a debt* (ṛṇa) N 6ᵇ.1; ~ pulë *to pay one's debt* V[1] 95ᵃ.2, ~ biya *id.* N 2ᵃ.1. — dānāgānas kāya *won through a wager* 20ᵃ.7; dānāgānas jwoṅa(ṃ) kayā (*a debtor*) *pledged for debt* 20ᵃ.6.

dānë, *v. t. to appoint* (*to an office*) N 50ᵃ.2; *to direct* (ch-g-s *to a work*) 19ᵇ.5.

dān-ghāṭ, *s. a toll-house* N 47ᵃ.5.

dāpho-svān, *s.* = dvāpho-° P 43ᵃ.3*.

dām [*S.* dāman *gift*], *s. money* N 7ᵃ.4, *valuables* B 3ᵇ.8, *price* N 24ᵇ.4, *fee* (*of a harlot*) 22ᵇ.4; ~ biya *to give, to bestow* Vi 93.30, *to pay one's debt* B 24ᵇ.11.

dāya¹ (-l¹), *v. t. to beat, to strike* H³ 25ᵇ.3, *to flog, to thrash* (*for punishment*) N 53ᵃ.4; dāyāwo syāya *to beat to death* Ś 148ᵃ.1.

dāya² (-l¹), *v. t. to cook, to boil* Vd 46ᵇ.2.

dāya³ (-t), *v. t. to measure* B 34ᵃ.10. dāya bastu *s. a measure* (māna) N 48ᵇ.3.

dāya⁴ (-t), *v. i. to decay*(?) N 27ᵃ.4*.

dāya⁵ (-t; *mostly spelt* ḍāya), *v. i.* = daya N 37ᵇ.5. — dā-kāle *in regard to* 27ᵃ.5; dātaṅāwo *id.* 9ᵇ.2.

dāyakë , *caus. of* dāya¹ B 49ᵃ.2.

dāyakë², *caus. of* dāya² Vd 15ᵇ.4.

dāyat [*cf. S.* dāyāda], *s. a descendant, heir* N 5ᵇ.8.

dāl, *s. a granary or store-room* (koṣṭha) AH 68ᵇ.

dās [*S.*], *s. a servant, slave* H² 88ᵃ.5. — dāsī [*S.*], *s. a female servant* B 8ᵇ.1.

dāh [*S.* dāha *s. burning*], ~ yāya *to set on fire* H² 102ᵇ.1; ~ juya *to be burnt* Vi 175.5.

dāhalapë [dāh], *v. t. to burn* H² 102ᵇ.4; *to destroy by fire* (mi·s) B 69ᵃ.7; *fig.: to torture* (*subj.* śokan *pain*) H² 91ᵇ.1.

dāhā [*S.* dāha *s. burning,* — *heat*], *s. heat* (*from fever*) Vd 41ᵇ.4. ~ yāya *v. i. to burn* Bh 106ᵇ.7*.

dikë, *v. t. to put, to place* H² 82ᵃ.6, *to pour in* M 14ᵃ.5.

dikwo, *see* **dakwo**.

dikhalapë [*H.* dikhānā], *v. t. to shew, to point out* N 19ᵃ.4*.

dig [*H.*], *s. a quarter of the horizon* H² 96ᵇ.5.

digaphal, *s. name of a medicinal plant* Vd 15ᵇ.4.

digu, *s. porridge* (odana) AH 55ᵇ.

digdhalapë [*S.* digdha *mixed*], *v. t. to mix* H³ 36ᵃ.8*.

dig-pāl [*S.* dikpāla], *s. the guardian of a quarter of the sky* B 36ᵃ.9.

dicakë¹ (*caus. of* diya¹), gaṅāwo ~ *to stop, to make an end to* Bh 83ᵇ.3; kwosas ~ *to break a bone* N 44ᵃ.7.

dicakë² = dikë V¹ 10ᵃ.2.

ditakë = dicakë² M 32ᵇ.8.

dit-lā, *s. the month Āṣādha* CW 1.50.

didi, *s. a midwife* Ś 154ᵃ.7. — ~-aji *id.* 148ᵃ.7.

din [*S.*], *s. a day, see* **thani, hnu**; dinas *during the day* N 22ᵇ.2, din *adv. daily* Vd 22ᵃ.5; ~ swoya *to appear in public* B 19ᵃ.7. — ~-p(r)atiṃ *every day* V¹ 13ᵃ.5.

dīnār [*H. from Arab.*], *s. a dinar, ducate* N 53ᵇ.2.

dinë [= **linë**], *v. t. to cut off* M 32ᵇ.4; *to cut to pieces* B 14ᵃ.3; *to hurt, to wound* H³ 16ᵇ.9; ghālan ~ *to inflict a wound* H² 31ᵃ.5.

din-belā [*S.* dina + velā], *s. an auspicious day* B 58ᵇ.7.

dīpalapë [*S.* dīp *to shine*], *v. i. to be splendid* N 46ᵇ.9*.

dibā, *ifc.* **tvāk-**

diya¹ (-t), *v. i. to cease, to stop* H³ 40ᵇ.4, *to halt* Ś 168ᵇ.7.

diya² (-l¹), *v. i. to sit, to stay* B 25ᵃ.5.

diya³ (-t), *v. i. it suits, it pleases* (yāya, yāṅa(ṃ), yāṅāwo *to do*) Ś 147ᵃ.3.

diś [*S.*], *s. a quarter, region* N 26ᵇ.3.

di-sanë, 1) [diya²] *please!* H¹ 80ᵇ.5. — 2) [diya²] *sit down!, stay!* 81ᵃ.5.

disā [diya²], ~ conë *to sit down* P 13ᵃ.6.

diśā [*S.*], *s. a region, direction, quarter of the compass* M 32ª.2.

dihi = dehe N 28ª.6.

du[1], ~ kaya *to take, to make one's own* B 34ᵇ.5. — ~ kāya *to drag into* B 47ᵇ.12, *to draw in* (*arms and legs*; (*of a tortoise*) C[1] 107; *to let in, to admit* H[3] 35ᵇ.10; *to collect* C[1] 91; *to embrace, to adopt* H[3] 49ᵇ.4; *to confiscate* N 17ª.3, *to receive* (*stolen goods*) 50ª.1. — ~ kunë *to shut in* N 29ª.1; *to surround, to hem in* 22ª.7. — ~ choya *to send into* H[2] 18ª.4, *to put into* B 34ᵇ 5. — ~ taya *to put into* B 20ª.1; ch-hm-yāke ~ taya *to bring to...* 4ª 4 (du ti *ipr.*). — ~ teya *to throw into* N 13ᵇ.8. — ~ thë (= thaya) *to put into* Vd 37ᵇ.1; ~ thakë *caus.* 38ᵇ.5. — ~ thanë *to put or place into* B 51ª.5; *to conceal, to hide* 34ᵇ.5. — ~ danë *to belong* (ch-g-s *to...*) N 11ᵇ.3; *to be acquainted* (ch-g-s *with...*) 9ª.6. — ~ dāya (*milit.*) *to storm* H[2] 96ᵇ.7. — ~ piya (-t) *to lead into* Ś 161ᵇ.7. — ~ phiya *to initiate in* Vi 141.3; ch-hm-yā basās, *to get into one's power* H[2] 32ᵇ.3; lobhas, *to make desirous ib.* — ~ phvāya *to attack* Bh 42ᵇ.1. — ~ biya (-t) *to enter* H[1] 48ª.2. — ~ biya (-l[1]) *to fly into* N 42ª.5. — ~ beya (-l[1]) *id.* H[2] 43ᵇ.3. — ~ bvāya *to leap into* H[1] 67ᵇ.1; ch-hm-yāke, *to rush at...* H[2] 41ª.4. — ~ lāya *to have intercourse* (strīyāke *with a woman*) N 3ª.6. — ~ hāya *to go into, to enter* H[1] 95ª.2.

du[2] (*5th form of* daya), *is* B 20ª.8; *can, may* 34ᵇ.12. *gen.*: ma ~ *is not* V[2] 32ᵇ.3; *must not* Vi 160.27; *is impossible, can't be* C[2] 164. chan(aṃ) putr ma ~ *you have no son* V[1] 98ª.2; ṅeṅā ma ~ *has not heard* Ś 150ª.5; mantri ma du rājā *a king who has no minister* C[2] 249. — ma dusāṃ *if not is* M 3ᵇ.2; ma duṅās *id.* B 24ᵇ.6.

duwāli [*M.* duār *door-way*], *s. a door* B 33ᵇ.10. — duwāli *a door-keeper* 4ª.5.

du-wonë, *adv. in, in the interior of* (ch-g-yā, *a few times* ch-g) H[3] 71ª.2.

duḥkh [*S.*], *s. misfortune, harm, trouble*; ~ siya *to suffer misfortune* M 13ᵇ.5, ~ naya *id.* Bh 156ª.7; ~ lāya *to get into trouble* H[3] 38ª.2; ~ biya *to cause misfortune* V[1] 129ᵇ.1, duḥkhan kaya (ch-hm-yāta) *id.* Bh 136ª.3. duḥkh tāya *to be unhappy* Vi 171.1 duḥkhan kāwo *unhappy* V[1] 91ª.1.

duḥkhi [*S.* duḥkhin], *adj. unhappy, unfortunate* H[2] 89ª.7; ~-hma *id.* B 7ᵇ.5.

du-kaṇṭhagiri, *s. name of a plant* (bṛhalī) Md 4ᵇ.3.

dukh, *s.* = duḥkh V[1] 125ª.3.

dukho, *s. a mushroom* (aticchatra) AH 33ᵇ.

dugaṁ, °**gan** [*M.* dugun], ~ chi *adj. twofold, double* H[3] 34ᵇ.7; ch-g-yā ~ *twice as much or many as* Bh 46ᵇ.12.

dugu[1], *s. a goat* Ś 157ᵇ.6.

dugu[2] [*s.* du-gan], *adj. another, a second* Vi 172.21*.

dugu[3], ~-chāhā *the Ichneumon plant* AH 31ᵇ; ~-svān-hā *id.* Md 11ª.1.

dugu-kwos, *s. the back-bone* AH 41ª (~koy).

dugun = dugaṃ H[2] 100ᵇ.6.

dugon = dugaṃ N 25ᵇ.2.

dugwo, *s. milk* H[1] 39ª.2*.

dugn = dugaṃ Bh 21ᵇ.3.

ducaritr [*S.* duśca°], *s. misbehaviour* H[1] 13ᵇ.4.

ducutī, *s. something to sit upon, a seat* B 25ᵇ.10.

dūt [*S.*], *s. a messenger* H[2] 79ª.5. ~-jan *id.* 77ᵇ.5.

du-ta, ~ kaya *to draw in* (*breath*?) M 23ª.3. — ~ kāya *to let in, to admit* B 44ᵇ.6. — ~biya *to bring in* 50ᵇ.5. — ~ boṅaṃ haya *to bring* 4ª.8; ~ boṅaṃ yanë *id. ib.*, *to lead into* Bh 120ª.7. — ~yanë *to lead into* B 3ᵇ.5.

— ~haya *id.* M 9b.5; *to collect* C¹ 139.

du-tal, ~ wonë *to enter* B 4b.5.

du-të, *v. t. to bring* (ch-hm-yāke *or* ~-yāta *to somebody*) V¹ 89a.5. ~ haya *id.* B 4a.4.

du-thë, *adj. being or to be found somewhere* B 47b.7.

duthwo, *adj.,* ~ lukhā *the inner door* CW 4.9.

dudu, *s.* 1) *milk* Bh 42a.2. — 2) *the breast of a woman* C¹ 285; *an udder* Bh 19a.7. — ~-wo-si *name of a plant* (kṣīrikā?, ms: chhyiriká) AH 31a. — ~-kol-se *a medicinal plant* Vd 41b.4. — ~-guṇ *quality of milk* B 43a.3. — ~-cokā *the nipple of the breast* AH 41b. — ~-pāy *a breast* (vakṣa) *ib.* — ~-pipilī *the nipple of the breast* Ś 148b.4. — ~-makadi *name of a plant* (dugdhikā) Md 17a.3. — ~-mā *a nurse* N 34b.4. — *ifc.* **colas-, phasi-, manuṣy-, mes-, sā-.**

dudhal, *s. name of a medicinal plant* Vd 26a.4. — ~-se *id.* 28b.1. — ~-svān *the thorn-apple* AH 31b (dudha-swáng).

dunë¹, *v. i. to enter, to penetrate* (ch-g-s *into*...) Vi 36.26; jala's ~ *to dive into the water* Bh 22a.1. — *v. t. to start* (*a car*) Bh 113b.6.

dunë², *adv.* ch-g-yā ~ *in* (*the interior of*) C² 153; dunëwo pinëwo *inside and outside* H² 96b.5. — *s. the interior* CW 1.38, *the stomach* (koṣṭha) AH 68b.

duṁ-ta, ~ yanë = du-ta ~ H² 62a.3.

duṁ-taṁ [= du-ta], ~ haya *to take back* N 22a.1*.

dupola, *s.* 1) *name of a plant* (piṇyā) AH 32. — 2) = dupoloḍ 65b.

dupoloḍ, *s. a sort of gourd* (mahā-koṣātakī) Md 47a.4.

dumbal [*cf. S.* uḍumbara], *s.,* ~-si *Ficus glomerata* P 18a.2.

dumbwol-jā, *s. who eats from the same dish* (ekasthālīsahāya) N 11a.4, *an apprentice* (antevāsin) 2b.3*.

duya (-l¹), *v. t. to put into* B 58b.2, *to put* (*an arrow on the bow*) Vi 34.16; hnasas duyāwo dhālaṃ *he said it into his ear* H² 58b.9.

duy-jhaṅgal, *s. a skylark* CW 7.7.

du-lā [*cf. M.* duī *two*], *s. the second day of the lunar fortnight* AH 10b.

durālambh [*S.* durāla(m)bhā], *s. name of a plant* Vd 3a.1.

duli¹ [*cf. S.* doli], *s. a sedan-chair, palanquin* V¹ 128b.1.

duli², *s. the twelfth day of the lunar fortnight* AH 10b.

durg [*S.*], *s. a citadel, stronghold* H² 87b.4.

durjan [*S.*], *s. a villain, scoundrel* H¹ 47b.3.

durnapury(-svān), *s. a medicinal plant* Vd 14b.1.

durbal [*S.*], *adj. weak, feeble* H² 58b.3.

durbyār, ~ yāya *to act wickedly* H² 79a.8.

durmati [*S. bad disposition of mind*], *adj. ill disposed* H² 54a.4.

dulyā, *s.* = duli¹ Bh 173b.1.

durlabh [*S.*], *adj. difficult to obtain* H² 40b.7.

dūṣaṇ [*cf. S.* dūṣaṇa *adj. corrupting*], *s. fault, blemish* N 21b.2*.

duskh, *s.* = duḥkh Bh 22b.5.

duṣṭ [*S.*], *adj. bad, wicked, false* B 5b.5.

du-svān, *s. name of a plant* (bakula) Md 31a.5.

du-hā, ~ wonë *to go into* (ch-g(-s)) V² 36b.4; ~ bi-jyāya *id.* B 20b.2. — du-hāṅ wonë *id.* H² 87a.1.

dṛḍh [*S.*], thawo citt ~ yāya *to compose oneself* Bh 163b.1.

dṛṣṭi [*S.*], *s. a look* B 12b.5; anyony ~ julaṃ *they looked at each-other* (*with amorous eyes*) V¹ 16a.4.

dewo¹ [*S.* deva], *s. a god* Vi 74.16. — *ifc.* (*goddess!*) **katāmahli-**.

dewo², *s.* = dewol Vi 88.3 (caity-dewo).

dewodāl [*H.* deodār], *s. Cedrus Deodara* CW 6.18.

de-wonë, *adv.* ch-g-(yā) ~ *outside* M 7ª.1, *out of* 5ᵇ.2.

dewol [*H.* deval *a small temple*], *s. a temple, sanctuary* V¹ 56ª.1.

de-kākë, *v. t.* = dekë N 44ª.2.

dekë, *v. t. to cut off* N 51ᵇ.5; *to bite off* V¹ 37ᵇ.6.

deguli, *s. a charm, incantation* V¹ 125ᵇ.1.

dedalapë [*H.* der *delay*], *v. t. to defer, to postpone* V² 63ª.1*.

dedh = dr̥dh V¹ 14ᵇ.2.

ḍenik, ~-kāle *if it is badly written* N 8ᵇ.8*.

denë, *v. t. to cut off* N 44ª.2.

de-pālak, *s. a guard of the town* V² 28ª.1*.

deb [*cf. S.* devana *dice*], ~ jwoṅ *a gambler* N 48ᵇ.4*.

debaṅg [*cf. S.* Devāṅga *name of the inventor of wearing*], *s. a kind of silk* N 41ª.6*.

debatā [*S.*], *s. a deity* H² 95ª.2.

debadāru [*S.*], *s. Cedrus Deodara* Vd 2ª.6.

debī [*S.*], *s. a goddess* V¹ 58ª.4.

debik [*S.* daivika *coming from the gods*], *s. fate* N 16ᵇ.3*.

delapā, *adj.*, ~ lāhāt *the right hand* B 63ᵇ.12.

deś [*S.*], *s. a country* H² 50ª.5, *a town* B 11ᵇ.9, *a village* P 48ª.5.

deśanā [*S. instruction*], ~ yāya *to point out, to make known* (pari-diś) P 16ᵇ.3*.

deśāntar [*S.*], *s. a foreign country* V¹ 39ᵇ.10.

deh [*S.*], *s. a body* V¹ 25ᵇ.3.

dehe, ~ biya *to bring about* N 28ª.6 (dihi); ~ bisëṃ haya *to procure* B 36ᵇ.5. — ~ yāya *to make look like* Bh 13ª.5*.

daib [*S.*], *s. fate* H² 49ᵇ.1.

daiyub, *s. a deity* C¹ 270*.

dë¹, ch-g-s ~ chāya *to place into...* B 55ᵇ.8. — ~ jāya *to ascend* (ch-g-s *something*): saṃśayas ~ jāya *to fall into doubt* H¹ 15ᵇ.3*.

dë², *after num. -fold*; pë ~ *four-fold* H³ 34ᵇ.8; suya-në ~ *thirty-two-fold* N 52ᵇ.7.

dëcakë, *v. t.*, caraṇ ~ *to use as spy or detective* N 48ᵇ.7.

dën = dë² C¹ 297.

dënë, *v. i. to sleep* V¹ 36ª.2; dëṅaṃ conë *to be sleeping, to be asleep* B 7ª.5; dën wonë *to go to sleep* H³ 33ª.1. — dëṅā kwothā *a bed-room* CW 4.5; dënë lāsā *a bed* 8.92.

dë-lāsā, *s. a bed, couch to sleep upon* V¹ 50ᵇ.1.

do = du²; laṃkha ~ bu *a field where water exists* N 27ᵇ.2. — *gen.*: ma ~ = ma du H¹ 16ᵇ.4; ma do-guli *unattainable* 75ª.5; ...ma do-hma *who is not in possession of...* 19ª.5; ...ma doṅ ma do ...*does not exist* C¹ 156; ma dosa *as it is impossible* H¹ 6ᵇ.4. — ch-g-yā do·n *because of..., on account of...* 66ᵇ.5; swoya don *because* (*I*) *saw* Bh 65ª.3.

dokh [*S.* doṣa], *s. a fault, defect* N 32ª.3; ch-hm-yāke ~ yāya *to be maliciously disposed against...* H³ 37ᵇ.3. *instr.*: dokhan *on account of, owing to* (ch-g-yā) H¹ 55ᵇ.4.

dokhan, *s.* = dokh H¹ 22ᵇ.4; ~ thwolwo *a criminal* N 26ª.5.

dokhal, *s. name of a plant* (bhū-str̥ṇa) CW 6.37.

dokhi, *adj.* = duḥkhi H¹ 75ª.4*.

doṅgā, *s. a boat* CW 2.6.

dophukh, *s. name of a plant* (kāla-śāka) Md 48ª.3.

doman [*cf. H.* du-māni *a double meaning*], *s. doubt* AH 13ᵇ (domang).

ḍor, ~ wonë *to go to, to go into* (ch-g-s)(?) N 33b.7*.

dośāpāśā [*cf.* S. pāśa *dice*], *s. a die, dice* (akṣa) N 44b.2*.

do-se̥, *s. name of a plant* (tuṇḍakerī) AH 32a.

doh [*S.* droha *mischief; treachery*], ch-hm-yāke ~ yāya *to betray someone* H² 69b.4.

doha, *s. a bull* AH 56a.

dohalapë [*cf. S.* duh *to milk,* — *to take advantage of?*], *v. t.* dakṣiṇā ~ *to give reward* N 19a.8.

dohi¹ [*cf. S.* doha *milk, milking*], ~ kāya *to milk* N 21b.9.

dohi² = drohi?; ~-khu *a kind of thief* N 41a.3*.

dwo, *s. a heap, stack* CW 7.17; *a mound* B 3b.2. ~ cinë *to heap up* Vi 27.2. — *ifc.* **ghās-, na-.**

dwoṁ-gu, *s. stammering* AH 17b.

dwokā [dwo], *s. cross-roads* B 11b.2. — *ifc.* **bidyā-, la-.**

dwogi [*cf. S.* dva- *two*], misāwo ~ padārth *joint property (of a wife)* N 17a.8; ~-cand *adopted* (labdha) 40b.4, në-hmasaṃ dwogi dwogi-cand kāy *a son belonging both to the bījin and the kṣetrika* 33b.5; dwogi-puñjā *(property of) a commercial partnership* 16b.1. — dwogi *adv. jointly, in common* 40a.4.

dwocit [*cf. H.* ducittā *doubtful*], ~ yāya *to be doubtful, to waver* Bh 69a.1*.

dwonwoṁ, *adv.* ~ ma ~ *at all events*(?) N 3a.6*.

dwoya (-l¹), *v. t. to put (an arrow to the bow)* Bh 114a.3*.

dwol, *num. a thousand*; ~ chi *one thousand* V² 70a.2, në ~ *two thousand* H¹ 57a.5; jimkhu ~ sat chiwo cyā *16 108* Bh 173b.1.

dyāk [dyāya], *s. loss (in bargaining)* N 7b.8.

dyāṅī, *s. a fence* (vṛtti) N 28a.7, *an enbankment for the purpose of irrigation* (kedāra) 26a.6, *an artificial mound* (setu) 26b.4. — ~-kha(ṃ) *dispute about* — — 27a.4.

dyāya (-t), *v. t. to lose (money)* V¹ 94b.6.

draby [*S.*], *s. wealth, property* H¹ 64a.1.

drohi [*S.* drohin], *adj. treacherous, hostile* B 28a.5.

dvayakë = dayakë N 8b.8.

dvā, *s. a pot, pan* (piṭhara) AH 54b.

dvāwo, *adj.*, ~ kā *large tissue* N 25b.2*.

dvākā, *s.* = dhvākā AH 67b.

dvākwo, *adj.* = dakwo N 25a.4.

dvāpho-svān, *s. a kind of jasmine* (kunda) AH 30a.

dvāya (-t), *v. i.* = daya N 4a.4. — dvātaṃ *as for...* 18a.5.

dvāyakë (*caus. of* dvāya) = dayakë N 27a.4.

dvār [*S.*], *s. a door, gate* H² 93b.4; mebayā dvāran ṅenë *hear something through another* V² 69b.5. — **dvāli** *a door-keeper* V¹ 40a.6.

dviguṇ [*S.*], *adj. double, twofold* N 24a.4.

dveṣ [*S. hatred*], ~ yāya *to hate* H² 70b.4.

dh (ḍh).

dhaṁ-gu, *s. confirmation*(? niṣṭhā) AH 68b.

dhakaṁ [dhaya], *stands in the end of the oratio recta* (= *Sa.* iti) H¹ 62a.2. — **biya** ~ *with an intention to give* H² 113b.2; yāya ~ *in order to do they intended killing* 53b.3. — **chu** ~ B 13a.6; syāya ~ **tayā rājā-cā** *the prince why?* 34b.7; thathë ~ *thus* P 10b.1. — **dhakāwo** = **dhakaṃ** B 27a.10; **dhakā** *id.* 59a.4.

dhago-cā, *s. a spoon* AH 55a.

dhacu, *adj. dried up, shrunk*(?) Vd 14ª.4.

dhan [*S.*], *s. riches, wealth* H¹ 11ᵇ.4, *fortune, property* N 2ª.7. — **~-byāhār** *lending of money* C² 250. — **~-śāsti** *a fine* N 53ª.2.

dhanaku, *s.* = dhanukh M 22ª.2*.

dhanabant [*S. adj.*], *adj. rich, wealthy* H² 49ª.7. — *s. wealth, riches* 3ᵇ.6.

dhanādy [*S.* dhanāḍhya], *adj. rich, opulent* Vi 33.27.

dhani [*S.* dhanin], *adj. rich* V¹ 74ª.5. *s. a rich man* H¹ 56ª.1, *a merchant* H² 36ᵇ.5; *a creditor* N 2ª.8.

dhanik [*S.*], *s. a rich man* N 5ª.6; *a creditor* 17ᵇ.4.

dhanu [*S.*], *s. a bow* (*for shooting*) Bh 99ᵇ.2; *a measure of length* 62ª.6.

dhanuk, *s. a bow* (*for shooting*) Ś 155ᵇ.1. — dhanukh *s. id.* H² 76ª.4.

dhanĕ, *v. i.*, cha-khe ~ *to keep to oneself*(?) Ś 157ᵇ.2. no ~ *to be taken with giddiness*(?) N 17ᵇ.6.

dhandā [*H. work, occupation*], *s. embarassement, dismay, perplexity* H² 81ª.1; ~ kāya *to be perplexed or dismayed* B 4ª.1, ~ kaya *id.* M 9ª.1. āmo ~ kāya chāy *why be so dismayed* Ś 166ª.5.

dhandhā, *s.* = dhandā Ś 163ᵇ.6. — *ifc.* **śok-**.

dhany [*S.*], *adj. happy* Ś 163ª.3.

dhap, *s.* = dhal-pa H³ 12ª.7. — *ifc.* **jati-**.

dhaban-bi, *s. a variegated snake* AH 19ª.

dhay, *s. a worm, an insect* (svedaja) AH 65ª.

dhaya (-l¹), *v. t.* = dhāya¹ H³ 19ᵇ.10.

dhal, *s. a channel, water course* CW 2.4. — dhalaṇ jāwo *well-watered* CW 3.4 (dhalaṃ-~).

dhalaṁ~dhā, *adj. firm*(? dṛḍha) AH 69ª.

dhalapĕ, *v. t.* = dhalalapĕ N 24ᵇ.1*.

dhalay [*M.* dhar *to hold, grasp, keep*], ~ yāya *to perform* (*a ceremony*) Vi 94.32.

dhalalapĕ [*M.* dhar *to hold, grasp, keep*], *v. t. to bear, to carry* Bh 139ᵇ.4; *to keep, to observe* (*law etc.*) H¹ 38ᵇ.1; doṣ ~ *to have faults* H³ 12ª.1; śāstr ~ *to study the śāstras* C¹ 2; -rup ~ *to take the form of*... Bh 62ᵇ.6; gati ~ *to beat, to throb* (*pulse*) Vd 3ᵇ.5; silas ~ *to keep in one's mind* V¹ 43ª.4. — *v. i.* simān ~ *to keep within the boundaries* C¹ 208; narakas ~ *to go to hell* P 23ᵇ.3.

dhalī, *s. coagulated milk* C¹ 40. — **~-ti** *buttermilk* Vd 22ª.2. — **~-thyākā** *a jar with coagulated milk* H³ 43ª.2. — *ifc.* **sā-**.

dhaliṅ, *s. a post, pillar* H³ 25ª.1.

dhali-svān, *s.* = dhāli-° Vd 50ᵇ.5.

dhal-wā, *s. a rain of saliva* (?) Vi 131.17*.

dhal-pa, *s.* = dhal-pwo H³ 12ª.6.

dhal-pwo, *s. a pot, vessel* Bh 12ª.7. — *ifc.* **cā-**, **laṁkha-**.

dharm [*S.*], *s. piety, righteousness* H² 50ª.2; *religious merit* N 29ᵇ.6.

dhā¹, *cl.-w., mod.* = dhāl¹ Ś 145ᵇ.3.

dhā-² (-n *or* -t? *only:* dhāṅāwo), *see* **kwo**.

dhāk [*M.* ḍhāk], *s. a large kind of drum* Vi 151.2.

dhākaḍ, *s. the son of a Śūdra-woman* N 11ª.5*.

dhāt, *s.* = dhāṃt V¹ 32ᵇ.1.

dhātuli, *s. name of several plants:* khāyu ~ (kośātakī) Md 47ª.2, māku ~ (rājakośātakī) *ib.* 3.

ḍhāḍakaṁ, ch-g s ~ jwoya *to infest a place* (*robbers, etc.*) N 48ᵇ.6*.

dhā-dhā, ~ yāya *to beat* (*repeatedly*), *to knock* H² 36ª.5.

dhāṁt, *s. a thief, robber*(?) V² 21ª.3*.

dhābay [*S.* dhāv *to run*], ~ yāya *to run* H³ 16ª.3. — dhābalapĕ *id.* H¹ 88ª.5.

dhāminī [*H.* dhāman *a bamboo, from which bows are made*], *s. name of a plant* (dhanvaga) Md 38[a].8.

dhāya[1] (-l[1]), *v. t. to say, to speak* (*before or after oratio recta*) H[1] 79[b].1, *to tell* V[2] 37[b].7, *to call, to name* H[1] 75[a].1. — (dhakaṃ) dhāyā *by name* 72[b].2, dhāyā nām *id.* 55[a].3; gathē dhālasā *as it is said* 3[b].2 (*usually interrogatifs with* **dhālasā** *are used in the sense of: for, or = our colon; lit.: "if you say how, why etc. (then I tell you)"* Vi 41.10); naya ma dhāsēṃ *not to speak of eating* Vi 111.10. — *Some forms of* dhāya *are used merely emphatically:* bidyā dhāyā = bidyā H[1] 2[a].4; tonēṃ ma dhāyā *I have nothing to drink* Vi 106.27; chatāṃ dhāyaṃ ma *nothing at all* V[2] 74[b].6.

dhāya[2] (-l[1]), *v. t. to beat, to knock* H[3] 13[b].3.

dhāyakē (*caus. of* dhāya[1]), *to (suffer oneself to) be called* Vi 4[a].3.

dhāl[1] [*H. a stream, current*], *cl. w.* Vi 98.10. — cha dhāranaṃ *at once* Vd 32[a].2. — *ifc.* **khwobi-, hi-, hiti-.**

dhāl[2] [*M.* ḍhāl], *s. a shield* Bh 106[b].4.

dhālat, *s.* = dhāl[2] H[2] 88[a].8.

dhāraṇā [*S. the act of holding*], prāṇ ~ yāya *to keep oneself alive* H[2] 84[a].3; mantran ~ yāya *to incantate* Bh 99[a].1.

dhāramuṁd, ~ jwoya *to appear in bad company*(?) N 42[a].2*.

dhārā[1] [*H.* dhār *a stream, current*], *s. a river* N 27[a].7. — *ifc.* **jal-, laṁkha-, su-sal-.**

dhārā[2] [*H.* dhār], *s. the edge* (*of a sword*) H[3] 87[b].1.

dhāli-svān, *s. Grislea tomentosa* (dhātakī) Md 13[b].2.

dhāle[1], *s. pome-granate* B 35[b].6. — ~-mā *a pome-granate tree* 35[a].10. — ~-pati-svān *id.* (dāḍima) AH 29.

dhāle[2] [dhāya[1]], *emphasizing part., even, just* (*lit.: "if you say"*) H[2] 66[b].1.

dhāhā-dewo, *n. pr. Hara* C[1] 255*.

dhi, *s. a rope, chain*(?) N 53[a].4*.

dhik, *s. the bank* (*of a river*) H[3] 38[b].8, *the coast* (*of the sea*) Vi 83.8. — *ifc.* **khusi-.**

dhikkār [*S. reproach, contempt*], *adj. vain, futile; contemptible* B 24[a].7.

dhiti [*S.* dhṛti], *s. firmness, resolution* H[1] 16[a].5*.

dhitkār = dhikkār Bh 101[a].5.

dhi-dhi, ~ yāya *to knock* B 43[b].1*.

dhinē, *v. t.* = dhēnē B 63[a].6.

dhir [*S. adj. steady*], *s. steadiness* Vi.

dhirj = dhairy; citt ~ yāya *to compose oneself* M 12[a].7.

dhiry = dhairy Ś 154[b].6; ch-hm-yāta ~ biya *to compose, to reassure* Vi 43.18. — ~-bal *firmness, fastness* M 34[a].3.

dhu[1], *s. a tiger* H[1] 16[a].1. — *ifc.* **cha-sipol-, ti-.**

dhu[2], *s. length* B 4[a].3.

dhu[3] = du[3] B 13[b].10.

ḍhukaṭ, ~ yāya *to meet, to assemble* (?) N 49[a].1*.

dhukuti [*cf. H.* dhukṛī *purse*], *s. a treasure*(?) Bh 184[a].5*.

dhuk-svān, *s. name of a plant* (nāgāhvā) Md 18[a].3.

dhunakē (*caus. of* dhunē) = *simpl.* 1) V[1] 10[a].3. — 2) naya dhunakāwo *having finished eating* V[2] 17[a].6.

dhunē, *v. t.* 1) *to finish, to complete* B 42[b].2. — 2) *in connection with the 4th form of a verb denoting that an action is completed:* ṅenē dhuna (*I*) *have heard* H[1] 51[b].3.

dhup [*S.* dhūpa], *s. incense;* ~ thanē *to burn incense* Vi 18.30.

dhupi, *s. a medicinal plant* Vd 37[b].1.

dhu-puruṣ, *s. a wicked person* (?) N 12[a].2*.

dhubiyā [dhobi], *s. a washerman* H[2] 76[a].1.

dhul[1], *s. dust* Bh 69[a].1. — *ifc.* **svān-**.

dhūl[2], ~ mi kuṅāwo *not to be recognized* B 38[b].9.

dhulë, *see* **tok**.

dhūrt [*S.*], *s. a rogue, knave* H[2] 108[b].8.

dhusalapë [*H.* dhūsnā *to beat, to punish*], *v. t. to offend, to slander; only:* dhusalapaṃ *in an offensive way* N 10[b].6.

dhusi [*cf.* jal-dhu], *adj. hunch-backed* C[1] 238.

dhusu, *s. roasted meat* (**śūlya**) AH 55[b].

dhe-dhe, ~ culë *v. i. to rock, to shake* Bh 12[a].3.

dheyan [*cf. S.* adhyayana], *s. studying* H[1] 16[a].4*.

dheṣ [*cf. S.* dveṣa], *s. hatred* N 4[b].3.

dhairy [*S. firmness*], ~ yāya *to be composed, to be steadfast* H[2] 16[a].6.

dhëk, *s. envy* CW 1.72.

dhë-kāke, *v. t. to cut off* N 13[b].7.

dhënakë, *caus. of* dhënë Vi 44.6.

dhënë, *v. t. to cut (off)* B 40[b].6. *fig. to destroy (a hope)* Bh 45[a].4. — dhënë-gu *s. a sickle* AH 53[b].

dhësal, *s. the bank (of a river)* Bh 12[a].4.

dhok, ~ phalakaṃ choya *to push* (ch-g-s *into*...) V[2] 17[a].3; ~ phelakaṃ ~ *id.* V[1] 26[a].3*.

dhoġi, *adj. musty, smelling of raw meat* (visra) AH 14[b].

dhobi [*M.*], *s. a washerman* V[1] 56[a].6. — dhobini *s. a washer-woman ib.*

dhoya, *v. t. to break through (a fence)* N 28[b].4*.

dholkhi-kāk-jhaṅgal, *s. a sea eagle* CW 7.10.

dhauti [*S.* dhauta *washed*], ~ cāya *to wash, to bath* P 16[a].1.

dhwoṁl, *s.* = dhwol H[2] 96[b].2.

dhwok-hma, *adj. eldest* V[1] 112[b].3.

dhwok-svān [= dhuk-°?], *s. a plant the root of which is used in medicine* Vd 27[b].3*.

dhwokwo-hma, *adj.* = dhwok-hma N 37[b].8.

dhwod, *s.* = dhwol H[2] 51[a].1.

dhwon, cha ~...në ~ *the first time... the second time* N 25[a].3*.

dhwoṁḍ, *s.* = dhwod H[2] 84$_2$[b].3.

dhwom-colas, *s. a kind of goat* Vd 36[a].3*.

dhwol, *s. a jackal* H[1] 46[b].4. — ~-bathān *a pack of jackals* H[2] 84[b].7.

dhyabā, *s. a coin, money* B 50[b].11.

dhyān [*S.*], *s. meditaion* B 46[b].7; ~ yāya *to meditate* V[1] 100[b].2.

dhyābalapë [*cf. S.* dhyāyati], *v. t. to consider* V[1] 28[b].1, *to think of* Bh 16[b].5, *to meditate* 95[b].4. dhyābalapaṃ ṅenë *to study* H[1] 17[a].4.

dhyāya (-t), *see* **kuṭ**.

dhvaṁsalapë [*S.* dhvaṃs *to decay*], *v. t. to destroy* N 41[a].4.

dhvākā, *s. a city gate* H[2] 96[b].5; dhvākāyā phal *a terrace before a house-door* AH 24[b]. — ~-phusa *a watch-tower* 25[a].

dhvāku-hma, *adj.* = dhwok-hma N 38[a].9.

dhvākhā, *s.* = dhvākā Bh 98[a].1; ~-pi-laṃ *the chief road through a village* AH 24[a].

n.

na[1], *s. smell, odour* V[2] 32[a].4. ~ tuya *v. t. to smell* H[3] 53[a].8, ~ tāya *to perceive a smell* V[2] 32[a].1. — *ifc.* **svān-**.

na[2], *s. morning;* ~ saṅāwo *when the morning dawns, when the day is breaking* H[1] 43[b].4, ~ sanakāwo *id.* H[2] 32[b].7.

na[3], *s. iron* B 59[a].3; nayā *made of iron* M 4[a].5.

na'u [*EH.* nauā, nāu], *s. a barber* H[2] 63[b].1.

na'uni (*subj.* na'uninin *and* na'uninan), *s. the wife of a barber* B 40b.5.

nawol [*cf. S.* nakula], *s. an ichneumon* H³ 54a.2. ~-cā *dimin.* H² 101b.6.

-naṁ, *see* **-nwoṁ**.

naka, *adv. this moment, just now* C¹ 296; nakas *at first, at the beginning* N 43a.3; nakan nisẽṃ *from the beginning* Vd 10b.1; naka yaṃ-tol *at once* N 20a.2.

na-karmi, *s. a smith* B 57a.2.

na-kālan, *adv. early in the morning* M 22a.1 (na-kāraṇ).

naki, *s. name of a plant* (nakha) CW 6.32.

nakiṁ, ~-cā *an old woman* HP 82.35a, ~-ju *id. ib.*

nakẽ (*caus. of* naya), *to let eat* V¹ 9b.2; *to feed* B 32b.2.

nakhi, *s. iron* Md 33a.4. — ~-pati *an iron plate* Vd 35a.1.

nagar [*S.*], *s. a town* V² 48b.1. — ~-cā *a small town* M 7a.5. — *ifc.* **kacā-**.

nagarī [*S.*], *s. a town* V¹ 59a.4.

nagu, *s. a star* (nakṣatra) CW 1.44.

nagn [*S.*], *adj. naked* H² 41a.2.

naṅā-gu, *s. thunder* CW 1.40.

naṅkyāl, *s. an ingredient of medicine* Vd 28b.2.

naciniyā [*cf. M.* nacanihār], *s. an actor, dancer* N 11a.4.

na-tu, *part.* = tu⁴ H¹ 68b.2.

natuwā [M. naṭvā *dancing boy*], *s. a dancer* B 46b.3, natuwāni *a dancing-girl* 22a.3, natuwā-misā *id.* 20a.12.

natrawā *s.* = natuwā V¹ 113a.4.

na-thẽṅ, *s. an iron club* AH 52a.

nadī¹ [*S.*], *s. a river* H³ 75a.1.

naḍī², *s. a public dancer* N 11a.5*.

na-dwo, *s. a mass of iron* M 4a.4.

na-dhā, *adj. bad smelling* CW 1.55.

nanā, *adv. once for all* N 31b.6. — nanānaṃ *adv. quickly, soon, at once* C¹ 126; nanāṃ *id.* H³ 29b.2.

nanẽ (*only:* naṅ, naṅā) *perhaps: to dream; used only in cases like this:* gwo belasaṃ swoya nāpaṃ ma naṅā ratn *a jewel I had never even dreamt of seeing* B 3a.1.

nani, *s. a town* B 41a.5, ~-katak *inhabitants of a t°* 45b.3, ~-cā *a small town* Vi 67.34.

nan-milā, *s. moonshine* CW 1.43.

napā = nāpa V¹.

napuṁsak [*S.*], *s. an eunuch* H³ 39a.5.

namaskār [*S. adoration, homage*], ~ yāya *to pay homage* (ch-hm-yāke *to*...) Bh 184b.3. namaskāra(ṃ) *used as verb. fin.* Vi 79.28; namaskā *id.*

na(ṁ)p-kāy, *s. a kṣetraja* N 38b.3.

naya (-l¹), *v. t. to eat* H¹ 19b.5, (*fire*) *to consume* H³ 96b.6. strī ~ *to enjoy a woman* H¹ 64a.4; cupā ~ *to kiss* V² 24a.5; duḥkh ~ *to suffer distress* M 28b.6. — nayuwo *s. an eater* H¹ 33a.3; naya *s. food* 20b.5.

nayakākẽ, *caus. of* naya V¹ 91b.6.

nay-khiṁ, *s. a sort of drum* Vi 151.2.

nal [*H. tube, pipe*], *s. a vein, artery* Bh 179b.5. — *ifc.* **pẽt-**, **hi-**.

narak [*S.*], *s. hell* N 52b.7.

nali¹, *s. ashes* C¹ 281.

nali², ~ ma saṃ-gwo *shy, timorous* (śālīna) N 30b.8.

nal-si, *s. name of a plant* (tiniśa) Md 38a.2.

na-sā¹, *s. food* V² 25a.5.

na-sā² = na-svāk C¹ 190.

na-sāk = na-svāk 1) Ś 169b.3. 2) *name of a plant* (māṃsī) CW 7.33.

na-sācakẽ [na-sāk], *v. t. to make sweet-scented* C² 190*.

na-sikhal, *s. an iron chain* Bh 54b.5.

na-su, *s. an iron rod* N 43b.9.

nas-cātis, *adv. in the morning* B 8a.11.

naṣṭ [*S.*], ~ juya *to perish* H³ 87a.3; ~-chāyā mantr *a mantra to make oneself invisible* Vi 135.18.

na-svāk 1) *adj. sweet-scented, fra-*

grant H[3] 100^{b}.8. *s. sweet scent, fragrance* B 49^{a}.5. 2) *name of several plants* (sahakāra, saptalā) AH 32^{b}.

nā[1], *s. water* AH 20^{a}.

nā[2], *s.* = na[1] V[1].

nā[3] = nāyo H[1] 7^{a}.1.

nāku, *s. membrum virile* AH 41^{b}.

nāk-chekani, *s. a medicinal plant* Vd 34^{a}.2.

nāgapāc [*S.* nāgapāśa], *s. the weapon of Varuṇa* Bh 100^{a}.1*.

nāth [*S.*], *s. a lord, husband* Bh 15^{b}.7.

nāḍ [*S.* nāla (*hollow*) *stalk* (*of a lotus*)], *s. ifc.* **palë-.**

nāḍi[1] [*S.*], *s. a vein, artery* Vd 42^{a}.4.

nāḍi[2], *s.* = nābhi P 4^{b}.2*.

nānā [*S.*], *adj. various, different* H[3] 9^{b}.7.

nān-se, *s. name of a plant used in medicine* Vd 50^{b}.5*.

nāpa [= nāpaṃ], ~ wonë *to come along with* Vi 68.9. — ~ chyāya *to put together, to join* (ch-g-wo ch-g-wo) M 38^{a}.4. — ~ jyāya *v. i. to unite* M 34^{b}.5, *to meet* Vi 159.10; ch-g-wo ~ *to be mixed with* Md 55^{b}.7. — ~ taya *to put together, to join* (ch-g-wo ch-g-wo) H[3] 38^{b}.1. — ~ lāya *to go, to proceed* H[1] 80^{a}.3; ch-hm-wo ~ *to go to...* 37^{a}.4, *to meet* 43^{a}.2; ch-hm ~ *to meet, to come across* V[2] 33^{a}.4, *to reach, to keep up with* Vi 34.15; *to meet, to assemble* H[2] 45^{b}.4. — ~ lācakë *to lead to* B 11^{a}.15, *to cause to meet* H[3] 47^{a}.3; ~ latakë *id.* Vi 161.26; ~ lākë *to put together (hands)* Vi 77.8. — ~ hanë *to unite, to put together* C[2] 152.

nāpa(ṁ), *adv.* 1) *completely* H[3] 34^{a}.1; ~...ma *not at all* Vi 34.4. 2) *mutually* H[1] 43^{a}.1; *together, jointly* B 65^{a}.6; *also, too* H[2] 89^{b}.5. ch-hm-wo ~ *together with...* V[1] 97^{b}.3, ch-hm-n *id.* V[2] 11^{a}.5; ch-hm-s *id.* Vi 162.14. ch-hm-wo nāpa-hma *being together with, the companion of...* B 66^{b}.5.

nāpik [*cf. Mr.* nāpīk (*for* nāpit)], *s. a barber* Vi 44.5. — nāpit [*S.*], *s. id.* H[2] 92^{b}.5*.

nābhi [*S.*], *s. the navel* Vd 10^{a}.4; nābhis coṅ bāyu *samāna* (*one of the five vital airs*) AH 6^{b}.

nām[1] (*S.* nāman], *s. a name* H[2] 10^{a}.6; ch-hm-yā ~ kāya *to name* B 43^{a}.9, *to call* 58^{b}.3, *to invoke* Vi 30.15; ~ chuya *to give a name* Bh 12^{a}.6; ~ danë *to be called* M 30^{b}.8.

nām[2], *s. a ship* V[1] 37^{b}.1. — nāma-wāl, *s. a shipmaster* CW 2.6.

nāy[1] [*cf. S.* nāga], *s. a serpent* N 49^{a}.4.

nāy[2], *s. a seller of flesh* (māṃsavikrī)(?) P 26^{a}.1*.

nāyi(wo), *adj.* = nāyu C[1] 240.

nāyikë, *v. t. to make mild* Vd 45^{a}.1*.

nāyu, *adj. soft, mild, lenient* C[1] 241; nāyuwo *id.* 240.

nāyo [*old ipr. of* nālë], *take* (*it*)! B 30^{a}.6; tiwo ~ *adorn yourself quickly* Ś 169^{a}.3.

nāy-bāhālaṁ, *s. a serpent-demon* CW 2.1.

nāl, *s. mud, clay* C[1] 199.

nālikyāl [*S.* nārikela], *s. a cocoa-nut* C[2] 212*.

nālu-col, *s. a pulse of hemp* C[1] 290.

nālë, *v. t. to recover* (*one's property*) N 5^{a}.7; mitr ~ *to form a friendship* B 62^{b}.8; puruṣ ~ *to take a husband* N 33^{a}.6; twoho ~ *to find an excuse* 32^{a}.2.

nāś [*S. loss, disappearance*], ~ juya *to perish, to be lost* H[2] 15^{a}.5. — *alone without* juya: (*a disease*) *ceases* Vd 13^{b}.6.

nāsalapë [nāś], *v. i.* nāsalapaṃ wonë *to cease* (*a disease*) Vd 18^{a}.2.

nāsi, *s. the privy parts of a woman* AH 41^{b}.

nāsti [*S.* nâsti *is not*], ~ juya *to perish* H[2] 48^{b}.2.

nāhā, *s. name of a plant* (saivāla) AH 22ᵃ.

nāhā-wā, *s.* 1) *wild rice* AH 54ᵇ. — 2) *new grain* Md 67ᵃ.3.

nāhāl, *s. a quiver* Bh 99ᵃ.4.

nāhālu, *s. name of a plant* (jambāla) AH 23ᵇ.

ni[1], *s. a rope, chain* H[1] 27ᵃ.4. — *ifc.* **sas-**.

ni[2], *prt. the meaning of which it is difficult to define: just, before all* H[1] 37ᵇ.4.

ni[3], *s. a sun* CW, Einl. p. 547.

ni[4], *num.* = nē H[3] 52ᵃ.2; ~-hma V[2] 61ᵃ.7; ~-hma-hma M 8ᵇ.3.

ni[5], *s.* = na[4] Ś 156ᵇ.6*.

ni-āśrā [*cf. S.* nir-āśa *and Ne.* āśrā], *adj. hopeless, desperate* Bh 69ᵃ.1*.

niwo, *ipr. of* naya H[3] 54ᵃ.10.

niṁ-ga [niṅ?], *s. a praiseworthy form of marriage*(?) N 38ᵃ.5*.

niḥśaṅkā = nisaṅkā H[2] 80ᵇ.7.

nik, ~ jāyakaṃ *unsurmountable* N 28ᵇ.4*.

ni-kaṁ, *part.* = ni[2] Vi 33.33.

nikaruṇā [*S.* niṣkaruṇa], *adj. pitiless, unmerciful* H[2] 108ᵇ.8*.

nikarṣan [*S.* nikaṣaṇa *rubbing* (*on the touch-stone*)], ~ yāya *fig. to use as a touch-stone* H[2] 57ᵃ.4*.

ni-guli, *s.* 1) *a pair* CW 7.16. — 2) *the privy parts* 8.58.

ni-gwo [niṅ], *healthy food* C[2] 146.

nigrah [*S.*], ~ yāya *to keep down, to restrain* H[2] 50ᵃ.2.

niṅ, *adj.* = ṅiṅ C[2] 119.

ni-tā, *num.* = ni[4] Vd 4ᵃ.6.

nīti [*S.*], *s. moral precepts* H[1] 28ᵃ.1.

nity [*S.* nṛtya], *s. dancing* V[1] 56ᵃ.3.

nityayā-thēṁ [*S.* nityam], *adv. always* H[2] 31ᵇ.2.

nidān[1] [*S.* —, *cause, motiv*], ~ yāya *to take care off, to keep orderly* H[2] 76ᵇ.2, ch-g-s *id.* B 1ᵇ.4.

nidān[2] [*H.*], *s. medical diagnosis* Vd 3ᵇ.5.

nidrā [*S.*], *s. sleep* H[3] 88ᵃ.3. — ~ yāya *to sleep* Bh 104ᵇ.1; ch-hm-yā ~ wowo *someone falls asleep* V[1] 19ᵃ.3, ch-hm-yā ~ juwo *id.* Ś 144ᵇ.7. — ~ *error for* nindā C[1] 37.

nin = niṅ H[2] 94ᵃ.1. ~ kha *truth* CW 1.59; ~-hma *chaste* 8.25.

ninakē [niṅ], *v. t.* cāku ~ *to make savoury or palatable* Vd 48ᵃ.2.

nini, *s. the husband's sister* P 60ᵇ.3, *the father's sister* N 34ᵇ.4.

nindalapē [*S.* nind-], *v. t. to blame, to reproach* Bh 57ᵃ.7.

nindā [*S. reproach*], ~ yāya *to treat with contempt* H[2] 107ᵃ.6.

nip, *s. a Nimba-tree* Vd 41ᵇ.1.

nipun [*S. adj.* nipuṇa *skillfull*], ~ kāya *to examine* (*thoroughly*) H[2] 10ᵃ.7, ~ yāya *id.* H[3] 5ᵇ.6.

nip-cikan, *s. oil from the Nimba-tree* Vd 15ᵃ.5. — ~-col *pulse from that* 15ᵃ.5.

nip-si, *s.* = nip P 30ᵇ.5; ~-simā *id.* CW 6.20.

nibastran [*S. adj.* nirvastra], *adv. with nothing on* B 18ᵃ.2.

ni-bāl, *adv. twice* Vi 33.33.

nibodhi [*S.* nirbuddhi], *adj. ignorant, stupid* Ś 147ᵇ.7.

ni-bhāl, *s. the sun* C[1] 149, *sunshine* C[1] 135.

nimitt [*S.*], *s. cause, reason* Vi 59.32; ch-hm-yā, ch-g-(yā) nimittin (°ttan, °ttis, °tt) *for the sake of* H[1] 17ᵇ.3; swoya(yā) ~ *in order to see* H[2] 83ᵃ.4; ṅeṅā ~ *because* (*he*) *had heard* Bh 16ᵇ.5. thwote(yā) ~ *therefore* P 40ᵇ.4; chu(yā) ~ *why?* Vi 124.14.

nimbal-si, *s. a Nimba-tree* C[1] 153*.

ni-hmati-puli [= nē-°], *s.*, kwokh ~ *a pair of crows* H[3] 35ᵃ.1; ~ *copulation* CW 7.16.

niya[1], *num. twenty* M 10ᵃ.5.

niya[2], *v. t.* = nēya Vd 7ᵇ.3.

niya-tā, *num.* = niya[1] C[1] 128.

nir, *adj. bad* H[1] 9[b].4*.

niradoṣi [*S.* nirdoṣin], *adj. innocent* N 49[b].3.

nirabarṇ [*S.* nīlavarṇa], *adj. blue-coloured* Vd 44[b].5.

nirabāhalapë [*S.* nirvāhaya- *to perform, to accomplish*], *v. t. to settle* (*the law*) N 46[a].1.*

nirāmāsi [*cf. S.* nirāmiṣāśin], ~ **yāya** *to eat no flesh* H[1] 38[b].1.

nilās, *s.* = nilāsā V[1] 14[a].6.

nilāsā [*S.* nirāśa], *s. hopelessness* H[1] 24[b].1; ~ juya *to lose hope* H[2] 48[b].3, ~ yāya *id.* H[1] 95[b].4.

nirāhār [*S. want of food, fasting*], ~ yāya *to abstain from food, to faste* H[2] 34[a].6.

nirūp [*S.* ni-rūp- *to search, to examinate*], ~ yāya *to prove, to examinate* H[2] 14[a].4; *to search; to aspire to* H[1] 87[b].1; ch-hm-yāke ~ ~ *to remind someone* (*of his obligations etc.*) N 14[b].6.

nirūpanā [*S.* nirūpaṇa *searching, examination*], ~ yāya *to search* H[3] 20[b].1; *to take into consideration* 29[b].10.

nirūpalapë [nirūp], *v. t. to prove, to examinate* N 24[b].6, *to reason* 10[b].66; *to remind* (*of one's obligations etc.*) 14[b].7.

niroġ [*S.* niroga], *adj. free from sickness* Vd 50[a].6; nirogi *id.* H[2] 5[a].1.

nilobh [*S.* nirlobha], *adj. free from desire* H[1] 40[a].4. nilobhi *id.* 79[b].2.

nirjan [*S.*], *adj. deserted, desolate* H[1] 70[a].3.

nirṇay [*S.*] *s. decision* H[2] 68[b].1. ~ **yāya** *to decide* V[1] 23[b].4.

nirnān, ~ yāya *to refresh, to comfort* H[2] 42[b].7*.

nirmal [*S.*], *adj. spotless, unstained, pure* H[2] 75[b].3; ~ yāya *to be pure* N 47[b].5.

nirmit [*S. formed, constructed*], ~ yāya *to make, to form* H[1] 29[b].2.

niryās, ~ yāya *to prevent* N 26[a].1*.

nirlajjā [*S. adj.* nirlajja], *adj. shameless* H[2] 87[a].3.

nisaṅkā [*S.* niḥ + śaṅkhā], ~ yāya *to be free from care, to be unconcerned* H[2] 60[b].6. — niśaṅkān *without scruples* V[1] 135[a].5.

nisāṁ, *s. a standard* (patākī) AH 51[b].

nisādhalapë [*S.* niḥ + sādhaya-], *v.t. to put out of order* Ś 152[b].1*.

nisëṁ, *adv. since, from:* thani ~ *from to-day* H[1] 89[b].5; thwo belasaṃ ~ *since this time* M 39[a].6; thalanaṃ ~ *from this time* H[1] 64[a].5; hṅawoṃ ~ *beforehand* 95[b].3; kāsëṃ ~ *since* (*I*) *took* H[3] 14[b].9. durabhubanaṃ ~ *from afar* M 10[b].4.

nisobhāgi [*S.* niḥ + saubhāgin], *adj. unfortunate, unlucky* (durbhaga) N 32[b].1*.

niścay [*S.*], *s. resolution, determination* H[2] 114[a].3. ~ yāya *to decide, to determine* Vi 175.10; ~ juya *to be determined* H[2] 114[a].2. niścayanaṃ *adv. surely, decidedly* Ś 163[b].2.

nistalapë [*S.* niṣṭha], *v. i. to be intent on, devoted to* V[1] 12[a].6.

nistār [*S. crossing, ... rescue*], jeta ~ julo *I have been saved* Bh 156[a].1*.

nisti, *s.* = nīti H[1] 21[b].1.

nisphal [*S.*], *adj. vain, fruitless* H[3] 54[b].11.

nismāyā [*S.* nirmāya *powerless, weak*], ~ yāya *to be dismayed* Ś 146[b].1.

nu = nuyo V[1] 49[b].1.

-nuṁ, *see* **-nwoṁ**.

nugal, *s.* = nugwoḍ B 57[b].9. *fig.: the heart, mind* Vi 58.12; nugalan kha hlāya *to speak freely* H[3] 44[a].9; thawo nugalas thaṅaṃ taya *to keep secret* H[2] 38[b].6.

nugwoḍ, *s. the heart* H[1] 54[b].2. — *ifc.* **u-**.

nūn, *s. a lord, master* H[2] 98[b].3.

nuya (-l[1], *but* nuṅāwo M, B), *v. t. to swallow, to devour* B 47[a].2.

nuyakë (*caus. of* nuya), *to let take (medicine)* Vd 43ᵃ.1.

nuyo, *after 4th form of the verb: let us*... V² 65ᵃ.5. nuyo nuyo *come, let us go* Vi 42.27.

nṛty [*S. dancing*], ~ yāya *to dance* V¹ 109ᵃ.3.

ne¹, *prt.* = ni² H² 71ᵇ.2.

ne² = naya N 18ᵇ.3.

neka- = neku: nekasēṃ *becoming low (pulse)* Vd 9ᵃ.2*.

neku, *adj.*, ~ kā *fine tissue* N 25ᵇ.2.

netāl, *s.* = ṅatāl CW 8.70.

netr [*S.*], *s. an eye* Bh 141ᵇ.7.

nenë¹, *v. t. to hear, to listen* (= ṅeṅë¹) Bh 1ᵇ.7.

nenë², *v. t. to ask* (= ṅeṅë²) B 22ᵇ.2.

nebaḍan, ~ kaya *to lock (a door)* Bh *11ᵇ.6; *to imprison* *12ᵇ.2.

ne-bhāl, *s.* = ni-bhāl H² 80ᵃ.1.

nem [*H.*], *s. religious observances* H² 42ᵃ.1.

nemalapë [nem], *v. t. to instruct* N 10ᵃ.8.

ner, *adj.*; ma ~ *the best* (uttama) Vd 11ᵇ.6*.

nelë, *only* nelāwo *becoming fatigued or weak*(?) Bh 179ᵃ.3, 26ᵇ.2*.

në, *num. two, both* V¹ 14ᵃ.3; ~-hma *id.* H¹ 54ᵃ.1; ~-hma-hma *ord. the second* H² 74ᵇ.2. në hnu kwo-hnu *on the second day* N 24ᵇ.4. në cā *a night and two days* (pakṣiṇī AH) Vd 8ᵇ.1.

në-tā, *num.* = në H¹ 70ᵇ.5.

në-hmati-puli, *s. man and wife* (dampatī) CW 8.34.

nëya (-l¹), *v. t.* ch-g-n ~ *to mix with*... Vd 14ᵇ.4.

no¹, *s. the tongue* N 44ᵃ.2; (*the cavity of the*) *mouth* Vd 35ᵇ.6, ~ siya *to rinse the mouth ritually* P 25ᵇ.1; non wāya *to utter (words), to speak* Ś 145ᵃ.2, non ma wāya *to keep silence* H² 44ᵇ.3; non wātakë *to cause to speak* Vd 49ᵃ.3, ~ wācakë, wākë *id.* B 25ᵃ.10. — ~ tuya *to kiss* Ś 150ᵃ.2.

no², *s.* ~ sal *gait and voice* N 30ᵇ.5*.

no³, *s.* = nol H³ 25ᵇ.3.

no⁴ = nuyo B 32ᵃ.10.

no-cā, *s. the dawn* (brāhmamuhūrtaka) CW 1.46.

noya (-l¹), *v. i.*, tāp noyāwo *having become hot* V² 32ᵃ.6; co beg ~ *if the urine is rich* N 30ᵇ.3; hma sa ~ *the body having got a cutaneous eruption, a blister* V² 32ᵃ.6; me sa noyiwo *the tongue will become foul* Vd 44ᵃ.4; si nowo kachu *cutaneous disease with blisters* 34ᵇ.5.

nol, *s. a stick* H³ 11ᵇ.3.

nobāl = nvāhāl Ś 155ᵃ.7 (°hān).

-nwoṃ (*in younger* MSS -naṃ, -nuṃ *or merely* -ṃ), 1) *suffix of the indefinite pronoun.* — 2) *part.: even* C² 45; -nwoṃ... -nwoṃ *both... and* N 30ᵇ.1. — chesa-ṃ *even in the house* H² 29ᵃ.1; bhatu-ṃ kwokha-ṃ *both parrot and crow* H³ 45ᵇ.9.

ntu, *part.* = na-tu C¹ 108.

nyanë¹ (*irr. ipr.* nyayo B 23ᵃ.8), *v. t.* = nenë¹ H³ 55ᵇ.2.

nyanë², *v. t.* = nenë² B 2ᵇ.5.

nyā¹, *s. a fish* (= ṅā¹) H³ 55ᵇ.8.

nyā², *s. iron* N 25ᵇ.1*.

nyāk, *adj. vehement* Vd 30ᵃ.1.

nyācakë (*caus. of* nyāya²), kwo ~ *to (suffer oneself to) be oppressed* B 13ᵃ.11*.

nyātu, *see* **nyāya²**.

nyā-pā, *num. five* B 11ᵃ.2.

nyāy [*S. right or fit manner*], ~ ma du deś *an ill-mannered, lawless country* B 48ᵇ.4.

nyāya¹, *v. t. to buy* (= ṅāya²) B 5ᵃ.3.

nyāya² (-t), *v. i. to move* (= ṅāya³) Bh 93ᵇ.4. nyātu ~ *id. intens.* C¹ 278.

nyālā-pu, *adj. ashamed* (= ṅālā-pu) B 20ᵇ.4.

nvāya (-t), *v. t.*, ch-hm-yāta ~ *to blame, to revile* N¹ 21ᵇ.4.

nvāhāl, ~ kaya *to make known, to proclaim* M 6ᵇ.2; ~ kayakë *id.* B 67ᵇ.2.

hn.

hnawo = hṅawo C¹ 4.

hnawol-bhu, *s. a watery country* CW 3.3.

hnatakaṁ, *adv. completely* P 20ᵇ.6*.

hna-pā, *adv.* = hṅa-pā.

hnay [*mod.* = hnas), *num., only:* ~-sal *seven hundred* Vi 125.11.

hnaya, *num. seventy* AH 57ᵃ.

hnal-pot, *s. a kind of reed:* ~-ban *a thicket of reeds* (naḍyā) CW 6.38.

hnas¹, *s. an ear* V¹ 125ᵃ.2. — ~-tisā *an ornament of the ear* AH 66ᵃ. — ~-syāk *ear-ache* Vd 15ᵇ.4.

hnas², *num. seven* Vi 127.11; ~-hma *id.* (*of living beings*) V² 32ᵃ.5; ~-guli *id.* (*of things*) Vi 81.10.

hnasi-bhu, *s. a region contiguous to water* AH 23ᵇ.

hnas-kan, *s. a mirror* H² 94ᵇ.6.

hnas-vā, *num.* = hnas² N 4ᵇ.4.

hnas-tvāk, *s. a medicinal plant* Vd 48ᵃ.5.

hnas-pat, *s.* = °-pot CW 8.72. — hnas-pan *id.* C¹ 275.

hnas-piri, *s. the drum membrane* (*of the ear*) Bh 99ᵃ.2*.

hnas-pot, *s. an ear* H¹ 48ᵃ.1. — ~-cokā *the tip of the ear* B 9ᵇ.7. — ~-tisā *an ornament of the ear* AH 43ᵃ.

hnas-bi, *s. a species of worms* (karṇajalaukā) CW 7.6.

hnā = hṅā B 8ᵃ.4.

hnākan, *s. name of a plant, used in medicine* Vd 28ᵇ.4.

hnā-co = hṅā-° B 44ᵃ.6; hnācoyā *previous* H³ 41ᵃ.3. — hnā-ca B 38ᵃ.5.

hnātikā, *s. a circle of hair between the eyebrows* Vi 16.22. — °khā *id.* Bh 83ᵃ.3.

hnāthu [= hṅathu?], *s. a wife* (patnī) AH 37ᵃ.

hnā-pā, *adv.* = hṅā-pā Ś 166ᵃ.7.

hnāya (-l¹), *v. t. to mix up, to stir about*(?) Vd 34ᵃ.6.

hnās, *s. the nose* V¹ 37ᵃ.5. — ~-co *the tip of the nose* Vd 10ᵃ.2. — ~-rog *catarhh of the nose* (pīnasa) AH 39ᵇ. — ~-pvāl *a nostril* AH 50ᵇ (nháyapoá). — ~-biṣay *the sense of smell* AH 14ᵃ.

hni¹, *s. a day* H² 66ᵃ.8. hni hni chiyā *every day* H³ 47ᵃ.4; hnin *id.* V¹ 91ᵃ.6; hni-noṃ cā-noṃ *day and night* N 21ᵇ.5. — *ifc.* **bā-**.

hni², *s. matter, pus* M 12ᵃ.6.

hni³, ~ thanë *to use incantations* Bh 12ᵃ.6.

hniṁ-gu, *adj.* = hneṃ-gwo C¹ 94*.

hnithaṁ, *adv. always* H¹ 21ᵃ.3; hnithakaṃ *id.* P 62ᵃ.2; hnithaṅ(aṃ) *id.* Bh 12ᵇ.2; hnithan(aṃ) *id.* Vi 85.20, *at once* 121.26.

hnid, *s.* = hṅeḍ C² 126.

hninakë = hṅi°.

hninë, *v. i. to ripen* Vd 18ᵃ.2*.

hniṁḍ, *s.* = hṅeḍ N 48ᵇ.5.

hni-pu, *s. the brain* CW 8.52.

hni-pot, *s. a tail* H² 49ᵇ.1.

hniyakë, *caus. of* hnilë H³ 23ᵃ.4.

hnilakë, *caus. of* hnilë H³ 40ᵇ.11.

hnilë, *v. i.* = hnëlë B 18ᵇ.7.

hni-sone, *s. a building ground* AH 25ᵃ.

hnu, *s. a day* (*used in connection with num. only*): cha hnuyā dinas *some day* H¹ 2ᵇ.2; ṅā hnuyā la *a journey of five days* B 47ᵃ.1.

hnuya¹ (-l¹), *v. t. to pay* (*debt*) N 8ᵃ.6; *to give as payment* N 20ᵃ.4.

hnuya² (-l¹), *v. t. to trample, to kick* (*with the feet*) B 17ᵃ.9.

hnul, *adj.* = hnol H² 100ᵇ.2.

hneṁ-gwo, *adj. ripe* C² 95*.

hneḍ, *s.* = hṅeḍ H¹ 23ᵃ.5.

hnen-paṁth, *s. a sort of reed* (naḍa) AH 33^b^.

hnel, *s.* = hṅeḍ Vi 106.18.

hnel-se, *s. a medicinal plant* (*Citrus medica*) Vd 29^a^.4.

hnë = hṅa H[3] 51^b^.2 (hne, hnye).

hnëwo = hṅewo H[3] 59^a^.9. — hnëwonë = hṅe° 14^a^.7.

hnëthu, *adj.* = hṅathu H[3] 2^b^.5.

hnëya[1] (-l[1]), *v. i.* ch-hm-wo ~ *to be superior to*... (= hṅeya[1]) H[3] 23^a^.7*.

hnëya[2] (-l[1]), *v. t.* = hṅeya[2] H[3] 11^a^.2.

hnëlë, *v. i. to laugh* (= hṅelë) H[3] 60^b^.5.

hnol, *adj. new, fresh* H[1] 84^b^.3.

hnyathu = hṅathu H[3] 2^b^.5.

hnyācakë = hṅācakë H[3] 2^b^.4.

hnyāya[1] (-t), *v. t.* = hṅāya[1] H[3] 16^b^.8.

hnyāya[2], *v. i.* = hṅāya[2] H[3] 22^b^.8.

hnyāya[3] (-t), *v. t.* = hṅāya[3] N 26^b^.7.

hnyeḍ, *s.* = hṅeḍ H[3] 54^b^.6.

p.

paṁ, *s. a painter* AH 59^b^ (pang).

paṁ-mā [= pat-?], *s. reeds:* ~ apā *abundant in reeds* (vetasvān) AH 23^b^ (pangmá —).

paṁlë, *s.* = palë C[1] 164.

pakawān, *s.* = pakvān B 15^a^.10.

pakasinī [*S.* pakṣiṇī], *s. a female bird* B 39^a^.1. — ~-misā *a woman who has become that ib.* 5.

pakë, *see* **tha**.

pakvān [*H.*], *s. pastry, sweat meats* V[1] 17^b^.2.

pakṣ [*S.*], *s. a side, party* H[2] 84~a~^b^.2; *an adherent, follower* H[3] 39^b^.6.

pakṣi [*S.* pakṣin], *s. a bird* H[1] 36^a^.4.

pak-si, *s. bamboo, reed*(?) N 50^b^.3*.

paṅk [*S.*], *s. a swamp* H[2] 43^b^.6. — *ifc.* **madhu-**.

paṁkṣi, *s.* = pakṣi Ś 137^b^.5.

paṅkh, *s.* = paṅk H[3] 20^a^.4.

paṅkhā [*M.* paṃkh, paṃkhā], *s. a fan* Bh 162^a^.6.

paṁgal, ~ biya *to aim at* H[3] 11^b^.3.

paṁgāl [= paṃgal?], haḍ-jaḍ ~ biyā *abuse combined with reproach* N 42^a^.4*.

pacay [*M.* pac *to be cooked*], ~ yāya *to cook, to boil* H[2] 90^b^.5.

paciṅ, *s. a finger* Vd 7^a^.1; kisiyā ~ *the trunk of an elephant* AH 66^a^.

pacinī, *s.* = paciṅ Bh 24^a^.2. — *ifc.* **hmālā-**, **siku-**.

pacol, *s. a bag or vessel* (puṭikā) P 18^b^.4*.

pa-chi, *s. a pair;* sā ~ *a pair of cows* N 32^b^.6.

pachim [*M. the west*], *s. the north* (*sic*) B 63^b^.9.

pajitā, *s. a sort of neck-ornament* CW 8.72.

pajr, *s.* = pañjar Ś 144^a^.2*.

pañc[1] [*S.* pañcan], *num. five* H[2] 50^a^.2.

pañc[2] [*H.*], *s. a village council* B 41^a^.5.

pañcajany [*S.* pā° *one of the 8 upa-dvīpas of Jambudvīpa*], *s. Panjāb* N 53^b^.2*.

pañca-tāḍ, *s. a musical instrument with five strings* Vi 151.3.

pañcaraṅg [*S.* pañca *five* + raṅga *colour*], *s. the five colours* Vi 17.9.

pañcāṅ-lā, *s. the little finger* N 51^a^.7.

pañcārī [*S.* pañcāla], *s. a certain savage tribe, or a Vedic school* N 25^b^.4*.

paṁchi, *s.* = pakṣi H[3] 9^a^.6. — ~-bhās *the language of the birds* B 10^a^.11.

pañjar [*S.*], *s. a cage* Ś 144^b^.7.

pat, *s. bamboo* H[2] 36^a^.6.

Paṭan, *n. pr. Patan* B 59^a^.9*.

patapë, *v. t.* = palapë H[1] 4^a^.3*.

paṭambar, *s.* = paṭāmbar Bh 173^b^.4.

patalā [*S.* paṭala *a roof, thatch*], *s. the edge of a thatched roof* CW 4.9.

paṭā(k) [*S.* paṭākā], *s. a flag, banner* Vi 89.11.

paṭāṁbar [*S.* paṭa *woven cloth* + ambara *garment*], *s. a cloth, garment*; *only ifc.* **pāt-**.

patāsi [*cf. S.* paṭa *cloth*], *s. the lower garment* B 17ᵇ.8.

pati¹ [*cf. H.* paṭṭī *leaf*], *s. a leaf, sheet (of paper), a document* N 8ᵇ.4. — *ifc.* (*sheet of metal*): **nakhi-, palë-, sijal-.**

pati², *s. a gnat, moschito* H¹ 47ᵇ.5.

pati³, ~ chik *adj. flat* CW 8.39; ~-jāwo *low* Wr. p. 304.

pati(ṁ) [*S.* prati], *adv.*, kacā ~ *on every branch* Vi 17.14; din ~ *every day* H² 9ᵇ.4. — patikaṃ *id.* Vi 67.34.

patigalapë [*cf. S.* prati + gar], *v. t. to protect* N 39ᵇ.2.

patini [*S.* patnī], *s. a wife* N 9ᵇ.3.

paṭutar [*S. compar. of* paṭu *eloquent*], *adj. eloquent* H² 34ᵇ.5.

paṭṭas [*cf. H.* paṭṭā], *s. a kind of sword* Bh 160ᵃ.3*.

paṭṭāmbar, *s.* = paṭāmbar Vi 150.30.

patyār = pratyār Vi 168.19.

patr [*S.* pattra], *s. a letter* B 61ᵃ.3.

pat-sili [*S.* paṭa *cloth* + *Ne.* silë *to wash*], *s. a washerman* H² 52ᵇ.3.

path [*S. a road; reach*], *s. road* B 12ᵇ.2; *a certain region:* meb ~ baniyā *a merchant from other parts* N 7ᵇ.8.

Pathuwā, *name of a man* B 39ᵇ.3.

pathuli, *s. one of the ten palāṇḍus* (mocikā Md) P 58ᵃ.1.

paḍapë, *v. t.* = palapë P 62ᵃ.6.

paḍapëkë, *caus. of* paḍapë P 62ᵃ.6*.

paḍalapë, *v. i.* = paralapë Bh 22ᵃ.4.

padārth [*S.*], *s. a thing, object* H¹ 7ᵇ.4, *property* N 15ᵇ.1.

paḍi, ~ sākṣi *an indirect witness* N 9ᵃ.5*.

paḍihāsalapë [*S.* parihāsa *s. joking, deriding*], *v. t. ro deride* N 10ᵇ.6*.

padm [*S.*], *s. a lotus* V¹ 9ᵃ.3.

pani, *s. a ladle* AH 55ᵃ.

panë, *v. t. to hold back, to prevent from running away* B 33ᵃ.10, *to keep off* B 27ᵇ.2; ch-g-s ~ *to prevent from…* M 14ᵃ.2, *to obstruct* (lukhā·s *a door*) B 32ᵃ.10, la(·s) ~ *to obstruct a way* H² 66ᵇ.3.

paṁt¹, *s.* = pat H² 36ᵃ.5.

paṁt² [= pañc?], *s. a company* (*of artisans etc.*; śreṇi) N 9ᵇ.2,3*.

panti, *s.* = pati² H² 32ᵇ.6.

paṁth, *s.* = pat AH 33ᵇ; — ~-bu *a thicket of bamboo* B 28ᵇ.4; ~-bho *id. ib.* — *ifc.* **hnen-.**

paṇḍit [*S.*], *s. a learned man, scholar* H¹ 65ᵇ.1.

pandu-seto [*S.* pāṅḍu?], *s. a plant, used medicinally* Vd 36ᵇ.2.

paṁdhān, ch-hm-wo ~ jwonë *to commit adultery with…* N 33ᵇ.7; ~ lāya *to be guilty of a°* 34ᵇ.1. — paṃdhan *id.* 34ᵃ.2.

paṇy [*S.*], *s. merchandise* N 23ᵇ.6; ~ thwolwo *the seller* 23ᵇ.5.

panyal-si, *s. name of a plant* (karamardaka) AH 29ᵇ.

papati, *s. the wing of a bird* H² 30ᵃ.6; paputi *id.* 80ᵃ.1. — *ifc.* **jhagal-.**

paban [*S.*], *s. wind* B 69ᵃ.1; *flatulence*(?) Vd 12ᵃ.1.

pabitr [*S. means of purification*], ~ yāya *to clean, to purify* P 48ᵇ.4; ~-śarīr yāya *to clean the body (ritually)* H² 32ᵃ.4. — *adj. clean, pure* Ś 167ᵃ.4.

pahm, *s.* = padm Ś 162ᵃ.6.

payinalapë [payini], *v. t. to settle, to set in order* N 45ᵇ.3. — payinalapayakë *caus.*, dharm-mārgas ~ *to cause to keep oneself on the way of righteousness ib.* 1.

payini [*cf. Mr.* paiṇ *bargain, agreement*], ~ lācakë *to maintain, to keep orderly*(?) N 17ᵇ.2*.

par[1] [*S.*], *adj. belonging to another* H[2] 75[b].5; *strange* B 17[a].8. *s. another, a stranger* H[2] 94[a].6. — paran *adv.*, ~...ma *only* H[1] 66[b].3.

pal[2] [*S.*], *s. a weight* V[2] 27[a].1.

palak [*S.* palakyā], *s. a kind of turnip:* ~-ke *a broth made from* palak Vd 47[a].1.

parakiri [*cf. H.* palaṅgṛī *a small bed or couch*], *s. a couch* Ś 159[a].5.

palakhāl [*cf. S.* prākāra], *s. a wall (enclosing a town, house etc.)* H[2] 84[b].2. — *ifc.* **gaḍh-**.

paraṅki [*cf. H.* palaṅg *bed, couch*], *s. a couch* Bh 174[a].6*.

paratr [*S. adv. in the other world*], *s. the other world* C[2] 14; paratras *in the other world* Bh 170[a].3.

paradeśi [*S.* °deśin], *s. a foreigner* B 52[b].7.

paraṁtu [*S.*], *adv. but, however* H[3] 102[a].8; *rather* 82[b].2.

parapasā, *s.* = parbasā(t) AH 8[a].

palapë [*for* paṭhalapë *from S.* paṭh- *to read?*], *v. t. to read, to recite* H[2] 91[a].6; *to study* N 48[a].2 (paḍapë).

parabī [*cf. S.* para], *s. a counterpart (in a lawsuit)* N 11[b].6. — ~-kajhet *a defendant* (pratyarthin) 6[a].6.

param [*S.*], *adj. highest, utmost, most excellent* Ś 163[a].4.

paramān [*pop. H.* parmān —, *authority*], *s. an official, chief (of a town or village)* B 13[b].5.

paraṁparā(n) [*S.* paraṃparā *succession, continuation*], *adv. successively* V[1] 55[a].4; ch-g-yā ~ *in continuation of...* N 26[b].3.

paray [*M.* paṛ, par], ~ juya *to fall* (ch-g-s *into...*) H[2] 94[a].6; ~ yākë *to cause to fall* 31[b].5.

paralapë [*see* paray], *v. i. to fall, to fall down* (ch-g-s *into...*) H[3] 37[b].9; *to plunge into ruin* H[1] 45[b].1.

paralok [*S.*], *s. the other world* V[1] 98[b].1; ~ wonë *to die* 98[a].6.

parākram [*S.*], *s. courage, strength* H[2] 89[a].4; ~ thul *courageous* 79[a].3.

palākh, *s. cause, opportunity(?)* H[2] 39[a].3; ~ taya *to place(?)* H[2] 71[b].3*.

parāg [*S.* parāñc —, *averted(?)*], khuya ~ juya *to have an aversion to stealing(?)* N 9[b].7*.

parādh [*formed by misinterpretation from* aparādha], ~ yāya *to do right* Vi 42.24.

parārth, *s.* = padārth H[2] 21[a].1.

palā-sawo, *s. a medicinal plant* Vd 38[b].3.

pari[1], *s. a bunch of flowers* H[1] 67[a].2*.

pali[2], *s. a sort of building (caravanseray?)* B 8[a].4.

pali[3], *s. a roof* (= pol[1]) AH 25[a].

palik, ~ bisëṃ taya *to deposit (a thing with a third person to be delivered ultimately to the owner)* (*cf.* anvāhita) N 17[a].8. — ~-kalantr *interest on loans* 6[b].7.

parīkṣā [*S. examination*], ~ swoya *to examine, to investigate* (ch-g-yā *into...*) H[1] 19[b].3; ~ siya *id.* (ch-g) B 49[b].2; ~ yāya *id.* (ch-g(-yā)) H[2] 95[a].3. — ~ yācakë *caus.* V[1] 62[a].2.

palikhan = palisā H[2] 63[a].2*.

parikhalapë [*S.* parīkṣ-], *v. t. to examine* N 24[b].8; — parikhalapayakë *caus.* 23[b].7.

palikhyā = parīkṣā V[1] 107[b].4.

parigati [*cf. S.* pari + gam *to go round* —; *to get, to attain?*], *s. control over one's actions, independence* N 4[b].5, *authority, warrant* 31[a].8; ch-hm-yāta ~ khāta(ṃ) *authority rests with...* 39[b].9.

palichā [H. paricchā *examination*] = parīkṣā V[2] 31[b].4.

parichedalapë [*S.* pariccheda —, *definition, decision*], *v. t. to define* N 33[a].9, *to decide* 49[b].7.

parijan [*S.*], *s. servants* H[2] 61[b].5.

parin, *adv. quickly, hastily(?)* H[1] 94[a].4.

paripāt[1], *s.* = paripāṭi Vi 89.6.

paripāt[2] [*cf. S.* paripāṭayati *to destroy*], *s. destruction* Vi 121.19*.

paripāṭi [*S.*], *s. method* N 14ᵇ.6.

parimāṇ [*S. a measure, measuring*], *s. method* H² 25ᵃ.6; ch-g-wo ch-g-wo ~ yāya *to compare a thing with...* H³ 40ᵇ.11.

palisā, *adv.*, ch-hm-yā ~ *in the place of...* H³ 33ᵃ.3; ~ wonë *to go in the place of another* B 12ᵃ.4*.

pariṣṭ [*S.* *pariṣṭha], *adj. most excellent* V¹ 17ᵃ.1.

pariśram [*S.*], *s. weariness, exhaustion* H² 76ᵃ.4; ~ cāya *to become exhausted* 88ᵇ.6; śarīran ~ yāya *to commit sensual excesses* N 42ᵃ.1.

parihāj, *s. compensation, damages* N 42ᵇ.3; ~ kāya *to get compensation* 15ᵇ.8; ~ yācakë *to cause to give compensation* 43ᵃ.1; parihājan taṅa(n) *or* taṅānaṃ *by the way of compensation* 21ᵇ.6. — parihājā = parihāj 51ᵃ.4.

parihājalapë, *only:* parihājalapaṃ taṅaṃ *by the way of compensation* N 50ᵇ.1*.

palë, *s. a lotus* C¹ 267. — ~-nāḍ *the stalk of a lotus* Vd 15ᵃ.4. — ~-pati *a lotus-leaf* C² 227. — ~-pu *the seed of a lotus* Md 30ᵃ.4. — ~-muni *the seed-vessel of a lotus* AH 66ᵃ. — ~-suki *a lotus-fibre ib.* — ~-svān *a lotus-flower* Ś 152ᵃ.5. — ~-svān-mā *a lotus-plant* 162ᵃ.4. — ~-hal *a lotus-leaf* Ns 2ᵃ.2. — ~-hā *the root of a lotus* Md 30ᵃ.4. — *ifc.* **kāth-**.

pal-kā, *s. a kind of mustard* Md 66ᵇ.8. — ~-cikan *mustard-oil* 59ᵃ.2.

palkhāl, *s.* = palakhāl V² 10ᵇ.4.

pal-thāk, *s. a freckle, mark* (piplu) AH 39ᵇ.

parbat [*S.*], *s. a mountain* Bh 136ᵇ.1. — ~-co *the top of a mountain* AH 26ᵃ. — ~-jol *a cave of a mountain* H² 98ᵇ.6. — ~-pākh *a slope, precipice* AH 26ᵃ.

parbasā(t), *s. lightning* CW 1.4; ~ tolaṃ *it lightened* Vi 17.25.

paryant(aṁ) [*S.* paryantam *adv.*], *adv. altogether* B 29ᵇ.1.

pal-se-ghās, *s. a fragrant grass* (katṛṇa) CW 6.37.

pahlābi-se, *s. a plant used medicinally* Vd 24ᵇ.2.

pasanan, ~ biya *to give away in marriage (a maiden)* N 31ᵇ.5; ~ wonë *to marry (of a maiden)* 33ᵃ.2.

pasal [*cf. H.* bāzār *from Pers.*(?)], *s. a shop* B 17ᵃ.5.

pasaliyā, *s. a shopkeeper* AH 56ᵇ.

paśu [*S.*], *s. an animal* H² 53ᵃ.8, *cattle* N 53ᵇ.3.

pasulī, *s. wood-sorrel* Vd 25ᵃ.4. — ~-ghās *id.* AH 32ᵇ (pusughánsa).

pahal[1] [*M.* pahar], *s. a quarter of a day or a night, a watch* B 21ᵃ.7.

pahal[2] [*H.*], *s. (mode of) beginning* P 2ᵃ.3.

pahiri [*cf. M.* pahāṛ *a mountain*], *s. a mountaineer, Pahṛī* N 25ᵇ.4*.

pā[1], *s. an axe* AH 52ᵃ.

pā[2] [*H. from Pers.*], *s. a leg* H² 29ᵇ.1.

pā[3], *s. the wing (of a bird)* CW 7.15. — *ifc.* **khā-**, **hmas-khā-**, **lā-**.

pā[4] [= pā³], *cl-w. for parts of the body found by pairs:* cha pā lā-hāt *one arm* H³ 9ᵇ.8, khu pā hnas-pot *six ears* H² 83ᵇ.2; *also:* lakām cha pā *one shoe* Ś 154ᵃ.7.

pā[5], ~ chāya (-l¹) *to take on one's shoulders* H³ 59ᵇ.2; pā chāyâwo haya *to carry on one's shoulders* H² 108ᵇ.8. — ~ dāya: lā ~ ~ *to clap one's hands, to raise one's hands*(?) B 16ᵃ.1.

pā[6] [= pā³?], *s.*, moḍ-sa buwo ~ *a comb* CW 7.14.

pā-[7] (*only* pās-tunuṃ), *v. i. to be cured* H² 47ᵇ.5*.

pā-[8] (*only* pāsëṃ), bal ~ *to gather the military forces*(?) H³ 50ᵇ.7*.

pā'u, *adj. mod.* = pāṅu AH 14.

pām-ti, *cl-w.* = pā[4] M 33[a].2.

pāk[1] [*S. s. cooking; ripening*], *adj. ripe* Vi 91.19. — ~ yāya *to prepare (food, by boiling, roasting etc.)* B 68[a].5; ~ wonakë *to boil out, to make a decoction from* Vd 52[b].4; ~ juya *to become digested* 10[a].5. — ~-thāy *a kitchen* AH 54[b].

pāk[2], *s. distance, difference; gen.* anta(r)-**pāk** *id.* H[1] 30[a].2.

pākal [*M. ripe?*], *adj. hard, harsh* H[2] 72[b].7*.

pāku, *s. a gully* CW 5.4. — *ifc.* **lwoha(m)-**.

pākë[1] (*caus. of* pā-[?]), *to cure* M 36[b].3*.

pākë[2] [pāk[2]], *v. t. to keep at a distance* C[1] 233*.

pākh[1], ~ te *to leave (husband or wife)* N 36[a].2.

pākh[2] = pāk[1] Bh 116[b].2; ~ wonë *to ripen* C[2] 202, ~ hanë *id.* C[1] 202; ~ juya *to become (sufficiently) boiled* Vd 47[b].6.

pākh[3], *s.* = pāku(?) N 29[a].5. — *ifc.* **parbat-**.

pākhān [*S.* pāṣāṇa], *s. a stone* Bh 163[a].2.

pāg [*H.*], *s. a turban* N 18[b].7*.

pāgā [*H. stable?*], ~-ci *a sort of salt* (bhūmija) Md 24[b].3.

pāṅu, *adj. sour* C[1] 281; ~ ci *a sort of salt* Vd 39[b].4.

pāc[1], *s.* = pāś Bh 100[a].1. — *ifc.* **nāg-**.

pāc[2], *only ifc.* **su-**.

pācakë[1] [pācu], cet ~ *to compose oneself* H[1] 75[a].5; cet ma pācakaṃ *adv. startled or alarmed* 4[a].4.

pācakë[2] = pākë[2] C[1] 273*.

pācu, *adj. composed, collected* V[1] 64[a].1. — pācula *is composed (subj. gen.* citt, cet *mind); mostly:* ma ~ *is startled or alarmed* V[2] 42[b].3.

pācukë = pācakë[1] H[2] 45[a].1.

pā-ju, *s. a maternal uncle* P 31[b].3.

pāt[1] [*M. leaf of a tree*], *cl-w. for flat objects* H[2] 105[a].5.

pāt[2] [*H.* pāṭ], *s. silk* N 25[b].1.

pātak [*cf. H.* pātak], *s. a medicinal plant* Vd 50[b].4.

pātaki [*S.* pātakin *guilty of a crime*], *adj. guilty of a minor offence* (aupapātika) N 39[a].1*.

pātakë, *caus. of* pāya[1] Vd 34[b].2.

pāṭā[1] [*S.*], *s. a vegetable, potherb* H[1] 41[a].5*.

pātā[2] [*cf. Mr.* pāṭ], *s. a watercourse for irrigating fields(?)* N 27[a].7*.

pā-ti, *cl-w.* = pā[4] M 16[a].6.

pātu, *see* **pālë**.

pāt-lāhāt [*M.* pāt *leaf?*], *s. a hand* CW 8.63.

pāt-le, *s.* = pā-li N 12[a].3*.

pāṭh [*S. recitation*], ~ yāya *to recite* H[2] 11[b].3.

pāḍ, *s. loss (in trade)* N 25[a].7; ~ juya *to be lost (in trade)* 25[a].3.

pādukā [*S.*], *s. a shoe (term of respect)* H[2] 59[a].2.

pādo, *s. a nostril* Vd 14[a].2.

pān [*S. s. drink*], ~ yāya *to drink* V[1] 99[b].6; ~ yātakë *to let drink* Ś 162[b].5.

pāp [*S.*], *s. a sin* B 17[a].3; ~ yāya *to commit a sin* H[2] 72[a].5; ~ lāya *to become guilty of a sin* N 13[b].3; ~ kāya *to make oneself guilty of a sin* V[1] 69[a].3. — ch-hm-yāta ~ lātaṃ *it is the fault of...* 108[a].5.

pā-pā [pālë], *interj.* cut, cut! Vi 158.19.

pāpi [*S.* pāpin], *adj. sinful, wicked* B 32[a].8, *id. fem.* H[2] 43[b].7. — **pāpini** [*S.*] *id. fem.* B 48[a].8.

pāpiṣṭh (*also:* °piṣṭ, °pist, °past) [*S.*], *adj. most sinful, most wicked* H[2] 63[b].4.

pā-phayakë, *caus. of* pā-phe N 50[a].8.

pā-phā-gu, *s. an oath* AH 15[b].

pā-phe, *v. i. to make an oath* N 12[a].2.

pāban [*S.* pāvana *purification*], ~ yāya *to purify* N 13b.3.

pā-mi, *s. a wood-cutter* H² 52a.5.

pāy, *s. marrow* H² 58a.8*.

pāya¹ (-t), *v. t. to warm, to heat* Vd 30b.4.

pāya² (-l¹) [= pālë?], *v. t. to cut open* Bh 116b.3*.

pāya³, *adv.*, ch-g ~ *like a thing* H¹ 79a.2, *in accordance with*... N 45a.4. ch-g ~-thëṃ, *adv. like a thing* H² 116a.5; ch-g ~-thiṃ-gwo *adj.* (*being*) *like a thing* 29b.5. — ch-g-yā senwoṃ ~ tawo-dhaṅ *greater than*... 66b.6. — ~-dhaṅ *adj. greater, surpassing* H¹ 78b.5.

pāya⁴, *s.* = pāyak V² 68b.7.

pāyak [*H.*], *s. an armed attendant* V¹ 122b.1; *a hangman, executioner* N 42a.8. — *ifc.* **ba-**.

pāyal [*M. ancle*], *s. an ornament of the ancle* B 26a.12. — *ifc.* **ti-**.

pāyukë (*error for* pācukë?), *v. t. to settle, to decide* V² 11b.3*.

pāl¹ [*S.* pāra *further shore; end, termination*], ~ yāya 1) *to cross* (*a river etc.*) H³ 21a.10; ~ yācakë *to convey across, to ferry across* N 47a.5, ~ yākë *id.* Vi 93.33; Yamunā ~ itāwo *after having crossed the* Y° Bh 12a.4. — 2) *to make an end to, to decide, to settle* (ch-g(-yā) *something e.g. a quarrel*) N 44b.3; ~-**kha hlāya** *to pronounce upon, to pass a judgement upon* 21a.4.

pāl² [= pāl¹?], suyā ~ *whose turn is it*? B 39a.9; ch-hm-yā ~ lātaṃ *it is the turn of*... H³ 35a.11, — — julaṃ *id.* B 17a.7; pāl wonë *to go by turns* 12a.2; ~ taya *successively* Vi 121.15; ~ lācakaṃ *by turns, successively* M 20a.5, ~ lākaṃ *id.* Vi 149.8; ~ lāk-thëṃ *by chance* 36.3; ~ yāya *to chance to be* (*somewhere*) H³ 26b.11.

pāl³ = pāḍ: ~ yāya *to destroy, to ruin* M 19a.4; ch-hm-yāta ~ yāya *to lay to one's charge* B 18a.11; pālan lipt juya *to disgrace oneself* N 48a.6.

pārak [*cf. Mr.* pārakh *examination, trial*], ch-hm-yāke ~ yāya *to bring a case before someone* (*as judge*) B 2a.4. — ~ *s. an antagonist* (*in a lawsuit*) N 11b.4.

pārakhi [= pārak?], *s. a judge* AH 62b.

pāraṅ [*S. eating and drinking after a fast*], ~ yāya *to eat or drink after a fast* P 51a.5; *to take food* Bh 57a.1.

pālanā [*S. protecting*], ~ yāya *to protect* H² 88b.5.

pālay [pāl¹], ~ yāya *to decide, to settle* B 26b.2.

pālāl (*cf. B.* pāṛāṛī *an indigo-plant*], *s. name of a plant* (bhallatakī) CW 6.15.

pā-lāhā, *s.* = pāt-lāhāt Vi 109.3.

pā-li (*mostly spelt* pā-ḷ) [pā = pāt¹, *see* ~-lāhāt *and cf.* pāt-le], *s. a foot* B 22a.8. — ~-tal *the sole of the foot* C¹ 109.

pālu, *adj. pungent, acrid* C¹ 111. — *s. ginger* Md 21b.6.

pāle, *s. crops*(?) Bh 18b.2*.

pālë, *v. t. to strike, to cut* (*with a sword*) B 14a.8.

pāś¹ [*S.*], *s. a net, snare* H¹ 12b.3.

pās² [*S.* pāśa], *s. a die* B 67a.8; pāsan lvāya *to play at dice ib.* 7.

pās³ = pāsā: ch-hm ~ yāya *to meddle with*..., *to have to do with*... B 8b.11.

pāsaṁtāp [*S.* paścāttāpa], *s. repentance* H¹ 26b.5. ~ cāya *to repent* H² 114a.2.

pāsar, *s.* 1) *the hollow of the hand* Vi 70.15; lā-hāt ni pānaṃ ~ jyāya *to put together both hands as to form a* (*drinking*) *vessel* M 14a.5. — 2) *as much as can be contained in the hollow of the hand*: *ifc.* **svān-**.

pāsas [*M.* pās *neighbourhood*], *adv.* ch-hm-yā ~ *beside, near* C¹ 177.

pāsā¹ [*M.* pās *neighbourhood*], *s. a friend, companion* V¹ 67ª.6, *a kinsman* C² 156; ch-hm(-wo) ~ yāya *to keep company with*... H¹ 12ª.2. — ~-khu *a thief's accomplice* B 5ᵇ.3. — ~-jan *kinsmen* C² 157. — *i/c.* **bandhu-**.

pāśā², *s.* = **pās²** N 44ᵇ.2*.

pāsĕṃ [*cf.* pāya³], jātiṃ ~ *regarding the caste* N 42ᵇ.1†.

pāhanā, ~ yāya = pāhān ~ M 30ᵇ.3.

pāhān [*H.* pāhunā, pāonā], *s. a guest* V¹ 26ᵇ.2. ~ yāya *to treat as guest, to entertain, to regale* H² 28ᵇ.5. — ch-g-s pāhānā woya *to take part in*... (*as guest*) 20ᵇ.6.

pi¹, ~ kaya — ~ kāya M 34ᵇ.7. — ~ kāya *to take out, to put out* C¹ 109, *to fetch out, to call out* Bh 63ª.2; *to collect (in one's mind)* Vi 15.28; *to display (strength etc.)* Bh 161ᵇ.3; krodh, *to fly into a passion* M 21ª.6; mikhān khobi, *to shed tears* 20ª.7. — pi cālë *to break out (a cutaneous disease)* Vd 43ᵇ.5. — ~ chosĕṃ haya *to send out, to show out* B 7ª.7; ~ ma choya *to hold back, to detain* H² 101ª.1. — ~ joya *to become known, to leak out (a secret)* 68ᵇ.6. ~ joyakë *to make known, to give away* 68ᵇ.5. — ~ tanë *to give away, to betray* H² 36ᵇ.11; pi tanaṃ choya *to turn out, to banish* V² 25ᵇ.3. — ~ taya *to give away (a secret)* C¹ 243; *to display (strength etc.)* H³ 39ª.1. — ~ tine *to turn out* Vi 96.34, *to banish* N 52ª.6; ~ tinaṃ choya *id.* V¹ 22ᵇ.3. — ~ thanë *to betray (a secret)* H¹ 53ª.2; *to commit a breach of confidence* H² 70ª.4. — ~ thaya: gu pi thā me *fire lighted in a wood* 40ᵇ.3. — ~ hyāya *to get out* Bh 34ᵇ.4. — ~ bvāya *to rush out of* H² 96ᵇ.1. — ~ lāya *to go out(?)* 50ᵇ.2. — ~ luya (-l¹) *to turn out* V¹ 15ᵇ.1, *to banish* N 41ᵇ.1. — ~ swoya *to look out of* H².7ª.1. — ~ hāya *to go out* V² 25ª.2; ~ hāsĕṃ wonë *to go away, to disappear* C¹ 50; ~ hāya thāy *issue, passage out* H¹ 25ᵇ.2.

pi², *s.* = pe AH 38ᵇ.

pi³, *num.* = pë H² 45ᵇ.5.

piwāl [piya¹], *s. a guard* B 31ª.8.

piwo, *adj. foremost, front* B 36ª.11.

piwonë, *adv. outside* C² 212, *on the outside* B 48ª.6; nagalayā ~ *outside the town* V¹ 68ª.5; ch-g ~ wonë *to go out of*... V² 48ᵇ.2. — ~-guli *adj. outer* Vi 143.19.

pikë (*caus. of* piya²), mikhā ~ *to shut the eyes (of another)* Vi 121.31.

pi-khā, *s. a spider* CW 7.6.

pical, *s. impurity of the eye* Vi 56.3. — *i/c.* **mikhā-**.

pi-jā, *s. a spark of fire(?)* Vi 174.34*.

pi-ta, ~ kaya *to shed (tears)* M 9ª.1. — ~ kāya *to display (vigour etc.)* Vi 82.32. — ~ choya *to send away* 104.19. — ~ biya *to give into marriage* B 50ᵇ.9. — ~ yanë *to lead out* Vi 104.29. — ~ haya *id.* B 64ᵇ.2.

pitā [*S.*], *s. a father* V¹ 51ª.4.

pītāmbar [*S. adj. dressed in yellow clothes, or corr. from* paṭāmbar], *s. (yellow) clothes; only i/c.* **pāt-**.

pi-të, *v. t. to give away, to betray (a secret)* C² 243; bacan ~ *to reject an advice* H² 52ᵇ.1.

pitti, *s.* = pritī V² 68ᵇ.7.

pit-mā, *s. a tree, the root of which is used medicinally* Vd 36ᵇ.3.

pi-tyāya, *v. i.* = pë-tyāya Vi 98.31. — pi-tyāk-hma *adj. hungry* 131.8.

pithu (*adv. outside*); ~-guli *adj. outer* CW 4.8.

pi-thyā, *adv. outside* P 12ᵇ.3*.

pīḍalapë [*S.* pīḍ- *to press; to torment*], *v. i.*, ch-g-n ~ *to be tormented by*..., *to suffer from*... V¹ 67ª.5.

pinun, *only:* wo ~ *for this reason* V² 11ª.1*.

pinë, *adv. outside* V² 74ᵇ.2; *on the outer side* C² 212; cheyā ~ *outside the* *house* Vi 84.6; deśanaṃ ~ *outside the town* B 48ª.3. — *adj. outer* B 48ª.5.

piṇḍ [*S.*], *s. a funeral ball* B 60ª.7.

pipi, *s. mod.* = pipili Md 22ª.3.

pipirāmul [*H.* piplāmūl], *s. the root of the long-pepper tree* Vd 33ᵇ.1.

pipili¹ [*H.* pipal], *s. long pepper* Vd 3ᵇ.4.

pipili², ~-khā *a kind of bird* (cātaka) CW 7.9. — *ifc.* **dudu-**.

pipihā, *adj. variegated* AH 67ª; ~ jhaṅgal *name of various birds* (śāraṅga) 35ª.

pippali [*S.*], *s. long pepper* Vd 4ª.4.

pibās [*cf. S.* pipāsā], *s. thirst* N 13ª.7.

piya¹ (-I¹), *v. t. to keep guard* Vi 148.13.

piya² (-I¹), *v. t.*, mikhā ~ *to shut one's eyes* V² 51ª.1.

piya³, *num. forty* H³ 44ª.1.

piya⁴ (-t), *v. t.* = pēya C¹ 153.

piyakĕ (*caus. of* piya¹), *to place as guards* Ś 155ᵇ.2.

piyat [= pĕt?], ~ juya *to be broken or crushed* H² 37ª.1*.

piyā, *s. foam* AH 58ᵇ; piyān jāya *to be foamy* Vd 6ᵇ.3.

piyāsāl [*cf. B.* piyāśāl *Pentaptera tomentosa*], *s. the sandal-tree* CW 6.16.

pilā, *s. a basket* AH 61ª.

pilāk-si [*cf. S.* plakṣa], *s. Ficus infectoria* Md 36ª.6.

pilāg-simā, *s.* = pilāk-si H² 9ª.5.

piri, *s. a membrane; only ifc.* **kapās-**, **chu-**, **hnas-**.

pilili, *s. the wife of the husband's sister* (yātar) CW 8.28.

pirtt [*S.* pitta], *s. bile, bilious humour* Vd 14ª.1.

pil-bhot [*cf. Mr.* pil *a young one in general*], *s. children* B 16ª.4.

pisi, *s. the privy parts of a woman* AH 41ᵇ.

pi-swo, *s. a nest (of a bird)* H² 40ª.8*.

pi-hā, ~ woya *to go or come out* (ch-g-n *of*...) H¹ 52ᵇ.2; ~ .wonĕ *id.* V² 77ª.2; ~ bi-jyāya *id.* M 18ª.1.

pu¹, *s. seed* B 61ᵇ.8. pu busĕṃ yanĕ *to bear fruit* B 61ᵇ.2. — *ifc.* **amb-**, **simā-**.

pu² [= pu¹?], *cl-w.* (*hair, sword, tooth, verse etc.*) V¹ 41ᵇ.1.

pu³, *s.* = pwo¹ C¹ 183.

pu⁴ [= pu¹?], ~ janā wonĕ *to have intercourse (with a woman)* N 35ª.2*.

pu-wā, *s. a sort of corn* N 41ᵇ.5! — ~-madhi *a cake, made of* pu-wā AH 55.

pukhu, *s. mod.* = pukhuli Bh 185ª.4.

pukhuli, °ḍi [*M.* pokharī], *s. a tank, pond* H² 73ᵇ.5.

pugār, ch-hm ~ yāya *to be on bad terms with*... H² 106ᵇ.7.

puṅkĕ = punakĕ B 27ᵇ.1.

pucakĕ (*caus. of* puya¹), ch-g-s ch-g ~ *to brand a thing with*... V² 13ª.3 = V¹ 19ª.4*.

puchālapĕ [*M.* pūch], *v. t. to ask, to consult* N 31ª.7.

pūjalapĕ [pūjā], *v. t. to worship, to pay respect* H² 27ᵇ.7.

pūjā [*S. honour, worship*], ~ yāya *to worship, to pay respect* H¹ 30ᵇ.4.

pūjāmān [*from* pūjā], ~ yāya *to worship* P 49ª.5.

puñjā [*S.* puñja *a heap*], ~ hlāya *to unite, to form a partnership* N 16ª.4. — *ifc.* **dwogi-**.

put [*S.* puṭa *fold?*], ~ thunā sa-pal *a braid of hair worn by widows* AH 43ª (putu thugná sapo).

putā [*cf. S.* putra], *s. a son (used as vocativ only)* Vi 111.13.

puti, *s. a part, fragment* Ś 144ª.2, *rest, arrears* N 8ª.6. ~ dayakĕ *to leave a rest* C² 257. — *ifc.* **lipā-**.

puṭi, chiyā puṭis wonĕ *to be in bad company* N 42ª.1*.

puṭuli, *s. a sort of silk* N 41ᵇ.6.

putr [*S.*], *s. a son* V[1] 48ª.5; *a daughter (sic)* V[2] 18ᵇ.4; ch-hm-s ~ yāya *to make a woman pregnant* Bh 116ª.5. — putrī [*S.*], *s. a daughter* V[1] 51ᵇ.3; *a son (sic)* V[2] 18ª.6. — *ifc.* **baṇik-, bāṇi-, mantri-, rā-.**

puthi [*H.* pothī], *s. a book* C[2] 155; puthis swoya *to refer to a book* 38. — *ifc.* **mantr-.**

puna [*S.* punar], *adv. again* Ś 154ᵇ.7.

punakë[1] (*caus. of* punë[1]), *to dress, to clothe (another)* H[2] 95ᵇ.2.

punakë[2] (*caus. of* puya[1]!), *to burn, to scorch* (min *with fire*) P 51ᵇ.5 (puṅakë)*.

punarapi [*S.*], *adv. again* V[1] 24ª.4.

punarbāl, °**bād** [bāl], *adv. again* B 63ᵇ.9; ~ hanaṃ *id.* M 21ᵇ.7. — punarbad *id.* V[2] 21ᵇ.5.

pu-ni [= pu-hni], *s. the day of the full moon* AH 10ᵇ.

punë[1], *v. i. to be covered* H[1] 45ª.1, *to be tainted* (pāpan *with sin*) B 17ª.4, *to be possessed (by evil spirits etc.)* P 58ᵇ.1; bastran ~ *to dress oneself in a garment* H[3] 38ª.5.

punë[2], *v. t.*, byājan ~ *to lose or to forfeit the profit* N 23ᵇ.9.

puṇy [*S.*], *s. religious merit* H[1] 49ᵇ.1.

pu-hni, ~-si *the day of the full moon* P 38ª.1; ~-kuhnu *id.* 42ª.7.

puya[1] (-t), *v. t. to burn (subj.: fire etc.)* V[1] 92ᵇ.5.

puya[2] (-l[1]), *v. t. to cover* B 29ᵇ.8; murchān ~ *to faint (lit.: "to be covered with fainting")* B 66ᵇ.5.

puya[3] (-l[1]), *v. i. to blow (of the wind)* H[3] 16ᵇ.3.

puyakë[1], *caus. of* puya[2] V[2] 56ᵇ.1*.

puyakë[2] (*caus. of* puya[3]), *to blow (a musical instrument)* M 25ᵇ.2.

pūl [*H. from Arab., a small piece of copper coin*], *s. a small coin* B 47ª.2.

pulakë[1], *caus. of* pulë[1] V[2] 10ᵇ.5; kāl ~ ma jiwo *time is not to be eluded* C[1] 202.

pulakë[2], *caus. of* pulë[2] B 56ᵇ.10.

pulay [*M.* pūr *to fill, fulfil*], ~ yāya *to make good (a loss)* N 50ᵇ.1, *to repay, to return (a service)* H[2] 91ª.8; *to keep (a promise)* Vi 57.25.

puralapë [puray], *v. t. to make good (a loss)* N 22ᵇ.1.

pulā [*S.* purā *formerly*], *adj.*, ~ wosat *a worn out garment* (paṭaccara) CW 8.83.

pu-li, *s.* = pwo-li M 32ᵇ.8; puli-to wosënaṃ *coming up to the knees* B 45ª.6.

puruṣ [*S.*], *s. a man* N 35ª.2, *a husband* Bh 20ᵇ.7, *a suitor* N 32ᵇ.1.

purus [= puruṣ?], *s. a degree of relationship* N 30ª.7.

pulë[1], *v. t. to mount over, to scale* V[2] 95ª.2, *to cross* B 22ª.9; ch-hm-yāke pulāwo wonë *to go over to…, to desert to…* H[3] 39ᵇ.4; ch-g-s pulā wonë *to desert somewhere* Vi 126.9.

pulë[2], *v. t.* = pwolë B 12ᵇ.10.

pūrṇ [*S.*], *adj. full* (ch-g-n *of…*) Vi 28.32, *abundant* 28.30. ~ yāya *to make abundant, to give plenty of* Ś 165ᵇ.2, *to fulfill (wish)* Vi 39.3. — pūrṇan *adv. completely* H[2] 84ᵇ.6.

pul-pulū-kelā, *s. a kind of insect* (khadyota) CW 7.13.

purb [*S.* pūrva *former; east*], 1) *adj. previous, former* H[1] 26ᵇ.4; purbaṃ *previously, before* Bh 57ª.6; purbayā deh *a body as before* 57ᵇ.3. — 2) *s. the east* B 22ᵇ.10.

pūl-māl [pūl], *s. a string of small coins* B 46ᵇ.2.

pusa-mi, *s.* = pusā-° H[3] 20ª.1; ~ kāya *to take for one's husband* H[2] 37ª.4.

pu-sā, *s. germ, seed* H[3] 36ᵇ.11; *fig. germ, root* Vi 85.4, *an individual* 121.27.

pusā-mi [pu-sā], *s. a husband* H[1] 59ᵇ.2.

puṣkalani, *s.* = puṣkariṇī V[1] 9ª.6.

puskarāmul [*S.* puṣkaramūla], *s. the edible root of a lotus* Vd 42ᵃ.1.

puṣkariṇī [*S.*], *s. a lotus-pond* Ś 169ᵃ.1.

pustak [*S.*], *s. a book* V¹ 26ᵇ.4.

puṣṭāṅg [*S.*], *adj. with fat limbs, fat, well-fed* H² 50ᵇ.5.

puṣṭi [*S. fatness, thriving*], ~ yāya *to thrive, to become fat* H² 35ᵃ.6.

puṣp [*S.*], *s. a flower* V¹ 78ᵃ.5.

pus-mi, *s.* = pusā-° V² 36ᵃ.6.

pṛthi, *s.* = pṛthvī B 32ᵇ.5.

pṛthibī, *s.* = pṛthvī V¹ 110ᵇ.6.

pṛthvī [*S.* pṛthivī, pṛthvī], *s. the earth* Ś 164ᵃ.5; *the ground* Bh 179ᵃ.7.

pṛṣṭh [*S.*], *s. the back (of the body)* Bh 114ᵃ.1.

pe, *s. the outer skin of an embryo* CW 8.36.

pewāl, *s.* = piwāl Bh 11ᵇ.7(?)

peyaṅgu, *s.* = priyaṅgu (gundrā) CW 6.18.

pel, *s. a morsel* Vd 43ᵇ.4.

perā [*H.* peṛā], *s. a ball of dough* Vd 47ᵇ.2.

pë, *num. four* N 2ᵃ.5; pë-hma *id. (of living beings)* V¹ 65ᵇ.4; pë-guli *id. (of things)* C¹ 293. — pë-hma-hma *ord. fourth* M 8ᵇ.5. — pë hnu pë hnus *every four days* Vd 19ᵃ.6.

pë-kā, ~ la(ṃ) *cross-roads* CW 3.7.

pë-kon-lāk, *adj. square* CW 4.3.

pë-khe, *adv. in four directions* B 22ᵇ.9*.

pët¹ [*H.* peṭ], *s. the belly, womb, stomach* H² 42ᵇ.6. ~ kwo dawo *diarrhoea* Vd 22ᵇ.6, ~ kwo do-hma *suffering from d°* CW 8.48; pëtas du-hmạ *pregnant* 8.13 (pe-taỹ-) — ~-nal *the coeliac artery* H³ 59ᵃ.8. — ~-roy *disease of the abdomen* Vd 51ᵃ.1.

pët², ~ gulë *v. i. to be broken (off)* H³ 86ᵇ.7. — ~ gwolë *v. i. to be broken or crushed* 68ᵇ.6. — ~ nanë *v. i. to be broken (leg)* B 21ᵇ.7. — ~ punë *to press oneself (closely) to* B 55ᵇ.8. — ~ punakë *caus. to press together* Bh 138ᵃ.1, *to tighten (a cord)* B 57ᵇ.3.

pë-tā, *num.* = pë H¹ 28ᵇ.2.

pë-tyāk (*5th form of* pë-tyāya), *adj. hungry* H³ 59ᵇ.4, ~-hma *id.* H² 109ᵃ.2. — *s. hunger* H² 108₂ᵇ.6.

pë-tyāya (-t), *v. i. to be or become hungry* H² 58ᵇ.2.

pëth, *s.* = pët¹ P 51ᵃ.6.

pën, *s. a buttock, rump* Ś 148ᵇ.4; misāyā ~ *a woman's waist* (āroha) AH 73ᵇ (pyong). — *ifc.* **khi-**.

pënakë, *v. t. to kick (with the feet)* Bh 44ᵇ.5.

pënë, *v. t. to fasten* Vi 71.19; *fig.: to appoint* N 22ᵇ.5.

pënwoṁ, *adv. as compared with, more than:* sākṣiyā ~ pramāṇ *more valid than a witness* N 5ᵃ.2, thawo ~ thaṃ *above her, (of) higher (caste) than she* 30ᵃ.5.

pënt, *s.* = pët¹ H¹ 68ᵃ.3.

pënḍ, *s.* = piṇḍ N 38ᵇ.6; *fruit (of a field)* 33ᵇ.1.

pën-pvāl, *s. a buttock, rump* Bh 162ᵇ.4 (-pvar).

pëya (-l¹), *v. t. to plant, to sow* H² 68ᵇ.6.

pëyakë, *v. t. to save, to treasure(?)* B 65ᵇ.6*.

përabhecā(?), ~ swoya *to have intercourse (with a woman)* N 35ᵃ.4*.

pok, ch-g-s ~ cinë *to wrap up in...* Vi 147.34.

pokhaḍi, *s.* = pukhuli H² 88ᵃ.1*.

pogān, *s. a musical instrument* Ś 169ᵇ.5*.

poḍ = pol³; ch-hm-yā citt ~ ceya *to infatuate someone* Bh 47ᵇ.4. — ~ dāya *to inspissate by boiling* Vd 2ᵇ.3. — ~ cisëṃ *secretly* Bh 21ᵇ.6.

podh, *s. a mixed caste* N 43ᵃ.4*.

ponakë (*caus. of* ponë) = *simpl.* Vi 26.35.

ponë, *v. t. to bring (of one's own accord)* H¹ 17ᵇ.3*.

poya (-l[1]), *v. t.* = puya[2] Bh 21ª.2.

poyakē = puyakē[1] V[1] 91ᵇ.5*.

poy-lā, *s. the month Mārgaśīrṣa* AH 12ª.

pol[1], *s. a roof* AH 25ª. — *ifc.* **cas-**.

pol[2], *s. time:* jim-hnas ~ *seventeen times* Bh 101ª.2, swo ~ thrice B 49ª.1; cha polan *at once* H[2] 29ᵇ.11.

pol[3], ~ ciya (-t), *v. t. to wrap up* (ch-g-s *in*...) B 57ᵇ.7; ~ ceya *id.* Vd 25ᵇ.5.

polakē = pulakē C[2] 202.

poli, *s. a kind of plant* (poṭaka) Md 48ᵇ.4.

pole, *s. a kind of antelope* AH 34ª.

polē[1], *v. t. to break asunder* Bh 63ª.2.

polē[2], *v. t.* = pulē[1] V[1] 16ª.2.

porodawoti, *s. a medicinal plant* (mahājālinī Md) Vd 43ª.2.

polol, *s. a roof* CW 4.10.

posalapē [*M.* pos *to nourish*], *v. t. to nourish, to feed* V[2] 64ᵇ.3, *to maintain, to support* H[2] 87ª.7.

posi, *s.*, posiyā kāy *one of the sons of lower caste* (*i. e. others than kṣetrajas*) N 38ᵇ.1,2*.

pos-lā, *s. the month Pauṣa* CW 1.48.

pau [*mod.* = pali[3]], *s. a roof* AH 25.

pauwā [pau *mod.* = pali[3]?], *s. a sort of building* B 8ª.2*.

pwo[1], *s. hail* Bh 33ª.3. — *ifc.* **cvā-**.

pwo[2], *s. a kind of vessel* N 41ᵇ.5. — *ifc.* **tāhā-**, **dhal-***.

pwo[3] [= pwot], ~ dvāya (-t), *v. i. to swell, to develop* (*breasts*) N 31ᵇ.9.

pwom-gu, *s. a desert* AH 70ª.

pwoṁ, *adj. empty:* ~-pwoṃ conē *to be empty* (*perpetually*) N 49ª.2.

pwociṭi, *adj.* = pwocilī H[1] 6ª.3*.

pwocilī, *adj. naked* Bh 24ª.2.

pwochālapē, *v. t.* = puchālapē(?) N 49ª.3*.

pwomciḍi, *adj.* = pwocili N 13ª.7*.

pwot, ~ dhanē *v. i. to swell, to become tense* B 19ª.7.

pwo-pwo [pwo[3]], ~ cinakē *v. t. to fill with wind, to blow out* M 14ᵇ.7*.

pwoy, ~ ceya *to remove the sweepings* N 35ᵇ.8*.

pwo-li (*mostly spelt* °-l), *s. a knee* Bh 179ᵇ.6 (pori).

pwo-le, *s.* = pwo-li N 30ᵇ.2.

pwolē, *v. t. to pay* (*debt*...) N 7ᵇ.5.

pyas = pyās M 14ᵇ.3.

pyā[1], *s. a leech*(?) Vd 1ᵇ.3.

pyā[2], *s. membrum virile* AH 41ᵇ.

pyākhan, °**khun** [*cf. H.* pekhnā *plaything*], *s. dancing* N 42ª.2; ~ huya *to dance* Bh 12ª.3, ~ huyakē *caus.* B 70ª.8: ~ juyakē *to arrange a dancing* Ś 170ª.1, ~ hātakē *id.* 169ᵇ.2. ~-hma *an actor, public dancer* AH 60ª (pyākhungma). pyākhun huya sawo *an Apsaras* CW 1.4.

pyāya (-t), *v. t. to put in order* Bh 185ª.2: sa-pul ~ *to dress one's hair* P 16ª.5.

pyāya-thwo(ṁ), *s. yeast, barm* AH 62ª.

pyāla [*H.* piyālah *cup, from Pers.*], ~-bān *looking like a dram-glass* N 52ª.7*.

pyās [*M.* piās], *s. thirst* B 64ª.10; ~ pheya *to quench one's thirst* H[2] 42ᵇ.2; ~ cāya *to be thirsty* H[3] 41ª.9, pyāscāwo-guli *the being thirsty, thirst* M 12ª.1.

pra, *s.* = pal[2] V[2] 58ᵇ.7.

prakaṭ [*S. evident, open*], ~ yāya *to elucidate* N 11ᵇ.2*.

prakār [*S.*], *s. mode, manner* H[1] 15ᵇ.1; *sort, kind* N 42ᵇ.7.

prakāś [*S. splendid, visible, manifest*], *adj. open, manifest* N 48ᵇ.2. ~ yāya *to make known* V[1] 53ª.2; ~ juya *to radiate* (ch-g-n *from*...) Vi 17.7, *to become visible* 17.10.

prakāśamān [*S. ppr. of* pra-kāś *to shine*], ~ yāya *to make shine* Vi 16.23: ~ juyakē *to light up* Vi 16.25.

prakhāl, *s.* = palakhāl C[2] 175.

prakhyā(n)ti [*S.* prakhyāti *fame, renown*], ~ juya *to be or to become known or famous* M 34^b.5; ~ yāya *id.* B 1^b.2, *to make known or famous* M 4^b.4.

pracakṣ [= pratyakṣ], ~ swoya *to see clearly, to see through*... H^3 43^a.6.

prajā [*S. people, subject*], *s.* (*common*) *people, subject* N 29^b.4; *a servant, campanion* B 66^b.3; ~-lok *pl.* (*common*) *people, subjects* H^2 52^a.1. — ~-bal-khuni *common pidgeons* H^3 6^a.1; ~-byāṅ *common frogs* H^3 60^a.11.

prajog [*S.* prayoga], ch-g-n ~ yāya *to use*... H^1 9^a.5.

prajvālyamān [*from S.* pra-jval- *to begin to flame*], ~ juya *to begin to flame* Bh *10^a.4.

pratakṣ = pracakṣ H^3 36^b.8.

pratāp [*S.*], *s. splendour, glory* H^2 95^a.5.

prati(ṁ), *adv.* = pati(ṃ) C^1 219.

pratīkār [*S. prevention, remedy*], ~ yāya *to afford relief, to remedy* H^2 50^b.2.

pratigrah [*S. acceptance of gifts*], ~ kāya *to accept gifts* (ch-hm-yāke *from*...) N 48^a.6.

pratijñā [*S. a promise*], ~ yāya *to promise* H^1 86^b.1.

pratīt [*S. p.p. of* prati + i *to believe*], ~~*adj. trustworthy, credible*~~ H^2 68^b.1. ~ juya *to believe* H^3 35^b.3; ~ yāya *to make believe, to convince* B 59^b.11, ~ dayakë *id.* B 2^a.7.

pratipāl [*S. s. protecting*], ~ yāya *to protect, to maintain* N 46^b.7, *to keep* (*a promise*) V^2 43^b.7.

pratibhāṣā [*S. answer*], *s. a pledge* N 5^b.1*.

pratyakṣ [*S.*], *adj. distinct, visible* Bh 161^a.4; ~-an *adv. clearly, distinctly* H^2 100^a.5.

pratyahaṁ [*S.* °ham], *adv. daily* Bh 136^a.2.

pratyār [*cf. S.* pratyaya *belief*(?)], ~ juya *to be convinced, to believe* Vi 167.29.

pratyās [*S.* pratyāśā *confidence, exspectation*], yāyas ~ yāya *to have a desire, to be minded to do* Bh 16^b.3.

prades [*S. pointing out, showing*], saṃdeś ~ dayakë *to point out; to give instructions* B 42^b.3.

pradhān [*S.*], *s. the main thing* V^1 58^b.5.

praṇām [*S. bowing, respectful salutation*], ~ yāya *to salute respectfully* H^2 102^b.2.

praṇidhi *S.*], *s. a spy* H^2 83^b.3.

prabādī [*cf. S.* pravādin *stating, declaring* (*ifc.*)], *s. an opponent, a defendent* N 11^b.7.

prabeś [*S. admittance*], ~ yāya *to gain admittance* V^1 123^a.6.

prabhā [*S.* prabhāta; *modern form*], *s. morning* V^2 68^a.4.

prabhāb [*S.*], *s. might, power* H^1 70^b.1.

prabhiti [*S.* prabhṛti], *adv. and so on* B 9^b.11.

prabhu [*S.*], *s. a lord, husband* Ś 153^b.4; ~-ju *id.* B 32^a.4.

prabhūt [*S.*], *s. might, power* H^2 49^a.5.

pramād [*S.*], *s. negligence* H^2 72^b.5.

pramāṇ [*S.* (*right*) *measure*, — —, ~~*authority*~~], *s. authority; having* (*the greater*) *authority or validity* N 4^a.7; *being decisive, having validity* 10^a.5; *means of proof* 4^b.7. — *adv. as much as* Vd 25^a.5. — ~ yāya *to take as decisive, to conform to*... Vi 23.19; ~ hanë *to prove* N 6^a.6; pramāṇ(as) wonë *to be decisive, to be valid* 5^a.7. — promāṇan *adv. decisively, definitively* 26^b.4.

pramukhan [*S.* pramukha *foremost*], *adv. as the first, and so on* M 9^b.4.

prayog [*S. application*], ch-g(-n) ~ yāya *to make use of; to stake* H^2 59^b.4.

prayojan [*S.*], *s. occasion; aim, end* N 17^b.4; ~ ma du (*constructed in* *various ways) is of no use or to no purpose* Vi 169.26. — ~ yāya *to want* H[3] 27^{b}.10. — ~ yācakaṃ *to some purpose, intentionally(?)* B 68^{a}.3.

pralkhāl, *s.* = pa° V[1] 15^{b}.1.

praśaṁsā [*S. praise*], ~ yāya *to praise* Vi 60.17.

prasaṅg [*S. connexion*], ch-hm(-wo) ~ yāya *to have connexion with..., to keep company with...* H[3] 65^{a}.5; ~ ma yācakaṃ *without having connexion with...* N 22^{b}.4.

prasan[1] [*S.* praśna *a question*], ~ yāya *to ask* (ch-hm-yāke *someone*) V[2] 18^{b}.2.

prasan[2] = prasann V[2] 56^{a}.4.

prasaṁtāp, *s.* = pāsaṃtāp H[3] 61^{a}.5.

prasann [*S.* —, *pleased, kind*], ~ juya *to give (term of respect)* Ś 170^{a}.5; yāṅaṃ ~ juya *to be as kind as to do, to have the goodness to do...* V[1] 58^{a}.3.

praśaṣṭ [*S.*], *adj. most excellent* H[2] 88^{b}.6.

prasād [*S.*], *s. favour* H[2] 1^{b}.3.

prasādalapē [prasād], *v. i. to be favourably disposed* N 28^{a}.6.

prasār = pratyār Vi 167.27*.

prasthān [*S. departure*], *s. appearance in public* B 10^{b}.11, ~ dayakē *to appear in public* 19^{a}.8; ~ yāya *to send, to despatch* H[2] 83^{a}.7, *to depart* Vi 30.26.

prasthāb [*S.* prastāva], *s. occasion* H[1] 10^{b}.5; cha hnuyā prasthābas *some day* 36^{b}.1.

prahār [*S. a blow, stroke*], ~ yāya *to beat, to strike* H[1] 48^{a}.2.

prācitt, *s. for* prāyaścitt Vi 44.6*.

prātakāl [*S.* prātaḥkāla], *s. the morning* V[1] 101^{a}.2.

prātas [*S.* prātar], *adv. in the early morning* V[1] 1?^{a}.6.

prāṇ [*S.*], *s. life* V[1] 17^{a}.1. ~ mocakē *to die* H[1] 67^{b}.1, ~ twol-tē *id.* V[1] 23^{a}.1, ~ tyāg yāya *id.* Ś 163^{b}.5.

prāpt [*S. attained*], ~ yāya *to procure* B 60^{b}.3; ~ juya *to attain, to obtain* Bh 156^{b}.1.

prāpti [*S. s. obtaining*], ~ juya *to obtain* H[2] 76^{b}.1.

prāmakhalapē, *v. t. to examine* N 51^{b}.6*.

prāyaścitt [*S.*], *s. penance* P 56^{a}.1; ~ conē *to do penance* 62^{a}.1.

prārthanā [*S. prayer, appeal*], ch-hm-yāke ~ yāya *to ask or beg (something) of... (term of respect)* H[3] 3^{a}.7.

prāsād [*S.*], *s. a palace* V[1] 61^{a}.2.

prīti [*S. love*], ~ yāya *to love, to be or become attached to* (ch-hm-yāke) H[2] 60^{a}.1; -·wo -·wo prītin juya *to be attached one to another* B 7^{b}.12.

priy [*S. adj.*], *adj. friendly* V[1] 13^{a}.4. *s. kindness* H[2] 106^{a}.2.

priyaṅgu [*S.*], *s. a medicinal plant* Vd 16^{b}.3.

pruhit, *s.* = prohit C[1] 51*.

prem [*S. love*], ch-hm-wo nāp ~ juya *to be in love with...* M 2^{a}.6. — *adj. beloved* Vi 55.28.

preraṇ [*S. setting in motion*], ~ yāya *to set in motion* H[2] 82^{b}.8.

prohit [*S.* purohita], *s. a family priest* C[2] 52.

pvākhane, hnas-pot ~ *ear-boring* (karṇavedha) P 7^{a}.4*.

pvāt, *s.* = pvāth M 15^{a}.5. — *ifc.* **mat-**.

pvāte, *s. name of a plant* (hilamocikā) AH 33^{a}.

pvāth, *s. the belly, abdomen* B 19^{b}.7: mā-kwokhayā pvāthas dayāwo *the she-crow having become pregnant* H[2] 35^{a}.1. — *ifc.* **cay-**.

pvāpal, *adj. full* (ch-g *or* ch-g-n *of...*) M 38^{b}.7; ch-g-s ch-g ~ yāya *to fill something with something* Bh 178^{a}.7, ch-g-s ch-g ~ thanē *id.* 4^{b}.6, ch-g-s ch-g pvāpalan taya *id.* B 55^{b}.10.

pvāpwol, *adj.* = pvāpal Vi 31.3.

pvāl, *s. a hole, cave* H[1] 25[b].2; ~ lāya *to make a hole, to inflict a wound* Vi 175.4. — ~-gu ghāl *a wound* CW 8.44. — ~-co *penis* N 44[a].4. — *i/c.* **cay-, cimi-sa-, chu-, hnās-, pën-, phahaṁ-, siṁ-.**

ph.

pha(ṁ), *s. a measure of capacity* (= prastha) N 48[b].3.

phakan, *s. garlic* Vd 46[b].1; tawo ~ *a kind of garlic* (sthūlakanda) Md 50[b].6. — *i/c.* **mā-.**

phacakë (*caus. of* phaya[2]), ma phacakaṃ *not being able to* H[1] 19[a].5.

phacit [*from Arab.* faḍīḥat? *cf. Mr.* phajitī], *s. shame, disgrace* Vi 69.5; ~ yāya *to disgrace, to dishonour* H[2] 49[b].1; — *i/c.* **lajyā-.**

phacet, *s.* = phacit Bh 22[b].4.

pha-chi, *adv.* = phā-chi P 38[b].6*.

phat, ~ pulë *to tear asunder.*

phaṭaki (*also spelt* phatki) [*cf. S.* sphaṭika], *s. crystal* V[1] 61[b]. — **phatakir** *id.* V[2] 37[b].5.

phat-si, *s. a kind of pumpkin* (kuṣmāṇḍaka) B 34[b].4; **phat-simā** *the pumpkin plant ib.* 5.

phan-se [*S.* paṇasa], *s. the bread-fruit-tree* CW 6.20.

phaya[1] (-l[1]), *v. t. to support* Vi 163.22; *to bear, to endure* H[1] 23[b].5, *to resist* V[2] 33[b].1; ch-hm-yāke ~ *to rely upon...* H[1] 68[b].2; ch-g-s ~ *to seize hold of...* B 34[a].10.

phaya[2] (phat-, *else* -l[1]), *v. i. to be able* (yāya *to do...*) H[1] 18[b].2. — āmo upāy jinaṃ phayā *this device I can make use of* B 63[a].12; phayān phayā-hë(ṃ) *to the utmost of one's ability* H[3] 44[b].5; pha-chi — *id.* P 38[b].6; phakwo *adv. to the best of one's ability* B 13[a].9.

phaya[3] (-l[1]), *v. t.* = phāya[1] H[3] 51[b].4.

phaya[4] (-t), *v. t.* = phuya[1] Bh 58[a].6*.

phayi, *s.* = phasi[2] B 29[b].1. — ~-jawāl *a shepherd* Vi 93.4.

phal[1] [*H.* phaṛ *yard*], *s. a verandah or pavilion* (vedikā) AH 25[a]; *a sacrificial ground* P 44[a].5. — *i/c.* **jhyā-.**

phal[2] [*S.*], *s. fruit, result* H[2] 51[a].4; ~ biya *to bear fruits* 59[b].6. — *i/c.* **amp-, sisā-.**

phal[3], *s.* = pahal B 26[b].2.

phal[4], *s.* = pal[2] N 25[a].7.

phalakë, *see* **dhwok.**

phalay [phal[2]], ~ juya *to bear fruits* Vi 121.23.

phalalapë [phal[2]], *v. i. to bear fruits* H[1] 27[a].1. — phalalapayakë *caus. to bear as fruit, to result in* C[2] 93; phalalapakë *id. ib.*

phale, *s.* = phal[1](?) B 5[a].10.

phas[1], *s. air, wind* C[1] 267. — ~-kha *a lie, falsehood* B 57[a].6. — *i/c.* **gwo-.**

phas[2], = phasi[2] Bh 14[a].1*.

pha-si[1], *s.* = phat-si B 34[b].3.

phasi[2], *s. a sheep* H[1] 50[b].1. — ~-dudu *milk of a sheep* Vd 34[a].6.

phasi-gvāl, *s. name of several trees* (dhava, nanditaru) Md 38[a].7.

phas-kan, *s. a medicinal plant* Vd 46[b].4. — ~-ke *a broth made from this plant* 47[a].1.

phahaṁ [= phahan?], ~ tāya (-t) *to split with a wedge* H[2] 52[a].3, ~ dāya *id.* H[3] 25[a].2; ~-pvāl *a split, made with a wedge ib.*

phahan, sa ~ yāya *to tear one's hair* M 15[a].8; ~ ~ taya *id.* Vi 160.14.

phā[1], *s. a hog, boar* H[1] 72[b].5. — *i/c.* **gu-, che-, mā-.**

phā[2], *s.* = pha(ṃ) P 5[a].7. — *i/c.* **la-.**

phāṁ-gā, *s.* = phā-gā AH 44[a].

phā-kākë [phāya[1]], *v. t. to cut out* (*tongue*) N 51[b].5; *to cut open* (*belly*) *ib.*

phāku, *adj. astringent* Vd 45[b].2.

phā-gā [phāya[3] + gā], *s. a cloak* V[2] 75[a].7.

phā-chi, *adv. very, in a high degree* C[1] 144; phā-chin(aṃ) *id.* Ś 152ᵇ.3.

phāt[1] [*H.* pāṭ *a plank, board*], *cl-w.* Vi 116.22. — ~-lwoha *a flattened stone, a stone-slab* B 64ᵇ.5.— *ifc.* **lwoha-.**

phāt[2], ~ ile *a kind of ordeal* B 17ᵇ.6*.

phāḍalapë [= pho°], *v. t.* garbh ~ *to bring about a criminal abortion* N 52ᵃ.7*.

phāya[1] (-l[1]), *v. t. to cut* M 33ᵇ.8, *to tear, to rend* B 57ᵇ.3; *to destroy (a friendship)* H[2] 3ᵇ.2.

phāya[2] (-t), *v. t.* co ~ *to urine* N 44ᵃ.4; khi ~ *to relieve the bowels* H[2] 80ᵃ.4.

phāya[3] (-l[1]), *v. t. to cover* M 31ᵇ.2.

phāya[4] (phāt-, *else* -l[1]), *v. t.* = phaya[2] N 23ᵃ.5.

phāyakë[1] (*caus. of* phāya[1]) *to (suffer oneself to) be cut* M 33ᵇ.6.

phāyakë[2], *caus. of* phāya[3] V[2] 75ᵃ.7.

phāl [*M.* phār], *s. a ploughshare* B 54ᵃ.7.

phi, *s. sand* CW 2.3.

phiṁ, *cl-w.:* cāmal ni ~ *two Yak-tails* Bh 14ᵃ.8*.

phikë (*caus. of* phiya[2]), *to cause to be shrouded* (ch-g-n *in...*) B 27ᵇ.1.

phi-pati, *s. camphor* (abhraka) Md 33ᵃ.7.

phi-bhuṁ, *s. a sand-bank* (saikaṭa) CW 2.3.

phiya[1] (-t *or* -l[1]?), *v. t. to let expire (time)* P 55ᵃ.7.

phiya[2] (-t), *v. t. to envelop, to fold up* (ch-g-n *in...*) Vd 15ᵇ.5; *to immerse* (ch-g-s *in...*) B 59ᵃ.2.

phīli, *s. menses* N 32ᵃ.1*.

phu[1], *s. the crown of the head* N 27ᵃ.3.

phu[2], ~ khāya (-t), *to get dark; evening is drawing nigh* N 29ᵃ.1. — ~khācakë *id.* 22ᵃ.1*.

phu[3], ~ yāya *to spit* N 44ᵃ.4*.

phui, *s.* = phasi[3] H[3] 11ᵇ.10*.

phu-kij, *s. a brother (gen.)* N 39ᵃ.8; *mostly coll.: brothers* H[1] 96ᵃ.2. — phu-kiṃj *id.* N 2ᵃ.4.

phukë = phutakë H[2] 73ᵃ.4.

phu-ga, *s. a pillow* Ś 166ᵇ.1.

phuṁga, *s.* = phu-ga H[2] 79ᵇ.8.

phut, wā ~ chiṅāwo *grinding one's teeth* Bh 162ᵇ.4*.

phutakë (*caus. of* phuya[1]), *to destroy* Ś 152ᵃ.5, *to break (a promise)* Vi 171.13.

phuṭi [*cf. H. to be separated*], *s. a drop; only ifc.* **laṁkha-, hi-.**

phu-daṁ, *s. satiety* (tṛpti) AH 50ᵃ (phudang).

phupa [phu(-kij)], *s. a brother* N 38ᵃ.7.

— ~-kijā *id.* 40ᵃ.4. — ~-kiṃj *id.* 39ᵃ.6. — *ifc.* **kijā-.**

phu-phu, ~ dhāya *to pant, to gasp* Ś 155ᵇ.3*.

phuphulapë, *v. i. a symptom of disorder in the bowels (flatulence?)* Vd 12ᵃ.4*.

phubā, *s. a drinking-vessel(?)* B 55ᵇ.10*.

phuya[1] (-t), *v. i. to perish, to be destroyed* C[1] 140, *to be consumed, to be wasted* H[3] 31ᵃ.3. — *v. t. to destroy* Bh 113ᵃ.7, *to ruin* B 2ᵃ.9.

phuya[2], *v. t.* = phaya[1](?) V[1] 52ᵃ.5*.

phuya[3] (phut-, *else* -l[1]; *fifth form, espec. after* ma, *mostly* phu; *1st form a few times in* N phulaṃ), *v. i.* = phaya[2] H[2]20ᵇ.5; phuwon phuwo-thëṃ *to be best of one's ability* Bh 165ᵇ.2.

phuyakë, *v. t.,* dāman ~ *to make good the expenses* N 28ᵃ.3.

phuli [*H.* phullī *anything swollen or* S. phuliṅga *syphilis?*], ~-kachu *a kind of cutaneous disease* Vd 30ᵃ.1. — *ifc.* **bis-, yas-.**

phu-sa, *s. the hair on the crown of the head* CW 8.75.

phusalapë [*M.* phusiā *one who whispers; a deceiver; one who speaks falsely*], *v. t. to speak falsely to, to deceive (with words)* Bh 63ᵃ.3.

phusi, *s.*; *ifc.* **mikhā-**.

phek, ~ tuya (-t), *to sit down* H² 86ª.1; ~ tucakë *caus.* Bh 108ᵇ.1, ~ tutakë *id.* Vd 50ª.3.

phekë [phenë], *v. t. to tear asunder* H¹ 30ᵇ.3.

pheṭak, *s. a kind of weapon (bow?)* Vi 158.13*.

phenakë, *caus. of* phenë H² 17ᵇ.6.

phenë, *v. t. to tear asunder* H¹ 24ᵇ.3, *to break off* N 10ᵇ.4; *to release (by tearing the bonds)* B 40ᵇ.3; phesëṃ woya *to evade* N 16ᵇ.7. — *fig.: to affect deeply* B 49ᵇ.6; prāçitt ~ *to do penance* Vi 44.6.

pheya¹ (-l¹), *v. t. to lick* H¹ 61ª.4.

pheya² (-l¹), *v. t.*, pyās ~ *to quench the thirst* H² 42ᵇ.2.

pheya³, *v. t.* = phaya³ Bh 179ª.4*.

pheyakë (*caus. of* pheya¹?), *to administer medicine (of a half-liquid state)* Vd 24ᵇ.6.

pher [*rust. H. again*], ~ yāya *to repeat* Ś 153ᵇ.4; ch-g ~ helë *to exchange for...* N 24ª.3*.

phelakë, *v. t., see* **dhwok**.

phelā, ~ ~ tu(k) *adv. very much*(?) B 55ᵇ.5,6*.

pherāt [*H. a walk; visit*], ~ wonë *to visit, to attend* (ch-g-s *to...*) B 17ᵇ.7.

phaisi, *s.* = phasi² Md 62ª.1.

pho¹, ~ ni phonë *to beg urgently* Bh 22ª.7.

pho-² (phosëṃ *only*), *v. t. to resolve, to decompose* (laṃkhas *in water*) Vd 11ᵇ.5.

pho³, **phowo**, *5th form of* phaya² (= phu, phuwo) H¹ 9ᵇ.4.

pho-gi(ṁ) [phonë], *s. a beggar* M 9ª.3. — *ifc.* **jācak-**.

phoj [*cf. Mr.* phauja *from Arab.* faug̃], *s. an army* H² 94ª.1. — *ifc.* **sainy-**.

phot, ~ cālë *to reach; to hit* H¹ 74ᵇ.3.

phoḍalapë [*M.* phor], *v. t. to break, to smash* V¹ 2ᵇ.2; biśvās ~ *to abuse one's confidence* N 15ᵇ.8.

phonakë, *caus. of* phonë Bh 172ª.1.

phonë, *v. t.*, ch-hm-yāke ~ *to ask, to beg (something) of...* V² 30ª.2; ch-hm-yāta ~ biya *to give as a present to...* H² 89ª.7.

phopa, *s.* = phupa N 17ª.1*.

phol¹ [*H.* phul *flower, blossom*], *s. a blossom* Ś 157ᵇ.2. *gen. cl-w. (for flowers)* B 15ª.3. — *ifc.* **madan-**, **madhan-**.

phol² [*M.* phor *to break, to smash*], *s. destruction* Bh 128ᵇ.2; ~ juya *to be destroyed, to perish* H² 20ª.2, *to be wasted (effort)* 38ᵇ.7.

phoray [*M.* phor *to break*], ~ yāya *to break (a fortification)* H² 106ª.1.

pho-si, *s. Hibiscus mutabilis* Md 29ᵇ.1.

phyācakë (*caus. of* phyāya) *to redeem* N 20ª.5*.

phyā-phal, *adj. flat-nosed* AH 39ª (phyáphulu).

phyāya (-t), *v. t. to bring (as an offering)* B 39ª.10, *to give (as a payment)* N 7ᵇ.4.

phvā- (-t *or* -l¹? *only:* phvāṅāwo), *see* **kwo**, **du**.

phvāya (-t), *v. i.* = phaya² N 5ᵇ.4.

b.

ba¹, *s. soil, ground* H² 36ª.5. — *ifc.* **cho-**.

ba², *s. half* (= bā²) Ś 143ª.5; *gen.:* ba chi V¹ 93ᵇ.1.

ba³, ~ thëlë *to anoint* H² 46ᵇ.5; ~ thëlakë *caus.* H¹ 89ᵇ.2; ~ thilakë *id.* H³ 20ᵇ.9*.

baṁ-cho-lā, *s. the month Vaiśākha* CW 1.49.

baṁś [*S.* vaṃśa], *s. offspring* B 22ª.6.

bak^1 [*S.*], *s. a crane* H^2 76^a.7.

bak^2, *s. a bundle, bunch*(?) Ś 145^a.3.

bakaci [*H.* bakcā], *s. a medicinal plant* (candralekhā Md) Vd 32^b.3.

bakan, *s. a medicinal plant* Vd 46^b.1.

ba-kāy, *s.* = bā-° V^2 58^a.2*.

bak-si, *s. a kind of plant* (mahā-nimba) Md 9^a.4. ~-sē *id.*(?) Vd 36^b.5.

bakhat [*H.* vaqt *from Arab.*], *s. time* P 16^a.3.

bakhān [*M. a tale, narrative*], *s. news* B 55^a.4.

ba-khuṁ, *s. mod.* = bal-khunī H^2 107^b.1.

baṁk, ~ puya *to bow down respectfully* Vi 19.12*.

bac^1 [*M.*], *s. a word, utterance* H^3 28^a.10.

bac^2 [*H.*], *s. the orris-root* Vd 31^b.3.

bacan [*S.* vacana], *s. a word, utterance* V^1 13^b.2; ~ biya *to send word* Ś 160^a.4; ~ thwol *able to speak* H^2 56^a.1. — *ifc.* **śrāp-.**

bacay [*M.* bacab *to escape*], ~ juya *to escape* B 60^b.3.

bacalapē, *v. t.* = bañcalapē H^1 47^b.1.

bachā, *s. a spear* Vi 159.14*.

baji, *s. rice or grain flattened* H^2 52^a.5. — *ifc.* **tāya-.**

baji-hluyā, *s. a rice-mortar* V^1 73^a.6.

bajr [*S.* vajra], *s. a precious stone* V^1 1^a.6. — ~-malak *a thunder-clap* H^2 71^a.4.

bañcan(ā) [*S. deception, fraud*], ~ yāya *to deceive, to cheat* H^2 108^a.8.

bañcalapē [*S.* vañc-], *v. t. to deceive, to cheat* H^3 39^b.7.

ba-tāya, *v. t.*, bo ~ *to divide* N 37^b.5*.

batīs = battīs V^2 28^a.5.

batuk, *s.* = bastuk M 9^a.7*.

batt^1 [*cf. S.* vartaka], *s. a quail* Vd 5^b.6.

batt^2, *s.* = bastr P 33^b.7*.

battīs [*H.*], *num. thirty two* V^1 86^a.6.

bathān [*M. an enclosure for cattle*], *s. a herd, flock* CW 7.17. — ~-kisi *elephant(s), who belong(s) to the herd* H^2 77^a.2. — *ifc.* **kisi-, calā-, dhwol-, bwohal-, misā-, saḍa-.**

baḍ^1 [= bal^6], *s. inhonest dealing* N 24^a.9. baḍan kāya *to practise usury* 7^a.5; baḍan kāwo mi *a usurer* 48^b.3.

baḍ^2, *s.* = bal^1 N 41^a.4 (baḍan)*.

baḍan [*S.*], *s. a face* V^1 37^a.4.

baḍasācan [bal^5], *by fraud* N 41^b.3*.

baḍahar [*H.* baṛhal, baṛhar], *s. name of a fruit* (lakuca) Md 42^b.7.

baḍā [*H.* baḍā], *adj. great* Ś 161^a.7.

baḍāyi [*H.* baḍāī *greatness*], *s. manhood, manly courage* H^3 57^b.9*.

baḍi, *s. a share, partition* N 38^b.7. ~ thaya *to divide* V^1 111^b.3; ~ thasēṃ biya *to distribute* N 37^b.7. — ~-baṃtā *a share* N 17^b.7.

badiyār, *s. name of a plant, the root of which is used medicinally* Vd 23^b.2. — ~-hā 41^a.3.

bad-khuni, *s.* = bal-° H^2 10^a.1.

badh [*S.* vadha *a killer, slayer*], ~ yāya *to kill, to slay* V^2 44^a.6.

badhay [*H.* badhāī *increase, development*], ~ juya *itrs. to develop, to increase* M 6^a.5; ~ yāya *trs. id.* H^3 23^a.5.

badhar [*S.* vadhri], *adj. one whose testicles have been cut out* N 30^b.6*.

ban [*S.* vana], *s. a wood, forest* H^1 67^a.3. — *ifc.* **ghās-, hnal-pot-.**

banaj [*H.*], *s. trade, bussiness, commerce* V^1 96^b.6, *merchandise* N 21^a.7. ~ woya *to go out on business* H^3 22^b.5; ~ choya *to send out on b°* B 54^b.7; ~ jyāya *to carry on trade* 1^b.5; ~ jwoya *id.* N 24^a.9; ch-g ~ yāya *to deal in...* H^2 105^a.8. — *ifc.* **woho-, sala-.**

banajāl, *s.* = banijāl N 11^a.3.

banabaj [S. *vanavraja], *s. an inhabitant of the woods* N 26^b.3.

banāntar [*S.* vanāntara *the interior of a wood*], *s. a wood* H^1 93^b.2.

bani, *s.* = banik V[1] 68^{b}.1.

banik [*S.* baṇij], *s. a merchant* Vi 18.5. — ~-putr *the son of a merchant* Vi 84.33.

banijāl [*H.* banjārā *grain-merchant*], *s. a merchant* B 2^{a}.2. — *ifc.* **sala-**.

baniyā [*H.* banyā *a grain-seller*], *s. a merchant* V[2] 66^{a}.7. — ~-cā *the son of a merchant* Ś 143^{a}.2. — baniyāni *s. the wife of a merchant* V[2] 17^{b}.6. — ~-tiri *id.* H[2] 100^{a}.5.

baniyāl, *s.* = banijāl B 65^{a}.12.

baṁtā [ba-tāya], **baḍi** ~ thaya *to divide* N 40^{a}.4. — baḍi baṃtālapë *id.* 39^{b}.6.

bandak [*S.* bandhaka], *s. a pledge* N 8^{a}.5; ~ te *to give as a pledge* 19^{b}.7; ~ jwonë *to take as a pledge* 20^{a}.5.

bandanā [*S.* vandanā], ~ yāya *to worship* H[2] 78^{a}.1.

bandāb (?), *s. a bridegroom*(?) N 38^{a}.4*.

bandh[1] [*S. connection*], *s. connection; mode, manner* Ś 157^{a}.2.

bandh[2] [*S. bond, tie*], yāya *to bar, to block up* H[2] 95^{a}.7.

bandh[3] [*S.* —, *damming up*], *s. a dike for regulating the irrigation* (setu) N 27^{b}.2.

bandhan [*S. s. binding*], ~ yāya *to bind, to tie* Bh 83^{b}.4.

bandhalaṇë [bandh], *v. t. to bind, to tie, to fetter* Bh 54^{b}.6.

bandhi [*S.* bandhin *adj. binding*], ~ yāya *to imprison* H[2] 68^{b}.2; ~ taya *id.* H[3] 36^{b}.8.

bandhiyā (?), *s. a (war-)prisoner* N 19^{b}.8*.

bandhu [*S.*], *s. a kinsman* H[2] 93^{a}.7. — ~-jan *kinsmen* 60^{b}.5.

bapā, *s. a box, chest* (mañjūṣā) AH 61^{a}.

ba-pāyak [ba[1]?], *s. infantery* H[2] 87^{b}.8.

bap-cā, *s. a wag-tail* AH 34^{b}.

bab, *s.* = babu CW 8.31 (*gen.:* babyā).

babā [bā[1]], *s. a father* N 2^{a}.4; tawo ~ *a paternal uncle* 2^{b}.4 (tabāṃ). — ~-gotr *relatives on the father's side* 30^{a}.8.

babī, *s. a relative, kinsman* N 33^{a}.2. — ~-got(r) *distant relations* N 31^{a}.7. — *ifc.* **thaṁkāḍi-**.

babu, *s. a father* H[1] 24^{b}.5. — ~-ju *id.* B 17^{a}.2. — *ifc.* **mām-**, **sasal-**.

babyah (?), ~ te *to treat with contempt* N 46^{b}.6*.

bahmaṇī, °**hmuṇī** [*cf. Mr.* bāmhaṇī], *s. a brahman* H[3] 56^{b}.4.

bay [*S.* vyaya], *s. expense, expenditure* N 16^{a}.8, *pay, salary* H[3] 47^{a}.4. — ~biya *to defray the expenses* H[3] 46^{a}.11; ~ yāya *id.* N 40^{a}.5, *to spend (much) money* 49^{a}.6; ~ yāk-hma *a spendthrift* C[1] 119.

bayal [*cf. H.* ber], *s. jujube* (badara) C[1] 212. — ~-se *id.* Vd 24^{b}.3.

bayas [*S.*], *s. age* H[2] 44^{b}.7.

bal[1] [*S.*], *s. power, strength* Ś 160^{b}.2; ~ lāk *vigorous* H[2] 88^{b}.4. **balan** *adv. by force* N 41^{a}.3; ~ kāya *to rape, to violate ib.* 6.

bal[2] [*H.* bāṛ, bār *margin, fence*], *s. a border, land-mark* N 28^{b}.3. — *ifc.* **bu-**.

bal[3], *s. hut made of leaves* CW 4.3.

bal[4] [*S.* vara], *s. a gift, present* B 50^{a}.2.

bal[5] [*H. crookedness*], balan ciṅā *false* H[2] 66^{a}.1.

bal[6] [*H.* bar *up, out*; *from Pers.*], ~ hluya *to lift* H[1] 24^{a}.1*.

bal[7], *s.* = bel H[1] 22^{b}.1*.

baratinī, *s. ointment* Vd 15^{b}.3.

bal-adhikār [*S.* balādhikār *rape*], ~ yāya *to rape, to violate* B 52^{a}.12.

balahni, *s. evening* H[1] 12^{b}.1.

balabant [*S.*], *adj. vigorous, powerful* H[2] 50^{a}.1.

balā, *s. an arrow* B 47^{a}.11. — ~-cin *a butt, mark* AH 51^{b} (-ching). — ~-thu = ~ Vi 34.16; balā khu thu *six arrows* Bh 114^{a}.4. — *ifc.* **kām-**

balātkār [*S.*], *s. employment of force* H[2] 82ª.2.

balābal [*S.*], *s. strength and weakness, weak and strong points* H[2] 75ᵇ.5.

bali[1] [*S.*], *s. a gift, offering* H[3] 47ᵇ.8.

bali[2] [*cf. S.* vaḍiśa], *s. a fish-hook* AH 20ᵇ.

balikhā [*H.* barkhā], *s. the rainy season* H[3] 40ª.10. — ~-laṃkha *rain-water* Vd 13ª.2*.

baluṁ-simā [*S.* varuṇa *name of a tree?*], *s. a plant* (tiktaśāka) CW 6.12.

balobal, *s.* = balābal H[3] 40ᵇ.11.

bal-khu, *s.* = °-khunī B 3ª.9.

bal-khunī, *s. a pidgeon* H[1] 13ᵇ.2. — ~-khi *pidgeon-dung* Vd 38ᵇ.5. — ~-che *a dovecot* CW 4.10. — *ifc.* **prajā-, rājā-**.

bartamān [*S. existing*], ~ juya *to live, to exist* Vi 101.26, ~ yāya *to earn one's livelihood* 112.19; samay ~ yāya *to wait (and see)* H[2] 104ᵇ.4.

bartalapë [*S.* vart-], *v. i. to be, to exist* C[2] 137. — bartalapayakë *caus. to behave oneself* C[1] 276.

bardhamān [*S. increasing*], ~ juya *to increase (itrs.)* C[1] 185; ~ yāya *to set a-going* H[3] 48ª.7.

barṇ [*S.*], *s. colour* H[2] 43ª.1; *a caste* N 9ᵇ.2.

barṇā [*S.* varṇanā *description*], ~ hlāya *to describe* Bh 184ᵇ.5.

bal-se, *s. a medicinal plant* Vd 23ª.4.

bas = basā C[2] 191; bas *for* basas V[1] 36ª.2.

basalapë [*S.* vas-], *v. i. to live, to dwell, to stay* H[2] 42ᵇ.5, *gen.:* basalapaṃ conë *id.* H[1] 86ª.2.

basā [*S.* vaśa *will, desire*], ch-hm-yā basās conë *to be in the power or under the influence of...* H[2] 51ᵇ.1, — — wonë *id.* H[1] 5ᵇ.1, — — juya *id.* H[2] 26ᵇ.5; — — taya *to bring* — — H[3] 26ª.9, — — wonakë *id.* H[1] 5ª.2; **śokayā basās bi-jyāya** *to be overpowered by grief* M 24ᵇ.3; tnawo basā yāya *to subdue, to subjugate* H[2] 42ᵇ.1.

bastu [*S.*], *s. a thing, object* V[1] 48ᵇ.6; biya ~ *what is to be given* H[1] 18ª.3, dāya ~ *a measure, an instrument for measuring* N 48ᵇ.3.

bastr [*S.*], *s. a garment, dress* H[1] 90ª.3. — *ifc.* **kāpaḍ-**.

basy [*S.* vaśya *subdued*], ch-hm-yā ~ yāya *to be in one's power* V[2] 15ᵇ.3; basyas taya *to get in one's power* H[3] 2ᵇ.1.

bahani, *s. evening* B 17ª.5.

bahal [*cf.* bahalapë[2]], ~ juya *to be used* (yāya *to do a thing*) Vi 20.31, ~ yāya *id.* 93.5; ~ yāṅa(ṃ) joya *to subsist on* N 26ᵇ.3.

bahalapë[1] [*M.* bah *to flow*], *v. i. to flow (water)* H[6] 13ª.1, *to blow (wind)* Bh 84ᵇ.1, *to beat (pulse)* Vd 44ª.6. bahalapaṃ choya *to let swim* Vi 140.14.

bahalapë[2], *v. i.* = behalapë H[2] 68ª.8.

bahili[1], *adj. barren* Ś 145ª.4.

bahili[2] [*cf. S.* vihāra], *s. a sanctuary, temple* H[2] 52ª.4.

bahuli, *s. a kind of musical instrument* Vi 151.2*.

bā[1], *s. a male (bird or animal)* H[2] 69ª.4; *a father* B 33ᵇ.4.

bā[2], *s. half* B 57ª.8; bā la chi *half a month* P 56ª.6.

bā[3], *s.* = ba[1] V[1] 49ᵇ.2.

bā[4], *s. for* cakhabā V[2] 71ª.2.

bāṁ-lā-hma, *adj., mod.* = bān-lāk Ś 157ª.7.

bā-kāy, *s. father and son* V[1] 95ª.2.

bākār, *s.* = bāhākār Vd 1ᵇ.6*.

bāki [*H.* bāqī *from Arab.*], *s. a rest, remnant* H[3] 13ᵇ.1.

bā-kos, *s. half a krośa* P 12ᵇ.3.

bā-kwokha, *s. a male crow* H[2] 65ᵇ.8.

bāky [*S.* vākya], *s. a word, speech* Ś 159ª.3.

bākhan(ā) [*f.* bakhān], *s. an ancient tale, story of the past* (purāṇa) AH 15^b.

bā-khel, *s. half waste land* (ardha-khila) N 28^a.5*.

bā-guṇ, *s. manly virtue* B 43^a.3.

bāgo [*mod.* = bā-gwol], *adj.*, ~-hma *crippled, mutilated* AH 39^a.

bāgh[1] [*M.*], *s. a tiger* B 49^b.5. — ~-chālā *a skin of a tiger* H[2] 75^b.8.

bāgh[2], *s. a flute* M 4^a.7*.

bā-ghali, *s. half a gharī, twelve minutes* M 19^a.7.

bā-cal-khunī, *s. a male sparrow* B 31^b.12.

bā-cā[1], *s. midnight* B 62^b.9.

bācā[2] [*S. speech*], ~ yāya *to negotiate* H[3] 52^a.3; ~ biya *to give notice* N 23^b.3. — *ifc.* **abhay-.**

bā-cāti, *s. midnight* (= bā-cā) B 44^b.5.

bāj, *s.* = byāj N 23^b.4.

bājan [*H. poet.*], *s. a musical instrument* CW 1.68; ~ thātakë *to let play a musical instrument* Ś 169^b.5, ~ hātakë *id.* 169^b.2; ~ thāk *a musician* N 45^a.6; ~ thāwo *a Gandharva* CW 1.5.

bā-ju [bā[1]], *s. a father* B 52^b.5.

bājhā, ~ woṅ-hma(?) *a middle aged widow in red clothes* (kātyāyanī) AH 37^b (bájháwangmha).

bāñchā [*S. wish*], ~ yāya *to wish* H[1] 75^a.3; ch-hm-yā ~ julaṃ *it is the wish of…, … has the wish* M 2^b.8.

bāt[1] [*S.* vāta], *s. wind* H[3] 40^b.2, *wind as one of the humours of the human body* Vd 10^a.5. — ~-log *a disease, arising from a disordered state of the wind in the body* CW 8.48. — ~-loy *id.* Vd 22^a.2. — ~-jwol *fever, arising from* …. 2^a.1.

bāṭ[2] [*M.*], *s. a path, road* N 42^a.1*.

bāt[3], *s.* = wāt V[2] 73^b.4. — ~-kut *id.* CW 1.58.

bātrā [*S.* vārtā], *s. report, news* Bh 91^a.1.

bāḍ[1] [*H.* bāṛ], *s. a fence* N 28^b.4.

bād[2] [*S.* vāda], ~ yāya *to speak, to talk* B 34^b.12; ~ lvāya *to argue* 35^b.7; ~ bibād yāya *id.* H[2] 114^b.1.

bā-da [da], *yes may-be* H[3] 27^a.6*.

bādapo, *s. name of a medicinal plant* Vd 55^a.1.

bādī[1] [*H. wicked person*], ch-g-s ~ yāya *to injure, to damage a thing* N 41^a.3,5*.

bādi[2] [*S.* vādin], *s. a plaintiff* N 9^b.7.

bādy [*S.* vādya], *s. a musical instrument* Ś 167^b.7.

bādhalapë [*H.* bādhā *increase, progress*], *v. i. to prosper* N 29^b.6, *to increase* 25^b.1. — bādhalapayakë *caus. to make prosper* 36^b.5, *to increase, to add to* 25^b.2; dharm ~ *to do one's duty* 52^a.4.

bādhā [*S.* bādhā *injury, damage*], ~ yāya *to hurt, to injure* V[1] 69^b.6.

bān[1] [*S.* vāṇa], *s. an arrow* Bh 99^a.7.

bān[2] [*H. character* —], *s. only ifc.* (*having the character of*): **cwok-, pyāla-, hma-.**

bānar [*S.* vānara], *s. a monkey* H[2] 55^b.6.

bāṇi [*cf. S.* vaṇij], *s. a merchant* H[2] 84^a.1. — ~-putr *the son of a merchant* H[2] 46^b.4.

bāṇik, *s.* = bāṇi H[1] 89^b.3.

bānë, *v. t. to use, to wear (apparel); or: to wash*(?) N 25^a.3.

bāndhab [*S.* bāndhava], *s. a relative, kinsman* H[1] 34^b.3.

bān-lāk, *adj. handsome, beautiful* B 40^a.1. — bān-lākë *v. t. to make beautiful* H[2] 81^b.3.

bā-hni, *s. noon* B 47^b.11.

bāp [*M.*], *s. a father* N 6^a.2. — ~-ajā *forefathers* 2^a.6. — *ifc.* **ajā-.**

bābā [bā], *s.* 1) "*father*"; *used only as a vocative: o venerable one* B 52^b.3. — 2) *brother, only ifc.* **abu-.**

bā-milā, *s. half a* milā Vd 50^a.3; bā-melā *id.* 38^b.4.

bā-hma [bā], *s. the (lower) half of the body* Vi 159.14.

bāya[1] (-l[1]), *v. i. to move* V[2] 54^{b}.6*.

bāya[2] (-l[1]), *v. i. to be, to stay somewhere* V[2] 54^{b}.6.

bāya[3] (-l[1]), *v. i. to go to pieces* H[1] 52^{a}.1, *to separate* B 57^{a}.7.

bāyak, *s.* = pāyak (*clerical error?*) V[2] 74^{a}.6*.

bāyal, *s.* = pāyal AH 43^{b}.

bāyī [*cf. Mr.* bāī *a term for respectful compellation for one's mother or an elderly female*], *adj. aged* N 46^{b}.7*.

bāyu [*S.*], *s. wind* H[2] 97^{b}.5.

bāyu(wo) [bāya[2]], *s. a being, person* V[1] 123^{b}.2.

bāyub, *s.* = bāyu Bh 33^{a}.3.

bāl[1] [*H.* **bār** *day, time*], *s. a day* V[2] 76^{a}.6; ~ hnin *every day* Vi 143.35, bālaṃ *id.* Vd 4^{b}.5; swo-bāl *thrice* Vi 33.33; bāl chi-toṃ *some time* N 38^{b}.8. — bāl-chi *the first lunar day* AH 10^{b}. — *ifc.* **tithi-**.

bāl[2], *s. a kind of lotus* (śrīvāsa) Md 27^{a}.7.

bāl[3] [*cf. H.* bār *a load, burden; from Pers.*], *s., only ifc.* **khwobhi-, laṁkha-, hi-**.

bāl[4] = bād[2]: ~ lvāya B 35^{a}.10.

bālak(h) [*S.* bālaka], *adj. young* C[1] 296. — *s. a boy* H[2] 78^{b}.5, *a young animal* Vi 35.6; *boyhood* H[1] 7^{b}.1.

bālatu, *see* bālë.

bāraṁbār [*H.*], *adv. continually, again and again* H[3] 35^{a}.5, *by degrees* H[1] 18^{b}.3.

bāralapë [*H.* bāṛ *a fence* — —], *v. i.* ch-hm-n *to withdraw from..., to keep aloof* N 32^{b}.1.

bā-lā[1], *s. half a month* H[3] 27^{a}.6.

bā-lā[2] [lā], *perhaps* H[3] 27^{a}.6*.

bālād, *s. name of a plant* (bhallātakī) Md 17^{a}.7.

bāli[1] [*H.* bāṛī], *s. a cotton-field* B 38^{b}.10. — **~-thuwāl** *the owner of a cotton-field ib**.

bāli[2] [*M.* **bāri** *young, tender*], *adj. under age* N 4^{a}.7. *s. a child* 17^{b}.6.

bālë, *v. t. to mix, to blend* (ch-g-n or ch-g-wo *with...*) Bh 31^{b}.1. — cikan ~ *a kind of ordeal* B 17^{b}.6.

bās[1] [*S.* **vāsa**], *s. an abode* H[2] 50^{b}.8. ~ biya *to give shelter* V[1] 11^{b}.5; ~ yāya *to make a stay, to take rest* B 49^{b}.3; ~ conë *to stay (for a longer space of time)* 12^{a}.11.

bās[2] [*S.* vāsas], *s. clothes* N 41^{a}.4*.

bā-saḍa-cā, *s. a horse-colt* B 33^{a}.9.

bāsanā [*H.* bāsnā *smell*], ch-g-yā ~ kāya *to smell at...* Ś 162^{a}.5.

bā-sā, *s. a bull* N 28^{b}.5.

bāsiris, *adv.* = bāhilis Vi 145.30*.

bāhan [*S.* vāhana], *s. a vehicle* H[2] 112^{a}.6.

bāhalapë [*S.* vāhaya- (*caus. of* vah-) *to cause to bear; to keep going*], *v. t. to transport* N 21^{b}.6; kṛśān ~ *to be engaged in agriculture* 19^{b}.3.

bāhā, *s.* = bāhu H[3] 47^{a}.5.

bāhākār, *s. hickup* Vd 4^{b}.3*.

bāhāl, *s. a shoulder* Vi 159.13.

bāhik[1] [*S.* vāhika], *s. a carrier* N 21^{b}.7.

bāhik[2] [*S.* bāhīka *being outside*], *adv.* (*mostly:* bāhikan(aṃ)) *besides, for the rest* N 34^{b}.5; ch-g ~ *besides...* H[2] 39^{a}.1; ch-hm ~ meb...ma *no other than...* Ś 163^{b}.2.

bāhiri [*H.* bāharī *exterior, outer*], *adv.*, ch-g ~ *out of...* P 12^{b}.2; ~ yāya *to get outside* N 30^{b}.3. — *usually:* bāhiris; ch-g(-yā) ~ *out of...* B 51^{b}.1, *outside...* H[2] 35^{a}.5.

bāhu [*S.*], *s. an arm* V[1] 10^{a}.2.

bi[1], *s. a serpent* H[3] 59^{b}.5. — *ifc.* **āyal-, dal-, dhaban-, hnas-, bolo-, mā-, sākhāl-**.

bi[2], *adv. aside:* ~ kaṅāwo swoya *to glance at* CW 8.72. — ~ phiya (-t) *to turn off* M 30^{a}.8. — netr ~ boya *to take the eyes off* Bh 72^{a}.6.

bi-ujhā, *s. snake-catcher* (ahituṇḍika) N 11ᵃ.5.

bikār [*S.* vikāra *change* — —], ~ lāya *to be disappointed* H² 34ᵃ.3; ~ yāya *to change, to alter* H³ 38ᵃ.11.

bikāsamān [*s.* bikāsalapë], ~ yāya *to open (eyes)* Ns 2ᵃ.2.

bikāsalapë [*S.* vi-kāś *to appear, to become visible*], *v. i. to bloom* Ns 2ᵃ.2.

bikṛti [*S. change, alteration*], ~ lāya *to fail, not succeed* H¹ 22ᵃ.2.

bikri [*S.* vikraya *sale*], ~ yāya *to sell* Vi 21.8*.

bikriyā [*S. change*], ~ wonë *to undergo a change* H¹ 50ᵃ.2; ~ yāya *id.* C¹ 64.

bikṣ, *s.* = bṛkṣ V² 26ᵃ.3.

bikhu, *s.* = bhikṣu H² 62ᵇ.5.

bi-khul, *s. the skin of a serpent* CW 2.1.

bigrah [*S.*], *s. a war* H² 84ᵃ.2; ~ yāya *to wage war* 69ᵃ.6.

bighn [*S.*], ch-g-s ~ yāya *to prevent from...* M 33ᵇ.2.

bicakṣaṇ [*S.*], *adj. wise, experienced* H² 54ᵃ.8.

bicār [*S.* vicāra *procedure, reflection, investigation*], *s. an affair, oncercn* B 33ᵇ.4. ~ yāya *to care for, to take charge of* (ch-g(-s) *a thing*) H³ 26ᵃ.1, *to investigate* V² 14ᵇ.2, *to inquire* H³ 33ᵃ.6; *to greet, to welcome* B 48ᵃ.4, *to visit* V¹ 31ᵃ.5; ch-g-s ~ yākë *to put in charge of...* B 55ᵃ.10; ~ yātakë *to let investigate* Ś 151ᵇ.1; ~ ṅenë *to make inquiries* H² 61ᵇ.8; ~ he *to examine as witness* N 10ᵇ.4. — ~-kha *an affair* V¹ 49ᵃ.3; ~ -kha hlācakë *to let make a deposition (as a witness)* N 12ᵃ.5. — ~-saṃcār yāya *to investigate* H³ 32ᵃ.8, *to inquire after one's health, to greet* Vi 79.11; ~ dayakë *id.* H² 35ᵃ.1.

bicitr [*S.*], *adj. splendid* V¹ 9ᵇ.4; ~ yāṅaṃ *splendidly* H² 32ᵇ.6.

bich [*Bhojp.* bichhī], *s. a scorpion* H³ 59ᵇ.4.

bīj [*S.*], *s. seed* B 60ᵇ.5. **bījan** jāyalapu kāy *a self-begotten son* N 39ᵃ.3. — *ifc.* **kuṭ-**.

bijay [*S. victory*], *s. victory* H² 117ᵇ.3; *defeat*(?) Vi 157.22.

bi-jyācakë (*caus. of* bi-jyāya), *to lead, to conduct* H² 95ᵃ.6; *to let sit down* Bh 40ᵃ.4.

bi-jyātakë = °-jyācakë Vi 167.10.

bi-jyāya (-t), *v. i.* (*a term of respect for* wonë, woya, conë) *to go* V¹ 118ᵃ.5, *to come* H¹ 88ᵃ.2, *to stay, to live* V² 61ᵇ.1, *to sit down* B 7ᵇ.4. — *In connection with the 9th or 10th form or the conv. in* ·āwo: *to deign to..., to condescend to...* H² 87ᵇ.2.

bitakë (*caus. of* biya³), tāuti ~ *to protract the time* Bh 23ᵇ.2*.

bitay [*M.* bit], ~ juya *to pass away, to elapse* M 8ᵃ.4.

bitānt, *s.* = bṛt(t)ānt V² 36ᵃ.3.

Bituwā, *name of a man* B 39ᵇ.3.

bitt [*S.* vitta], *s. property* N 37ᵇ.4. — ~-bhaṇḍār *id.* 19ᵇ.4.

bithī, *s. the earth* V² 81ᵇ.2*.

bidamān [*from S.* vid- *to know*], *adj.*, ~ puruṣ *an eye-witness* N 10ᵃ.7. — ~ yāya *to know* 9ᵃ.5.

bidāran [*S.* vidāraṇa *s. tearing asunder*], ~ yāya *to go to pieces* Bh 62ᵃ.2.

biḍe-, ~-se = beḍe-° Vd 25ᵇ.3; ~-ke *broth made from this plant* 47ᵃ.1.

bideś [*S.* videśa], *s. a foreign country* H² 37ᵃ.5. ~ wonë *to go abroad* B 65ᵃ.5.

bidy [*S.* vidya *adj. finding*], ~ yāya *to find, to procure* B 23ᵇ.6.

bidyamān = bida° N 8ᵇ.1*.

bidyā [*S.*], *s. knowledge, science* H² 2ᵃ.1, *art* N 19ᵃ.7. ~ sawo *a Vidyādhara* CW 1.4. — **bidyābant** [*S.*] *adj. learned* H² 28ᵃ.6.

bidvāṁsi [*S.* vidvān], *s. a knowing person* N 53ᵃ.1; *a learned man* C² 141.

bidhātā [*S.* vidhātṛ], *s. a creator* H² 43ᵃ.2.

bidhān [*S.* vidhāna *s. arranging*], ~ yāya *to arrange, to prepare* B 46b.4.

bidhi [*S.*], *s. a rule, prescription* N 24a.7, *mode, manner* C¹ 72, *a sort, kind* N 9a.4. pē-tā ~ *fourfold ib.* 7; bigrahayā ~ yāya *to act in accordance with the rules for war* H² 83b.7.

bidhu [*S.* vidhu *lonely*], ~ cāya *to feel lonely, to be dejected* H² 54b.1; bidhun cāya *id.* H³ 45b.1*.

binatalapē [*S.* vinata *humble, modest*], *v. i. to be humble or modest* H¹ 10a.1*.

binati [*S.* vinati *humility, modesty*] = bimati H² 7b.5.

binā [*M. without*], *adv.*, ~...ma *if... not, unless* M 11b.5; ~ ch-g-s *without*... Vi 37.5, ~ ch-g-n *id.* 42.10. — binān(aṃ) *adv. besides, otherwise* H³ 39a.7; ch-g ~ *without*... Vi 23.6, *besides*... 26.16.

binun = pinu V¹ 15b.4*.

binti [*corrupt. from* binati] = bimati B 48b.8.

bipakṣ [*S.* vipakṣa], *s. an adversary* H³ 45a.3; ~ yāya *to act as an opponent, to be an opponent* H² 84₂b.1.

bipat(t)i [*S.* vipatti], *s. misfortune* H¹ 23a.1.

bipadā [*S.*], *s. misfortune* H² 106b.6.

biparīt [*S.*], *adj. wrong* Vi 76.33. *s. adversity* 55.27. — biparītan *adv. wrongly* Bh 47a.7.

biphot [*cf. S.* visphoṭa *a blister*], ~-kachu *a cutaneous disease with blisters* Vd 32a.3.

bibaṭalapē, *v. t. to find out* N 48b.2*.

bibahār [*H.* bevhār *practice, custom*], *s.* 1) *custom* H³ 30a.3, *conduct* 33b.2. — 2) (*cf.* bibāhār) *marriage* H³ 32b.5; ~ yāya *to arrange a marriage* (ch-hm-yāta *for*...) Vi 53.8; ~ yāñā biya *to give into wedlock* B 6a.3.

bibād [*S.* vivāda], *s. quarrel, dispute* N 10a.2; ~ yāya *to raise a dispute* V¹ 111b.5.

bibāh(ā) [*S.* vivāha], *s. marriage, wedding* H² 95b.3. —~yāya *to marry* (ch-hm(-wo) *somebody*) V¹ 85b.4; ~ yāñāwo biya *to give into wedlock* (ch-hm-wo *to*...) B 47a.8, *to arrange a marriage* (ch-hm-yāta *for*...) Vi 63.10; ~ yāñaṃ taya *to give into wedlock* H³ 14a.1. — ~-karm yāya *to celebrate a wedding* Vi 63.7. — **bibāhi** [*cf. S.* vivāhika], *s. a husband* N 35b.6; ~ strī *a married woman ib.* 7.

bibāhār *s.* = bibāhā, *through confusion with* bibahār Vi 53.8.

bibidh [*S.* vividha], *adj. manifold* V¹ 1a.5.

bibek [*S.* viveka *discrimination*], ~ ma du *not different* H¹ 4a.1; ~ ma yāsēṃ *thoughtlessly* H³ 31a.5.

bi-bol [bol], ch-hm-yāta ~ biya *to abuse, to revile*... N 43a.8; ch-hm ~ hlāya *id.* 46b.6.

bibhūti [*S.* —, *great power*], *s. magical power*(?) B 46a.6.

bimati [*corrupt. from* binati], *s. humble, most obedient words* H² 86a.7; ~-kha *id.* M 1a.6. — bimati yāya *to bow down, to pay reverence* Vi 67.10; sebā ~ yāya *id.* H³ 20a.7; ch-hm-yāke ~ yāya *to say, to tell, to ask deferentially* B 60a.2; kha ~ yāya *to tell, to make known* H³ 40a.1; ~ thēnakē *to send word* (*deferentially*) Ś 151b.1.

bimarṣ [*S. reflection; examination*], ~ yāya *to reflect* H² 67b.7, *to examine* 59b.3.

bimān [*S.*], *s. a charriot* B 24b.12. — ~-khat *id.* Vi 59.23.

bimukh [*S.* vimukha], *adj. averse, opposed* H¹ 38b.7.

bi-moc, *s. a small house-lizard* CW 7.5.

bi-mvāc, *s.* = °-moc AH 34b.

biya¹ (-l¹), *v. t. to give, to present*

(ch-hm-yāta *to*...) H[1] 78[a].2; *to cause (pain etc.)* V[1] 129[b].2; *to permit* B 7[b].7. trās ~ *to frighten* C[1] 82; utal ~ *to answer* V[2] 46[a].7; dānāgān ~ *to pay a debt* N 2[a].1; aparādh ~ *to charge with a crime* Vi 42.22. — *Used as an auxiliary after the conv. in* ·āwo *denoting that an action is performed for the benefit of another:* jin... thwo rājy jitay yāṅāwo biya *I shall conquer this kingdom (for you)* Vi 155.16.

biya[2] (-l[1]), *v. i.* = bëya Vi 37.27; bisëṃ wonë *to fly, to run away* V[2] 49[a].4, bisëṃ woya *id.* B 5[a].8; biyāwo choya *to despatch* H[3] 57[b].3.

biya[3] (-t), *v. i. to pass away, to elapse (time)* C[1] 179, *to set (as the sun)* CW 5.1.

biyakë[1], *caus. of* biya[1] H[1] 85[b].2.

biyakë[2] (*caus. of* biya[2]) = bëyakë H[3] 51[b].4; biyakal haya = bëyakaṃ yanë V[2] 50[b].4.

biyog [*S.*], *s. separation* H[2] 90[a].1; biyogan woya *to become separated* B 56[b].5.

bīr [*S.* vīra], *s. a (brave) man, hero* V[1] 7[a].6.

bilamb [*S. hesitation*], ~ juya *to hesitate, to be delayed* Vi 79.14; ~ yāya *id.* H[2] 90[b].1.

bilambh, *s.* = bilamb M 20[a].8; ~ yāya *to delay, to protract* Vi 54.35.

biras [*S. without taste; loathsome*], ~ yāya *to be reluctant or refractory* H[1] 81[a].1.

birah [*S. separation*], *s. longing* V[1] 67[a].5; ~ cāya *to become affected with longing* (ch-hm-yā *for*...) B 40[a].4.

birahalapë [birah], *v. t.*, bilahalapaṃ choya *to desire (profit)* N 15[b].7*.

birahinī [*S.* virahinī *adj. fem. separated from*], *s. longing* V[2] 49[a].5. *adj. longing (masc.)* V[1] 11[a].5.

bilāgo, *s. a wooden bolt for fastening a door* AH 25[a].

bilāp [*S. lamentation*], ~ yāya *to lament* H[1] 42[a].1.

bilās [*S. flirt*], ~ yāya *to flirt* H[1] 62[b].5. — bilāsalapë *v. i. id.* Bh 58[a].2.

bili, *s. a wasp* AH 35[b].

bili-si, *s.* = beḍe-se AH 31[a].

biruddh [*S.*], *adj.*, ch-hm-wo ~ *objectionable to*... V[1] 57[a].3.

birodh [*S.*], *s. hostility* H[2] 72[a].4.

birodhī [*S.* virodhin *obstructing*], ~ yāya *to obstruct* N 27[a].7.

birj [*S.* virya], *s. seed (of a man)* V[1] 96[b].1.

biṣ [*S.*], *s. poison* V[2] 12[a].2; biṣayā *poisoned ib.* 5.

bis [= biṣ?], ~-phuri *a cutaneous disease, caused by poison*(?) Vd 35[a].4*.

biṣay [*S.* viṣaya *thing, object*], *s.* 1) *property* N 5[b].4; ṅyāṅā ~ *merchandise* 24[b].6. 2) *a sense:* hnās-~ *the sense of smell,* meyā ~ *the sense of taste,* hmayā ~ *the sense of touch* AH 14[a]. — stribiṣayan *for the sake of a wife* N 2[b].1.

bisaralapë [*M.* bisar], *v. t. to forget* N 10[b].1*.

biṣād [*S.*], *s. consternation, amazement* H[2] 94[a].1; ~ yāya *to be disconcerted, amazed* 85[a].5. — biṣādi [*S.* viṣādin], *adj. disconcerted, amazed* H[1] 92[a].1; biṣādin conë *to be disconcerted, amazed* Bh 82[a].4.

biśeṣ [*S.* viśeṣa *difference, peculiarity*], biśeṣan(aṃ) *adv. especially, particularly* H[2] 84[a].5; ch-g(-yā) ~ *in accordance with*... Vi 49.30.

biśeṣalapë [biśeṣ], *v. i. to take special care* N 37[b].3; biśeṣalapaṃ *adv. especially* 14[a].4*.

bisëkë (*irreg. caus. of* biya[2]), *to let escape* Vi 119.22*.

biṣṭā [*S.*], *s. faeces* Vd 9[b].1.

bistār [vistāra *spreading* —, *detailed description*], *s. progress of events* Vi 123.23; ~-āyuṣ *lengthening of life, lengthened life* 122.24. — bistāran *adv. at length* 136.15.

bismay [*S.*], *s. a wonder, surprise* H² 50ᵇ.3; ~ yāya *to wonder, to be surprised* M 7ᵇ.1; ~ cāya *to become astonished or surprised* H¹ 12ᵇ.1.

biśrām [*S. rest, repose*], ~ yāya *to rest, to repose* H¹ 43ᵇ.2.

biśvās [*S.*], *s. trust, confidence* H² 73ᵇ.3; ch-hm-yā ~ siya *to enjoy the confidence of...* B 58ᵃ.7. — biśvāsas conë *id.* H³ 36ᵇ.1; ch-hm-yāke biśvās(an) siya *to commit (a thing) to one's charge* Bh 128ᵃ.3, — — seya *id.* N 15ᵇ.4; ch-hm-wo biśvās yāya *to place one's confidence in..., to trust...* H¹ 38ᵇ.4, ch-hm-yāke(n) — — *id.* V² 16ᵃ.3; biśvās yāk *trustworthy* H¹ 38ᵇ.4, ~ yākwo *id.* H² 47ᵇ.3.

bihaṁg [*S.*], *s. a bird* B 23ᵃ.8. — bihaṃgam [*S.*], *s. id.* 23ᵃ.4.

bihaḍ [*H.* bihaṛ *land broken into ravines*], *s. a pit* (viṣama) N 22ᵃ.4*.

bihalapë, *v. i.* = behalapë V² 62ᵃ.3*.

bihili, *adj. barren* (= bahili) N 36ᵃ.2.

bu¹, *s. a field* H¹ 48ᵃ.4. — *ifc.* **taṁ-, paṁth-, bleṅe-.**

bu², *s.* = bo²; ~ hoya B 35ᵃ.2; ~ huya *id.* 28ᵃ.1. — *ifc.* **kuhnali-, cha-si-.**

bu³ = pu⁴; ~ jaṅaṃ wonë N 33ᵇ.8*.

bu-kha, *s.* = bo-kha V² 38ᵃ.1; ~ hak-hma *a go-between* (dūtī) CW 8.12. — bu-khā = °-kha (V¹ *only*) 61ᵃ.6.

bu-khat, ~ kān *born blind* C¹ 178*.

bu-khā, *s.* = bhu-khā AH 25ᵃ.

bu-gāl, *s.* = bo-gād(?) Md 52ᵃ.7.

bucakë (*caus. of* buya¹) = buyakë¹ C² 288.

bu-cal-khunī [bu¹], *s. a sort of sparrow* Md 73ᵇ.3.

bujalapë [*M.* būjh *to know, under-stand*], *v. t. to know, to understand, to consider* N 51ᵇ.6.

bujār, *ifc.* **gal-.**

bu-jyā, *s. agriculture* AH 53ᵃ.

bu-jhamar-si, *s. name of a plant* (bhūmijambukā) AH 28ᵇ (bujhamasi).

bujhay [*H.* bujhānā *to cause to believe, to convince*], ~ yāya *to give notice, to instruct* H² 72ᵇ.8.

bujhik [*s.* bujhay], *s. a wise, sensible man* H² 82ᵇ.4.

butu, ~ bulë *to fall down* H² 113ᵇ.8.

buto-se, *s. a medicinal plant* Vd 24ᵃ.3.

bu-thuwāl, *s. the owner of a field* H³ 10ᵇ.2.

budalapë [*M.* būṛ *to drown, be drowned*], *v. i. to sink, to go down (ship)* V¹ 60ᵇ.3.

bude-kasulī, *s. a medicinal plant* (bhadramustaka AH) Vd 40ᵇ.5.

budhān [*S.*], *adj. knowing, wise* B 20ᵇ.13.

buddhi [*S.*], *s. cleverness, sagacity* V¹ 129ᵃ.1, *a trick* N 50ᵃ.1, *a purpose, design* Ś 163ᵃ.5; ~ biya *to give good advice* H³ 21ᵇ.4. — buddhiwont [*S.* buddhivat], *adj. wise, intelligent* Ś 167ᵃ.3. — *ifc.* **kapat-, mithyā-.**

bunë, *v. t.* = bonë B 43ᵇ.7.

bu-baṁ, *s. agricultural implements* N 41ᵃ.4*.

buya¹ (-l¹), *v. i. to be born* B 35ᵃ.8; *to grow (of plants)* Vd 45ᵇ.4. — gvāy buwo-hma misā *a hermaphrodite* CW 8.12.

buya² (-l¹), *v. t. to bear, to carry* N 21ᵇ.7; *to take with him* M 5ᵇ.2; *to help, to support* C¹ 110. busëṃ yanë *to carry (away) with him* B 54ᵇ.4.

buya³ (-t *or* -l¹?), *v. t. to recognize (a debt)* N 2ᵇ.4*.

buya⁴ (-l¹), *v. t. to rub* P 14ᵃ.7; wā ~ *to clean one's teeth* C¹ 290; hmas cikanan ~ *to rub oil on the body* B 28ᵃ.4.

buya⁵ (-t), *v. t. to lose (julan at play)* V¹ 90ᵇ.5; khan ~ *to lose a law-suit* N 15ᵃ.4; annan buk *without food* H² 93ᵇ.6.

buya[6] (-l[1]), *see* **lāy**.

buyakë[1] (*caus. of* **buya**[1]), *to bear (a child)* C[1] 171.

buyakë[2], *caus. of* **buya**[2]; *see* **ku**.

buyakë[3], *caus. of* buya[4] B 17[b].9.

buyalkā, *s. name of a plant* (droṇapuṣpaka) CW 6.25.

bulu, *adj. unclear, turbid* CW 2.5.

bulu-hun, *adv. slowly* H[2] 66[b].2; *cautiously* Vi 118.20.

bulë[1], *v. i. to shake*(?) B 38[b].9. — *v. t. to shake* Vd 15[a].2. — botu ~ *to shake violently (itrs.)* H[3] 61[a].2.

bulë[2], *v. i.* = bolë H[3] 61[a].8.

bu-sā, *s.* = bo-sā H[3] 59[b].7.

bṛkṣ [*S.*], *s. a tree* H[1] 27[a].1. — *ifc.* **aśok-**.

bṛt(t)ānt [*S.* vṛttānta], *s. an event, proceedings* H[2] 92[b].2. — ~-kha *a story* M 21[b].7.

bṛt(t)āntal, *s.* = bṛt(t)ānt H[2] 22[b].6.

bṛthā-kha [*cf. S.* vṛthā-vāc], *s. untrue speech, a lie* Bh 22[a].4*.

bṛdhamān [*S.* vardhamāna *p. pr. of* vardhate *to increase*], ~ **yāya** *to promote, to advance* H[2] 55[b].2*.

bṛddh [*S.* vṛddha], *s. an old man* H[2] 95[a].2. — bṛddhā *s. an old woman* V[1] 13[a].5.

bṛddhi [*S. growth, prosperity*], ~ juya *to thrive, to grow* V[1] 41[b].4. — *ifc.* (*interest*): **cākal-**.

bṛṣ, *s.* = biṣ, bikh H[1] 70[b].3.

bṛṣṭi [*S.*], *s. rain* H[2] 93[b].6.

be, *s. a fringe* CW 8.82.

beg [*S.* vega *hurry*; *violence*], ~ thaya *to spur (a horse)* B 47[a].10. began *adv. quickly, fast* H[2] 98[a].1; ~ sanë *to beat fast (pulse)* Vd 6[b].5; tawo ~ yāṅa(ṃ) woya *to be severe or serious (disease)* 14[b].4.

bejamān [*cf. S.* vy-añj *to decorate*], *s. decoration* Ś 169[b].3*.

bed = beḍā Vi 152.10.

bedanā [*S.*], *s. pain, ache* N 13[a].8; *pains of child-birth* Vd 26[a].4.

beḍā [*S.* velā?], ~ kāya *to take leave* Bh 184[b].3; ~ phonë *to ask leave, to ask permission* Ś 155[a].1; ~ biya *to grant permission* Vi 171.26, *to dismiss* 100.8; ~ biyāwo choya *id.* 27.5.

beḍe-se, *s. a medicinal plant* (viḍaṅga AH) Vd 43[a].6. — ~-pu *the seed of this plant* 47[b].5.

beḍ-ci [*S.* viḍa + ci], *s. a kind of salt* (viḍa Md.) Vd 22[a].3.

bedhalapë [*cf. S.* vedhas *pious*?], cett ~ *to be in spirits to* N 18[b].4*.

ben [*H.* bīn], *s. a stringed musical instrument* H[2] 62[a].4.

bey, *s.* = bay H[3] 31[a].10.

beya (-t), *v. i.* = biya[3] C[2] 180*.

bel [*S.* velā *point of time*], *s. the right time, right moment* H[2] 55[a].6; belas *in time* N 22[a].1, thwo belas *at this time, at this juncture* V[2] 6[b].3, *after 5th or 6th form: when, while* V[2] 50[b].2; yāya belas *when is to be done* H[1] 15[a].4; bel abel ma dayakaṃ *always* C[1] 16, bel = belas B 4[a].1. — *ifc.* **utār-**, **sani-**.

be-lā[1], *s. see* **toyu**.

belā[2] = beḍā M 20[b].6.

belā[3] = bel Vi 70.32. — *ifc.* **asuni-**, **din-**.

bes = bhes B 6[a].4.

beṣṭan [*S.* veṣṭana *encircling, surrounding*], ~ yāya *to surround, to encircle* Bh 14[a].2; ~ yācakë *to (suffer oneself to) be surrounded or enclosed* 184[a].4.

beṣṭhan = beṣṭan Bh 10[b].4.

be-haraḍ, *s. name of a plant* (vibhītaka) Vd 13[b].5. — be-halal *id.* CW 6.19.

be-hā, *s. a kind of aromatic root* (vacā) AH 31[a].

baid [*H.*], *s. a physician* CW 8.46.

baidy [*S.*], *s. a doctor, medical man* H[1] 56[a].1.

bairāgy [*S. change of colour, grow-*

ing pale], *s. faint-heartedness* H^2 70^a.8. ~ yāya *to become disheartened* 41^b.7.

bairi [*S.* vairin], *s. an enemy* H^1 7^b.1.

bais, *s.* = bayas V^1 125^b.4.

baiśy^1 [*S.* veśyā], *s. a harlot* N 30^a.4. — baiśyā-misā *id.* 22^b.5*.

baisy^2, *s.* = bayas H^3 14^a.2.

bĕ, *s. orris-root* (vacā) CW 6.29 (bye).

bĕkat = bĕkt H^2 68^b.3. *s. admission* (aṅgīkāra) CW 1.60.

bĕko, *s. a side, flank* CW 8.61. — ~-kwos *a rib* 8.55.

bĕkt [*S.* vyakta], *adj. manifest, evident* V^2 17^b.5; bĕktanaṃ *adv. evidently* B 69^b.2. — ~ yāya *to explain* V^1 87^b.3, *to elucidate* H^3 30^a.9, *to make up one's mind* V^2 54^a.2; ~ dayakĕ *to elucidate* H^2 68^b.3.

bĕktalapĕ [bĕkt], *v. i. to become manifest or evident* Vd 11^a.1*.

bĕ-gaṅ-guli, *s. name of a plant* (citrā) CW 6.35.

bĕgat = bĕkt V^1 27^a.5; bĕgatan *adv.* 102^a.4.

bĕṃgu, *s.,* ~ laṃgu *vegetables*(?) N 50^b.4.

bĕcakĕ (*caus. of* bĕya^1), *to let pass by* N 31^b.6; ch-g ~ *to act wrongly with...* 43^a.1.

bĕtāli, *s. a turban* B 55^b.4.

bĕtt, *s.* = bitt N 42^a.5. — *ifc.* **sarbasva-.**

bĕthā [*S.* vyathā], *s. pain, ache* Bh 178^b.2, *grief, affliction* AH 18^a. — ~ biya *to cause pain* C^1 231; ~ yāya *to feel grief* H^1 84^a.5.

bĕnakĕ (*caus. of* bĕnĕ), *to take away, to remove* B 68^b.7; *to let off* (*a culprit etc.*) N 15^a.6.

bĕnĕ, *v. i. to be taken off, to be removed* P 32^a.2; *to be released* (*as a slave*) N 20^a.4; *to be loosened, to be dishevelled* (*hair*) Bh 49^b.1.

bĕbasāy [*S.* vyavasāya], *s. exertion* H^3 22^b.9; ~ yāya *to exert oneself* H^3 49^b.1; ch-g ~ yāya *to be engaged in...* N 7^b.7.

bĕya^1 (-t), *v. i. to pass by* N 35^b.1; *to go too far, to act wrongly* 44^a.2.

bĕya^2 (-l^1), *v. i. to fly, to run away, to escape* H^1 95^a.4; *gen.:* bĕsĕ(ṃ) wonĕ *id.* V^1 78^b.5, bĕsĕ(ṃ) woya *id.* H^2 63^b.3.

bĕyakĕ (*caus. of* bĕya^2), bĕyakal choya *to let escape* H^2 63^a.3, bĕyakaṃ ~ *id.* H^1 61^b.1; ~ yanĕ *to lead away hurriedly, to escape together with* V^1 78^b.6.

bĕsan [*S.* vyasana], *s. sexual desire* N 37^b.7. — bĕsani [*S.* vyasanin], *adj. lustful* H^2 8^b.2.

bĕsyā [*S.* veśyā], *s. a harlot* V^2 67^b.3. — ~-misā *an open prostitute* N 48^b.4.

bĕharan [*cf. S.* vyavaharaṇa], *s. manner of proceeding; conduct* CW 1.73 (behalaṃ). — *ifc.* **ku-.**

bĕhalapĕ [bĕharan], *v. i. to conduct oneself* C^1 21; *to act* H^2 58^a.2. — *v. t. to settle* (*an affair*) H^2 44^b.3.

bo^1, *s. a part, share* N 38^a.8; pĕ bos chi bo *from four parts one* 2^a 5. — bo thaya *to divide* V^1 111^b.5; ~ taya *id.* B 23^a.4, pĕ bo taya *to divide into four parts* 58^a.6.

bo^2, *s. a flower:* ~ hoya (-l^1) *to bear flowers* C^2 276. — *ifc.* **gĕl-, gyālā-, ta-cho-, svān-, hāmal-.**

bo^3, ~ daya *to become extinct* H^1 66^b.5; ~ cāya *to turn away, to forsake* N 3^a.4.

bo^4, *s.* = bu^1; *only ifc.* **cho-, muṃ-.**

bo-kha [bo^3?], *s. a secret message* Bh 91^a.4; bo-khā *id.* (V^1 *only*) 61^a.6.

bo-gād, *s. a small well* AH 21^b.

bojār = bujār.

boti-si, *s. Calamus Rotang* CW 7.13.

botu, *see* **bulĕ.**

bodān, ~ taya *to perform a purificatory rite* (*a saṃskāra*) P 32^a.5.

bodh [*S. s. awakening, understanding*], ch-hm-yāta ~ yāya *to instruct* C[1] 211, *to convince* H[3] 34[a].11, *to persuade, to make obey* Vi 34.4; *to encourage* V[1] 52[b].1, *to compose, to console* Vi 44.1. ~ juya *to be convinced, to believe* Vi 87.7, *to be persuaded, to obey* 34.2; *to be consoled* H[3] 60[a].2. ~ biya *to encourage* H[1] 18[b].4.

bodhalapë [*S.* bodhaya- *to awaken; to instruct*], *v. t. to persuade, to convince* H[3] 46[a].4, *to compose, to reassure* Bh 89[b].4.

bonakë (*caus. of* bonë[1]), *to cause to fetch; to send for* Ś 145[b].7.

bonë[1], *v. t. to go for, to fetch* V[2] 46[a].1, *to take with one* H[3] 62[a].7, *to bring* H[2] 46[b].6. — bonaṃ yanë *to lead to, to conduct to* H[1] 56[a].2, *to lead away* B 47[b].8; ~ yanakë *to take with one* Vi 175.13; ~ haya *to bring* H[1] 90[b].4.

bonë[2], *v. t. to read, to recite* M 17[a].7.

bob, *s.* = baub Vi 177.25*.

bo-bo, lā-hāt ~ syāya *to shake one's fists at* B 37[b].8.

bobol, *s. ifc.* **laṁkha-.**

boy, *s.* = bos: **~-pa** = bos-paṃ C[1] 237*

boya[1] (-l[1]), *v. i. to fly (birds, etc.)* H[1] 24[a].1; bosë(ṃ) wonë *to fly away* B 53[a].3, *to run away* V[2] 30[a].4; ~ woya *to fly towards one* M 36[b].7; ~ juya = boya Vi 61.24.

boya[2] (-l[1]), *v. i.* = buya[1] H[1] 6[b].4.

boya[3] (-l[1]), *v. t.* = buya[4] C[1] 281.

boya[4], ~ ~ = bo-bo Vi 131.19.

boyakë (*caus. of* boya[1]), *to let fly, to let wave (a banner)* M 23[a].2; boyakaṃ yanë *to fly away with* V[1] 81[b].3, boyakal yanë *id.* M 23[b].2.

bol[1] [*M.*], *s. a word, speech* N 26[b].4; ~ biya *to abuse* 42[b].4; ch-hm-yāta ~ biya ëwo *speaking kindly to…* 36[a].2; ~-bācā bhiṃgwo *pleasant spoken* 36[a].4. — *ifc.* **saty-.**

bor[2] [= bāl[1]?], *only:* hnas-~ *sevenfold* Vi 87.24*.

boli [bo[1] *or* = baḍi], ~ thanë *to divide* B 32[a].7.

bolu, *adj.* = bulu; bolusëṃ wonë *to become turbid or muddy* C[1] 199.

bolë, *v. i.*, ch-hm-wo (nāp) ~ *to associate with…, to keep company with…* H[2] 6[b].7.

bolo-bi, *s. a water snake* AH 19[a].

bos[1], *s. grass* N 50[b].3. — ~-paṃ *id.* C[1] 237.

bos[2], ~ ~ yāya *to rub, to mash* Vd 46[b].3.

bo-sā [bo[2]], *s. ifc.* **se-sā-.**

bo-si, *s. a wood-cutter (a Newārī caste)* Vi 96.17; bo-si-ta *id. pl.* H[3] 25[a].1*.

bosighāli, *s. a medicinal plant* (nirguṇḍī CW) Vd 29[b].4.

bosobon [bos[2]], *adv. by rubbing*(?) N 35[a].5*.

boha-, bohaṃ-bohaṃn jāya *to bristle (of the hair of the body)* M 34[b].2. — bohaṃ-bohaṃ jāyakë *to make (the hair of the body) bristle* 36[b].7. — bohon jāyakë *id.* Bh 174[b].7.

boh-ṅā, *s. a kind of fish* (śāla) AH 21[a].

bau, *s.* = baub Pg 13[a].2*.

baub, *s. a father* H[3] 59[b].9. — ~-ju *id.* Vi 153.17.

bwo, *s. a wood* (ārāma) N 34[a].1*.

bwok, ~ jā *cooked food* (kṛtānna) N 50[b].4*.

bwokwo, *found*(?) N 23[b].1*.

bwohal[1], *s.* = bwohol[1] H[2] 108[b].6.

bwohal[2], *s.* = bwohol[2] C[1] 123. — ~-cā *a young heron* H[3] 54[a].4. — ~-bathān *a flock of herons* H[2] 101[b].3.

bwohoḍ, *s.* = bwohol[1] N 30[b].2.

bwohol[1], *s. a shoulder* V[1] 27[b].4.

bwohol[2], *s. a heron* H[1] 7[b].2.

byaglā, *s. a measure of time* (pala) CW 1.47.

byaṅgī, *s. a closet*(?) B 44[a].2.

byapāl, *s.* = byāpāl H³ 53ᵇ.8.

byabahalapĕ [*S.* vy-ava-har-], *v.i. to act, to proceed* N 46ᵇ.7. — byabahalapayakĕ *caus. to cause to act*; ~ ma tewo (*he*) *may cause* (*them*) *not to act* N 45ᵇ.1.

byabahār [*S.* vyavahāra *common practise*], *s. law, rule* N 6ᵇ.7; *conduct* V¹ 17ᵇ.4. — ~ yāya 1) *to conduct oneself, to behave* H³ 62ᵃ.5, *to arrange, to make an arrangement* N 8ᵃ.1. 2) (*through confusion with* bibāhā): *to marry* (*a girl*) H³ 56ᵇ.4, *to woo for* Vi 169.17.

byabahāralapĕ [byabahār], *v. t. to make a transaction* N 4ᵇ.5*.

byarth [*S.*], *adj. useless, to no purpose, of no consequence* H² 113ᵃ.6. byarthan *adv.* Vi 168.24.

byā, *s. breadth, width* B 4ᵃ.11.

byākul [*S. amazed, disconserted*], *s. amazement, consternation* H³ 31ᵃ.7. — ~ yāya *to be amazed or disconcerted* H² 69ᵃ.2.

byāghr [*S.*], *s. a tiger* H¹ 15ᵃ.2.

byāgal, *adv.*, ~ ~('an) *separately* Bh 92ᵇ.1 (byāgl 2 an), *each for himself* N 40ᵃ.4; byāgalan conĕ *to be divided in interests* (*heirs*; vibhakta) 39ᵃ.5.

byāgwol, *adv.* = byāgal P 34ᵃ.5.

byāṅ, *s. a frog* Bh 12ᵇ.1. — ~-rājā *the king of the frogs* H² 112ᵇ.3. — *ifc.* **kwo-kwo-, prajā-, mā-, rājā-.**

byācakĕ (*caus. of* byāya) *to dress* (*the hair*) Bh 49ᵇ.1.

byāj¹ [*H. interest, dividend*], *s. amount* N 25ᵃ.3; *proceeds, earnings* 24ᵃ.1. byājan punĕ *to lose the profit* 21ᵇ.5.

byāj², *s. a rein* (*of a horse*) AH 71ᵇ.

byāḍ, *s.* = byāl¹ Vd 24ᵃ.3*.

byādhā [*S.* vyādha], *s. a hunter* V¹ 119ᵃ.2.

byādhi [*S.*], *s. disease* Vd 14ᵇ.5.

byān, *s.* = byāṅ H³ 60ᵃ.6.

byāpalapĕ [*S.* vyā-pṛ], *v. i. to be occupied, to be busy* P 11ᵃ.7*.

byāpāl [*S.* vyāpāra], *s. an occupation* N 18ᵃ.6, *duty* 46ᵇ.7, *an affair, concern* H² 52ᵃ.6, *work, doing* B 45ᵇ.4; byāpāl yāya *to make use of* P 7ᵃ.1, ~ yācakĕ *to assign as occupation* N 35ᵇ.8, ~ biya *id.* B 52ᵇ.5. banaj ~ yāya *to do business* V¹ 96ᵇ.6.

byāpāri [*S.* vyāpārin *busy, engaged*], *s. a tradesman, merchant* V¹ 66ᵇ.5.

byāptamān [*cf. S.* vyāpta *filled*], ~ juya *to be filled with, to abound in* Bh 178ᵃ.6; ~ yāya *to fill* Ns 39ᵃ.6.

byāptalapĕ [*S.* vyāpta *filled*], *v. i. to be filled, to abound* (ch-g-s ch-g-n *something with or in*...) Bh 139ᵇ.7.

byāya (-t), *v. i.*, ch-g-s ~ *to agree with*... H³ 11ᵃ.7; *to take advantage of*... B 2ᵃ.9.

byāl¹, *s. Aegle Marmelos* (bilva) C¹ 229. — ~-si *id.* Vd 30ᵇ.3. — ~-hā *the root of* — 21ᵇ.2. — *ifc.* **kaṁci-.**

byāl², *ifc.* **dhan-.**

byāhār, *s.* = byabahār H² 58ᵇ.8. — *ifc.* **dhan-.**

brat [*S.*], *s. a vow* H¹ 40ᵃ.4.

brahma-hathyā, *s. slaying or murder of a Brahman* V² 16ᵇ.3. — ~-hatyā *id.* N 12ᵇ.1.

brahmā [*S.* brahman], *n. pr. Brahma* Ś 153ᵇ.1.

brāṇ, *s.* = brāhmaṇ H³ 57ᵇ.11.

brāhmaṇ [*S.*], *s. a Brahman* V¹ 52ᵇ.2.

brīhi [*S.*], *s. rice* Vi 83.18.

bvācakĕ (*caus. of* bvāya) *only:* bvācakaṃ *adv. quickly, hurriedly* B 52ᵃ.4.

bvāj, *ifc.* **kwo-, thaṁ-.**

bvātakĕ (*caus. of* bvāya) = bvācakĕ Ś 169ᵃ.5.

bvāya (-t), *v. t. to run* V² 49ᵃ.2, *to leap* Bh 184ᵇ.7.

bh.

bhawor, *s. a bee* C¹ 44*.

bhak, ~ danë *v. i. to accumulate, to lie in heaps* Bh 11ᵇ.7.

bhakt [*S. liked, worshipped*], ch-hm-yāke ~ yāya *to adore, to worship* Bh 116ᵃ.3. — **bhakti** [*S. worship*] *used in the same sense* H² 98ᵇ.3; ~-bhāb yāya = bhakt yāya Vi 23.11.

bhakṣ [*S.*], *s. food* H² 33ᵇ.2; ~ yāya *to eat* Vi 130.27; ~ bhojan yācakë *to give food* H² 82ᵃ.7.

bhakṣaṇ [*S. s. eating*], ~ yāya *to eat* Bh 78ᵇ.2.

bhakṣalapë [bhakṣ], *v. t. to eat* V² 62ᵃ.4.

bhagat, *s. a medicinal plant* Vd 14ᵃ.2. — *i/c.* **suya-**.

bhagabant [*S.* bhagavant], *adj. glorious, illustrious* H² 69ᵇ.2; *holy, venerable* H³ 41ᵇ.7.

bhagn [*S. broken*], ~ yāya *to break (asunder)* Bh 35ᵇ.5.

bhaṅg [*S. a breach, rupture*], ~ yāya *to break (a promise)* V¹ 69ᵃ.2; nidrā ~ ~ *to interrupt the sleep* Bh 105ᵃ.5. ~ yālakë *to cause to break* Ś 146ᵃ.7.

bhajanā [*S.* bhañjana *breaking*, — — *causing pain*], ~ yāya *to cause pain* B 42ᵇ.10*.

bhajalapë [*S.* bhaj- *to love, to worship*, —], *v. t. to love (carnally)* V¹ 29ᵃ.3; ch-hm-yāke ~ *to be attached or devoted to* V² 70ᵇ.2.

bhajyāli, *s. a sword, scimitar* AH 51ᵇ.

bhaṭā¹, ~ luya *symptom of a disease of the yoni* Vd 38ᵇ.2.

bhaṭā-², ~-kimi *name of a plant* (kākamācī) Md 15ᵇ.8. — ~-mā *a kind of tree* Bh 106ᵃ.6. — ~-mūl *the root of a medicinal plant* Vd 46ᵇ.6.

bhati¹, *adj. some, a little* M 8ᵇ.1. *adv. a moment* H² 83ᵇ.6; bhati bhati *very little* 48ᵃ.3; bhatin *soon* V² 61ᵇ.1; bhati-khu-nu *id.* B 58ᵇ.4; ~-ku-hnu tā *a short time* Vi 119.9; ~-oā *id.* M 22ᵇ.8.

bhati² [*cf. Mr.* bhatī — —, *art, method*], *s. a sort, kind:* swotā ~ *of three sorts* N 41ᵇ.4; bhatin *in case of* 45ᵃ.9. — *i/c.* **anek-**.

bhaṭi³, *s. a cat* H¹ 36ᵇ.2. — ~-cā *id. dim.* H² 103ᵃ.6.

bhatu, *s. a parrot* H¹ 78ᵃ.2; ~-ju *id.* H² 82ᵃ.7. — ~-cā *id. dim.* (*used contemptuously*) H² 86ᵃ.6.

bhaṭṭarāu [*cf. S.* bhaṭṭāraka], *s. a learned man* V¹ 127ᵇ.1.

bhaḍini, *s. i/c.* **guru-**.

bhan-cā, *s. a crucible* AH 61ᵇ (bhongchá).

bhantā, *s. the egg-plant* CW 6.30.

bhaṁti¹, *adv.* = bhati¹ N 32ᵃ.5.

bhaṁti², *s.* = bhati² N 53ᵃ.2; thwo bhaṃtin *in this case* 15ᵃ.3.

bhantili [bhati²?], *adv.*, lithwo lithwo ~ *more and more* N 33ᵃ.8.

bhaṇḍ [*S. a jester, mime*], ~-an *adv. unter false pretences* N 17ᵇ.6.

bhaṇḍā, *s.* 1) = bhāṇḍā H² 40ᵇ.4. — ~-kuḍā *a vessel, jar* 105ᵃ.5; ~-kuṇḍā *id.* 106ᵃ.3; ~-kuṇḍhā *a well* N 26ᵇ.4. — 2) = bhaṇḍāl N 17ᵇ.2; ~-kuṇḍā *a treasure* Bh 141ᵃ.5. — *i/c.* **kaṁha-**.

bhaṇḍāl [*M.* bhaṃḍār], *s.* 1) *a treasure* N 23ᵇ.1. — 2) = bhaṇḍā 1) H² 67ᵃ.6. — *i/c.* **bitt-**.

bhaṇḍili [*cf. H.* bhaṇḍārī], *s. a store-keeper* C² 64.

bhay¹ [*S.*], *s. fear* (ch-g-wo *of...*) H² 34ᵃ.3; *danger* B 66ᵇ.2. — ~-māl *adj. dangerous* 27ᵃ.6.

bhay², ~ phāya *v. t. to rise, to swell.* M 36ᵃ.4; ch-g-n ~ *to abound in...* Vi 51.11. — ~ phāyakë *v. t. to overflow* Vi 126.4; ch-g-n ~ ~ *to (suffer oneself to) be swelled or to be filled with...* M 34ᵃ.4.

bhayānak [*S.*], *adj. terrible* H² 71ᵃ.3.

bhalaḍi, *s.*, ~-sā *a cow* N 29^{b}.1. — *ifc.* **guru-**.

bharaṇ [*S. wages, hire*], *s. cost, price* N 24^{b}.4.

bharam [*H. perplexity*], *see* **khwolay**.

bharay [*H.* bharnā *to fill, to perform*], ~ yāya *to perform* Vi 145.12, *to prepare, to arrange* H² 84^{b}.6.

bharalapē [bharay], *v. t.* śūlas ~ *to fasten to a stake* N 44^{a}.8.

bhalasā, *s.* = bhalosā Vi 113.24.

bhalāḍ [*H.* bhalā *good, virtuous*], *s. a term of respect: the venerable or the honourable one* N 52^{b}.5.

bhali, *s. a daughter-in-law* B 50^{b}.10. — ~-cā *id.* Vi 177.25. — ~-mocā *id.* B 50^{b}.3. — *ifc.* **tvāc-**.

bhariyā [*M.* bharlā], *s. a carrier* N 21^{b}.7.

bhalosā [*H.* bharosā], *s. hope* Bh 179^{a}.1; ch-hm-yāta ~ biya *to inspire with hope, to encourage* B 23^{a}.6; ~ cāya *to take hope* Bh 179^{a}.2 (bharo!). — *ifc.* **āsā-**, **āśrā-**.

bhalyā, *s.* — bhariyā B 35^{b}.1.

bhas = bhay²: ~ cāya *to be overpowered, to be stunned* B 45^{b}.6; ~ phāya = bhay ~ Vd 38^{a}.3.

bhasm [*S.* bhasman], *s. ashes* V¹ 25^{b}.3.

bhākhā [*S.* bhāṣā], *s. speech, utterance* Bh 54^{a}.6; ~ yāya *to say* B 51^{b}.10, *to come to an agreement* (ch-hm-wo *with*...) B 15^{b}.11. — *ifc.* **saty-**.

bhāg [*S.*], *s. a part, portion* Vd 16^{a}.1, *proportion* 12^{a}.5.

bhāgi [*S.* bhāgin], *s. an owner, partner* B 10^{a}.7; *a fortunate man* 24^{b}.3.

bhāgi-hā, *s. a medicinal root* Vd 38^{b}.6.

bhāgy [*S.*], *s. fate* Ś 163^{a}.3.

bhājan [*H. basin*], *s. a frying pan* AH 54^{b}.

bhāju [*P.*?], *s. a lord, master* B 39^{a}.5. — ~-cā (*used in addressing a man*) 60^{b}.8, (*used in addressing a woman*) 8^{a}.3.

bhāṭ [*H.* bhāṭ], *s. a bard, herald* B 45^{a}.9.

bhātin(aṁ), *adv.* — bhatin V¹ 100^{a}.3.

bhānas [*cf. Mr.* bhāṇas], *s. an earthen vessel (for cooking food)* C² 282*.

bhāṇḍā [*H.* bhāṅrā], *s. a vessel*: ~-kuḍā *id.* H² 105^{a}.3. — *ifc.* **sijal-**.

bhāb [*S. condition; manner of being*], *s. manners, demeanour* N 32^{a}.8; *might, power* Ś 167^{b}.3. — ~ taya *to feel affection* (ch-hm-yāke *for*...) H² 82^{b}.2; ~ yāya *id.* Vi 135.32. — *ifc.* **mikhā-**.

bhābi [*S.* bhāvin *predestined, future*] *s.* 1) *the future* H³ 101^{a}.2. — 2) *bygone things (sic!)* Vi 137.4.

bhāy¹, *s. an expression; only ifc.* **mikhā-**, **mol-**.

bhāy², *s.* — bhās C¹ 257*.

bhāyi [*H.* bhāī], *s. a brother, companion* Ś 149^{a}.6.

bhār¹ [*S.*], *s.* = bhārā N 2^{a}.5; ~ buya *to maintain* 39^{a}.7.

bhāl² [*S. splendour*], *ifc.* **ni-**.

bhālato, °ta [*cf. S.* bhārtā], *s. a husband* H² 100^{b}.2.

bhālapē, *v. t. to think* Ś 168^{a}.3, *to regard as* H² 49^{a}.6, *to think of* B 33^{a}.1, *to deliberate* H² 5^{b}.10, *to intent to* H¹ 54^{a}.5. — priy ~ *to be kindly disposed* M 14^{a}.3; lajyā ~ *to feel ashamed* Bh 184^{b}.6.

bhārā¹ [*cf. Mr. a load, bundle*], *s. a burden* Bh 139^{b}.3; *fig.: a burden, task, duty* B 85^{b}.7. ~ kāya *to take upon oneself a task* Ś 168^{a}.6, ch-hm-yāta ~ biya *to throw a burden or a responsibility upon*... Vi 40.29.

bhālā² [*rust. H.* bhāṅrā], *s. an earthen pot or vessel* H³ 56^{a}.11. — *ifc.* **kaṁs-**, **thālā-**.

bhālu, *s. a bear* H² 85^{a}.3.

bhās, *s.* = bhāsā C² 257; chatā

bhāsaṃ ma siwo (*she*) *doesn't know what to say* V[1] 37[b].4. — *ifc.* **paṁchi-**.

bhāsalapē [*M.* bhāsā *speech*], *v. t. to promise* N 21[b].1.

bhāsā [*M.*], *s. speech, language* CW 1.57.

bhi, *adv.* = bhin[1]: cha-~ Bh 184[b].6.

bhiṁ, *adj.* = bhiṅ H[2] 74[a].7. — ~-hma (*of living beings*) *id.* B 10[a].1, *good, excellent* V[2] 42[a].6. — ~-gwo (*of things*) *good* V[2] 79[b].1, *fine* Bh 179[a].6; (*of living beings!*) *good* V[1] 67[a].2, *faultless, without blemish* N 24[a].3. — ~-gu (*of things*) *good* B 3[b].5, *auspicious* H[3] 20[b].3.

bhiṁ-pu, *s. a coral* P 27[b].3.

bhikwo [bhinē], *adj. good* Bh 107[a].1*.

bhikṣab [*from* bhikṣavaḥ *pl. of S.* bhikṣu], *s. religious mendicants* Vi 90.5.

bhikṣā [*S.*], *s. alms* H[3] 49[a].6.

bhikṣu [*S.*], *s. a religious mendicant* H[3] 92[b].6. — bhikṣuk [*S.*], *s. id.* 93[a].5. — bhikṣuṇī [*S.*], *s. a female mendicant* N 34[b].4.

bhiṅ [bhinē], *adj. good* H[1] 68[a].3; *beautiful* C[1] 181; *auspicious* H[1] 88[a].2. ma ~ *bad* V[2] 26[a].1, *improper* H[1] 35[b].1. — ch-hm-yāta bhiṅ-thēṃ yāya *to be of advantage to…* N 4[b].6, ch-hm-yāta ma bhiṅ-thēṃ *to the disadvantage of… ib.*

bhiṅalāy [*cf. S.* bhṛṅgarāja], *s. a species of large bee* AH 33[a].

bhitakhā-che [*cf. H.* bhit *a cave, den*], *s. a hut or cave of a hermit* M 24[b].3*.

bhin[1], *adv.*, ch-hm-yā ~ wonē *to go to…* H[2] 72[a].1; cha ~ *at some place, somewhere* B 31[b].8; cha-bhinaṃ *id.* Bh 169[a].1.

bhin[2], *s.* = bhen; ~-cā *id.* AH 38[b]; ~-macā *id.* P 46[b].7*.

bhinakē (*caus. of* bhinē), *to make good or noble* C[1] 190, *to make agreeable or pleasant* V[1] 98[b].1; *to adorn, to embellish* B 62[a].5; *to cure* V[2] 79[b].1. — bhinakaṃ *adv. well* H[1] 20[a].4; *thoroughly, severely* N 36[a].4.

bhinalapē [bhinē], *only:* ma bhinalapu *a fault, defect* H[2] 16[b].1*.

bhinē, *v. i. to be or become good, fine etc.* (*see* bhiṅ, bhiṃ) C[1] 16; ma ~ *to become bad* H[1] 20[a].5.

bhinn [*S. broken,* — —, *distinct*], ~ yāya *to make clear, to expose* Vi 90.3.

bhimarāj, *s. a medicinal plant* Vd 13[b].1.

bhīmili, *s. a fan* CW 8.94.

bhu, *s. a distance* V[1] 70[a].2; śat-chi jojan ~ *a distance of 100 Yojanas* M 5[a].3.

bhuṁ, *s. a field* N 27[b].2; *a ground* C[2] 279. — ~-jvālā *a mirage* CW 1.45. — *ifc.* **khapali-**, **gvāk-**, **che-**, **hnawol-**, **hnasi-**, **paṁth-**, **phi-**, **yajñ-**.

bhūwon [*S.* bhuvana], *s. a world* Vi 73.4.

bhuktamān [*from S.* bhukta *enjoyed*], *s. enjoying* Vi 123.26; ~ yāya *to enjoy* 51.25.

bhuktalapē [*S.* bhukta *enjoyed*], *v. t. to enjoy* V[2] 56[b].3, *to suffer* (*distress*) N 13[b].8; *fur.:* bhuktalapaṃ yanē *to have the actual or the legitimate enjoyment of a thing* 8[a].6, ~ taya *id.* 5[b].8. — bhuktalapēkē *caus. to let enjoy* (ch-hm-yāta ch-g *somebody something*) V[1] 91[b].5.

bhūkh [*H.*], *s. hunger* N 13[a].7.

bhu-khā, *s.* = bhwo-khāy Vi 83.6*.

bhuguti [*S.* bhukti *possession*], ~ yāya *to hire* N 19[b].3. — ~-bhṛti *a hired servant ib.* 2*.

bhuglu-jhaṅgal, *s. an owl* CW 7.7.

bhujapatal [*cf. S.* bhūrjapattra], *s. a birch-tree* CW 6.17.

bhujiṁ, *s.* = bhojinī; *only ifc.* **sā-**.

bhut [*M.* bhūt], *s. a ghost, goblin* V[1] 37[a].5.

bhu-ti[1], *s. the sap of flowers* CW 6.11.

bhuti[2], *s. a species of beans* (mukuṣṭhaka) Md 65[b].6.

bhutu, *s. a kitchen* AH 54.

bhutu-wā, *s.,* toyu, hyāṅu ~ *two kinds of plants* (vāstuka *and* jīvantaka) Md 47b.8.

bhunakë (*caus. of* bhunë), *to* (*suffer to*) *be coated or covered* Vi 56.3*.

bhunë[1], *v. t.,* ch-g-s ch-g-n ~ *to wrap a thing up in...* Vi 150.31; *to face, to coat* (*a building*) Vi 93.16.

bhunë[2], *v. t.* = bhonë Bh 163a.4.

bhūmā- [*cf. H.* bhūm], ~-sīmā *the boundary of a field* N 27a.1. — ~-sīmā-kha *a lawsuit with regard to the boundaries of fields* 13b.2.

bhūmi [*S.*], *s. a ground, soil* Bh 185a.6; *a land, country* H[2] 57a.3.

bhuya [*S.* bhūyas], *adv.,* ~ bhuyaṃ *again and again* C[1] 11*.

bhuray [*S.* bhur- *to stir, to struggle*], ~ yāya *to move, to stir* (*itrs.*) Bh 15b.2.

bhulalapë [*H.* bhulnā *to mistake, to err*], *v. i.* ch-hm-yāke ~ *to be infatuated by...* V[1] 87b.2; kāmas bhulalapāwo juwo-hma *blind from love* C[1] 178.

bhuruṅg, *s. a top:* ~ hilakë *to spin a top* B 53a.5.

bhūsanā, *s. humming:* ~-kha hlāya *to hum* (*as a bee*) Bh 95b.7.

bhuṣalapë [*S.* bhūṣaya- *to adorn*], *v. i. to be adorned* Bh 110b.2.

bhūsalapë, *v. i. to hum* (*as a bee*) Bh 173a.3.

bhusā-ṅā, *s. a sort of fish* (nalamīna) AH 20b.

bhṛti [*S.* bhṛtya], *s. a servant; ifc.* **bhuguti-.**

bhet, ~ bulë (Vi *a few times 5th form:* buwo) *v. i. to fall down, to tumble down* V[2] 24a.4; ~ bolë *id.* V[1] 37a.2.

bhetalas [*cf. H.* bhītar *within*], *adv.;* ch-hm(-yā) ~ *as for..., concerning...* N 40a.7.

bhed [*S. s. breaking*], *s. distinction* H[2] 87b.3. ~ yāya *to cause dissension* N 11a.7; ch-hm-yāke ~ yācakë *to cause to break with...* H[3] 57b.2.

bhedalapë [bhed], *v. t. to break* Bh 114a.1.

bhen, *s. the son of a sister* N 45b.6.

bhel [*H.* bhīṛ *a crowd, throng*], ~ ṅoya *to surround* (*in crowds*) Bh 139a.3; ~ thunë *id.* 98a.1; ~ punë *id.* 101a.7. — ~ bheyā kāy *many children* N 38b.8.

bhes [*M. a form, dress, disguise*], *s.,* ch-hm(-yā) ~ *disguised as, made up as...* V[1] 81b.5; ~ yāya *to disguise oneself* Ś 159b.2; ...bhesan *in the disguise of...* B 9b.1. — *ifc.* **misā-.**

bhënu, *s. a species of antelope* (ruru) Md 72b.3.

bho [*S.*], *interj. oh!* Ś 153b.4.

bhok, ~ puya (-l[1]), *v. i. to bend down* H[3] 56b.6, *to do reverence* (*by bending down to the ground*) (ch-hm-yāke *to...*) V[2] 80b.7. — ~ sunë *v. i. to prostrate oneself to the ground* Vi 58.5; *v. t. to bend down* 58.32.

bhog [*S. enjoyment*], ~ kāya *to accept as offering* H[3] 48a.5; ~ biya *to give as offering ib.;* ~ yāya *to eat* (*term of respect*) Vi 122.21, *to enjoy* H[3] 18b.4, *to suffer* Vi 46.14.

bhogy [*S. to be enjoyed*], ~ biya *to give as food* B 30a.6; ch-g ~ kāya *to take as food, to eat* 26b.6.

bhocā-simā, *s. a bush, shrub* AH 27a.

bhochi, *s. a household, family* B 60a.3.

bhoj [*S.*], *s. enjoyment, pleasure* H[2] 41b.1.

bhojan [*S. s. eating*], ~ yāya *to eat* (*term of respect*) H[2] 45b.5, ~ yācakë (yākë, yātakë) *to give to eat* V[2] 31b.4.

bhojā [*cf. S.* bhojana], *s. food* P 18b.1. ~ taya *to eat* 18a.6*.

bhojini, *s. a fly* V[1] 17b.2.

bhojy [*S. to be eaten or enjoyed*], ~ biya *to give food* H[2] 70a.6; ch-g ~ yācakë *to give something to eat* 43b.6.

bhot, *s., ifc.* **tvāc-, tvāy-, pil-.**

bhotan, *adv.*, pacini ~ swoya *to look through the space between the fingers* Bh 24ª.3.

bhonë, *v. t.* ch-hm(-yāke) ch-g-n *to throw a thing at...* H¹ 49ª.4.

bho-pakë = °-payakë Bh 162ª.7.

bho-payakë (*caus. of* bho-pë) *to give to eat* V¹ 75ᵇ.2.

bho-pë (*only ipr.:* bho-pi(wo), bho-piṅe), *v. t. to eat* B 44ᵇ.12.

bho-pëkë = °-payakë V² 47ª.4.

bho-bho, ~ dhāya *to suffer from flatulence* Vd 24ª.5.

bhoyu, *adj. whitish, grey* AH 14ᵇ; ~ mal *a medicinal plant* Vd 26ᵇ.5; ~ ragat hāwo *a particular disease of a woman* 38ª.4; ~ svān *a kind of jasmine* Md 31ª.7. — bhoyuwo = bhoyu; ~ sa *grey hair* CW 8.37. — bhoyuyu *becomes grey* Vd 9ᵇ.6.

bhau-cā [*mod.* = bhali-°], *s. a daughter-in-law* AH 37.

bhwo-khāy, *s. sweepings* CW 4.13; *dust* M 17ᵇ.1.

bhyā¹, *s. a sheep, ram* Wr p. 301.

bhyā², ~ nuya *to grow tired*(?) Ś 143ᵇ.2*.

bhyāl¹, ~ juya *to reach a mature age*(?) N 4ª.6*.

bhyāl², *s.* = byāl¹ B 25ª.12.

bhramaṇ [*S. s.* —, *turning*], ~ yāya *to cause to whirl round* Bh 62ª.6.

bhramar [*S.*], *s. a bee* V¹ 8ª.4.

bhramalapë [*S.* bhram-], *v. i. to roam about, to wander through* H¹ 33ᵇ.5 (*mostly* °lapaṃ juya *or* jwoya).

bhraṣṭ [*S. fallen down*], *adj. expelled from caste* H² 99ᵇ.1; jāti-~ *id.* N 36ª.7. bhraṣṭ juya *to be destroyed* H³ 40ª.8.

bhrātā [*S.*], *s. a brother* Bh 143ª.2.

bhvā, ~ ~ puya *to cause dissension* N 26ª.3*.

bhvātal, *s. a chest, box* B 51ª.5.

bhvāti, *s. a kind of musical instrument* M 25ᵇ.2*.

bhvātini, *s. a maid-servant* Bh 147ª.6.

bhvāl, *s. a hole, cave* B 38ᵇ.12. — *ifc.* **si-, simā-.**

m.

ma, *not* H¹ 37ª.2; ~ bhiṅ *not good, bad* 13ª.1; gwo belasa-ṃ...ma *never* H² 14ª.5; ma daya ma pho *it must be (there)* 64ª.1; ma yākë *to make undone* Vi 129.29; ma yāya *to prevent, to avert* H³ 47ᵇ.3.

maṁ, *s. the chaff (of grain)* N 26ᵇ.3*.

maṁ-gwo [manë¹], *s. swelling* Vd 27ᵇ.3; ~ cāya *to swell, a tumor arises* Vd 39ª.3; — ~-loy *a disease accompanied by tumors* 55ª.1. — *ifc.* **kvāsë-, khvāl-, tote-, pvāt-, lāhāt-.**

maṁś, *s. a particular measure* Vd 19ª.1.

makhā, *adv.* (*placed mostly after the verb. fin.*) *surely, decidedly* H¹ 27ᵇ.3.

makhi, *s. the rust of iron* Vd 35ª.6.

ma-khu, *adj. wrong, unjust; improper* N 47ᵇ.4; ~-guli *id.* H³ 38ª.8. ma-khu yāya *to act unjustly, improperly* P 22ᵇ.5. — ~ bidyā *ignorance* P 24ᵇ.5.

ma-khwo [= ma-khu], *adj. wrong; unjust* N 45ᵇ.3. ~ yāya *to do wrong, to act unjustly ib.* 2*.

magal [*cf. S.* makara], *ifc.* **hiti-.**

magnapaṅk, *s. for* mahā° H² 45ᵇ.2*.

maṅ [manë²?], *adj. loving, affectionate* N 3ᵇ.4. — maṅā *id.* 51ᵇ.7. — maṅan *adv. from affection* 17ᵇ.3.

maṅā-pu, *s. mixing, distilling* (saṃdhāna) AH 62ª (manápu).

maṅgal [*S. anything auspicious*], *s.*

bliss, happiness B 67a.2, *a sacred object* N 48a.8.

macā[1], *s.* = mocā H[3] 60b.8. — *ifc.* **kāy-, bhari-, bhin-.**

ma-cā[2], *s.* = mā-cā V[2] 80a.4.

machawāl [*H.* machvā], *s. a fisherman* CW 2.6.

machi, ~ ma machin yāya *to do as one likes*(?) N 46b.3.

mat [*S.*], *s. belief, idea* B 46a.6, *meaning* Vi 175.7.

mata, *s. a lamp, lantern* C[1] 18; ~ cyāya *to kindle a lamp* V[2] 80b.4. — ~-pvāt = ~ B 31a.7.

matawāl [*H.* matvālā *intoxicated*], *s. a drunkard* H[2] 109a.1.

mati [*S. thought, opinion*], *s. mind* Bh 13a.5, *way of thinking* B 10b.9. — matimān [*S.*] *adj. understanding* H[1] 75b.5.

matuwāl, *s.* = matawāl C[1] 254*.

ma-tëṅë (*only 5th, 6th and 10th form*), *v. t. to love* H[1] 16a.1, *to like* (yāya *to do*) V[1] 109b.2; ma-tëṃsëṃ tayā *beloved* H[3] 58b.3, ma-tëṅëwo tayā *id.* Vi 52.4. — *gen.:* ma-tëṅ *adj. beloved* (ch-hm-yā *by*...) H[3] 14a.3; ma-tëṅā *id.* H[2] 45a.3, ~-pu *id.* 82a.5; ~ bhāb *s. love* P 56a.3, ch-hm-yā uparas ma-tëṅā bhāb taya *to have love for*... Vi 52.14.

matt [*S.*], *adj.* 1) *intoxicated* H[2] 78b.5. 2) *furious* (*of elephants only*) V[1] 78b.3 (martt). — ~-hā *adj.* = matt 2) B 47b.8; ~-hāwo *id.* H[2] 16b.6.

maṭṭalapayakë, *v. i.,* mūl ~ *to get over a period of want*(?) N 7a.4*.

mat-pvāt, *s.* = mat B 31a.7.

maty, *s.* = marty B 28b.12.

matsy [*S.*], *s. a fish* H[3] 35a.6.

maṭh [*S.*], *s.; ifc.* **agni-.**

mathan[1], ~ woṅ *dry land* AH 23a.

mathan[2] [*S. s. churning*], ~ yāya 1) *to churn* Bh 35b.3; 2) *to destroy* H[2] 95a.5; ~ yācakë *to cause to overcome* (*a difficulty*) 88a.1.

mathanaṁ, *adv.* = manthān H[2] 113b.3*.

mathān, *adv.* = manthān H[1] 45a.3.

ma-thë [ma], *adj. improper, inconvenient* P 39b.7; ~-guli *id.* 28a.1.

mad[1] [*S.*], *s. passion* H[2] 105b.5.

mad[2] [*H.*], *s. spirituous liquor* H[2] 76b.7.

maḍa, *s.* = mala(k) N 29a.5.

madan [*S. id.*], ~-phol *name of a plant* (phaṇijjhakā) AH 30a.

madapān [= madya°], *s. drinking of spirituous liquor* H[2] 94a.7.

madu-ke, *s. one of the ten palāṇḍus* P 58a.1*.

madyapān [*S. a drinker of spirituous liquor*], ~ yāya *to be a drinker of spirituos liquor* Ś 147b.4.

madhan- = madan- AH 29a.

madhi, *s. a cake, sweetmeat* H[3] 30b.8. — *ifc.* **cho-, pu-wā-.**

madhu-paṅk, *s. for* mahā-° H[2] 13a.4 = H[3] 5a.8*.

madhë, *s.* = madhi V[2] 12a.5*.

madhyapān [= madya°], *s. spirituous liquor* H[3] 41a.1*.

madhyas [*S.* madhya *s. middle*], *adv.,* ch-g-yā ~ *in the middle of*... V[1] 61b.1.

madhyast [*S.* madhyastha], *s. an arbitrator, umpire* N 12a.6.

madhyān [*S.* madhyāhna], *s. midday, noon* V[1] 78a.2.

man[1] [*S.* manas], *s. mind* V[2] 66b.4; *inclination, disposition* M 11a.6. ~ cañcal-hma *fickle-minded* H[3] 11b.9; thawo manan *of one's own accord* V[2] 62a.6; manas *or* manan (bhālapë) (*to think*) *in one's mind* V[1] 43a.4. — ch-hm-yā man wonaṃ (*he*) *was seized with desire* B 53a.7; ch-hm-yāta (*or* -yāke) man wonaṃ *he took a fancy to*... M 18a.8; manas taya *to keep in one's mind* C[1] 108. — manas daya *to like* (yāya *to*...) Vi 169.29; man dayakë *to feel inclined* (yāya *to*...)

Ś 147ᵃ.7. — man thācakĕ *to offer guarantee* (ch-hm-s *to*...) N 7ᵇ.2, ~ dvayakĕ *id. ib.*

man² [*S.* maṇa], *s. a particular measure of grain* Vd 16ᵇ.5.

mana, *s. a chin* M 32ᵇ.8.

manathān, *adv.* = manthān H² 37ᵇ.5.

manathi, *s. a medicinal plant, Indian madder* Vd 34ᵇ.2.

manapaban-si, *s. a kind of tree* B 68ᵃ.2.

manabāñchā [*S.* manovāñchā], *s. mind's desire* H¹ 44ᵇ.5.

Manamohoni [*S.* manomohanī], *n. pr. of a woman* B 34ᵇ.12.

manasagg [*S.* manaḥsaṅga *attachment of the mind*], ~ juya *to be devoted or attached to* Ś 147ᵃ.7*.

manasā [*H.* mansā *wish, desire*], *s. mind* Ś 148ᵃ.2. yāya manasās daya *to be inclined to*... H³ 59ᵃ.1.

manasil [*S.* manaḥśilā], *s. orpiment* Vd 26ᵃ.1.

maṇi [*S.*], *s. a gem, pearl* H² 56ᵃ.3.

maṇik [*S.* maṇika *a jewel, gem*], *s. a ruby* (= *S.* māṇikya) B 68ᵇ.6.

manukh [*S.* manuṣa], *s. a man, human being* Vd 49ᵃ.2.

manu-mi, *s. a man* V² 62ᵃ.3*.

manuṣy [*S.*], *s. a man, human being* H² 57ᵇ.6.

manĕ¹, *v. i. to swell* Vd 11ᵇ.3.

manĕ², *v. t. to pardon* N 52ᵃ.2.

manoram [*S.*], *adj. delightful* Vi 143.1; ~ yāya *to enjoy* 135.26.

manohar [*S.*], *adj. charming* V¹ 9ᵃ.4.

mantr [*S.*], *s. a magical formula* Ś 164ᵇ.1; *an advice* H² 68ᵇ.5. — ~ yāya *to make incantations* B 39ᵃ.1. — ~-puṭhi *book containing magical formulas* V¹ 26ᵇ.1.

mantraṇā [*S.*], *s. advice* H² 87ᵇ.3.

mantri [*S.* mantrin], *s. a minister* V¹ 20ᵃ.3. — ~-cā *the son of a minister* B 63ᵇ.9. — ~-putr *id.* V¹ 16ᵃ.3. — *ifc.* **mūl-**.

manthān, *adv. quickly, hurriedly* H¹ 94ᵇ.3.

maṇḍap [*S. open hall*], *s. a pavilion* V¹ 72ᵇ.1, *a shop* H² 105ᵃ.6.

maṇḍal [*S.*], *s. a magical circle* V¹ 138ᵇ.4.

maṇḍalapĕ [*S.* manda *slow*], *v. i. to be slow, tardy, negligent* N 19ᵃ.5, *to be paralysed* (*with awe*) 48ᵃ.6. — maṇḍalapayakĕ *caus. to paralyse* (*with fear*) 49ᵇ.2.

mandil [*Bhojp. house, temple*], *s. a house* V¹ 11ᵇ.2.

maṇḍo [= maṇḍapa?], *s. a sanctuary of a deity* N 27ᵃ.7.

maṇḍhe [*H.* maṇḍī], *s. a medicinal herb* N 11ᵃ.7.

mayadān [*H.* maidān *from Pers.*], *s. a plain, flat country* B 62ᵇ.4.

mayādal¹, *s.* = marjāt C² 207.

ma-yādal² [=¹; *but* ma *has been taken for the negation* ma], *s. wrong course of action* C² 199; ~ yāya *to do wrong* N 11ᵃ.5.

mayi, *s.* = may(-ju) B 32ᵃ.8.

mayūr [*S.*], *s. a peacock* H² 74ᵃ.5. — *ifc.* **rājā-**.

may-ju, *s.* (*used in addressing a woman of superior rank*): *mylady, mistress* Ś 147ᵃ.5.

mal, *s. a man, human being* H³ 42ᵃ.4*.

mala, *s.* = malak C¹ 267.

malak [*S.* maraka], *s. lightning* C¹ 145. — *ifc.* **bajr-**.

marakat [*S.*], *s. emerald* H² 6ᵇ.5.

malakhedaṁ, *s. loss of colour* CW 1.75.

marac [*S.* marica], *s. pepper* Vd 2ᵃ.5. — *ifc.* **sit-**.

maraṇ [*S. death*], ~ juya *to die* V¹ 22ᵃ.6.

malaṁbhe, *ifc.* **mām-**.

mali [*H.* mirī *from Pers.* mīr?], *s. a chief, eminent man(?)* B 19ᵃ.1.

malin [*cf. Mr. dull, dim*], khvāl ~ yāya *to look gloomily* Vi 173.2.

mari-svān, *s. name of several plants* Md 32ᵃ.2.

male[1], *s. the wife of a maternal uncle* CW 8.29.

male[2], *s.* 1) *emerald* AH 57ᵇ. — 2) *black pepper* 59ᵃ.

markaṭ [*S.*], *s. a monkey* Bh 162ᵇ.7.

mal-kāji, *s. a minister* AH 48ᵃ (malakájee).

margu, margus coṅ bāyu *one of the five vital airs* (apāna) AH 6ᵇ.

marjāt(ā) [*S.* maryādā], *s. right course of action* V¹ 101ᵃ.6, *usage, custom* H³ 32ᵃ.8, *nature, habit, practice* B 68ᵇ.4.

marty [*S.*], *s. the earth* H² 62ᵇ.5.

mard, *s. manner of sexual intercourse* Ś 168ᵃ.2*.

mardan [*S. s. crushing, rubbing*], ~ yāya *to crush* Bh 99ᵇ.2, *to rub* Vd 54ᵃ.2.

marm [*S.* marman], *s. a limb* V¹ 33ᵃ.1.

maryādā [*S.*], *s. morality* N 1ᵇ.4.

masamo-, ~-cā *having reached the age of puberty* N 31ᵇ.3; ~-lyāsēṃ swobhāb *marks of puberty ib.* 9*.

masān [*M.*], *s. a burying ground* V¹ 21ᵃ.3.

mastak [*S.*], *s. the head* V¹ 56ᵇ.1.

mastri, *s.* = mantri V² 9ᵇ.3.

mahant- [*cf. S.* mahant-], ~-puruṣ *an eminent man* H³ 57ᵃ.10.

mahā [*S.* mahā- *great (in comp.)*], *adv. very, in a high degree* H¹ 11ᵇ.4.

mahārāj(ā) [*S.* mahārāja], *s. a great king, supreme sovereign* V¹ 108ᵇ.3.

mahinā [*H.* mahinā *month, monthly wages*], *s. wages* H² 89ᵃ.1.

mā[1], *s. a female (animal or bird)* B 32ᵃ.4. — *ifc.* (*a mother*) **ajī-, tutu-, dudu-**.

mā[2], *s. a tree* B 35ᵃ.1; *gen. cl-w. for trees* H¹ 36ᵃ.2. — *ifc.* **ap-, ambal-, aśvasth-, kusi-, kelā-, khokhar-, dhāle-, pit-, bhatā, yesi-, sisāphal-, svān-**.

mā[3] = māl (*5th form of* mālē²) H³ 60ᵃ.4.

ma-[4] (-n *or* -t? *only* mān), *v. t. to love* V¹ 117ᵃ.5.

mā-ut[1], *s. a female camel* Bh 79ᵃ.5.

mā'ut[2] [*cf. EH.* mahāut], *s. an elephant-driver* Bh 79ᵃ.5*.

māwo = māl (*5th form of* mālē²) H³ 47ᵃ.4.

māṁs [*S.*], *s. meat* B 109ᵇ.5.

mākaḍ [*cf. Mr.* mākaḍa], *s. a monkey* C² 131. — mākal *id.* C¹ 131.

mā-kas(a)mili, *s. a female parrot* V¹ 28ᵇ.4.

māku, *adj. sweet* Vd 10ᵇ.1.

mā-kwokha, *s. a female crow* H³ 35ᵃ.1.

mākraḍ, *s.* = mākaḍ N 44ᵇ.1.

mā-khā-pi-khā, *s. a spider* CW 7.6.

mākhi [*cf. S.* mākṣika], *s.*, subarṇ-~ *a kind of honey-like mineral substance* (mākṣika) Md 33ᵇ.3.

mā-khicā, *s. a bitch* AH 60ᵇ.

mā-gāḍhu, *s. a female donkey* H² 76ᵃ.5.

mā-cal-khuni, *s. a female sparrow* B 31ᵇ.12.

mā-cā, *s. mother and child (daughter)* V¹ 137ᵃ.1.

mā-colas, *s. a she-goat* AH 21ᵇ (má-cholay).

māchāwāl, *s.* = machawāl Bh 116ᵇ.1*.

māchi, *adv.* = machi; ~ ma māchin... ma *on no account whatever* N 49ᵇ.3*.

mā-ju [mā¹], *s. used in addressing a woman* Ś 148ᵇ.2. — *ifc.* **rā-**.

mā-jhaṅgal, *s. a hen-bird* B 65ᵃ.7.

mājhi [*H.* māñjhī *the steer-man of a boat*], *s. a ferry-man* **Vi 92.30**, *a* *fisher-man* H^2 99^b.5, *a steer-man* 73^b.7; *a barbarous tribe* (pulinda) AH 60^b.

mājhet, *s. the plaintiff* N 14^b.5.

mātan [*H.* māṭ], *s. a large earthen jar*(?) B 51^a.5.

mātā [*S. mother*], *s. a woman* B 44^a.8.

-mā-tāne, *forming neg. imperatives; only:* kha-~ *don't be* H^3 50^b.2, ju-~ *don't become ib.* — kha-~ *is also used in the sense: "as for..."* 64^a.4.

mā-titihudi, *s. a female sandpiper* H^3 37^a.9.

mātin-si, *s. a kind of ebony-tree* (tinduka) AH 28^b.

mātr [*S. measure, quantity*], *adv. only* H^2 53^a.8; ~ jukwo *id.* P 33^a.2. mātranaṃ *after a subst. or 6th form of a verb: merely through...* H^2 77^b.1; mātrasaṃ *id.* 92^a.7. cha-hnu-yā mātras *some day* B 7^b.12.

māthan, ~ wonë *to be level, to be plain* C^2 151.

māthan(aṁ) [*cf. S.* mātra *measure*], *adv., only:* nānā ~ *in manifold ways* H^2 50^a.4.

māthal [māthan], *adj. level, plain* CW 5.3.

māthasindhar, *s. a medicinal plant* Vd 54^b.5.

mādalapë [*S.* mādaya-], *v. t. to delight, to satisfy*(?) N 40^b.4; *to mock, to deride* H^2 57^b.6.

mādhi, *s.* = madhi B 3^a.3.

mān [*S. respect, honour*], ~ yāya *to honour* B 7^b.9.

mānabant, *adj.* = māni° H^2 39^a.3.

mānay [mān], ~ yāya *to honour* Ś 144^b.6.

mānik [*M.*], *s. a ruby* H^2 56^a.2.

mānibant [*cf. S.* mānavant- *rich in honour*], *adj. sensible, intelligent* H^3 15^a.9; ~-hma *id.* H^2 39^a.1.

mānukh [*M.*], *s. a man* H^2 56^a.7.

mānus, *s.* = mānukh N 13^b.7.

mān-mi, *s. a man* V^1 101^a.8.

māny [*S. adj. to be honoured*], ~ yāya *to honour* H^3 22^b.8; ~ kāya *to be honoured* (ch-hm-yāke *by...*) H^2 52^a.1.

māp [*H. measurement*], ~ yāya *to consider, to take into account* B 63^b.6*.

mā-phakan [mā^2], *s. a sort of bulbuous plant* (grāmakanda) Md 51^a.1.

mā-phā, *s. a she-boar* Bh 11^b.4.

mā-bi, *s. a female serpent* H^3 58^b.4.

mā-byāṅ, *s. a female tortoise* (kamaṭhī) AH 21^b.

mām, *s. a mother* H^1 24^b.5. — ~-ju *id.* B 22^a.12; *a paternal uncle's wife* P 59^a.2. — ~-malaṃbhe *id.* N 34^b.3. — *ifc.* **guru-, sasal-.**

mā-mes, *s. a female buffalo* N 28^b.6.

mā-hma, *s.* = mā^1 B 64^a.9.

māyakë, *irreg. caus. of* mālë B 50^b.3*.

māyā [*S. illusion, deception*], ch-hm-yāke ~ taya *to set one's heart upon...* Vi 46.10; ch-hm-yā(ke) ~ daya *to be attached to...* Bh 22^a.6; ch-hm-wo ~ kāya *to care about, to mind* H^3 31^b.11. — māyān *adv. deceitfully* Bh 61^b.7, *under a delusion* Vi 131.17. — ~-citt H^3 55^b.11 *and* ~-sneh Vi 57.29 *are used like* māyā.

mār^1 [*S. killing; death*], *s. contrast; an antidote* Vd 46^a.3.

māl^2 [*H. a necklace*], *cl-w. for necklace* Vi 103.28. — *ifc. (a garland):* **pūl-, mut-, svān-, hāre-.**

mālakë^1, *caus. of* mālë^1 B 8^b.2.

mālakë^2 (*caus. of* mālë^2), *to contract (a debt)* N 2^b.1. — mu mālakë *to prevent, to avert* C^1 97. — mālakwo *necessary* B 14^a.6. — biśeṣ ma mālakaṃ *without making any distinction (between)* H^1 81^a.5.

mālapë [māl^2], *v. t. to twist round, to encircle* C^2 178. — mālapayakë *caus.* N 21^a.3.

māray [*S.* māraya- *to kill*], ~ yāya

to kill, to destroy, to exstirpate H²71ª.7; ~ yācakē *caus.* 93ᵇ.8.

māralapē [*S.* māra *death*], *v. t. to slay, to kill* N 25ᵇ.4.

mālā [*S.*], *s. a wreath, necklace* Vi 103.28. — *ifc.* **kawoḍi-, moti-, svān-.**

mārāmārī [*cf. H.* mārāmār *struggle*], ~ yāya *to cause struggle or quarrel* N 26ª.3*.

mālē¹, *v. t. to seek, to search for...* V¹ 9ª.1. mālā haya *to find* H² 109ª.3; mālaṃ luyakē *to search, to scour* N 42ª.5. — māl mil woya *to go to seek everywhere* B 61ᵇ.1.

mālē² (*5th form also: old* mālwo, *younger* māwo), *v. i. to be necessary* H² 97ᵇ.3, ch-hm-yāta māl *it is necessary for someone, i.e. someone wants or needs* V² 62ª.5; *to wish, to want* B 40ᵇ.2; *must, shall* H¹ 51ª.2; *may (optativ):* hlāya māl *may (he) tell* V² 9ᵇ.5, bi-jyāya ~ *(you) may come* B 13ᵇ.12. — *The negation generally is* mu: mu māl *after 4th form usually has the force of a (polite) negative imper.:* gyāya mu māl *(you) need not be afraid, don't be afraid* V² 73ª.3.

mārg [*S.*], *s. a road* H² 79ᵇ.5.

mās [*S.*], *s. a month* Vd 45ª.3.

mā-salām-jhaṅgal, *s. the female of a certain bird* (lakṣmaṇā) AH 35ᵇ.

mā-sā, *s. a cow* C¹ 77.

māsik [*S. adj. monthly*], *s. menstruation* Vd 27ª.2. — ~-hi *blood of the m° ib.* 4.

mā-haṁs, *s. a goose* CW 7.12.

mā-haraḍi, *s. a kind of turmeric* Vd 21ª.6.

māhā = mahā Bh 23ᵇ.3.

māhān, *s. a kind of official* B 30ᵇ.2.

māhut, *s.* = mā'ut H² 105ᵇ.6*.

mi¹, *s. an eye* H¹ 24ᵇ.1; ~ pikē *to cause to shut the eyes* Vi 121.31.

mi², *s. a man* H¹ 62ª.4. — *ifc.* **ku-lāh-, jyā-, pā-, pusā-, manu-, mān-.**

mi³, *s.* = me¹ V¹ 92ᵇ.5; ~ syāya *to extinguish fire* V² 75ᵇ.1; ch-g-s ~ taya *to set a thing on fire* V¹ 127ᵇ.6; mi thanē *to light a fire* Vi 74.50; ~ lācakē *to let be destroyed by fire* B 21ᵇ.5.

mi-kā, *s.* = mi-khā Ç² 238.

miku-si, *s. name of a plant* (dārvī) AH 31ª.

mi-kha(ṁ), *s. a lawsuit concerning a man* N 13ᵇ.2.

mi-khā, *s. an eye* H¹ 4ᵇ.1; ~ miya *to shut the eyes* V¹ 82ª.3; ~ kanē *to open the eyes* M 10ᵇ.2; ~ kān-hma *blind* CW 8.50; ~ ma du-hma *who has lost his sight* H² 94ᵇ.6; ~ ma bhiṅ *timid* (kaśmala) C² 182. — ~-koṇ *the outer corner of the eye* CW 8.72. — ~-jhyāl *the pupil of the eye* AH 42ᵇ. — ~-pical *impurity of the eye* 41ª. — ~-phusi *the eyebrows* 42ᵇ. — ~-bhāb *a look of the eyes* Ś 159ª.6. — ~-bhāy *id.* H² 82ᵇ.5. — ~-loy *a disease of the eyes* AH 40ª. — ~ syāk-hma *blear-eyed* CW 8.49.

mi-khuti, *s. a disease of the eye* Vd 15ª.3.

mi-guli, *s. a spark* H² 96ᵇ.6.

micake, °ki, *s. Curcuma aromatica* Vd 23ᵇ.2. — ~-si *id.* 15ª.5.

mi-cikil, *s. a spark* CW 1.25.

mi-jan, *s.* = mi² B 59ª.1.

mi-jalā, *s. a flame* AH 6ª.

mi-jvālā, *s. a flame* AH 70ª.

mitaki-si, *s.* = micaki-° CW 6.28.

mitr [*S.*], *s. a friend* H¹ 25ª.3; ch-hm-wo ~ yāya *to form a friendship with...* 33ª.8. — *ifc.* **suheti-**

mit-se, *s. a gr[illegible]* CW 6.29. — ~-thw[illegible] *a kind of in[illegible]ting drink* (maireya) AH 62ª (mitsithoṇ).

mi-thap, *s. a chimney* (culli) AH 54ᵇ.

mithī [*H.* methī *fenugreek*], *s. a medicinal plant* Vd 39ª.6.

mithun [*S.*], *s. sexual intercourse* C² 125.

mithyā [*S.*], *adv. falsely* Bh 42ª.5. — ~-buddhi *falsehood, slyness* H² 32ᵇ.3.

mīn [*H.* mīnā *a caste of Hindu robbers of Rajputāna*], *s. a robber* N 11ª.7.

miya¹ (-l¹), *v. t. to sell* H² 105ª.7.

miya² (-l¹), mikhā ~ *to shut the eyes* V¹ 82ª.3; mi ~ *id., i. e. to die*(?) B 23ᵇ.2. mikhā mi (= ma?) miya *not to blink with the eyes* Bh 53ᵇ.3.

mil, *see* **mālë**.

milakhā, *s. the back of the neck* CW 8.68.

milay [*s.* milalapë], ~ juya *to meet, to assemble* H³ 35ª.10; ~ yāya *to unite* Vi 99.6.

milapë, *v. i.* = milalapë Vd 33ᵇ.5.

milalapë [*M.* mil *to unite, to meet*], *v. i. to meet, to assemble* H² 66ª.7.

milā¹, *s. a measure for liquids* Vd 2ᵇ.3. — *ifc.* **bā-**.

mi-lā², *s. the moon*; *see* **khin, toyi, toyu, nan, siṅu**. — *ifc.* **sasi-**.

mi-lāp, *s. a flame* CW 1.24.

mili-hma, *s.* = mel-° V¹ 108ª.1.

mi-sa, *s. the eyebrows* Vi 56.28.

misā, *s. a woman, wife* H¹ 61ª.1. — ~-jan *women* C¹ 216. — ~-jāt *womankind, woman* B 1ᵇ.7. — ~-pāsā *a female friend* CW 8.10. — ~-bathān *an assemblance of courtesans* AH 37ᵇ. — ~-bhes *disguised as a woman* Ś 159ᵇ.2. — ~-hyo *desiring, lustful* AH 63ᵇ. — ~-lan *a bodice* CW 8.84. — *ifc.* **kutal-, cedi-, natuwā-, pakasini-, baiśyā-, bësyā-, mo-**.

miśr [*S.* miśr- *to mix*], tāmran ~ ciṅaṃ-tayā *inlaid*(?) *with copper* Bh 73ᵇ.4*.

misray [*S.* miśr-], ~ yāya *to mix, to mingle* P 63ª.7.

mi-haraḍī, *s. a kind of turmeric* Vd 55ª.6.

mihi-loy, *s. stone-disease* AH 40ª.

mu¹, *s. a sort of pulse* M 8ᵇ.3*.

mu² = ma Vd 19ᵇ.6. — *The usual form before* mālë *and* mvālë H² 97ᵇ.2.

muṁ-bo, *s.* (*a field*) *sown with beans* AH 53ᵇ.

muk, *s. a medicinal plant* Vd 46ᵇ.4. — ~-yuṣ *a pulse made from this plant* Md 68ᵇ.5.

mukt [*S. liberated*] = **mukti¹** Bh *2ª.1.

muktalapë [*S.* mukta *released*], *v. t. to set free, to release* (*a prisoner*) N 52ª.2.

mukti¹ [*S. liberation*], ~ juya *to become released, to be saved* (*from sin, obligations a. s. o.*) N 2ª.7; ~ yāya *to save from, to rid of* H² 48ᵇ.3; ṛṇ ~ ~ *to discharge a debt* N 2ª.7.

mukti² [*S.* muktā], *s. a pearl* C² 219.

mukh [*S.*], *s. the face* V¹ 10ª.1; ch-g-s ~ yāya *to go in the direction of...* M 22ª.3.

mukhar [*S.* talkative], ~ juya *to be silent* (*sic*) H³ 39ª.5*

mukhu [*S.* mukura], *s. a bud* AH 27ª.

muguti [*cf. S.* mukti *release, liberation*], ~ juya *to be released* (*said of a slave*) N 20ª.1. ~ wonë *id.* 20ᵇ.6; ~ yācakë *to release* 20ª.3.

mugutilapayakë [muguti], *v. t. to cause to be released* (*a slave*) N 20ᵇ.5*.

mu-cā, *s.* = mo-cā Vi 122.19.

mujarā [*H.* mujrā *respects, from Arab.*], ch-hm-yā ~ yāya *to pay respect to...* Vi 40.1*.

mutī, *s.* = moti B 25ª.7.

mut-khul, *s. a pearl-oyster* CW 2.8.

mutti [*S.* muṣṭi], *s. a fist* Bh 81ᵇ.4.

mut-māl, *s. a necklace of pearls* CW 8.79.

mūtr [*S.*], *s. urine* Vd 3ᵇ.2.

mud [*cf. S.* mudrā], **mudan teya** *to seal* N 15ᵇ.1*.

mude, *s. the hollow above the hip, lap* Bh 169ª.4. — ~-si *id.* AH 65ª.

mūḍh [*S.*], *adj. foolish, stupid* H² 93ᵇ.3.

munakë (*caus. of* munë), *to assemble* B 62ᵇ.3.

muni¹ [*S.*], *s. a monk, hermit* H² 103ª.2.

muni², *s. the pericarp* (*of a lotus*) M 5ª.7. — *ifc.* **palë-**.

munë, *v. t. to assemble* B 60ª.3, *to collect* H² 118ª.5, *to join, to put together* H¹ 23ᵇ.5. — *v. i. to assemble, to meet* V¹ 26ᵇ.4.

mu-pā, *s. a maternal uncle* V¹ 107ª.2.

mul¹ [*S.* mūla], *s. a root* Vd 47ª.3, *main thing* H¹ 19ª.2. — mūlanaṃ *adv. above all* Vi 171.2. — ~-hma rānī *the first wife of a king* CW 8.5. — ~-kacā *a principal branch* 6.8. — ~-kuṭumb *a family* N 2ᵇ.2. — ~-nāyak *a householder* 4ª.1. — ~-mantri *a principal minister* B 53ª.2. — ~-laṃ *a main road* CW 3.9.

— *ifc.* **ambal-, u-, simalas-**.

mūl² [*S.* mūlya], *s. price, value* N 23ᵇ.5; ~ woṅ-gu *previous, valuable* B 2ᵇ.2; ~ wokwo *id.* N 50ᵇ.4. ~ kāya *to sell* 17ᵇ.3; ~ biya *to buy* 24ª.6; ~ yāya *to deal in* B 55ª.5. — *ifc.* **hmo-**.

mūrkh [*S.*], *s. a fool* H² 74ᵇ.5; ~-hma *id.* H¹ 65ᵇ.3.

mūrchā [*S. fainting fit*]; ch-hm-yā ~ juya *to faint* V¹ 56ª.5; mūrchān puya (-I¹) *id.* B 66ᵇ.5; mūrchān kawo *fainted* Bh 147ᵇ.3.

musān [*M.* masān], *s. a burial ground* B 14ª.6.

musumān [*H.* musalmān *Mahomedan*], *s. Mahomedan, a low-caste man* Ś 147ª.6.

musur [*S.* masura], *s. a sort of lentil or pulse* Vd 47ª.1.

musu-hun, *adv., only:* ~ hṅelë (hṅilë, hnilë) *to smile* H² 113ª.4.

must, *s. the forehead* (lalāṭa) N 12ª.3*.

muhubartt, ~ yāya *to keep silence* H¹ 68ª.2*.

mṛg [*S.*], *s. a gazelle* H¹ 33ᵇ.4.

mṛtak [*S.*], *s. a dead body, corpse* B 15ᵇ.9.

mṛtu = mṛtyu V² 55ª.5.

mṛtyu [*S.*], *s. death* H¹ 79ª.2. ~ juya *to die* V¹ 25ᵇ.1, ~ yāya *to kill* Vi 123.4. — mṛtyuk *adj. dead* Vi 107.9. — mṛty = mṛtyu Bh 13ᵇ.1.

me¹, *s. fire* H¹ 50ª.3. — *ifc.* **so-**.

me², *s. the tongue* H¹ 57ª.5; me sa noyiwo *the tongue becomes foul* Vd 44ª.4. — *ifc.* **ca-**.

me³, *s. a song* CW 1.68; ~ hālë *to sing* P 8ᵇ.6.

mewo = meba (*only* Vi) **123.19.**

megh [*S.*], *s. a cloud* H² 50ᵇ.7.

me-co, *s. the tip of the tongue* Vd 10ª.2.

me-cok, *s. who forsakes the fire* (agnityāga) N 11ª.4.

me-cokā, *s.* = °-co Ns 39ª.7.

me-col, *s.*, ~ juwo-hma *an incendiary* C¹ 114, ~ jowo *id.* N 10ᵇ.3.

mech, ~ munë *to conceal* N 15ª.8, *to deny* 15ª.3; ~ ma munë *to confess* 15ª.6.

met-se, *s.* = mit-° Vd 13ª.3.

medā(ṁ)giri, *s. a medicinal plant* Vd 51ª.2.

me-pu, *s. fire* N 50ª.1.

me-pukhuri, *s. a flame* N 13ᵇ.8.

meba, *s. and adj. other, another* H¹ 25ª.1. ~-tā *id.* V¹ 72ᵇ.2; ~-hma *id.* (*of persons only*) V¹ 49ª.1; ~-gu *id.* (*of things only*) B 47ᵇ.8. — ~-thëṃ *adv. otherwise* N 35ᵇ.4; mebanaṃ *id., else* M 7ª.8.

mebu = meba B 60ᵇ.4; mebunaṃ = meba° H² 51ᵇ.8.

melapë, *v. i.* = milapë H¹ 87ª.1.

melalapë, *v. i.* = milalapë H¹ 42ᵇ.2.

me-lā¹, *s.* = mi-lā² H² 28ᵇ.7.

melā² [*S. company*], khawo melāwo pāsā yāya *to keep bad company* N 49ᵇ.6*.

melā³, *s.* = milā¹ Vd 26ᵃ.6*.

mele, *adv. elsewhere, in another place* H¹ 66ᵃ.3, *to another place* V¹ 69ᵃ.5; ~ gananaṃ ma *from nowhere else* Vi 70.33. ~ *to another* (*man*) B 26ᵃ.3, ~ (pasanan) wonë *to go to another i.e. to marry again* (*of a widow*) N 40ᵇ.9. — *adj. other* H² 80ᵇ.6.

mel-hma, *s. the other* [illegible]e V¹ 111ᵃ.4.

mes, *s. a buffalo* Bh 13[illegible]. — ~-dudu *milk of a buffalo* Vd 38ᵃ.1. — ~-dhali *coagulated milk of a buffal*[illegible]ᵇ.2. — *ifc.* **gal-**, **doha-**, **mā-**, **sā-**.

mesāl, *s. the thigh*(?) N 30ᵇ.2*.

mes-galad, *s. a species of tree* (meṣaśṛṅga) Md 10ᵇ.3.

meherī [*H.* mehdī?], *s. a myrtle*(?) Vd 33ᵃ.5*.

maithun [*S.*], *s. sexual intercourse* H¹ 68ᵇ.3.

mĕ(ṁ)ba = meba (*only* N) 17ᵃ.4.

mo = ma Bh 33ᵇ.6.

mokṣ [*S.*], *s. liberation, deliverance* H¹ 28ᵇ.2; pāp ~ yāya *to deliver from sin* Bh 23ᵇ.4; ch-hm-yāta ~ choya *to liberate, to deliver* M 16ᵇ.8.

moc, *s.*, *ifc.* **bi-**.

moca, *s. a woman* C² 124*.

mocakë (*caus. of* moya), *to kill* Bh 137ᵃ.3, *to consume* H² 60ᵃ.4, *to squander* V² 55ᵇ.5, *to overcome* (*grief*) H³ 47ᵇ.4; saṃśay ~ *to solve a doubt* H¹ 3ᵇ.3; ch-hm-yā prāṇ ~ *to kill* 57ᵇ.4.

mocan [*S. adj. releasing from; for the meaning of the word in Ne. cf.* **mocakë**], ~ yāya *to destroy* P 58ᵇ.3, ~ juya *to be destroyed, to perish* H² 92ᵇ.6. — mocanā = mocan H¹ 93ᵇ.3.

mo-cā, *s. a child* P 57ᵃ.5, *a young animal or bird* H³ 35ᵃ.1. mocā-to *pl. children* V¹ 137ᵇ.1, *young animals or birds* H¹ 42ᵇ.2. — mocā buwo-hma *a lying-in woman* Vd 52ᵃ.6, ~ **thwol** *id.* N 33ᵃ.4 (mvacā-~). — *ifc.* **kāy-**, **tas-**, **bālak-**, **yili-**.

moti [*M.*], *s. a pearl* Bh 167ᵇ.4. — ~-thuco *a string of pearls* Bh 173ᵇ.2. — ~-mālā *a garland of pearls* AH 43.

moḍ¹ = mol¹ Bh 82ᵇ.3. — ~-sa *the hair of the head* Bh 50ᵃ.6. — ~-syāk *headache* Vd 13ᵃ.5.

moḍ² = mol²; ~ hluya H² 13ᵃ.3; ~ hluyakë *to bathe* (*trs.*), *to let bathe* N 35ᵇ.3.

moḍalapë [*S.* moda *delight, pleasure*], *v. t. to love, to appreciate* N 4ᵇ.3*.

mo-misā [*cf.* mo-cā], *s. women* N 5ᵃ.4.

mo-hma [moya], *s. loss* (?) N 21ᵇ.7*.

moya (-l¹, *but* mok, mocakë), *v. i. to perish, to be destroyed* H¹ 30ᵃ.2, *to perish, do die* V¹ 90ᵇ.6, *to be lost* H² 64ᵇ.2; ch-hm-yā prāṇ molaṃ *somebody has lost his life, has died* V² 59ᵇ.4.

mol¹, *s. the head* V¹ 58ᵃ.4. — ~-bhāy *expression of countenance* H² 82ᵇ.5.

mol², ~ hluya (-l¹), *v. i. to bathe* H¹ 18ᵃ.2.

mol³, *s.* = mwoṃd²; *ifc.* **gā-***.

mo-swo, *s. cough* Vd 52ᵃ.1; *gen.*: *mo-swok* 4ᵃ.2.

moh [*S.*], *s. delusion, infatuation* H² 15ᵃ.4. — ~ yāya *to delude, to infatuate* H³ 37ᵇ.6; ch-g-s ~ ~ *to suffer oneself to be infatuated by*... H¹ 78ᵃ.5.

mohalapë [moh], *v. t. to delude, to infatuate* B 70ᵃ.5.

mohit [*S.*], *adj. infatuated* H² 54ᵃ.6.

moho = moh Bh 143ᵇ.1*.

mohol, °**hal**, *s. copper* B 50ᵇ.12.

maun [*S. silence*], ~ yāya *to keep silence* V¹ 23ᵇ.1.

mwoṃḍ¹, *s.* = mol¹ N 13ᵃ.7.

mwoṃḍ², *s. a substitute* N 2[illegible]ᵃ.8. — *ifc.* **gā-***.

mwo-pā, *s.* = mupā CW 8.29 (m-bapā).

mwol-swol, ~ **dhāseṃ** *stammering*(?) N 12ᵃ.2*.

mye, *s.* = me[2] Pg 24ª.8*.

mvākë = mvācakë H[2] 92ª.3.

mvāc[1], *s. plantain* Md 41ᵇ.4.

mvāc[2], *s. a kind of drug (opposed to* cicun) Vd 46ª.3.

mvāc[3], *s.* = moc; *ifc.* **bi-**.

mvāca [= mocā?], *s. an unmarried girl* N 40ᵇ.3*.

mvācakë (*caus. of* mvāya), *to keep alive* H[1] 36ª.4; *to bring back to life* V[1] 93ᵇ.2; *to animate, to vivify* B 27ᵇ.3.

mvāt, *s. a sort of lac* (yāvaka) AH 54ª.

mvātakë = mvācakë H[3] 48ᵇ.1.

mvāya (-t), *v. i. to live, to be alive* H[1] 36ª.5; *to revive* V[1] 26ᵇ.5; *to be, to exist* N 48ª.8, jusëṃ ~ *id.* 13ᵇ.6.

mvālakë (*caus. of* mvālë), mu ~ = mu mālakë M 6ᵇ.6. — śaṅkhā kāya mu **mvālakaṃ** *enough of these scrouples* H[3] 35ª.6.

mvālë, *v. i.* = mālë[2] B 6ᵇ.1.

mvāhāli, *s. a musical instrument* Ś 169ᵇ.5*.

hm.

hma[1], *s. a body* V[2] 32ª.1; hmayā kwos *a skeleton* CW 8.54, ~-biṣay *the sense of touch* AH 14ª. — *ifc.* **bā-**.

hma[2], *s.* = hme[1]; *ifc.* **tarawāl-**.

hma[3], ~ pulë *to have sexual intercourse* Vi 143.10*.

-hma[4] [= hma[1]], *suffix which may be added to pronouns, adjectives, numerals and participles when they refer to persons:* thwo-hma kanyā *this girl* V[2] 52ᵇ.2; jñāni-hma *a knowing one* H[1] 62ª.5; ma ṅeṅ-hma *who does not hear* 46ᵇ.2; tawo kvāc-hma *the one with large foot-prints* V[1] 137ª.2.

hma-gas, *s. a dream*(?) Vi 83.28*.

hmaca-mo, *s. a wife* H[1] 75ª.1; ~ yāya *to espouse* N 34ᵇ.2.

hma-cā, *s. a daughter* V[2] 28ᵇ.6*.

hmati-puli, *s. a pair, couple* H[3] 65ᵇ.7; ni ~ *id.* B 59ᵇ.11. ni hmati-pu *man and wife* AH 38ᵇ; *copulation* 36ᵇ.

hma-të, *v. i.* = hmë-të H[1] 75ª.1.

hmanë, *v. i. to dream* B 37ª.12; *to sleep* P 17ª.7. — hmaṅā *s. a dream* CW 1.76.

hma-bān, *s. a brand shaped like the body (of a man)* N 52ª.7*.

hmaya[1] (-l[1]), *v. t.*, ch-hm ~ *to long for...* Ś 161ª.7.

hmaya[2] (-l[1]) [hma[1]], *v. t. to embody, to show, to display* M 22ᵇ.2; pyās ~ *to show symptoms of thirst* Vd 19ᵇ.2.

hmaya[3] (-t), *v. t.* = hmoya[1] H[3] 16ᵇ.5*.

hmayakë, *caus. of* hmaya[1] H[3] 41ᵇ.5*.

hmal, *s. lead (metal)* Vd 32ᵇ.1. — ~-mudr *id.* N 25ª.7.

hmas-khā, *s.* = hmas-khā B 47ª.1. — *ifc.* **rājā-**.

hmā-ca, *s.* = hmyā-ca V[1] 25ª.2.

hmā-tāne, thathë hlāk ju-~ *as it was said* H[1] 82ª.5*.

hmā-lā, *s. the thumb* B 46ª.5. — ~-pacinī *id.* Ns 26ª.4.

hmā-lā-milā, *s.* = hmā-ḷ-mudo AH 34ᵇ.

hmā-ḷ-mudo, *s. a lizard, chameleon* CW 7.5.

hmiga, *adv.* = hmegwo M 15ᵇ.3.

hmigwo, *adv.* = hmegwo B 32ª.11.

hmi-cā (hmi = hme[1]), *s., only ifc.* **khul-**.

hmi-të, *v. t.* = hmë-të B 53ª.5. — hmi-tëkë *caus. to divert* Vi 151.14.

hmukan, *s. a kind of garlic* Md 50ᵇ.7.

hmu-ku-chi, *s. a measure, from the elbow to the closed hand* (saratni) AH 42ª.

hmu-jyā, *s.* = hmo-° Vi 101.23*.

hmuti, *s. a handful*(?) H[2] 61ᵇ.1 = H[3] 32ª.2*.

hmutu, *s. the mouth* V[2] 47ᵇ.1, *the*

face C^2 226; hmutun dhāya *to speak aloud* Vi 133.5. — ~-si Bh 53^b.2.

hmuṭhi, *s. little staves of ivory* (śalākā) N 44^b.2*.

hmuthu, *s.* = hmutu Bh 35^b.6.

hmuya^1 (-l^1), *v. t. to dig* H^1 64^a.4.

hmuya^2 (-t), *v. t.* = hmoya^2 C^1 221.

hmuyakë, *caus. of* hmuya^1 H^2 84^b.6.

hmul, *s. a fist;* ~-kuchi *an ell* CW 8.67.

hmus-khā, *s.* = hmos-khā H^2 43^a.1.

hme^1, *s. a bag* B 49^a.5.

hme^2, *s. engagement, liability (to pay)* N 2^b.7; ~ ṅoya *to act up to one's engagements* (?) 4^a.8.

hmegwo, *adv. yesterday* V^1 21^a.6; hmegwoyā lā *the meat from yesterday* H^2 60^a.3.

hmeya (-t *or* -l^1?), *v. t.*, pu ~ *to sow the seed* N 33^b.2.

hmë-tayakë, *caus. of* hmë-të Bh 147^a.6.

hmë-të, *v. i. to play, to sport* Bh 12^b.2; *to divert oneself* H^2 62^a.2.

hmo^1, *adj. little, less, lesser* N 38^b.4; *youngest* AH 68^b; ~ mūl *of small value* N 50^b.4.

hmo^2, *s. profit, gains* (?) N 44^b.4.

hmokh-khā, *s.* = hmos-khā H^3 18^a.6.

hmo-co, *s. a woman, wife* H^2 20^a.1; hmo-ca *id.* H^1 17^a.2; hmo-cā *id.* V^1 32^b.6.

hmo-jyā [hmoya^1], *s. agriculture, farming* C^1 200; ~ wonë *to carry on agriculture* 282, ~ yāya *id.* 225.

hmoya^1 (-l^1), *v. t.* = hmuya^1 N 27^b.2.

hmoya^2 (-l), *v. t. to efface, to oblitterate* N 8^b.8, *to extinguish (fire)* H^1 51^a.1.

hmorukë [hmo^1], *v. t. to make subside* Vd 35^b.2.

hmos-khā, *s. a peacock* H^1 78^a.1. — ~-pā *the tail of a peacock* CW 7.14.

hmwost, *s. the forehead* N 52^a.7*.

hmyā-ca, *s. a daughter* H^1 84^a.1, *a girl* C^1 13.

hmyā-ya, *s.* = hmyā-ca P 54^b.7.

hmyi-takë = hmi° (*caus. of* hmi-të) *to divert* H^3 17^a.8.

hmyo, *adj.* = hmo^1 N 16^a.7,8*.

y.

Ya, *n. pr. Kathmandu* AH 24,101(ä).

yaṁ-kuli, *s. north-east* CW 1.34.

yaṁ-kel, *s. a cricket* CW 7.12.

yaṁ-tā, *s. the north* CW 1.33.

yaṁ-lā, *s. the month Bhādrapada* CW 1.50.

yaguḍi-siṁ, *s. name of several plants* (dīrghapattra) Md 18^a.8.

yaṁkë = yanakë; banaj ~ *to cause to carry on trade; to use as an apprentice (of a merchant)* N 21^a.7*.

ya-chi = ye-chi Vd 11^a.5*.

yajñ [*S.*], *s. an offering, sacrifice* H^2 95^b.3.

yaṁja = yanë N 21^a.6.

yate, *s. a short arrow* (bhindipāla) AH 52^a.

yatn [*S. exertion*], ~ yāya *to exert oneself* B 13^a.5.

yathāśakyan [*S.* yathā + śakya], *adv. to the utmost of one's power* H^3 50^b.10; ~ cāwo-thë *id.* 61^b.6.

yathë, *adv.*, ~ julasanwoṃ *whatever it may be, at all events* H^1 59^a.1; ~ yāṅānaṃ *whatever (you) may do* H^3 36^b.1; ~ bhinasāṃ *however good it may be* 24^b.9. — yathënaṃ *however, nevertheless* B 40^a.1.

yanakë, *caus. of* yanë Vi 134.17.

yanë, *v. t. to lead to, to conduct to* B 8^b.12; *to lead away* V^1 126^b.5. — *In connection with other verbs (mostly in the 9th or 10th form or the conv. in*

·āwo) yanë *mainly denotes a motion away from the subject:* haralapāwo yanë *to carry off, to abduct* V[1] 75[a].3; boyakaṃ ~ *to fly away with* H[1] 24[a].5; bhuktalapaṃ ~ *to take possession of* N 4[b].7. — *After the reduplicated form of a verb* yanë *denotes, that an action is done repeatedly:* to-to ~ *to drink repeatedly* Vd 52[b].6; wo-wo ~ *to come frequently* V[2] 74[a].6.

yamas-khāl, *s. a kind of alkali* (yavakṣāra) Vd 24[a].6.

yal, ~ khuya (-t *or* -l[1]?) *v. t. to bend, to bow* C[2] 49.

yalakuṭ, *s. the fork-tailed shrike* CW 7.8.

yal-yal, ~ gāya (-t *and* -l[1]) *to get blisters* V[1] 73[a].3.

yas [*S.* yaśas], *s. fame, renown* H[1] 29[b].5.

yasvāl, *s. coldnes* CW 1.42.

yā'u, *adj.* = yāṅu H[3] 10[a].8; yā'uṃsë(ṃ) wonë *to become light* M 2[b].6; yā'uyāya ~ *id.* 3[b].5.

yākāt [*cf. S.* ekānta], *adj. only* M 8[b].4; *adv. alone, by himself* V[1] 78[b].5; yākātan *id.* V[2] 77[b].4.

yākë, *caus. of* yāya Vi 26.18; *to let be done* 173.9, *to let be made or produced* B 31[a].1.

yāko, *s. the armpit* CW 8.61.

yākwo [yāya], *s. a case, affair;* ~ yāya *to settle an affair* Ns 47[b].12.

yāṅa(ṁ) [*9th form of* yāya], *after the 4th form of verbs: in order to...* H[1] 36[b].2.

yāṅu, *adj. light (not heavy)* H[2] 30[b].7.

yācakë, *caus. of* yāya H[2] 88[a].1.

yācalapë [*S.* yāc-], *v. t. to beg, to entreat* H[1] 67[a].4.

yāt[1] [*cf. S.* yātrā], *s. a feast, festival* V[2] 48[b].1.

yāt[2], ~ yāya *to drive out* N 44[b].8*.

yātakë = yācakë M 28[a].5.

yātrā [*S.*], *s. a festival* B 56[b].9.

yādal [*abstracted from* ma-yādal[2]], *s. the right course of action* C[2] 199.

yān, *s. distance* H[3] 13[b].7. yānanaṃ *from afar* M 30[b].2; yānasa(ṃ) *id.* C[1] 242.

yāya (-t), *v. t. to do, to make, to act* H[2] 77[b].6, *to arrange* B 31[a].1; rājā ~ *to make a king* H[1] 83[b].4. — *v. i. to be, to conduct oneself like...* B 7[a].8, *to be personified as...* N 46[a].2. — *In connection with nouns from Sa. or modern Indian languages* yāya *very largely forms verbal expressions with the sense of a transitivum, less frequently with that of an intransitivum (in this case the proper meaning of* yāya *seems to be "to act like..., to conduct oneself like...").*

yāl, *adj. squint-eyed* C[1] 238; ~ dhu-si *id.* CW 8.41.

yāle [= yāl?], *s. a kind of disease or bodily defect* N 32[a].8*.

yās, *s. a kind of deer* (rauhiṣa) CW 7.2.

yā-sā, *s. a sort of antelope* (go-karṇa) AH 34[a].

yi[1], *s. evening* (sāya) AH 11[a].

yi[2], *adv.* = i V[1] 114[b].4.

yiku, *adj. dry* Vd 11[a].4.—yikayuwo *becomes dry* 37[b].4.

yi-tā = i-tā Bh 166[b].1.

yitikan, *s. a kind of pot-herb* (cillī) Md 48[a].2.

yi-dā, *adv.*, ~ thi-dān dāya *to beat one another* Bh 46[b].5.

yinaka- [yinë], yinakā *the beginning of the night* CW 1.46; yinakwo *during the night* Md 55[a].8*.

yinā, *adv. there* V[1] 95[b].2*.

yināp, ~ yāya *to say, to speak* (= ināp) Bh 73[a].5. — yināpalapë *v.t. id.* Bh 171[a].6.

yināpë, *v. t. to say, to speak* (= inā-lapë) H[1] 10[a].1.

yinë, *v. t.*, cā ~ *to pass the night* B 22[b].8.

yi-pol, *adv.*, ~ thi-pol *to and fro* Bh 12ª.5.

yi-bi, *adv.* = i-bil H² 35ª.1.

yimunī, *s.* = imunī Vd 11ᵇ.5.

yiya (-t *or* -l¹?), *v. t.* = yinë: cā ~ H² 44ª.6*.

yili(ṁ), *s. a daughter-in-law* V¹ 56ᵇ.4.

— ~-mocā *id.* N 32ª.4.

yilë, *v. t. to obliterate* B 59ᵇ.5,6*.

yi-sār, *adv.*, ~ thi-sār yāya *to drag hither and thither* Bh 133ᵇ.3.

yukt [*S. joined*], ~ yāya *to join, to fasten* Bh 170ᵇ.1.

yuguti, *s.* = juguti AH 66ᵇ.

yuddh [*S. battle*], ~ yāya *to fight a battle* B 13ᵇ.7.

yubarāj [*S.* yuvarāja], *s. a young king, prince* V¹ 10ᵇ.5.

yuṣ [*S.* yūṣa], *s. soup, broth*; *ifc.* **muk-**.

ye- (-n *or* -t?), *v.*, ma yeṅā ma yeṅā *without being asked* N 12ª.4*.

yekwo, *adj. many, much*(?) N 9ª.5.

yecakë, *v. t.*, bhuṃ ~ *to determine the boundaries of a field* N 26ᵇ.3*.

ye-chi, *adj. different* (ch-g-yā *from*..) N 15ª.8; ~ ma ~ yāṅa(ṃ) *one by one* 26ᵇ.6; ~ ... ~ *what... what* Vd 11ª.5.

yenë, *v. t.* = yanë Ś 154ª.3,4*.

yeya (-l¹), *v. i. coire* N 31ª.1.

yeyakë, *caus. of* yeya N 34ᵇ.1*.

yeyu, *adj. yellow* CW 1.56. — ~ kwolot *yellow Barleria* 6.24.

yesi-mā, *s. a medicinal plant* Vd 30ª.5.

yehe, *s.* = ehe CW 8.23.

yai-kuli, *s. the south-west* CW 1.33.

yai-tā, *s. the south* CW 1.32.

yogy [*S.*], *adj. proper, becoming* (ch-hm-yāta *for*...) Bh 141ª.7.

yojalapë [*S.* yojaya- (*caus. of* yuj)], *v. t. to use, to employ* C¹ 67; *to lead* (ch-g-s *to*...) 31.

yoni [*S.*], *s. the privy parts of a woman* Vd 38ᵇ.2; *womb* Bh 57ᵇ.1.

yau-kuli, *s. the north-west* CW 1.34.

yau-tā, *s. the west* CW 1.33.

yauban [*S.*], *s. youth, adolescence* H² 37ª.3.

hy.

hyando, thawo ~-cār *independence* N 39ᵇ.5*.

hyā'u, *adj.* = hyāṅu Ns 26ᵇ.5; hyā'un *id.* Ś 148ᵇ.4; hyā'uk *id.* M 34ᵇ.7.

hyāṅu, *adj. red* Bh 102ª.3. — ~ kusyāl-tu *the red sugar-cane* Md 62ᵇ.6; ~ cāk *a cutaneous disease with circular spots* CW 8.44. — hyāṅayu *becomes red* Vd 9ᵇ.5; hyāṅasëṃ *becoming red* 15ᵇ.1; hyāṅa(ṃ) woya *to become red* 38ª.6; hyāṅucakë *to make red* 22ª.6; mikhā hyāṅukaṃ kanë *to open the eyes so that they become red* Bh 68ᵇ.3.

hyāpu, *s. a medicinal plant* Vd 13ᵇ.4.

hyāmuk, *adj. red* (= hyā'uk) Vi 56.28*.

hyāya, *v. t.* = hṅāya¹(?) M 33ᵇ.8*.

l (r).

la¹, ~ woya *to get at* H² 13ᵇ.7. — ~ thyāya (-t) *to seize hold of* B 54ª.10. — ~ saya (-l¹) = *foll.* Vi 167.1. — ~ swoya *to greet, to welcome* M 30ᵇ.2. — ~ hiya (-t) *to support, to maintain* V¹ 50ª.3. — ~hicakë *caus. of foreg.* B 43ª.7.

la², *s.* = lā⁴ P 6ᵇ.5; *gen.*: ~ chi *one month* Vi 147.4; ~ chi-toṃ *for one month* H² 41ᵇ.2. la *cl-w. for month* Vi 133.17.

la³, ~ hlāya = lawo ~ B 52ᵇ.11.

la'unī, *s. fresh butter* Bh 35ᵇ.3.

lawo, ~ hlāya (-t *and* -l¹) *to hand over* (ch-hm-yāta *to*...) Bh 116ᵇ.4; ch-hm-yā hastas ~ ~ *to deliver into* *the hands of...*, *to hand over to...* H² 113ᵇ.2. — ~ suyakë *to give to eat* P 4ᵇ.5.

lawoṅ [*S.* lavaṅga], *s. a clove tree* Vd 3ᵃ.1. — ~-tvāc *s. Laurus Cassia* 51ᵃ.3.

lawotinī, *s. a low-caste woman* (vṛṣali) B 20ᵃ.4, *the concubine of a king* (bhogini) AH 37ᵃ (lawating).

la(ṁ), *s. a road* Bh 134ᵃ.5, *a way, direction* H¹ 24ᵃ.1, *a journey* B 47ᵃ.10, *fig.*: dharmayā ~ *the way of righteousness* H¹ 16ᵃ.5. — lan wowo (puruṣ) *a traveller* 15ᵃ.2; las *on the road* V² 61ᵇ.7, lan *id.* Bh 74ᵃ.6; thwo las *in this manner* V¹ 80ᵃ.4; ch-hm-yā lan *through, by (means of)* N 38ᵇ.2. — *ifc.* **mūl-**.

laṁ, *s. water* Bh *10ᵃ.3.

laṁ-hṅe, *s. a yard, court* CW 4.8.

laṁ-chi, *s. the principal road through a town* CW 4.2.

laṃ-sī, *adj. facing the road* N 28ᵇ.3*.

lak¹, *s. amount, value* N 44ᵇ.4; thawo lakan *at one's own expenses* 21ᵇ.7. — lak-lak *s. surety, bail* N 7ᵇ.2; lak-lak yāya *to put in bail* 40ᵃ.6.

lak², *num.* = lakh B 55ᵃ.5.

lakay, *s. name of a plant* (naktamāla) CW 6.17.

la-kā [la = lā²], *s. the palm of the hand with the fingers extended* (capeṭa) CW 8.66.

lakām, *s. a shoe, sandal* B 11ᵇ.8.

lak-dal, *s. the upper part of the arm* CW 8.62.

rakṣ¹ [*S. adj. guarding*], ~ yāya *to guard* N 43ᵇ.6.

lakṣ² [*S.*], *num. one hundred thousand* Bh 155ᵇ.1.

lakṣaṇ [*S.*], *s. a mark, sign* H² 16ᵃ.4; *med.*: *symptom* Vd 2ᵇ.6.

rakṣalapē [rakṣā], *v. t. to protect, to guard, to watch over* V² 50ᵃ.4.

rakṣā [*S. protection*], ~ yāya *to protect, to guard, to watch over* H¹ 45ᵇ.1.

ḷak-si, *s. name of a plant* (bhūdātrī) Md 2ᵇ.4.

Lakṣmī [*S.*], *n. pr. the goddess of fortune* H² 44ᵇ.5. — ~-svān *a plant, the root of which is used medicinally* Vd 14ᵃ.1.

lakh [*M.*], *num. one hundred thousand* N 13ᵃ.8.

lakha, *s.* = laṃkha C² 221. — ~-bāl *a current of water* AH 67ᵃ.

lakhalapē, *v. t.* = rakṣalapē B 31ᵃ.6.

lakhā¹, *s. rice*(?) B 26ᵃ.3.

lakhā², ~ biya *to pay toll* (śulka) AH 49ᵇ.

lakhā-khi [lakha], *s. a leather bucket for drawing up water* (udghāṭana) AH 61ᵃ.

lakhā-pwoṁ = lā° N 40ᵇ.3.

la-khuṁ [khu²?], *s. cross-roads* N 17ᵃ.7*.

lakhvā, *s. a field* (kedāra) Md 65ᵃ.3.

lag, *adj. good, right* V¹ 107ᵃ.6. — *s. a charm* Bh 24ᵃ.3.

ragat [*illit. H.*], *s. blood* Vd 38ᵃ.5. — ~-adasār [*cf. S.* raktātisāra], *bloody flux* 37ᵇ.4.

lagudā, *s.*, khāyu ~ *a plant* (kaṭutumbī) Md 46ᵇ.5.

lage, *adj.* = lag H³ 56ᵇ.8.

laṅ, *s. a bodice* Bh 184ᵇ.6. — *ifc.* **misā-**, **sa-**.

laṁkha, *s. water* H¹ 50ᵃ.3; ~ kāya *to bathe* Ś 148ᵇ.6. — ~-kuthi *a fountain, cistern* (prapā) AH 24. — ~-gu *a water-reservoir* AH 21ᵇ. — ~-thal *a drinking vessel* B 25ᵇ.9. — ~-dhalapwo *a water-pot* Vi 24.26. — ~-dhārā *a stream of water* 98.12. — ~-phuti *rain* AH 8ᵃ, *a drop of water* 20ᵃ. — ~-bobol *a billow* H² 97ᵇ.5. — ~-sā-li-gu *a rainbow* CW 1.41. — ~-hul *a billow* H² 97ᵇ.5. — *ifc.* **balikhā-**.

laṁkhwo, *s.* = laṃkha N 48ᵇ.3.

laṅghan(ā) [*S. s. crossing, transgressing*], ~ yāya *to surpass (boundary)*

N 25^b.6, *to transgress (order)* H² 87^b.4; ~ yācakë *to let surpass* N 25^b.6.

laṅghalapë [*S.* laṅgh-], *v. t. to leap over, to scale (wall)* V¹ 16^a.1, *to transgress (compact f. i.)* N 25^b.4.

laj, *s. a kind of weapon* Vi 157.28*.

rajanā [*S.* rañjanā *s. charming, pleasing*], ~ yāya *to charm, to please* Vi 133.3*.

rajaputanī [*M.* rajpūt *rajput*], *s. a woman of the kṣatriya-caste* P 56^b.1*.

rajayi [*H.* rajnā *to be filled, satisfied*], ~ yāya *to fill, to satisfy*(?) Vi 94.15.

lajjā, *s.* = lajyā H² 87^b.3.

lajyā [*S.* lajjā], *s. shame, disgrace* Vi 22.1, *sense of shame* V¹ 37^b.5; ~ cāya *to become ashamed* Bh 185^a.2. — ~-phacit yāya *to disgrace* Vi 143.31, ~-phacit juya *to be ashamed* Vi 40.20.

rañjan [*S. s. charming*], ~ yāya *to appease, to conciliate* H³ 61^a.11.

rañjalapë [*S.* rañjaya- *to make glad*], *v. t. to appease, to conciliate* H³ 43^b.7.

rat [*S. devoted, attached*], puruṣawo ~ misā *a lover of men* C¹ 245.

ratak [*S.* *rataka = rata?], *adj. beloved*(?) Bh 22^b.1*.

lati [*M.* ratī], *s. a grain, small portion* Vd 16^b.6.

ratikrīḍā [*S.*], *s. the pleasure of love* H² 75^b.4.

ratn [*S.*], *s. a jewel, precious stone* V¹ 111^b.5.

la-tyā, *s. a month and a half* H¹ 49^b.1. — la-tyāt *id.* P 48^b.3.

la-tvāk [la = lā²], *s. an elbow* CW 8.62.

rath [*S.*], *s. a carriage* H² 98^b.5.

la-thyāṁthi, *s.* = °-tyā H³ 11^b.4*.

laḍabalālapë [*H.* laṛbaṛānā], *v. i. to stammer, to falter* N 12^a.4*.

lan, *s.* = laṅ B 27^b.1.

lanakë¹ (*caus. of* lanë¹), *to let wait, to keep waiting* H³ 44^b.1; lanakaṃ tiwo *wait!* H³ 44^b.1.

lanakë² = lenakë C¹ 258.

raṇi [*S.* ṛṇin], *s. a debtor* N 7^b.3.

raṇī, *s.* = raṇiyā N 14^b.5.

lanikunī, *s. Hayagrīva* HP 24,105*.

raṇiyā [*H.* riṇyā], *s. a debtor* N 6^b.6.

lanë¹, *v. i. to wait* B 31^a.11; tā-kāl ma lasëṃ *ere long* H² 107^b.1.

lanë² [= lenë¹?], *v. i. to cease* H² 76^a.4.

lanë³, *v. t. to weigh* N 50^b.5. ~ bastu *weighing implement* 48^b.3.

laṁḍ, *s.* = lwoṃḍ H² 33^a.6.

la-pate, *s. a leaf* B 57^b.8.

lapāl, ~ conë *to be on the outlook* B 6^b.7; ~ taya *to put on the outlook* 6^b.6.

la-pu, *s. a way, path (fig.)* H² 11^b.4.

la-phā [la = lā²], *s. a fathom* CW 8.67.

rabat-kāy, *s. one of the sons of lower caste (i.e. others than kṣetrajas)* N 38^b.1,3*.

labadhab, ~ yāya *to act incautiously* N 16^b.1*.

labhā, *s. garlic* AH 32.

ramalapë [*S.* ram- *to enjoy*], ch-hm-s ~ *to take delight in...* C² 181.

rambat, *s. luck*(?) H² 38^a.2*.

laṁbhā, *s.* = labhā CW 6.33.

lay¹ [*mod.* = ras], *s. joy, delight* H¹ 11^a.5.

lay² = lāy² M 26^b.4.

laya (-l¹), *v. t.*, ghās ~ *to cut grass* Vi 20.27.

lalik, *s. a medicinal plant (a palāṇḍu)* P 58^a.1. — ~-ke *broth made from this plant* Vd 47^a.1. — *ifc.* **khel-.**

ras [*S.*], *s. joy, pleasure, delight* (ch-g-yāke, -s, -wo *in...*) M 4^b.6; rasan danë *to live in joy* Vi 81.19; ch-hm-wo nāp rasan conë *to be in love with...* H³ 47^a.1; ras siya *to feel joy* H² 81^a.7; ch-g-wo ~ yāya *to take delight in..* M 3^b.3; ch-g-yā ~ kāya *to taste a thing* Vi 136.27. — ~ tāya (-l¹) *to be glad* V² 69^b.1; ~ tāyakë *to* *make glad, to cheer* V¹ 88ª.1. — *ifc.* **svān-.**

rasarasāgr [*cf. S.* rasa *taste*], *s. delicious things* Vi 28 27.

rasānaj [*S.* rasāñjana], *s. a sort of collyrium* Vd 36ª.6. — rasānañju *id.* 15ᵇ.1.

rasik [*S. adj.*], *adj. passionate* V¹ 153ª.6. — *s. passion* H² 49ᵇ.2.

rahasy [*S.*], *adj. secret* H² 43ª.2.

la-hān, *s. water* AH 20.

la-huli, *s. a billow* Bh 11ᵇ.4.

rā¹, *s. a king* H¹ 83ᵇ.3. rā-hma kisi *the king of elephants* H³ 41ᵇ.6.

lā², *s. a hand, arm* N 44ª.2. — *ifc. (finger):* **aṅgulī-, anā-, cā-, co-, datho-, pañcāṅ-, hmā-.**

lā³, *s. flesh, meat* H¹ 29ᵇ.2. — *ifc.* **khā-, sala-, sā-, së-.**

lā⁴, *s. a month* H¹ 49ᵇ.1. — *ifc.* **kati-, kas-, kos-, gun-, camgu-, cet-, cho-, ta-cho-, tamcho-, this-, dit-, poy-, pos-, yam-, si-.**

lā⁵, *s.* = la(ṃ) V¹ 32ª.

lā⁶, *a particle of interrogation:* marjāt dawo lā *is it right?* V¹ 102ᵇ.2; lā ama-thë *much as this* H¹ 28ᵇ.5; *if:* lā juraṃ *if... is* N 50ᵇ.2, *(mostly with conv. in* ·asā)*:* lā kālasā *if... takes* B 35ª.5. — lā... lā *is it (so)... or is it (so)?* V² 25ᵇ.6; *either... or* N 28ᵇ.4; *be it... be it* 22ª.6.

rā'ut [*Mr.* rāūt], *s. a horse-soldier* V¹ 127ª.2.

lāk [lāya¹], *s. property* Vi 153.17.

lākam = lā⁶ Vi 64.9.

lākām, *s.* = lakām Ś 148ª.1.

lākë¹ *(caus. of* lāya¹*), to cause to obtain* M 26ª.6; hastas ~ *to let fall into the hands of* H³ 51ª.10.

lākë²; *caus. of* lāya² V¹ 50ª.6.

lākha, *s.* = laṃkha Vd 36ª.2. — ~-kuthi *a well, cistern* CW 3.2.

lākhalapë [*cf. Mr.* rākhaṇeṃ], *v. t. to protect, to save, to preserve* N 16ᵇ.8.

lākhā-pwom, ~ jwoña(ṃ) woyā *(a son) brought with a woman pregnant at the marriage* (sahōḍha) N 38ᵇ.1; ~ wowo *id.* 38ᵇ.2.

rāg [*S. feeling, passion*], ~ cāya *to become angry* N 46ª.8.

lāgalapë [*M.* lāg *to adhere to, to stick to*], *v. i.*, ch-g-s ~ *to stick to...* N 19ª.8, *to be interested in..., to be engrossed in...* 22ª.7; *to act on..., to influence...* Bh 7ᵇ.1. yāya ~ *to desire to do...* N 35ª.5. — lāgalapayakë *caus. to make interested in, to make stick to* N 19ª.4.

lāgā-bhāgā [*H.* lāg *animosity* —, *a plot*], ~ yāya *to insult, to commence a quarrel* N 42ᵇ.8. — lāgā-bhāṃ yāya *to follow up an attack* 43ª.3.

lā-gwoḍā, *s. a lump of flesh* Vi 147.33.

lā-gwoy, *s. a medicinal plant* Vd 50ᵇ.4.

lāmkha, *s.* = laṃkha Md 52ª.2.

lāca = lāya¹ N 18ᵇ.7.

lācakë¹ *(caus. of* lāya¹*), to cause to obtain* N 39ª.8; *to cause to get hold of* Bh 20ᵇ.7; *to cause to hit* N 18ᵇ.6.

lācakë² *(caus. of* lāya³*), to cure* N 26ª.4*.

lāch, *s.* = lāchi N 27ª.7.

lāchi [*cf. S.* rathyā], *s. a main-road* V¹ 97ª.2. — lāche *id.* Vd 45ᵇ.3.

lāj [*H.*], *s. shame* C² 9.

rājakul [*S.*], *s. a king's palace* H³ 47ᵇ.1.

rājagṛh [*S.*], *s. a royal palace* B 10ª.5.

rājahams [*S.*], *s. a kind of swan* H² 73ᵇ.4.

rājā [*S.*], *s. a king* V¹ 77ª.5. — ~-kisi *the king of elephants* H² 77ª.2; ~-ghal *the palace of a king* B 5ᵇ.1; ~-cā *a royal prince* B 9ª.6; ~-bal-khuni *the king of pidgeons* H³ 4ª.8; ~-byāñ *the king of frogs* H² 112ᵇ.1; ~-mayūr *the king of peacocks* 78ᵇ.8; ~-hmaskhā *id.* 79ª.5.

rājy [*S.*], *s. a kingdom* Ś 168ᵃ.6. — ~ yāya *to exercise government* B 19ᵃ.10.

lātakē (= lācakē¹), *to cause to obtain* Vi 66.11; *to lead, to conduct* 76.16.

lā-ti, *s. flesh-broth* Md 70ᵇ.4.

lā-to, *pl. of* lā⁴ H¹ 86ᵃ.5; lā-ta *id.* H³ 20ᵃ.5.

rātri [*S.* rātri], *s. night* V¹ 18ᵇ.4.

lāth, *s.* = lvāth H³ 25ᵇ.7*.

lā-thē, ~ juya ēwo *a Rākṣasa* CW 1.4; ~ naya ēwo *a Piśāca ib.* 5.

lāḍ [*EH.*], *s. saliva* N 43ᵇ.7.

lādan [*M.* lād *to load*], ~-sā *an animal of burden* N 24ᵇ.8.

lānakē (= lenakē?), *v. t. to cause to cease, to cure (a disease)* V¹ 135ᵇ.2*.

rāni [*M.* rānī], *s. a queen* V² 79ᵇ.7. — ~-cā *a young queen* Vi 173.4, *a princess* Ś 160ᵇ.7.

lānē, *v. i.* = lanē¹ N 31ᵃ.2.

lā-pā, *s. a bat* CW 7.13; *a cricket* AH 35ᵇ.

rā-putr, *s. a prince* H³ 47ᵃ.2.

lābh [*S. acquisition, gain*], ch-g ~ daya *to obtain* Vi 88.33; ~ dayakē *id.* 78.4.

lābhā, *s.* = labhā P 58ᵃ.1.

rā-māju, *s. a princess* B 46ᵇ.11.

lāy¹ [*cf. H.* lāg — —, *ill-feeling*], ch-hm-yāta ~ biya *to bear malice to..., to retaliate* Vi 129.5*.

lāy², ~ buya (-l¹), *to shout, to set up a cry* M 17ᵇ.2; ~ boya (-l¹) *id.* Bh 99ᵇ.5.

lāy³ [*H.* rāē *a prince, chief*], *s. a king:* ~-kul *the palace of a king* CW 4.6. — ~-ghal *id.* Ś 170ᵃ.3.

lāya¹ (-t, lāyāwo B 5ᵇ.4), 1) *v. t. to obtain, to attain* H¹ 70ᵇ.2, *to get hold of, to catch* V¹ 48ᵇ.3; *to hit* (ch-g-s *in..., on...*) H² 105ᵇ.3; *to possess, to be endowed with* Vi 130.10. — **suhṛd** ~ *to form a friendship* H¹ 11ᵇ.5; **li** ~ *to find an opportunity* H¹ 62ᵃ.1; āpadā ~ *to bring on oneself distress* C¹ 97; **bandhan** ~ *to become captured* H¹ 31ᵃ.3; do ma lāya *to commit adultery* N 35ᵇ.7. — 2) *v. i.*, hastas ~ *to fall into the hands of* Bh 13ᵃ.6; ch-hm-yāta ~ *to fall to one's lot* Vi 86.6.

lāya² (-l¹), *v. t. to prepare, to arrange (bed, couch)* V¹ 130ᵇ.3.

lāya³ (-l¹), *v. i. to be cured (a disease)* Vd 14ᵃ.2.

lāyakē (*caus. of* lāya³) *to cure (a disease)* B 9ᵃ.12.

lāya-pu, *s. a weaver's loom* AH 61ᵃ.

lāyalapē [*H.* lāg *affection, love*], *v. t. to love* C² 94*.

lāl, *s.* = lāḍ B 63ᵇ.5.

lās¹ [*corr. from S.* nirāśa *hopeless?*], ~ cāya *to lose courage* V¹ 33ᵃ.4.

lās² [*H.* rās *heap?*], *s. a capital, stock* H² 49ᵃ.4.

lā-sā [lāya²], *s. a couch, seat* V¹ 130ᵇ.3. — *ifc.* **cheguli-, dē-, liba-, li-.**

lā-hā¹, *s.* = lā-hāth B 21ᵇ.6. — *ifc.* **li-.**

lāhā² [*B.*], *s. a kind of red dye, lac* Md 29ᵃ.7. — ~-si *Butea frondosa* H² 6ᵃ.5.

lā-hāti, *s.* = lā-hāth V¹ 73ᵃ.1. — *ifc.* **li-.**

lā-hāth, *s. a hand, arm* H¹ 16ᵇ.2.

lā-hul, *s.* = la-huli CW 2.3.

li¹, *adv. thereafter* V² 67ᵃ.7; ch-g-n ~ *after (a lapse of)...* 19ᵇ.1. (yāṅā(wo), yāṅānam, yāsēṃ, yāsēn) li *after having..., since...* N 39ᵃ.8.

li² [= li¹], ~ kāya *to take back* N 17ᵃ.4, *to pull out (an arrow from the wound)* Vi 36.27; *to restore* 89.3; *to abandon, to give up (hope etc.)* H¹ 78ᵇ.5; mikhā ~ *to avert the eyes* M 28ᵇ.2. — ~ hṅyācakē *to drive back (a car)* Bh 112ᵇ.1. — ~ cāya *to restore* N 26ᵇ.3. — ~ cilē *to retreat, to retire* Bh 139ᵇ.2. ~ cilakē *caus.* 152ᵃ.5. — ~ coya *to rewrite* C² 270. — ~ choya *to send back* V¹ 52ᵇ.2, *to dismiss* H² 47ᵃ.2, *to dispatch* H³ 46ᵃ.4. — ~ juya *to come back* Bh 123ᵃ.2. — ~ tanē *to rebound* (ch-g-s *from*...) 141ᵇ.7. — ~ taya: ~ tal woya *to return* (*trs.*), *to give back* N 24ᵇ.3. — ~ thënë *to return* (*itrs.*) V² 72ᵇ.6. — ~ danë *to place oneself with the back against* (ch-g-s) B 40ᵇ.6. — ~ dhanë *id. ib.* 5. — ~ piya (-t) *to be left* M 15ᵃ.1. ~ pikë *caus.* V¹ 97ᵇ.1. — ~ picakë *to abandon, to give up* (*hope etc.*) H² 40ᵃ.1, *to master* (*passion*) H³ 49ᵇ.1. — ~ phiya (-t) *to overtake* C¹ 34. — ~ pheya (-t) *id.* C² 34. — ~ phyāya *to get back, to recover* M 25ᵃ.5. — ~ biya *to give back* N 21ᵇ.1. ~ biyakë *caus.* 22ᵇ.4. — ~ bvācakë; *only:* ~ bvācakaṃ *adv. leaping back* H² 66ᵇ.3. — ~ lanakë *to cease, to stop* (*trs.*) Vi 172.29. — ~ lāya (-t) *to be left* Vi 106.15. — ~ lācakë *to keep pace with* B 47ᵃ.10; ch-hm ~ *to* (*suffer oneself to*) *be followed or accompanied by*... V¹ 22ᵇ.5; ch-hm-yāke ~ *to deliver* (*back*) *to*... N 32ᵃ.4. — ~ lāyakë *to fetch back* 20ᵇ.1. — ~ liya *to follow* N 42ᵃ.5. — ~ hlāya (-t) *to give back* 15ᵇ.5. ~ hlācakë *id. ib.* 6. — ~ sālë *to draw or pull back or backwards* Bh 70ᵇ.3. — ~ swoya *to look back* M 29ᵇ.7. — ~ hāya *to return, to come back* H¹ 24ᵇ.1.

li³, *s. a bow* (*for shooting*) H¹ 74ᵇ.2.

li⁴ (*gen. spelt* ḷ), *s. a leg, foot* B 49ᵃ.8.

li-uttarā, *s. an answer* Vi 35.29.

liwo (*mostly:* liwo liwo), *adv. afterwards* H¹ 24ᵃ.3; ch-hm-yā ~ *behind, after* V² 28ᵃ.4, ch-hm-wo ~ *id.* B 47ᵇ.8; ch-g-n ~ *after* (*a lapse of*)... V² 72ᵃ.5; ·sëṃ ~ *after having*... Vi 147.5. — ~ ~ *repeatedly* H³ 58ᵃ.5. — liwo-coṃ *afterwards* N 39ᵇ.6; liwo coṃ-gwo *a heir* 2ᵃ.4, liwo coṃ-gwo strī *a widow* 2ᵇ.8.

li-wonë, *adv.*; ch-g-yā ~ *behind a thing* V² 56ᵃ.5.

li-kaṭakit, *s. a medicinal plant* (bṛhatī) CW 7.27.

li-ke, ~ woya *to return* B 27ᵇ.9*.

li-kyāṁ, ~ beya *to run back* B 169ᵃ.1*.

likhiti [*cf.* *M.* likh *to write*], *s. a scribe* N 8ᵃ.5.

li-khvāc, *s. a foot-print* Bh 48ᵇ.3.

li-guṇ, *s.* = °-gwon H³ 17ᵃ.5*.

li-gwon, *s. a bow-string* Bh 99ᵃ.5.

liṅ, *s. a radish* AH 33ᵃ (ling).

licakë (*caus. of* liya), *to* (*suffer oneself to*) *be followed or accompanied* V² 73ᵇ.5.

li-co, 1) *adv. afterwards* N 26ᵃ.4; li-cos *id.* 3ᵇ.4; li-cos ma dātaṃ *they are quits* 7ᵇ.1. — 2) *adj. later, second* 10ᵃ.3.

lijyā, *s.* = lajyā V² 40ᵃ.4*.

li-ta, ~ kaya *to stop* (*blood*) M 14ᵇ.3; ~ kayāwo biya *to give back* 21ᵃ.3. — ~ kāya *to take back* 21ᵇ.7. — ~ choya *to send back* 20ᵇ.7. — ~ taya *to put back* Vi 78.29. — ~ phyāya (-t) *to get back, to recover* M 22ᵇ.5. — ~ biya *to give back* B 9ᵃ.9; *to barter, to exchange* AH 56ᵇ. — ~ bonë *to bring back* B 48ᵇ.9. — ~ yanë *to lead back* Bh 161ᵇ.4. — ~ haya *to bring back* 114ᵃ.2.

litakë = licakë Vi 71.8.

li-than, *adv.*, ch-g-n ~ *after* (*the lapse of*).. V² 64ᵇ.7.

li-thinaṁ, *adv.* = li-than Bh 157ᵇ.3*.

lithu, *adj. later, subsequent* V¹ 69ᵇ.4, *younger, the younger one* B 51ᵇ.9. ~-hma (kalāt) *the second wife* B 17ᵇ.7.

li-thë(ṁ), *adv. thereon, after that* V¹ 10ᵃ.3, lithë-ṅanakaṃ *later on, afterwards* V² 43ᵃ.5. — lithë-gwo *adj. following* Vd 14ᵇ.4.

lithwo, *adj.* = lithu; *the last* (*act*) N 6ᵇ.1.

lin, ~ wonë *to go behind, to follow*

V^2 6ᵇ.2: ~ juyāwo woya *to go back* Vi 80.29.

līn [*S. clung together; devoted*], ~ juya *to be composed* (ch-g-s *of...*) H^2 111ᵇ.2; ~ yāya *to be intent on* P 37ᵇ.4.

lina-suthi, *s. a medicinal plant* Vd 55ᵃ.3 (ḷna-).

linë (liyāwo V^1), *v. t. to cut down, to slay* V^2 71ᵇ.3; *to cut off* Vi 74.31.

li-patas, *adv.* = °-potas H^2 103ᵇ.3; li-pat ~ *immediately afterwards* C^2 164.

li-pā¹, *s. a bow (for shooting)* H^1 91ᵇ.4. — ~-put *a fragment of a bow* Bh 78ᵃ.4.

li-pā², ~ taya *to place behind; to let follow* B 49ᵃ.6. — ~ lāya *to stay behind, not to be able to keep pace with* C^1 34; ~lātakë *to keep back* Vi 120.21.

li-pi, ~ hṅe-pi bibek ma yāk *not caring for the past nor the future* H^3 31ᵃ.5. = li-pe hna-pe apekṣā ma yāk H^2 60ᵃ.5*.

li-pukh, *s.* = °-pwokh H^2 41ᵃ.1. — li-puṃkh *id.* 41ᵇ.3.

li-pe, *adv.* = li-pi.

li-potas, *adv. afterwards, later on* N 43ᵃ.2; ~ coya *to rewrite* C^1 270. — li-pot *id.* CW 8.18.

li-pwokh, *s. a bow (for shooting)* H^1 72ᵃ.4.

lipt [*S.*], *adj. soiled* H^2 97ᵃ.6; *fig. tainted* Bh *2ᵃ.2.

liptalapë [lipt], *v. i. to be tainted* N 13ᵇ.1.

liba, *s. a couch, bed* H^1 91ᵃ.1 (ḷba). — ~-lāsā *id.* (śayyā) AH 44ᵇ.

libi, *s. a park(?)* Vi 16.31.

libi-lukhā, *s. a side-door* (pakṣa-dvāra) CW 4.9.

liya (-t), *v. t. to pursue* H^3 43ᵃ.3; *to conform to* C^1 274. — *(of a woman): to attach oneself to (another man than the husband)* N 33ᵃ.4.

li-yā, *adv.*, ch-g-n ~ *after (the lapse of)...* N 7ᵃ.2; siṅan ~ *after he has died* 6ᵇ.8; thanin ~ *from to-day* V^1 70ᵇ.2.

lil¹ [*S.* rirī], *s. yellow brass* AH 58ᵃ.

lil², ~ wonë *to come back* V^1 59ᵇ.2; *to go behind, to follow* 8ᵇ.4.

li-lanā, ~ wonë *to disappear, to vanish* M 11ᵇ.4*.

li-lā¹, *s. hands and feet* N 48ᵃ.7.

li-lā², ~ woya *to come back* N 31ᵇ.3.

li-lāsā, *s. a couch, bed* (śayana) AH 44ᵇ.

li-lāhā(t), *s. hands and feet* P 15ᵃ.2.

li-lusi, *s. the nails of the feet* Vi 44.6.

lis, *adv. afterwards* N 18ᵇ.2; ·sëṃ ~ *after having...* 14ᵃ.3; ~ ma dāca-kaṃ *in order to become quits* 7ᵇ.2. — lisaṃ = lis 15ᵇ.8; ~ puya *to repeat* H^2 105ᵇ.8.

lisan, ~ taya *to restore, to repair* H^3 61ᵃ.9.

li-sal, *s. an answer:* ~ kanë *to give an answer* V^2 23ᵃ.2, ~ biya *id.* B 14ᵇ.3.

lisëṁ (*10th form of* liya?], *adv. behind* (ch-hm-yā, ~-s, ~-wo) Vi 37.2; ch-hm-wo ~ wonë *to keep up with* Vi 37.22; ~ conë *to be left* N 33ᵃ.5; khusi ~ *along a river* B 58ᵇ.5.

li-hā, ~ wonë *to return* H^1 24ᵇ.2. — ~ woya *id.* B 62ᵇ.4. — ~ jhāya *id.* B 1ᵇ.6. — ~ bi-jyāya *id.* M 18ᵇ.5.

lu- (*only:* luṅāwo, luyā), *v. t. to pour* C^1 158; khaḍg ~ *to draw a sword* H^2 91ᵇ.7.

lu(ṁ)¹, *s. gold* C^1 70. lu(ṃ)yā *golden* N 25ᵃ.7.

lu(ṁ)², ~ wonë *to know, to understand* N 10ᵇ.1. — ~ thanë *to satisfy, to make content* H^3 44ᵃ.5. — ~ daṃja (= danë) *to be content* (ch-g-n *with...*) N 38ᵇ.5.

lu-karmi, *s. a goldsmith* AH 59ᵇ.

luku (*also:* °ṃ, °ḍi, °n, °ni, °l), ~ chiya (-t) *v. t. to carry on the shoulders* H^2 110ᵇ.3 (lukuṃ). — ~ duya (-t) *v. i. to drive, to plunge into* Vi 31.32 (luku). — ~ **biya** (-t) *v. i. id.* V^2 38ᵃ.4

(lukun), *to set (of the sun)* H³ 24ᵃ.6 (luku). — ~ biya (-l¹) *v. t. to dive, to plunge into* V¹ 92ᵇ.4 (lukun). *to be plunged, to be let down into* Bh 12ᵃ.7 (lukuḍi).

lu-khā, *s. a door, gate* B 32ᵃ.10. — ~-khadu *a threshold* Vd 47ᵇ.1. — *i/c.* **libi-**.

lugati-svān, *s. name of a plant* (gaṇeruka) Md 31ᵇ.4.

lucakē, *v. t.*, me ~ *to cause to bite one's tongue* Bh 84ᵃ.4.

lu-catāk, *s. a golden whip* B 16ᵇ.10.

ruci [*S.*], *s. liking* Vd 4ᵇ.2.

lu-culyā, *s. a bracelet of gold* Bh 173ᵇ.4.

lutu, *see* **luya.**²

lu-two, *s. a piece of gold(?)* B 51ᵇ.7.

rudhir [*S.*], *s. blood* V¹ 107ᵇ.6.

luṁdati, *s. a noble part of the body* N 18ᵇ.7*.

luṁḍi, *s.* = lwoṃḍ Bh 106ᵇ.4.

rūp [*S.*], *s. a form, shape*; ~ yāya *to take the form of...* H³ 29ᵃ.7. — ~-chand *beauty* N 24ᵃ.7. — ~-jaubhan [*S.* rūpayauvana] *youth and beauty* V² 43ᵃ.5; ~-jauban *id.* V¹ 68ᵇ.4.

rupalapē [*S.* rūp- *to form; to contemplate*], *v. t. to consider, to reflect upon* N 45ᵃ.9.

lubdh [*S.*], *adj. greedy, covetous* H² 39ᵇ.5.

lumakē [lumu], *v. t. to make warm or hot* Vd 43ᵃ.1.

lu manakē (*caus. of* lu manē) = *simpl.: to think of* M 17ᵇ.6, *to remember, to recall* V² 72ᵇ.1; *to collect one's thoughts* Vi 173.34.

lu manē, *v. t. to think of* V² 68ᵃ.6, *to remember, to recall* H³ 27ᵃ.5.

lu mānakē = lu manakē V¹ 122ᵇ.6.

lu mānē, *v. t.* = lu manē V¹ 113ᵇ.3.

lumu, *adj. warm, hot* Vd 10ᵇ.4; lumuyāwo *having become hot* M 4ᵃ.2.

luya¹ (-l¹), *v. t. to turn up, to appear*; *to be found* V¹ 128ᵇ.2; *to rise (sun, moon)* H³ 51ᵃ.1; ch-hm-yā manas ~ *to strike..., to occur to...* M 2ᵇ.4, nugalas ~ *id.* Vi 119.1. — ma luseṃ joya *to raise difficulties* N 21ᵇ.6.

luya² (-l¹), *v. t. to drag, to trail* Bh 84ᵃ.4. — lutu ~ *id. intens.* M 26ᵇ.8.

luya³ (-l¹), *v. t.*, ch-hm-yāke lā ~ *to lay hands on...* N 44ᵃ.2.

luyakē (*caus. of* luya¹), *to bring to light* V² 13ᵃ.3, *to produce* H³ 2ᵇ.7; *to find out, to make out* B 64ᵃ.7, *to find* V¹ 20ᵃ.4. — hi ~ *to shed blood* N 42ᵇ.6; luyakaṃ *adv. in public* N 23ᵃ.3, ma ~ *in secret ib.* 1.

lusi¹, *s. a nail, claw* H¹ 16ᵃ.3. — ~-karmi *a barber* H² 93ᵃ.3. — *i/c.* **li-**.

lusi², *s. a pestle* AH 59ᵇ.

lu-sikhal, *s. gold thread* H² 65ᵇ.5.

re [*S.*], *vocative particle* H² 76ᵇ.3; re re *id.* 102ᵃ.6.

leṁ-leṁ, ~ puya (-l¹) *to swim* B 35ᵃ.3.

lekhā¹ [*S.*], *s. a territory* H³ 42ᵃ.9.

lekhā² [*P.*], *s. an account, narrative* Pg 12ᵇ.6*.

leṁja = lenē N 36ᵇ.4.

lenē, *v. i.* = lanē¹ N 36ᵃ.8.

lepan [*S. act of smearing, ointment*], ~ yāya *to smear* Vd 13ᵃ.6, *to anoint* B 25ᵇ.12.

lepalapē [*S.* lepaya-], *v. t. to smear* V¹ 25ᵇ.3.

lebu, *s. the common lime* Md 44ᵇ.8; cāku ~ *a kind of lime* (rājanimbūka) *ib.*

leya, *v. i. to be approved, to be praised* (praśasyate) C¹ 65 = C² 66*.

leyakē (*caus. of* leya), *to approve, to praise* H² 55ᵃ.1*.

leyā, ~ deyā *giving and taking* N 40ᵃ.5,6*.

leye, *s. mod.* = las CW 1.61.

le-san, *adv.* = li-san H¹ 52ᵃ.2.

resalapē [*H.* ris karnā *to vie, compete with*], *v. t. to protest against* N 38ᵃ.3*.

leh [*S. s. licking*], ~ yāya *to take (a medicine) by licking or sipping* Vd 24^{b}.5.

le-hane [leṃ-leṃ], ~ puya *to swim* N 30^{b}.3*.

le-he [leṃ-leṃ], ~ puya *to swim* B 35^{b}.3*.

lëwoḍ, *s.* = lëwol N 22^{b}.4.

lëwol, *s. a paramour* H[1]63^{a}.3; ~-hma *id.* B 8^{a}.7; ~-puruṣ *id.* 45^{b}.1. ch-hm ~ yāya (*of a woman*): *to have illicit intercourse with...* H[2] 65^{a}.1; ch-hm-yāke ~ wonë (*of a man*) *id.* N 35^{a}.6.

lëkwo [lënë], *s. a rest, remnant* V[1] 42^{a}.5; *adj. remaining* H[2] 94^{b}.8.

lëṁkā [= lënakā], *s. a rest, remnant* P 20^{a}.3*.

lënakë (*caus. of* lënë), *to leave, to spare* V[1] 42^{a}.5.

lënë, *v. i. to be left* P 57^{b}.4, *to be spared* Vi 117.26.

lok[1] [*S.*], *s. the world, people* H[1] 16^{b}.3. — *forming plurals* M 13^{b}.4.

lok[2], ~ phyāya = lwoc ~ M 26^{b}.4*.

loġ [*S.* roga], *s. a sickness, disease* H[2] 87^{b}.3. — *ifc.* **bāt-**.

roġi [*S.* rogin], *adj. sick; s. a patient* Vd 8^{b}.4.

loṅ, ~ conë *to be immersed* Ns 3^{a}.5*.

rot [*cf. M.* lūṭa *pillage*], *s. a robber* V[2] 77^{a}.3*.

ronë, *v. t. to forge (metal)* N 25^{a}.7.

lop, ~ tu- (-n *or* -t?) *v. i. to sink, to be submerged* H[2] 12^{a}.4. — ~ thu- (-n *or* -t) *v. i. id.* H[3] 5^{a}.8*.

lobh [*S.*], *s. desire, greed* (ch-g-yā *after...*) H[1] 88^{a}.4. ch-g-s ~ taya *to desire..., to crave for...* Vi 126.7, ~ ~ cāya *to be seized with desire for...* H[2] 13^{a}.3. — lobhi [*S.* lobhin] *adj. desirous, lustful* H[2] 93^{b}.3.

romañc [*S.* romāñca], *s. the thrill of the hair* N 36^{b}.7.

loy[1], *s.* = log C[2] 51; loyan kawo *adj. sick* H[1] 68^{b}.5. — *ifc.* **alë-, kimi-, kuṣṭ-, kwo-, ciku-, pët-, maṁġwo-, mikhā-, mihi-**.

loy[2] = lwoc: ~ byāya Vi 98.31*

loya (-l[1]), *v. i.*, ji manas ma lowo *it does not please me* Vi 41.32; nītis ma lowo *it is not in accordance with the Niti* H[1] 28^{a}.2.

loyakë (*caus. of* loya), ch-g-s ~ *to make agree with...* Ś 149^{b}.1; lokawo loyaka(ṃ) bacan *pleasant or friendly words* C[1] 166.

loyamand [*cf. S.* rogavat], *adj. sick, ill* N 22^{a}.2*.

lol, ~ manakë *to forget* B 37^{a}.3.

loh-ṅā, *s. a kind of fish* (lohita) AH 21^{a}.

lwoc, ~ phyāya (-t[1]) *v. t. to tear off, to detach* Bh 59^{b}.6, *to tear out, to uproot* B 16^{b}.5. — ~ byāya (-t[1]) *v. i. to leap, to jump* H[1] 59^{a}.4, *to run, to dart* Bh 12^{a}.5. — ~ byāya (-t) *v. t.* = ~ phyāya C[1] 117.

lwo-twok, *adj. strongly made* N 30^{b}.2*.

lwo(ṁ)ḍ, *s. a stick, cudgel* H[2] 33^{a}.1.

lwo-pāt, *s. a kind of weapon* Bh 81^{b}.6*.

lwoha(ṁ), *s.* = lwohwo C[1] 85. — ~-karmi *a stone-cutter* 39. — ~-cā *a small stone* B 2^{b}.10. — ~-pāku *a cave* (guhā) AH 26^{b}. — ~-phāt *a stone-slab* M 33^{b}.8.

lwohwo, *s. a stone* V[1] 130^{b}.1. — ~-wā *rain of stones* Bh 33^{a}.3. — ~-cā *a small stone* B 35^{a}.4.

lyākh [*H.* lekhā *account, reckoning*], *s. a number, multitude* Ś 145^{a}.7. ~ yāya *to calculate; to take into account* (ch-g(-n) *something*) N 23^{b}.9; ~ swoya *id.* P 7^{a}.5. — je mṛtakayā ~ *I may be reckoned as dead* V[1] 81^{b}.5.

lyā-ca-, *adj. young* (*of male beings only*): ~-mo *id.* H[1] 35^{b}.4, ~-hma *id.* H[3] 19^{b}.3, ~-hmo *id.* H[1] 56^{b}.3. — ~-hma juya *to grow up* B 20^{b}.13.

lyā-ya-hma, *adj.* = lyā-ca-hma H^3 43^a.4.

lyā-sa, *adj. young, fresh (of things)* C^2 294*.

lyā-sẽ, *adj. young (of female beings only)* C^1 296, ~-hma *id.* H^2 105^b.1. — ~ juya *to grow up* 39^b.5.

lvākāl [*cf. S.* lohakāra], *s. a blacksmith* C^2 197*.

lvācakẽ (*caus. of* lvāya) *to cause to quarrel* B 25^a.12; jul ~ *to cause to gamble* B 43^b.3; yuddh ~ *to cause to wage war* Bh 82^a.3.

lvāth, *s. the bill (of a bird)* H^2 53^a.5*.

lvāḍ [*cf. S.* lodhra], *s. Symplocos racemosa* Vd 21^a.3. — ~-si *id.* AH 28^a. — *ifc.* **gu-**.

lvāpu, *s. a quarrel* C^1 129.

lvāya (-t), *v. i. to quarrel, to wrangle* B 59^b.11, *to fight* H^3 50^b.6; bigrah ~ *to wage war* C^2 5, jul ~ *to gamble* N 44^b.7. — lvāya ẽwo *quarrelsome* C^1 119.

hl.

hlanẽ, *v. t. to bear* H^1 47.2, *to lift* Bh 36^b.1. hlaṅa(ṃ) thwotanās *when it is rising (in price)*(?) N 25^b.1.

hlamāwānyo, *s. an eye in a peacock's tail* CW 7.14.

hlākẽ, *caus. of* hlāya^1 M 39^b.5.

hlākwo (*7th form of* hlāya^1), *s. a text* N 28^b.8.

hlāca = hlāya^1 N 12^a.4.

hlācakẽ^1 (*caus. of* hlāya^1), *to question* N 10^a.1; sīmā-khaṃ ~ *to settle a dispute about boundaries* N 26^b.3; guṇ-kha ~ *to (suffer oneself to) be praised* H^3 27^b.2.

hlācakẽ^2, *caus. of* hlāya^2 N 15^b.6.

hlātakẽ, *caus. of* hlāya^1 Bh 184^b.5.

hlāy, *s., only ifc.* **sit-**, **set-**.

hlāya^1 (-t *and* -l^1), *v. t. to say (before or after oratio recta)* H^1 82^b.4; *to speak, to tell, to utter* 53^a.2; *to picture, to describe* H^2 86^b.8. kha ~ *to tell something, to tell a tale* V^1 40^a.2.

hlāya^2 (-t *and* -l^1), *v. t. to hand over; to give back* N 15^b.6.

hlā-sal [hlāya^1 + sal], *s., ifc.* **kha-**.

hlu-kāpal, *s. a new and unbleached cloth* AH 43^b.

hluk-si, *s. name of several plants containing a milky sap* (kṣīrī) Md 42^a.2.

hluya^1 (-l^1), *v. t. to pay (out)* N 38^b.8.

hluya^2 (-l^1), *v. i. to bathe* N 27^a.2*.

hluya^3 (-l^1), *see* **baji**, **bal**.

hluyakẽ, *caus. of* hluya^1 N 43^b.4.

hleṅe, *s. a place for rubbish* N 18^a.8. — ~-bu *id.* 27^a.7*.

hleya (-l^1), *v. i. to move* Ś 143^b.7. — *v. t. to move, to transfer* B 58^a.12.

hlonakẽ (*caus. of* hlonẽ^2), *to make fat* H^2 58^b.1*.

hlonẽ^1, *v. t. to raise, to lift* N 12^a.3; *to repair, to put in order* Vi 93.16.

hlonẽ^2, *v. i. to become fat* Vd 50^b.1. hloṅ *adj. fat* H^3 24^a.2; ~-hma *id.* CW 8.38.

hloya^1 (-l^1), *v. t. to vomit* Bh 59^b.7.

hloya^2 (-t *or* -l^1?), *v. t.*, mikhā ~ *to prick the eyes* N 51^b.5*.

s (ś).

sa, *num.* = sat V^2 27^a.1.

sa(ṃ), *s. hair* H^1 75^b.5. ~ yāya *to dress the hair* Md 79^b.4; ~ khāṅ muḍā *bald* CW 8.41 (khāṃ). — *ifc.* **āgan-**, **āgam-**, **kukuli-**, **cimi-**, **phu-**, **mi-**, **moḍ-**.

sawāḍ, °l, *s.* = sabāḍ, °l H^3 56^a.5.

sawol, *s.* = sabal H^1 7^a.5.

saṃ-kokhā, *s. a raven* CW 7.4.

saṃ-khul, *s. a shell, conch* CW 2.8.

saṃ-gā [sa(ṃ)], *s. a blanket* AH 58^b.

saṁ-ci, *s. a kind of salt* Vd 29ᵃ.6.

saṁ-pārok, *adj. thick-haired* C¹ 242*.

saṁyukt [*S. conjoined together*], *adj. supplied with* H² 62ᵇ.4.

saṁyog [*S.*], *s. union, conjunction* H² 90ᵃ.1.

saṁla, *s.* = sala C¹ 244.

saṁśay [*S.*], *s. doubt* H¹ 21ᵇ.1; ~ yāya *to rouse doubt* H³ 58ᵃ.6.

saṁsarg [*S. union, association*], ~ yāya *to keep company* (ch-hm-wo *with*...) H¹ 88ᵇ.5. saṃsarg(an) *adv.*; ch-hm-wo (nāpa) ~ *together with* H³ 44ᵃ.2.

saṁsār [*S.*], *s. the existence, world* H¹ 78ᵇ.5.

saṁsul-si, *s. name of a plant* (kampilya) Md 7ᵃ.5.

saṁskār [*S.*], *s. a ceremony of purification* V¹ 109ᵃ.1.

saṁhār [*S. accumulation*], ~ juyakë *to collect, to gather* H² 98ᵇ.5.

saka (*gen.* sakasyā, *subj.* sakasë-naṃ) = sakal Vi 118.18. — ~-tā(ṃ) = sakal-tā(ṃ) B 58ᵃ.11.

saka-bhanaṁ, *adv. everywhere* Vi 19.33. ~-bhinaṃ *id.* M 4ᵃ.1.

sakal (*genitiv:* ~·asaṃ, ~·ayāṃ, ~·asayāṃ) [*S.*], *all, adj.* H² 73ᵇ.5; *id. s.* Ś 143ᵇ.3. — ~-tā(ṃ) *everything* V¹ 30ᵇ.5.

sakalë (*s., and adj. after the subst.:* sakalëṃ) = sakal; *s.* H¹ 25ᵃ.5; *adj.* B 62ᵇ.3. — sakalëṃ dayakë *to gather completely* H³ 48ᵇ.7.

sakāṁt [*cf.* saka], *all*(?) M 36ᵇ.8*.

sakwo, ~...ma ~ *some ... some* Bh 12ᵃ.3*.

śakti [*S. ability*], tham ~ jukwo *to the best of one's ability* N 19ᵃ.1.

saky [*S.* śakya *able, possible*], ~ dawo-thëṃ *to the best of one's ability* Vi 23.31; sakyan cāwo-thëṃ *id.* H¹ 27ᵇ.5.

sakhā [*S.* sakhi], *s. a friend* V² 7ᵃ.6. — sakhāy *id.* B 9ᵃ.5. — sakhe *id.* (*voc. only*) V² 8ᵃ.3.

sa-khi¹, *s. cow-dung* P 51ᵃ.5. — ~-ti *water, in which cow-dung has been dissolved* Vd 15ᵃ.5. — *ifc.* **sā-**.

sakhi² [*S.* sakhī], *s. a female friend* V¹ 78ᵃ.3.

sagat [*cf. S.* śakta], ~-noṃ *adv. to the best of one's ability*(?) Bh 67ᵇ.3*.

sa-gu, *s. a rope of hair* V² 32ᵃ.7.

saṁkalp [*S. desire, intention*], ch-hm-yāta ~ yāya *to promise* Bh *10ᵇ.4.

saṁkaṣṭ [*S.*], *s. distress, trouble* Bh 10ᵃ.7; ~ yāya *to be in distress* 79ᵇ.6.

śaṁkā, *s.* = saṃkhā H² 114ᵇ.4.

saṁket [*S.*], *s. an appointment* V¹ 10ᵇ.1.

saṁkoc [*S. shyness*], ~ ma thwolwo *shameless* N 132ᵃ.8.

saṁkhā [*S.* śaṃkā], *s. care* H¹ 20ᵇ.5, *suspicion* N 49ᵇ.8. ~ kāya *to be anxious or alarmed* H² 80ᵃ.6; ~ yāya *id.* H³ 26ᵇ.9; ~ cāya *to become anxious or alarmed* 6ᵃ.10, *to become suspicious* 46ᵇ.8; śaṃkhā cāya ëwo *procrastination, dilatoriness* H³ 6ᵃ.10.

śaṁkhuli, *s.*, kvāṅu ~ *the indigo-plant* Md 8ᵃ.8, hāku ~ *a medicinal plant* (nīlikā) *ib.*

saṁkhvār, *s. a medicinal plant or drogue* Vd 39ᵃ.1.

saṅg = saṅgh H³ 42ᵇ.5.

saṁgam [*S.*], *s. intercourse* H² 80ᵇ.5; ch-hm ~ yāya *to keep company with* 116ᵇ.2. ch-hm-wo saṃgaman *together with*... 40ᵇ.1.

saṁgrah [*S. collection*], ~ yāya *to collect* H¹ 2ᵇ.4.

saṁgrahaṇ [*S. s. seizing, obtaining*], ch-hm ~ yāya *to take* (*a husband or wife*) N 33ᵃ.9; ch-hm-wo ~ yāya *ro have sexual intercourse with*... 35ᵇ.4. — saṃgrahaṇī yāya *id.* 30ᵃ.6.

saṁgrām [*S.*], *s. a war, struggle* H¹ 23ᵃ.1.

saṁñāsi, *s.* = saṃnyāsi B 46a.1.

sac, *s.* = sas[1] H[1] 74b.2; *the spine, backbone* CW 8.52.

saccalapë, *v. t.* = sañcalapë Bh 62b.7.

sa-cā, *s. a calf* N 28b.1, *a heifer* 21b.8.

sacān, *s.* = sâcān CW 7.7.

sacun, *s. barley-flour:* ~-sarāb *a śarāva of barley-flour* H[2] 105a.5.

sacchi, *num.* = sat-chi C[2] 223.

sa-jawāl, *s. a cowherd* N 22a.1.

sa-jik, *adj. clever, able* V[1] 31a.1.

sajyā [*S.* śayyā], *s a couch, bed* V[1] 50a.4.

sañc, *s. name of a plant* (tāḍī) CW 6.39.

saṁcanā [*S.* saṃcayana *s. heaping together*], ~ yāya *to heap together, to accumulate* H[2] 2b.2.

saṁcayī [*S.* saṃcaya *collection, accumulation*], ~ yāya *to collect, to accumulate* H[1] 64a.4.

sañcalapë [*S.* sac *to be associated with*], *v. t. to gather, to collect* Bh 110a.7.

saṁcār [*S. mode, manner*], ~ yāya *to use* N 41a.5.

saṁja = sanë N 25b.4.

saṁjukt, *adj.* = saṃyukt H[2] 5a.2; ~ yāya *to supply oneself* (ch-g-n *with*...) Vi 168.12.

saṁjog [*S.* saṃyoga *union*], daibayā ~-an *through divine ordinance* Vi 132.35.

sat [*S.* śatam], *num. a hundred* V[1] 78b.4; *gen.:* ~-chi B 52a.2; ~-chi-tā *id.* H[2] 70b.6; ~-chi-hma (*of persons*) *id.* C[1] 133; ~-chiwo cyā *108* Ś 151b.7.

satal, *s. a hut of an ascetic* (maṭha) CW 4.5.

satān, *s.* = sātān H[2] 107a.8.

sa-tāni, *s. a woman's braided and ornamented hair wound round the head* (dhammila) AH 43a.

sati, *adv.*: ~ ku-hnu (*or* khu-hnu, khu-nu) *on the next day* V[2] 31b.3; thwonaṃ ~ ku-hnu *on the next day from this* H[3] 31a.2; thwoyāṃ ~ ku-hnu *id.* B 9a.8.

satī [*S. a good and faithful wife*], ~ wonë *to become a satī, to burn oneself together with the husband's corpse* H[2] 37b.1.

sa-tupatak, *s. a braid* (*of hair*) CW 8.74.

satë [*S.* satya *just, true*], *s. virtue* V[1] 71a.2; *an oath, solemn promise* Ś 160b.3. ~ yāya *to make an oath or a solemn promise* Vi 171.35; ch-hm-wo ~ yāya *to make a solemn agreement with*... V[1] 68b.6; ch-hm-yāta ~ biya *to give a solemn promise to* .. Ś 144b.1. satën(aṃ) *adv. justly* N 27a.2; ~ khawo *it is true* Vi 47.5. — satë-thëṃ *adv. truthfully* Vi 99.32. — *adj. true* Ś 153b.4. — satëwont [*S.* satyavat] *adj. truthful, veracious* H[2] 34b.1.

satpuruṣ [*S.*], *s. a good or noble man* H[2] 42a.5.

śatru [*S.*], *s. an enemy* H[1] 46b.3; ~ yāya *to treat as an enemy* H[3] 2b.8.

sad [= sabad?], *s. an oath* N 49b.8.

saḍa (*often spelt with* ś), *s.* = sala B 5a.11.

saḍa-bathān, *s. a herd of horses* B 33a.9.

sadā [*S.*], *adv. always* B 7b.5; sadāṃ *id.* C[2] 262; sadān(aṃ) *id.* B 27b.9; sadāñ *id.* H[2] 66b.8; sadākālaṃ *id.* H[1] 68b.4, sadāyā-thëṃ *as always* B 13b.1.

sadābati [*H.* sadā-barat], *s. alms distributed daily to the poor* B 52a.12.

saḍhāl, cittayā ~ yāya *to be of good cheer* N 46b.2*.

sanakë (*caus. of* sanë), ch-hm ch-g-s ~ *to let someone treat or serve something* H[2] 51b.3.

sanā [*H. from Arab.*], *s. senna, a sort of condiment* (vesavāra) AH 55a (sunáng).

sanān = snān B 57^b.8.

sanil, *s. evening* CW 1.46. — ~-bel *id.* C² 50 (sani-).

saneh [*M.*], *s. love* H² 30^b.6.

sanĕ, *v. i. to be (somehow)* C¹ 78, *to behave, to conduct oneself* H³ 34^b.1; began ~ *to throb vehemently (pulse)* Vd 42^a.1. — ch-hm-wo ~ *to have sexual intercourse with...* N 30^b.7.

saṁtān [*S. coherence, connection; offspring*], *s. offspring* N 31^a.5. — ~-phal *profits* 24^a.1.

saṁtāp [*S.*], *s. affliction, remorse* H² 38^b.5; ~ yāya *to repent* H² 72^a.8, *to be in suspense* N 14^a.2; ~ cāya *to repent* Bh 142^a.1; ~ lāya *id.* H³ 39^a.4.

saṁti, *adv.* = sati Ś 159^b.5.

saṁtuṣṭ [*S.*], *adj. satisfied, content* V¹ 130^a.4; ~ yāya *to satisfy, to propitiate* H³ 47^b.7.

saṁtoṣ [*S. satisfaction*], ~ yāya *to satisfy* H² 36^b.7; ~ juya *to be satisfied, to be content* (ch-g-n *with...*) 79^a.4.

saṁḍa, *s.* = saḍa C¹ 234.

saṁdeś [*S.*], *s. instruction, information* V¹ 14^a.2, *a proposal* B 24^a.9. — ~-pati *a written information* 61^a.2.

saṁdeh [*S.*], *doubt, suspense, uneasiness* Vi 39.27; ~ kāya *to lose confidence* H² 77^a.1, ~ cāya *id.* Ś 147^a.4, ~ tāya *to be in doubt or in suspense* Vi 155.7.

saṁdhalapë [*S.* sam-dhṛ- *to support, to restrain*], *v. t. to hold back, to detain* Bh 74^b.1.

sandhi [*S.*], *s. agreement, peace* H¹ 3^a.1; ~ yāya *to make peace* H² 99^a.2; ~ juya *to come to an agreement* N 35^b.6.

saṁdhyākāl [*S.*], *s. the evening time* H² 80^b.8.

sanyāyī [*S.* sa + nyāyin?], *adj. self-possessed* N 52^b.4*.

saṁnyāsi [*S.* saṃnyāsin], *s. an ascetic, devotee* B 17^b.11.

sap, ~ tinë *to go towards, to approach* H¹ 95^a.3.

sapan [*M.*], *s. a dream* B 22^a.11.

sapāni, *s. an ant* C² 34.

sa-pāl, *s.* = sa-pwol V² 45^b.4.

sa-purāk, *adj.* = saṃ-pārok C² 243*.

sa-pwol, *s. a braid of hair* Bh 49^b.1.

saphal [*S.*], *adj. fruitful, successful* V¹ 12^b.4.

saphali, *s.* = saphuli C¹ 154.

saphuḍā, *s. a round box* (samudga) CW 8.93.

saphuli, *s. a book* C¹ 38.

sabad [*cf. S.* śapatha *an oath*], *s. an ordeal* N 14^b.8; ~ phāya *to cause to undergo an ordeal* 15^a.1. — *ifc.* **agni-**.

sabal [*S.* śabara], *s. a mountaineer* H² 9^a.5.

sabāḍ, °l [*H.* savād], *s. taste* H² 104^b.1. — *ifc.* **ci-**.

śabd [*S.*], *s. a voice* H¹ 49^a.2; ~ dayakë *to recite* Bh *10^a.4.

sabhā [*S.*], *s. the court of a king, court of justice* N 12^a.2. ~ yāya *to give audience* V¹ 40^a.4; ~ dayakë *id.* V² 26^a.6, *to sit in judgement* B 7^b.4.

sam [*S. same, equal*], ch-g-wo ~ tuly *like a thing, equal to a thing* M 24^a.3.

samakhuli, *s.* = (hāku) saṃkhuli Vd 37^a.5.

samacār, *s.* = samācār Vi 47.9.

samajhalapë [*H.* samajhnā *to understand*], *v. t. to remember* N 10^a.9. — samajhalapayakë *caus. to remind* 10^a.8.

samadalapayakë [*M.* samad *to remember*], *v. t. to remind* N 9^a.5*.

samadhāl, ~ yāya *to consult* (ch-hm-wo *somebody*) B 32^a.7; (thithi) ~ yāya *to consult together* V¹ 87^a.6; ~-sāhuti yāya *id.* Bh 20^b.7.

samabhāg [*S. an equal share*], ~-an *in equal parts* Vd 26^b.4.

samay [*S.*], *s. time, juncture* H² 95^b.5. — *ifc.* **godhu-**.

samarth [*S. able, capable*], *adj.*

able, competent N 38b.4; ch-hm-yā ~ dawo *somebody is able* (yāya(s) *to*...) H3 33b.2.

samast [*S.*], *adj. all* H1 86a.3, *whole* V2 31a.1. — samastaṃ s. *id.* B 64a.1; *adj.* (*after the noun*) H1 10a.4.

samasvān [*cf. S.* śmaśāna], *s. a graveyard* B 14b.1.

samācār [*S. custom, usage*], *s. news, intelligence* B 60a.3. — ~-kha *id.* Ś 169b.2.

samān [*S.*], *adj. alike* H2 108a.7; ch-hm-wo ~ *like, equal with*... Ś 164a.4. ~ yāya *to deem alike* M 5a.3.

samāl [*M.* śamār *to adorn*], *s. embellishment* AH 43a. ~ yāya *to adorn oneself* CW 8.21; ~ yākë *to adorn* (*another*) B 31a.1.

samīp [*S. neighbourhood*], ch-g-yā samīpas *near to*... H1 36a.1; ch-hm-yā samīp(as) wonë *to go to*... H2 27a.7.

sami-si, *s. name of a plant* (śaktuphala) AH 29a.

samudr [*S.*], *s. the sea, ocean* V1 48b.2.

samet [*S. having come together*], *adv.*, ch-hm samet(an) *together with*... H2 57a.2.

saṁpat(t)i [*S.*], *s. good fortune* H2 16a.6; *wealth* V2 67a.6.

saṁpann [*S.*], *adj. provided, endowed* (ch-g-n *with*...) H3 34b.2.

saṁpāni, *s.* = sapāni C1 34. — ~-cā-dwo *an ant-hill* Vd 45b.3.

saṁpūrṇ [*S. filled; complete*], ~ yāya *to make complete, to procure* (*completely*) Vi 27.31, *to fulfill* (*a wish*) M 3b.5. ~ juya *to elapse, to expire* Vi 63.19, ch-g-n ~ juya *to be provided with*... 116.31. saṃpūrṇan *adv. completely* 89.23.

saṁbandh [*S.*], *s. connection, union* N 30a.8; śarīrawo ~ *bodily contact* V1 73b.5. mitr-~ yāya *to form a friendship* H2 44a.2.

saṁbā, *s. an oath* N 15a.5*.

saṁbhāṣaṇ [*S. conversation*], ~ yāya *to converse* B 15a.10.

saṁbhuri-ci, *s. a kind of salt* Vd 39b.4.

saṁbhog [*S. pleasure*], ~ yāya *to enjoy oneself* V1 74b.3.

samm [*P. during*], cha-bāl ~ *once* Pg 24a.4; mās la chi ~ *for one month* Vi 52.33; la chi sammayā hmin *every day during a month* 144.24.

saṁmat [*S. opinion, consent*], ~ yāya *to deliberate, to consult together* H2 114b.3, *to give one's consent* Vi 47.35. ch-hm-yā saṃmatan *with the consent of* H2 106a.4.

saṁmukh [*S.* saṃmukham], *adv. towards* (ch-hm-yā) H2 76a.5; juddhayā ~ yāya *to enter into a war* 107a.3.

saṁmeti [*clerical corruption of* saṃpati], *s.* = saṃpatti V2 31a.1.

sa-hmā, *s.* = sā-° M 39a.6.

sahmār [*M.* samār *to arrange*], ~ yāya *to arrange, to put in order* H2 102a.8.

say, *s.* = sac AH 40.

saya1 (-l1), *v. t. to know, to understand, to be conversant with* H1 73b.4, *to learn* N 19a.7. kha sawo *eloquent* V2 33b.2.

saya2 (-l1), *v. t. to bring* V1 32a.4; (se) ~ *to bear* (*fruit*), *to yield* (*fruits*) Ĉ1 47.

sayakë1 (*caus. of* saya1), *to teach* H1 10b.1.

sayakë2 (*caus. of* saya2), *to make fruitful* H1 9a.5.

saya-tā, *num.* = suya-tā M 10a.7*.

śayan [*S. rest, repose*], ~ yāya *to rest, to repose* H2 5b.5.

say-mbāc, *s.* = say H3 17a.6.

sal1 [*S.* svara], *s. a voice* V3 58b.5, *a sound* H3 105b.3. ~ kanë *to send word, to give notice* B 59a.8. — *ifc.* **ca-, thwok-, li-, su-.**

sal2, ~ payakë *to redress* (*an injustice*) N 45a.5. — ~ phāya (-l1) *to* *be taken with dizziness*(?) B 38ª.2; ~ ~ phāya *id.* Vd 44ª.1.

sal³, *num.* = sat; ~-chi V¹ 78ᵇ.4; në sal *two hundred* N 21ᵇ.9 (~ śar).

sala (*often spelt with ś*), *s. a horse* V² 7ª.2; ~-to *pl.* B 38ᵇ.11.

sala-khvāl, *s.*, Kuberayā ~ *a Kinnara* CW 1.31.

salag [*M.* sarag], *s. the sky* CW 3.4.

sala-gal, *s. a horse-stable* B 6ᵇ.11.

sa-laṅ, *s. a blanket* (kambala) AH 43ᵇ.

sala-cā, *s. a foal* B 38ᵇ.10.

sala-jhawāl, *s. a horse-minder* B 38ᵇ.10.

saradār, *s.* = sardār AH 51ª.

śaraṇ¹ [*S. refuge, protection*], ch-hm-yāke ~ kāya *to take refuge with...* Bh 113ᵇ.7, ~ ~ woya *id.* N 34ᵇ.4, ~ ~ yāya *id.* P 7ᵇ.7.

salan², *s.*, svānayā ~ *fragrance*(?) Vi 18.32*.

salapi, *s. name of a plant* (śathī) AH 33ª.

sala-banaj, *s. dealing in horses* C¹ 225.

sala-banijāl, *s. a horse-dealer* C² 225.

saram-, ~-chi *the Rudras* CW 1.3. — ~-nasī *the Ādityas* 1.1, the *Sādhyas* 1.3.

salalapë [*S.* sar], *v. i. to flow* N 30ᵇ.8.

sala-lā, *s. horse-flesh* Md 71ª.4.

sala-hāl-sal, *s. neighing* CW 1.63.

salā, *s.* = sala V¹ 11ª.6.

salāṁ-jhaṅgal, *s. a crane* H² 93ᵇ.5. — salān-jhaṅgal *id.* H² 82₂ª.1.

śarāp, *s.* = śrāp H² 112ª.7.

sarāb [*S.* śarāva], *s. a measure* H² 105ª.6. — *ifc.* **sacun-**.

salām, *s. a painter's brush* B 29ᵇ.8.

sali¹, *s. a strainer* Bh 166ᵇ.1. — ~-cā *id.* AH 54ᵇ (salingchá).

sali², *s. fruit, crop*(?) CW 3.1.

sali³, *s. a shield* (phalaka) AH 52ª (saling).

śarīḍ, *s.* = śarīr H¹ 29ᵇ.4.

salil, *s.* = śarīr V² 60ª.1.

śarīr [*S.*], *s. the body* H² 98ª.3; śarīras daya *to be pregnant* V¹ 97ᵇ.4. — ~-śāsti *corporal punishment* N 53ª.2.

salo, *s.* = sala AH 53.

sarobal [*S.*], *s. a pond, lake* V¹ 136ᵇ.5.

sarjjan¹ [*S.* sajana], *s. a kinsman* H³ 28ᵇ.6.

sarjjan² [*S.* saj-jana], *s. a good or virtuous man* H¹ 39ᵇ.1.

sal-të [*sal*¹], *v. t. to shout* B 57ª.12, *to address* 2ᵇ.5, *to say* (ch-hm *to...*) Vi 41.9; *to call, to summon* 165.2, sal-tāwo haya *id.* V¹ 95ᵇ.1. — sal-takë *caus. to cause to be summoned* M 8ª.4.

sardār [*H. a general, from Pers.*], *s. a general, chief-commander* H² 87ᵇ.5.

sarp [*S.*], *s. a serpent* V¹ 93ª.3.

sarbasa(ṁ), *s.* = sarbasva(ṃ) V² 59ᵇ.6.

sarbasva(ṁ) [*S.* sarvasva], *s. entire wealth* V¹ 97ᵇ.2; ~ bëtt *id.* N 52ª.4.

saryyā [*S.* śayyā], *s. a bed, couch* H¹ 62ᵇ.5.

sas¹, *s. a sinew; a bow-string* H¹ 74ᵇ.1.

sas² [*S.* sasya], *s. grain* N 29ª.1 (śaś).

śaś³ [*S.*], *s. a hare* H² 76ª.6. — ~-cā *id. dim.* 77ᵇ.5.

sasal, *s.* = sasul V² 20ª.6. — ~-babu *id.* B 47ª.3. — ~-mām *a mother-in-law* CW 8.29.

sa-si¹, *s. name of a plant* (āmlavetasa) Md 44ᵇ.5.

sasi² [*S.* śaśin], ~-milā *the moon* B 63ª.8.

sasul [*EH.* sasur], *s. a father-in-law* V¹ 31ª.4.

sast, *adj.* = samast V¹ 31ᵇ.5.

śastr [*S.*], *s. a weapon* N 12ª.8. — *see* **astr**.

sasy [*S.*], *s. seed, produce of the field* H² 88ª.8.

sah [*S. bearing, enduring*], ~ yāya *to bear, to endure* H² 84ᵃ.7. — ~-thēṃ *as much as one can bear* Vd 35ᵇ.4.

sahaj [*S. innate*], *s. character, disposition* H² 53ᵇ.3. sahajan *adv. by nature* N 11ᵃ.8.

sahan¹, *s. a signal*; ~ dayakë *to make a signal* B 40ᵃ.9; ~ biya *id.* 48ᵃ.7.

sahan², *num. ten* AH 57ᵃ.

sahar [*H.* śahr, *from Pers.* šähr], *s. a town* Vi 25.16.

sahalapë [*S.* sah-], *v. t. to bear, to endure* H³ 40ᵃ.11*.

sahasr [*S.*], *num. thousand* V¹ 1ᵃ.3.

sa-hān, *s. a herd of cows* N 29ᵃ.3.

sahāy [*S.*], *s. a companion, associate* H² 106ᵃ.3. ~ yāya *to take with him (as companions)* Vi 154.9.

sahās [*hypercorrect* = sahāy], ~ yāya *to utilize* C¹ 9.

sahi [*cf. Mr.* saī karaṇeṃ *to approve*], *adj. good, right* Ś 151ᵇ.3.

sahit [*S. joined, united*], ch-hm ~ *together with* B 5ᵃ.12; ~ yāya *to take with one* Vi 79.12; ~ conë *to be assembled* M 9ᵃ.6. — sahitan = sahit V¹ 40ᵃ.4.

sā¹, *s. a cow* H¹ 19ᵃ.2; sā-to *pl.* Bh 26ᵇ.2. — *ifc.* **kāl-, hnyā-, cāhmal-, thu-, thwo-, bā-, mā-, lādan-, yā-.**

sā², *s. breath(?)* M 23ᵃ.3*.

sā³, *s. wages(?)* N 21ᵇ.5*.

sā⁴, ~ wāya (-t) *to plough* N 29ᵇ.3; sā wāṅā la *a furrow* AH 54.

sā⁵, *num.* = sat H¹ 9ᵃ.5.

sāk, *adj. savoury, palatable* B 30ᵃ.11. — *ifc.* **na-.**

śākapāk, *s.* = °pāt M 11ᵃ.2.

śākapāt [*S.* śākapātra], *s. a vegetable dish* H² 29ᵇ.7.

sākṣi [*S.* sākṣin], *s. a witness* N 9ᵃ.2; *a proof* Ś 150ᵇ.4. — ~ kenë *to produce witnesses* N 22ᵇ.8; ~ yāya *to appoint as witness* 10ᵃ.4.

sākh¹, *s. distant connections* (?) N 7ᵃ.7.

sākh² [*H.*], *s. authority, trust* N 20ᵃ.2*.

sākhar [*cf. Mr.*], *s. sugar* C¹ 153.

sākhāl-bi, *s. a boa* AH 19ᵃ.

sā-khi, *s. cowdung* AH 55ᵇ.

sāgar [*S.*], *s. an ocean* H³ 33ᵇ.5.

sā-gvāth, *s. a cow-pen* Bh 12ᵃ.5.

sā-ghel, *s. clarified cow-butter* Vd 24ᵇ.5.

sā-cā, *s. a calf* C¹ 77.

sācān, *s. a falcon* V¹ 76ᵇ.

sāchi, *s.* = sākṣi *a proof* Ś 150ᵃ.6.

sāj [*M. preparation*], ~ tāl lācakë *to make ready* H³ 42ᵇ.1; sājan tāl lāya *to be ready* 45ᵇ.8; sājan jiyakë *to make oneself ready* H² 59ᵃ.6.

sā-jawāl, *s.* = °-jhawāl Vi 93.4.

sā-jhawāl, *s. a cow-keeper* H³ 54ᵃ.8.

sātān, *s. a falcon* V² 47ᵇ.1.

sāti, *adv.* = sati V¹ 47ᵃ.1.

sātu, *see* **sālë.**

sāth-saṅgh [*H.* sāth *company*] *s. a caravan* Vi 93.27.

sā-dudu, *s. cow-milk* P 64ᵃ.2.

sādeś, *s.* = saṃdeś V¹ 15ᵃ.3,4*.

sādhan(ā) [*S.* sādhanā *accomplishment; gain*], ~ yāya *to accomplish* H³ 2ᵇ.8, *to get ready* H³ 78ᵇ.7, *to gain, to acquire* Vi 22.5.

sādhalapë [*S.* sādhaya-], *v. t. to accomplish* V¹ 123ᵃ.5, *to settle, to finish* H³ 30ᵇ.6, *to gain, to acquire* N 38ᵃ.2; yāyayāta kāry ~ *to get ready for doing* H² 67ᵇ.3.

sā-dhali, *s. coagulated cow-milk* P 4ᵃ.2.

sādhu [*S.*], *adj. powerfull, excellent* H¹ 30ᵃ.4.

sānë, *v. i.* = sanë N 26ᵃ.1.

śānt [*S. tranquil, calm*], ~ juya *to be restored to reason* H³ 74ᵇ.5; ~ yāya *to appease (anger)* Bh 185ᵇ.4, *to cure (disease)* M 8ᵇ.3.

śānti [*S. calming*], ~ juya *to be cured (disease)* H³ 87ᵇ.4.

sāhno, *n. pr. the Viśvas* CW 1.1.

sāphaly [*S.*], *s. fruitfulness; success* H³ 51ᵃ.7.

sābadhān [*S.* sāvadhāna *attentive*], ~ yāya *to be attentive* B 69ᵇ.10; sābadhānan *adv. attentively* V¹ 8ᵇ.5.

sā-bhujiṁ, *s. a gadfly* CW 7.12.

sāmagrī [*S.*], *s. a complete collection of implements or materials* H² 85ᵇ.8.

sāmant [*S. neighbourhood*], ~-lok *neighbours* N 26ᵇ.1.

sāmarth, *adj.* = samartn N 48ᵃ.5. ~ ma du *it is impossible* H² 89ᵃ.3. — sāmarthī *adj. able* H³ 78ᵃ.5. — sāmarthāyi *adj. fitted, suitable* N 38ᵃ.1.

sāmāgrī, *s.* = sāmagrī Vi 24.1.

sāmāny [*S.*], *adj. common, ordinary* Vi 23.22; *less heavy* (agariyān) N 51ᵇ.3.

sā-mes, *s. milch-cattle* N 24ᵇ.8.

sā-hmā [sā¹], *s. a dairy produce* Bh 68ᵇ.1.

sāhmāgrī, *s.* = sāmagrī Bh 28ᵇ.1*.

sāl [*H. from Pers.* šāl *shawl*], *s. a coarse cloth* AH 43ᵇ.

sāras [*S.*], *s. a crane* H² 98ᵃ.8.

sā-lā, *s. cow-flesh, beef* C² 290.

sāri [*S.*], *s. a thrust-like bird* B 53ᵇ.4.

sālē¹, *v. t. to drag* Bh 81ᵇ.6; lā-hāt ~ *to drag along by the hand* 120ᵃ.7; (dudus) ~ *to pinch, to squeeze (the breast)* H¹ 83ᵃ.5; laṃkha ~ *to draw water* B 5ᵇ.8. — sātu sālē (*intens.*) *to drag vehemently* 8ᵇ.3.

sālē², *v. t.*, rājā ~ *to proclaim king* H³ 39ᵇ.9.

sārthī [*S.* ~ kṛ *to make a gain out of a thing*], yāyas ~ juya *to be eager to..., to be intent upon* Vi 18.8*.

sār-phal [*S.* sāra + phala], *s. profit* N 19ᵃ.7.

sā-sakhi, *s. cow-dung* Vd 16ᵃ.1. — ~-ti *the juice from it* 15ᵃ.6.

sāsalapē [*S* śās], *v. t. to punish* N 43ᵃ.1; *to educate* H¹ 20ᵃ.4.

sā-sā¹ [sā²], *s. the price of a bride, a nuptial gift* N 33ᵃ.9; sā-sā luṃ *id.* 32ᵇ.6; sā-sā pulalapē *to give the nuptial gift* 32ᵃ.2.

sā-sā² [sālē?], ~ conē *to squeeze, to caress (repeatedly)* N 34ᵃ.3*.

śāsti [*S. punishment*]; ~ yāya *to punish* V² 76ᵃ.6; ~ yātakē *to cause to punish* M 28ᵃ.5; ~ naya *to be punished* Ś 153ᵇ.5. — *ifc.* **dhan-, śarīr-.**

śāstr [*S.*], *s. a compendium of rules* H² 3ᵃ.2.

sāhas [*S.*], *s.* 1) *a reckless act* N 41ᵃ.4. 2) *fine, punishment* 51ᵃ.4.

sā-hān, *s. a drove (of cattle)* N 28ᵇ.7.

sāhi [*H.* sāī *current money*], *s. money* Vi 25.9; *a unit of coin* H² 89ᵃ.6.

sāhu, *s. a plough* AH 53ᵇ. — ~-dand *the pole of a plough* (īṣā) *ib.* 54ᵃ.

sāhuti, ~ biya *to give advice* Ś 161ᵃ.3; ~ yāya *to consult together, to deliberate* H³ 59ᵃ.3; ~ saṃmat yāya *id.* H² 108ᵇ.1.

sāheb [*H.* sāhib *from Arab.* ṣāḥib], *s. a lord, master* Ś 145ᵃ.6; ~-ju *id.* Vi 155.12.

si¹, *s. a bank, coast, shore* H³ 41ᵇ.4. — *ifc.* **khu-, khusi-, khwo-, grām-, pukhuli-, mude-, hmutu-, laṁ-.**

si², *s.* = se² AH 41ᵇ.

si³, *s.* = se¹ H¹ 44ᵇ.3. — *ifc.* **atamb-, abāli-, amp-, ambal-, alaṇḍ-, ul-, karkaṭā-, kuhnali-, kol-, khayal-, khwol-, gaṁbhāli-, ginār-, guṁ-, gulāp-, cikay-, chu-¹, jawo-, jal-, jhama-, titu-, thaṁ-, duṁbal-, nal-, nip-, nimbal-, pak-, panyal-, pilāk-, pha-, phat-, pho-, bak-, bili-, bujham-, boti-, byāl-, manapaban-, mātin-, miku-, micaki-, mitaki-, yaguḍi-, lak-, lāhā-, lvāḍ-, hluk-, sa-, saṁsul-, sami-.**

si(ṁ), *s. wood (as building material or fuel)* C¹ 85; *a tree* N 26ᵇ.4. — siyā *wooden, made from wood* Vi 44.15. — *ifc.* **chu-².**

si'u(ṁ), *adj.* = siṁu AH 11ᵃ (sheewon).

siwā = sibā Ś 159ᵇ.3.

siṁ = sinwoṃ H¹ 31ᵇ.2.

siṁ-tvāk-jhaṅgal, *s. a woodpecker* CW 7.8.

śiṁśapā [*S.*], *s. name of a tree* V¹ 27ᵇ.4.

siṁsalyā, *s. name of a tree* (śiṃśapā) V² 16ᵃ.1.

siṁh [*S.*], *s. a lion* H² 49ᵃ.2. — ~-tisā *an ornament for the hair* (vālapāśyā) CW 8.76.

siṁ-hal, *s. a leaf of a tree* Ś 166ᵇ.1.

siṁhāsan [*S.*], *s. a (king's) throne* H² 72ᵃ.5.

sik (*5th form of* siya¹), *adj. dead* V² 24ᵇ.1; ~-hma *id.* C¹ 290.

si-kacā, *s. a branch of a tree* H³ 52ᵇ.1.

si-karmi, *s. a worker in wood* B 33ᵇ.8.

sikiri, *s.* = sikhal H² 36ᵃ.4*.

siku-pacini, *s. the little finger* AH 42ᵃ.

sikwo (*7th form of* siya¹), *adj. dead* V² 79ᵃ.7.

sikha, *s.* = sikhalī H³ 35ᵇ.7. — sikhani *id.* H² 67ᵃ.1.

sikhani, *s.* = sikhalī H² 67ᵃ.1.

sikhalapë [*H.* sikhānā *to teach; to advise*], *v. t. to guide, to control* H¹ 62ᵇ.2; *to encourage* N 18ᵇ.7.

sikhalī, *s. a line, string* B 34ᵃ.1. — *ifc.* na-, lu-.

sikhāl [*H. from Pers.* šikār], *s. hunting* Ś 155ᵃ.6.

si-khul, *s. the bark of a tree* C 6.8.

si-khoṭ, *s. a stem, trunk (of a tree)* CW 6.6.

sikhy [*S.* śiṣya], *s. a pupil, apprentice* N 37ᵇ.3.

si-ghāli, *s. a (wooden?) chest* B 4ᵃ.6.

śīghr [*S. quick, fast*], ~ yāya *to hasten* Bh 82ᵃ.7. śīghranaṃ *adv. quick* V¹ 137ᵇ.3.

siṅu, *adj. dark:* ~ milā *dark night* CW 1.47.

siṅgāl, *s.* = śṛṅgār CW 8.2.

siṅghātak [*S.* śṛṅghāṭaka], *s. a medicinal plant* Vd 46ᵇ.5.

sicakë¹, *v. t. to cause to put on (an article of dress)* B 27ᵇ.1*.

sicakë², *caus. of* siya² Bh 142ᵃ.2.

si-cataṁ, *s. a wooden ladle* AH 55ᵃ.

sicalapë, *v. t. to efface, to oblitterate* C² 221*.

siʾal, *s. copper* Vi 83.19. — ~-pati *a copper-plate* B 32ᵇ.11. — ~-khorā *a cup of copper* Vd 29ᵃ.4. — ~-bhāṁḍā *a copper-vessel* C¹ 281.

si-jhāwo, *s. a multitude of young buds* (kṣāraka) AH 27ᵃ.

śīt [*S.*], *s. cold, frost* H³ 40ᵇ 2.

śītal [*S.*], *adj. cool, cold* Ś 162ᵇ.4; ~ yāya *to cool* H² 28ᵇ.6.

situ, *s. a sort of grass* (durvā) Md 20ᵇ.4; tawo ~ *id.* (gandhadurvā) *ib.* 6.

sit-khāl, *s. a medicinal plant* (snuhī AH) Vd 48ᵇ.6.

sit-marac, *s. a kind of plant* (veṇukā) Md 27ᵇ.3.

sit-hlāy, *s. resin of a tree* (rāla) Md 28ᵃ.4.

sithi, *s. 7th day of the lunar fortnight* AH 10ᵇ.

sithi-svān, *s. Vitex Negundo* AH 29ᵇ.

sidhu [siddh], ~-guli *adj. safe, secure* H¹ 95ᵇ.2; ~-tole *while... is safe* H² 84ᵇ.2, *while... prospers* C¹ 108. — sidho *(a wish) is fulfilled* H¹ 78ᵇ.1.

siddh [*S. accomplished*], ~ yāya *to accomplish, to carry out* H² 79ᵃ.6; ~ juya *to be accomplished, to be fulfilled* Ś 162ᵇ.7, buddh ~ juya *to become a Buddha* Vi 146.16. — siddhalaṅāwo *if... succeeds* C¹ 108; siddhayuwo *will succeed* H¹ 6ᵇ.5.

siddhayakë (*not seldom:* °dha°) [siddh], *v. t. to accomplish, to carry out* H² 6ᵃ.2.

siddhalapë [siddh], *v. t. to accomplish, to bring about* H[1] 96ª.1.

sina(ṁ), *adv.* = sinwoṃ V[2] 34ᵇ.4.

sineh(ā), *s.* = saneh C[1] 288; ~ taya *to love* H[2] 105ᵇ.1; ch-hm-wo ~ yāya *to enjoy love with...* H[3] 27ª.1.

sinwoṁ, *adv. more, better, in a higher degree than:* striyā ~ *better than a wife* H[1] 28ª.5; ratnayā ~ (ati) jhyātu (*fare*) *more valuable than jewels* C[1] 169.

sihnal, *s. red lead, vermillion* Md 34ª.7.

si-pā, *s. the testicles* AH 41ᵇ.

sipā'i, sipāyi, sipāhi [*H. from Pers.* sipāh], *s. a soldier* H[2] 87ᵇ.6.

sipi, *s. name of a plant* (cavya Md) Vd 50ᵇ.4.

sib, *s.* = seb H[3] 51ᵇ.12*.

sibak, *s.* = sebak V[2] 31ª.2.

sibakāl, ~ yāya *to stipulate* B 34ᵇ.12; ~ biya *id.* 37ª.2*.

sibay, *s. a dowry*(?) Vi 53.9*.

sibā = sebā B 63ª.9.

si-bho, *s. a creeper* AH 70ᵇ.

si-bhvāl, *s. the hollow of a tree* B 43ª.7.

simal [*M.* simar], ~-simā *the silk-cotton tree* CW 6.16.

simalas, *s. name of a medicinal plant* (rohītaka Md) Vd 54ᵇ.5. — ~-mūl *the root of this plant* 47ª.3.

simā, *s. a tree* H[1] 36ª.1. — ~-apā *a grove of trees* (vṛkṣavāṭikā) AH 26ᵇ. — ~-kacā *the branch of a tree* CW 6.4. — ~-kholā *the bark of a tree* AH 27ª. — ~-cā *a bush* CW 6.4. — ~-jhol *a row of trees* AH 26ᵇ. — ~-pu *the seed of a tree* B 61ᵇ.2. — ~-bhvāl *a hollow of a tree* B 43ª.6. — *ifc.* **alal-, arkaṭi-, ul-, wolagat-, khayal-, tāyago-, nip-, pilāg-, phat-, bhocā-, simal-.**

sīmā [*S.* sīman], *s. a border, boundary* N 27ª.4. — *ifc.* **bhūmā-.**

simān [*M. boundary, limit*], *s. a boundary* C[1] 208; *a territory* Vi 35.2; ~ yāya *to bound, to limit* M 16ᵇ.7.

simi, *s. a kind of crop* N 41ᵇ.5.

siya[1] (-t), *v. i. to die* H[1] 49ª.4.

siya[2] (-t, siyāwo V[1]), *v. t. to wash, to cleanse* V[2] 47ª.7.

siya[3] (-l[1]), *v. t.* = sëya H[3] 61ᵇ.1.

siya[4] (-l), *v. t.*, mikhā ~ *to shut the eyes* M 32ª.2.

siyakë = sëyakë; 1) Vi 140.22. 2) Ś 146ᵇ.5. 3) *to know, to learn* (= *simpl.*) Vi 30.12.

siyiwo, *adj.* = siyuwo C[1] 283.

siyu, *adj. reddish brown, tawny* V[1] 123ᵇ.6; siyuwo *id.* V[2] 73ᵇ.2.

sil[1] [*M.* sir], *s. the head* V[1] 45ᵇ.4. silas taya *to impress (a thing) on one's mind, to keep in mind* V[2] 28ª.4; ~ dhalalapë *id.* V[1] 43ª.4; ~ juya *to be kept in mind* Vi 115.26. ch-g-yā ~ taya *to be at the head of...* H[1] 67ª.3.

sil[2] [*S.* śīla], *s. a character* H[1] 45ª.5.

sil[3], *s. leprosy* CW 8.43; ~-do-hma *leprous ib.* 49.

si-lā, *s. the month Māgha* CW 1.49. — ~-cet-lā *the cold season* (śiśira) AH 12ª.

silis [*M.* siris], *s. a kind of tree* (śirīṣa) CW 6.20.

silë[1], *v. t. to wash* B 59ᵇ.6.

silë[2], *v. i.* = siya[1] P 17ª.7*.

silok [*cf. S.* śloka], *s. a verse* H[2] 90ª.6.

silopā, ~ biya *to give presents* B 52ª.9; silopāwo ~ *id.* 12ª.12; silopā'u ~ *id.* Vi 152.9.

sil-khāl, *s.* = sit-° CW 6.29.

śilpakār [*S.* artisan], *s. a pupil* (sic; śiṣya) N 53ᵇ.4*.

śilpī [*S.* śilpin], *s. an artisan* V[1] 53ª.6.

si-sā, *s.* = se-sā; ~-phal *id.* H[3] 30ᵇ.8. ~-phal-mā *a fruit-tree* Vi 83.24. — ~-bosā = sesā-~ B 23ª.4.

sisi, *s.* = sise Vd 42ᵇ.1.

sisi-cā, *s. a small phial* HP 82, 31ª.

sisu-ṅā, *s. a marine animal* (ulupin) AH 20^b^.

sise, *s. a medicinal plant* Vd 15^b^.5.

sisĕṁ = sesĕṃ V² 52^a^.5.

siso-puti [*H.* sisu], *s. name of a tree* (śiṃśapā) AH 29^b^.

si-hal, *s.* = siṃ-hal AH 27.

su¹, *int. who?* (*of persons only*) H¹ 36^b^.5. — *rel.* (*corr.* wo) 65^a^.5. — *indef.* (= su-ṃ) V² 70^b^.6. — ~ gwo-hma *int. who?* H² 71^b^.7; ~ julasa-nwoṃ *whoever it may be* H¹ 38^a^.1.

su², *s. a cloud* H³ 40^a^.11; sun puṅ *a rainy day* (*lit.: covered with clouds*) CW 1.42.

su³, *ifc.* **na-**.

su-ṁ (*gen.:* suyā-ṃ H¹ 19^a^.2) = su-nwoṃ; ~...ma *nobody* Vi 117.22. — ~ gwo-hma-ṃ *some* (*adj.*) 64.9. — ~ cha-hma...ma *nobody* 92.31.

suwāl, *s. a cook* V¹ 49^a^.5.

śuk [*S.*], *s. a parrot* Ś 146^b^.5.

sukapāl, *s. a kind of sedan-chair* Ś 168^a^.1*.

sukĕ¹, *v. t.*, dudu ~ *to milk*(?) B 52^b^.4*.

sukĕ², *v. t.* = sucakĕ¹ V¹ 130^b^.5*.

suk-myāl, *s. a kind of plant* (koraṅgī) CW 6.31.

sukh [*S.*], *s. luck, happiness* H¹ 43^b^.2; thawo ~ *independence* H³ 24^a^.6. — sukhi [*S.* sukhin], *adj. happy* H² 51^a^.6; ~ yāya *to make happy* N 53^b^.5. — *ifc.* **sulat-**.

sukhapāl, *s.* = suka° Bh 173^b^.6*.

sukhay [*M.* sukhā *to dry up*], ~ juya *to dry up* M 15^b^.6*.

sukhu, *adj.* = sukhulī; ~ ciṅāwo *being withered* Vi 98.31*.

sukhulī [*M.* sukhal], *adj. dry, withered* B 16^b^.5.

su-khol, *adv.*, hmigwo ~ *yesterday morning* B 21^b^.9*.

sugandh [*S.*], *s. perfumes* B 25^b^.12.

sucakāl [suya¹], *s. a tailor* B 27^a^.5.

sucakĕ¹, *v. t. to wash* V² 76^b^.6.

sucakĕ², *v. t. to boil* Vd 24^b^.5.

śuci [*S.*], *adj. reliable* H² 79^a^.2. ~ yāya *to become innocent* N 48^a^.5; *to purify* P 28^a^.2; ~ juya *to become pure* (*in a religious sense*) 57^a^.7.

su-chi-, ~·yāta jusĕ(ṃ) harasa-nwoṃ *to anybody* H¹ 16^b^.2. — ~-nwoṃ *somebody* 15^a^.2; ~-naṃ *id.* H² 61^b^.8.

sutakĕ, *v. t.* = sucakĕ² Vd 55^a^.3.

su-ti [su²], *s. rain-water* Vd 14^b^.4.

su-tuppā, *s. a leech* CW 2.8.

su-tha, *s. morning* P 17^b^.6. *adv. in the morning* C¹ 295; ~ tewolaṃ *early in the morning* H² 92^b^.8, ~ hnāpāṃ *id.* B 17^b^.9. — su-thā *s.* = su-tha CW 1.45.

suthī [*S.* śuṇṭhī], *s. dry ginger* Vd 28^a^.4.

su-ḍaṁ, *adv. in the morning* N 22^a^.1*.

sudās, *s. a sort of hemp* (mūrvā) Md 14^a^.5.

śūdr [*S.*], *s. a Śūdra* N 52^b^.6.

sudhā, *adv.* = suddhā C¹ 149.

sudho [*cf. S.* śuddha *clean, pure*], *adj. free from blame* N 22^b^.3.

śuddh [*S. clean; pure*], *adj. plain, distinct* N 8^b^.4; ~ kāy *a legitimate son* 39^a^.1. ~ yāya *to purify* P 28^a^.2.

suddhā [*H.* sudha *straight, right?*], *adv. quite, completely* H² 103^b^.6. ~... ma *not at all* Vi 84.12.

suddhāṁt, *adv.*, ~...ma = suddhā...ma M 15^b^.4; *not even* 19^a^.7.

su-naṁ (*gen.:* suyā-naṃ B 63^a^.1) = °-nwoṃ: ~...ma *nobody* V² 28^a^.2. — su-naṅ *id.* Ś 160^b^.2.

sunaterī, *s. a kind of plant* (mahāmuṇḍī) Md 6^b^.7.

sunā, *pr. int. who?* H² 29^b^.7. — sunānaṃ *int. who after all* H¹ 41^b^.1; *rel. whoever* 5^a^.2; *indef.:* ~...ma *nobody* Vi 35.4; ~ gwo-hma *int.* H² 71^a^.2. — sunānwoṃ = sunānaṃ N 23^a^.3.

su-nilā, *adv. in the morning* N 47^a^.1.

su-num = su-nwom H[1] 84^b.2. — su-nuṅ *id.* Ś 164^a.4.

sunĕ, *v., see* **bhok.**

su-nwoṁ, *indef. someone* H[2] 47^b.3.

sundar [*S.*], *adj. beautiful* V[1] 55^b.6. — sundarī [*S.*] *id. fem.* Ś 153^b.4.

suṇḍini [*S.* śuṇḍin, *fem.* śuṇḍinī], *s.* 1) *a seller of spirituous liquor* N 49^a.1. — 2) *his wife* 3^a.1.

śūny [*S.*], *adj. empty* H[2] 38^b.1; ~ ~ juya *to be destroyed* Vi 123.12.

su-hniṁ, *adv. in the morning* Vd 51^b.4.

su-hnithaṁ, *adv. every morning* Vd 50^a.6*.

su-pāc, *s.* (*a heavy*) *cloud* H[3] 20^b.2.

supi, *s. a knife, dagger* (= cupi) B 28^a.8*.

subarṇ [*S.*], *s. gold* H[2] 11^a.3.

subāchar, *s.* = subhāchar Md 24^a.2.

su-bāṭī [*cf.* a-bāṭī], *adj. law-abiding* N 46^b.3.

subhā [*S.* śubha], *adj. agreeable, pleasant* M 24^b.7.

Subhā'ṛt, *n. pr.* B 39^b.3.

subhāchar [*S.* sauvarcala], *s. natron; alkali* Vd 29^b.1.

subhūri-ci, *s. sea-salt* Md 24^b.1.

sumakaṁ, *adv.* = sohmakaṃ B 14^a.10.

sumar(a)ṇā [*S.* smaraṇa *remembrance*], ~ yāya *to remember, to bear in mind* Vi 25.49; *to invoke* (ch-hm-(-yāta)) 80.19; ch-hm-yā nām ~ ~ *id.* 30.24. — sumaranāyāo = sumarṇā yāṅāwo 84.23.

sumalapĕ [*cf. S.* smar-], *v. t. to worship* B 68^a.8.

sumarṇ = sumar(a)ṇā Ś 151^b.6.

sumukaṁ, *adv.* = sohmakaṃ H[2] 94^b.6.

suhmakaṁ, °hmu°, *adv.* = sohmakaṃ H[1] 63^b.5.

suya[1] (-l[1]), *v. t. to sew* B 27^b.1.

suya[2], *num. thirty* N 24^b.4; ~ ni dor *32000* Ś 146^b.2.

suya[3] (-l[1]), *v. t. to hit, to stab* Bh 136^b.4. — *v. i. to stick to* B 43^b.9.

suyakĕ[1], *caus. of suya*[1] Ś 147^b.6.

suyakĕ[2], *v. t.* = sucakĕ[1] V[1] 130^b.4*.

suyacun, *c. a plant* (amlikā) Md 45^a.3.

suya-bhagat, *s. a medicinal plant* Vd 14^a.2.

śūr [*S.*], *s. a brave, valiant man* H[2] 34^b.1.

sulakĕ (*caus. of* sulĕ), *to let somebody hide himself* H[2] 65^a.5.

sulat-sukh [*cf. S.* surata-saukhya], *s. tse pleasure of sexual intercourse* V[1] 72^a.6.

sulā [*S.* śūla], *s. a pale* V[2] 59^a.4; ch-hm ~ biya *to impale somebody* V[1] 132^b.2.

sulin [*cf. M.* sūṁḍi *a distiller*], *s. a seller of spirituous liquors* AH 60^a (suling). — sulini *his wife* H[2] 76^b.6, *a low-caste woman* C[2] 254.

sulĕ, *v. t. to hide, to conceal* V[2] 24^b.1. *v. i. to hide oneself* H[2] 76^a.4.

surg [*pop. H.* surag], *s. heaven* Ś 167^b.5.

sūry [*S.*], *s. a sun* H[1] 60^b.3.

sulyā, *s.* = sulā Ś 146^a.5.

su-sal [su[2]], *s. a deep, hollow sound* CW 1.64. — ~-dhārā *a storm of rain* Vi 159.4.

susār [*H. a cook*], *s. food* Vi 151.11.

śuśrūṣā [*S. obedience*], ch-hm-yāke ~ yāya *to obey* N 18^a.3. — ~-byapār *done by labourers* (karmakṛta) 18^a.7.

suhit [*S. very good*], ~ yāya *to treat well* H[2] 53^a.2.

suhṛd [*S.*], *s. a friend* H[1] 46^a.5. — suhṛt *id.*: ~ yāya *to form a friendship* H[3] 25^b.5.

suhṛday [*S. good-hearted*], ~ yāya *to make somebody one's friend* (*cf. S.* suhṛd) H[1] 51^b.3.

suheti [*cf. S.* suhṛd], *s.* 1) *a friend*

H² 32ᵇ.1; ~-mitr = ~ 40ᵃ.7. ~-hma *adj. friendly* C¹ 186. — 2) *s. friendship* 254.

śṛṅgār [*S.*], *s. love raptures* B 17ᵃ.9. — ~-kathā yāya *to pass words of love* V¹ 73ᵃ.5.

sṛṣṭi [*S. creation, formation*], ~ yāya *to form, to create* H³ 111ᵇ.1.

se¹, *s. fruit, corn, grain* V¹ 2ᵃ.1. — *ifc.* (*plant, vegetable*): **kaṁci-, koḍ-, khajur-, khabij-, japu-, jau-, jhatu-jhamar-, tawo-, titul-, tu-, tur-, tëbhuli-, to-, dudhal-, do-, nān-, hnel-, phat-, phan-, bayal-, bal-, buto-, beḍe-, mit-, met-.**

se² [= se¹?], *s. a testicle* CW 8.58.

se³ = saya¹ N 19ᵃ.1.

sewā = sebā Vi 21.33 (sewā yāt!). — sewāyāo = sewā yāṅāwo 105.5.

secakë [sesëṃ], thawoke secakaṃ tā padārth *a deposit* N 15ᵇ.7*.

seja = sëya N 19ᵃ.4.

set, *s. resin*(?) Vd 32ᵃ.6.

setamale [*cf. S.* śvetamarica], *s. white pepper* AH 58ᵇ.

seti, *s. a Śūdra* H³ 60ᵇ.5.

seto, *s. a medicinal plant* Vd 47ᵇ.4.

set-khāl, *s.* = sit-° Vd 35ᵃ.5.

set-hlāy, *s.* = sit-hlāy CW 8.87. — set-lāch *id.* Vd 32ᵇ.2; seth-lāch *id.* 30ᵃ.2, seth-hlāch *id.* 38ᵇ.4.

sedhu [*cf. S.* saindhava], *s. a kind of rock salt* Vd 21ᵃ.1. — ~-ci *id.* Md 24ᵃ.6.

senāpati [*S.*], *s. a commander of an army* H² 59ᵃ.1.

senwoṁ, *adv.* = sinwoṃ H³ 66ᵇ.6.

se-puṭ, *s. grass* C² 152*.

seb¹ [= sebā], *s. service* H³ 51ᵇ.12*.

seb² [*H. apple, from Arab.*], *s. the jujube-plant* Md 43ᵃ.3. — ~-ti *juice from this plant ib.* 4.

sebak [*S.*], *s. a servant* H³ 52ᵃ.7.

sebalapē [*S.* sev-], *v. t. to serve, to attend to* (ch-hm, *seldom* ch-hm-yāke) V¹ 41ᵃ.5; *to pay homage to*… V² 69ᵃ.4, *to make love* H² 39ᵃ.5, *to enjoy, to partake of* P 58ᵃ.5.

sebā [*S. service, homage*], ~ yāya *to serve, to attend upon* (ch-hm-yāke, ch-hm-yā) H² 52ᵇ.6; *to pay homage to* (—·yāke, —·yāta) V¹ 115ᵇ.5; *to indulge in*… (—·yā) C¹ 259. — ~ dhāya *to pay homage* (—·yāke) B 69ᵇ.4.

se-bu, *s. leather* N 41ᵇ.5*.

seyaku, *adj. shrivelled, wrinkled* AH 39ᵃ.

sel, *s. marrow* H² 21ᵃ.1, *pith* (*of a tree*) AH 27ᵃ.

selë, *v. t.* = silë¹ V¹ 117ᵃ.2.

se-sā [se¹], *s. fruits* H² 59ᵇ.6. — ~-bo-sā *id.* H³ 30ᵇ.9.

sesëṁ, ch-hm-yāke ch-g ~ taya *to commit something to one's charge* V² 50ᵃ.4; — — tāthë *id.* Bh 130ᵃ.5.

sainy [*S.*], *s. an army* Ś 155ᵃ.6. — ~-phoj *id.* H² 94ᵇ.8.

sairithi(?), *s. fuel* (samidh) N 47ᵃ.3*.

sëṁ-kul, *s. a leathern oil-bottle* (kuṭū) AH 54ᵇ (syankulu).

së-ghāli, *s.* = si-° B 4ᵃ.5 (sye-°).

sëṁjakë = sënakë; khvāl ~ N 12ᵃ.3*.

sëtu, *s. a kind of plant* (dūrvā) CW 7.36.

sënakë¹ (*caus. of* sënë¹), *to* (*suffer oneself to*) *be taught or instructed* B 47ᵃ.7.

sënakë² (*caus. of* sënë²), *to hurt, to damage* Vi 74.30; *to hinder, to obstruct* M 14ᵃ.1. khvāl ~ *to distort one's face, to change colour* N 49ᵇ.5.

sënë¹, *v. t.* 1) *to teach, to instruct* H¹ 48ᵇ.5. — 2) *to learn* (ch-hm-yāke *from*…) C¹ 121. — kha ~ *to give instructions* H³ 34ᵇ.4.

sënë², *v. i. to decay* N 30ᵇ.7, *to be damaged* Vi 73.14.

sënd = sën (*8th form of* sënë¹) N 19ᵃ.3.

sëndhu, *s.* = sedhu Vd 25ᵃ.1.

sëya (-l[1]), *v. t. to know, to understand* V[1] 41b.6, *to know, to recognize* 121b.1, *to learn, to ascertain* Bh 109b.4, *to perceive, to become aware of* H[1] 37a.1, *to accept, to recognize* N 26a.7; *to suffer, to experience* C[2] 164. biśvās ~ *to have confidence in* N 15b.4.

sëyakë (*caus. of* sëya) 1) *to instruct, to teach* H[2] 117b.1, *to tell, to communicate to* 106b.3. 2) ch-hm-yāke ~ *to ask somebody* Bh 47b.3.

së-lā, *s. the liver* CW 8.52.

sëhalapë, °he°, *v. t.* = sahalapë Bh 11a.4, *to be master of, to control* Vi 136.1, *to withstand* 150.11.

śok [*S.*], *s. sorrow, grief* V[1] 120b.2; ~ yāya *to mourn, to lament* H[1] 42a.1, ~ kaya *to grieve* M 13b.7, ~ kāya *id.* Vi 52.2.

sog [*M.*], *s. sorrow* Vd 19b.2*.

śocanā [*S. complaint, lamentation*], ~ yāya *to lament, to be sorry for* H[2] 41b.6.

socay [*S.* śocaya-], ~ yāya *to clean* P 56b.7.

sotabāt [*cf. S.* śotha], *s. a swelling, tumour* CW 8.42.

sodha [*cf. S.* svadhā *self-power —, own home*], *s. property*(?) N 23b.2; ~ yāya *to take charge of*(?) 16a.3.

śodhan [*S. purification*], ~ yāya *to purify* B 67a.8.

śodhalapë [śodhan], *v. t. to put in order* H[3] 46b.5*.

śobhā [*S.*], *s. ornament, distinction* C[1] 289, *splendour* H[2] 1b.4. ~ lāk *splendid, beautifull* Vi 167.22.

so-me *s. a fire, lit on grass* H[1] 50a.3.

soya, *v. i.* = suya[3]: simā sowo simā *a parasitical plant* CW 6.27.

soy-cā, *s. a kind of plant* (tailapāyikā) AH 35b.

solë, *v. t. and i.* = sulë V[1] 37a.6.

sohāne, *s.* = svāhāne AH 25a.

soho-gā, *s. borax* Vd 39a.1.

sohon, *s. a medicinal plant* Vd 36b.5. — *ifc.* **gwoḍ-**.

sohmaṁ, *adv. secretly* N 23a.1; ~ taya *to be silent, to keep silence* 5a.6.

sohmakaṁ [sohmaṃ], *adv.*, ~ conë *to be silent, to keep silence* H[1] 25b.4.

soh-ṅā, *s. a kind of fish* (gaḍaka) AH 20b.

swo[1], *s. a nest* H[2] 75a.6. — *ifc.* **jhaṅgal-, pi-**.

swo[2], *s. the lungs* CW 8.52 (soṁ).

swo[3], *num. three* H[1] 49b.1; ~-hma *id.* V[2] 16a.5. — ~-hma-hma *ord. third* H[3] 59a.9. — ~-guli = swo P 11b.2.

swok, ~ hṅyāya (-t), *v. t. to loosen*(?) Vi 93.6. — ~ thanë *to put into, to insert* B 34a.2. — ~ pyāya (-t) *v. t. to instil into* Vd 16a.5. — ~ luya (-t) *to pour forth*(?) Vi 131.18.

swocakë (*caus. of* swoya), *to let look on* Bh 81a.5; *to cause to select* B 6a.11; *to cause to investigate* H[3] 44b.6.

swojan [*S.* svajana], *s. a kinsman* N 14a.1.

swoṁja = swonë N 40b.1*.

swot, khaḍg ~ phyāya (-t) *to draw one's sword* B 54a.11.

swotakë = swocakë Ś 155b.6.

swo-tā, *num.* = swo[3] H[1] 24b.5.

swodhë, °dhi, *s. a kind of sour gruel* (kāñjika Md) Vd 34b.2.

swonë, *v. i. to live, to dwell* N 22b.7.

swoṁḍ [*cf. S.* śuṇḍā], *s. the trunk of an elephant* Bh 79a.2.

swobhā, *s.* = śobhā H[3] 43b.9.

swobhāb [*S.* svabhāva], *s. nature, character, disposition* H[1] 19a.1; swobhābanaṃ, *adv. by nature, naturally* H[2] 97a.1.

swobhāyamān [*from S.* śobhā], *adj. splendid, excellent* Vi 17.2.

swobhit [*S.* śobhita *adorned*], ~ yāya *to shine* H[1] 12b.2.

swoya (-l[1]; *but some forms also* -t: swotaṃ, swotasāṃ, swotaṅāsëṃ, *and always caus.*), *v. t. to look at, to view,* *to regard* H^1 86^b.5, *to witness* B 25^b.1, *to observe, to notice* V^1 17^b.4, *to look for, to investigate* H^1 54^b.3, *to look for, to select* V^1 67^a.2; *to look out* Vi 148.25; *to visit* V^2 52^a.2; *to regard as* C^1 87; *to stand, to submit to* Vi 168.27; *to have (sexual) intercourse with* N 35^a.4.

swolo-hon, *adv. slowly* Vd 5^b.5.

swost [*S.* svastha], *adj. healthy* V^1 88^b.3; ~ juya *to recover one's health* Vd 33^a.3.

stan [*S.*], *s. the breast of a woman* V^1 68^b.5.

stu, *adv.* = tu^4 N 38^a.4.

stuti [*S. praise*], ch-hm-yāke ~ yāya *to praise, to glorify…* Bh 175^a.1.

strī [*S.*], *s. a woman, wife* H^1 28^a.5; ch-hm-wo ~ puruṣ yāya *to marry someone* Vi 132.26. — ~-jan *women* V^1 134^a.4.

sthal [*S.*], *s. dry land* H^2 88^a.8.

sthān [*S.*], *s. a place, abode* V^1 55^b.6.

sthāpanā [*S.* sthāpana *s. causing to stand*], ~ yāya *to place* Vi 177.10.

sthāpit [*cf. S.* sthāpaka], *s. the erector of an image* Vi 44.9.

sthābar [*S.*], *s. immovables* N 23^b.9.

sthir [*S.*], *adj. safe, lasting* Vi 55.8; indriy ~ yāya *to restrain one's senses* 16.7; citt ~ yācakë *to make up one's mind* Bh 95^b.4. — sthiran taya *to make secure* Vi 94.16; ~ conë *to be fixed, to be immovable* Ś 153^b.1.

sthiralapë [sthir], *v. t. to cause security* N 23^a.8.

snān [*S. bath*], ~ yāya *to bathe* H^1 18^a.5; ~ yācakë *to let bathe* Vi 24.20; ~ yākë *id.* 26.18.

sneh(e) [*S.* sneha *love*], *s. a love-affair* Ś 149^b.5. *adj. beloved* Vi 57.17. — ~ yāya *to form a friendship* H^1 50^a.4, *to love, to be in love* (ch-hm-wo *with…*) Ś 153^a.6; ch-hm-yāke ~ yāya *to make love to…* V^1 17^a.5.

spaṣṭ [*S. clear, evident*], ~ jwoṃ-gwo *attested (by witnesses)* N 6^a.8. — ~-kha *the testimony of a witness ib.*

smadhāl = sama° Ś 143^a.7.

smabhāgan = sama° Vd 49^b.3.

smaśān [*S.*], *s. a cemetery* V^1 19^a.2.

syāk [syāya], *s. pain, ache* Vd 9^b.5.

syākë (*caus. of* syāya), *to let kill* Vi 42.15.

syākwo [syāya], *s. ache, pain* Vd 15^b.6.

syāca = syāya N 49^b.3.

syacakë (*caus. of* syāya), *to let kill* V^2 25^b.4; *to inflict pain* H^3 1^b.7.

syātakë (*caus. of* syāya), *to let kill* Vi 53.7.

syāya (-t), *v. t.* 1) *to kill, to slay* H^1 86^a.4; *to extinguish (fire)* V^2 75^b.2. — 2) *to hurt, to ache, to pain* H^3 50^a.8.

syuwo = siyuwo, *3rd form of* $siya^3$ M 12^b.7.

śla[1], *num.* = sat: jim-cyā ~ *1800* Ś 157^a.1.

sra[2] = sal^2 Vd 19^a.6.

śraddhā [*S. a wish, desire*]; ~ yāya *to desire; to be willing* H^2 11^b.2.

śrāp [*S.* śāpa *curse*], ~ biya *to curse* B 63^a.8. — ~-bacan *a curse* Bh 10^a.1.

śrīkhaṇḍ [*S.*], *s. sandal-wood* Ś 152^a.6.

śreṣṭi [*S.* śreṣṭhin], *s. a guildmaster* Vi 144.9.

śreṣṭi [*S.* śreṣṭha], *adj. most excellent* H^2 35^b.6. ~ yāya *to raise, to exalt* B 64^b.7.

śreṣṭhi [*cf. S.* sṛṣṭi *creation*], ~ yāya *to create* H^1 5^b.5*.

ślok [*S.*], *s. a verse* H^1 11^b.3.

śroti [*cf. S.* śrotriya], *s. a brahman versed in the Veda* H^1 56^a.1.

svakāry [*S.*], *s. one's own business or duty* H^2 110^b.3.

svat, *num.* = sat M 4^a.8*.

svapn [*S.*], *s. a dream* Ś 161^b.1; ch-hm-yāta svapn(as) biya *to communicate something to somebody through a dream* V^1 97^b.5.

svar^{1}, *s.* = sal^{1} H^{2} 76^{a}.5. — svar-të *v. t.* = sal-të N 50^{a}.1.

sval^{2}, ~ tiya *v. t. to bind* H^{1} 45^{b}.2.

svarg [*S.*], *s. heaven* B 29^{b}.3.

svasur [*S.* śvaśura], *s. a father-in-law* P 60^{b}.4. — śvasuriṇī [*cf. S.* śvaśrū] *s. a mother-in-law* N 34^{b}.3.

svāwol, *s. a weapon* (śastra) C^{1} 114*.

svāṁ, *s. mod.* = svân B 16^{b}.7.

svākë (*caus. of* svāya) = *simpl.* V^{1} 58^{a}.4.

svācakë (*caus. of* svāya), *see* **tihiṁ**.

svād, *s.* = sabāḍ H^{2} 40^{a}.7*.

svān, *s. a flower, blossom* H^{1} 7^{b}.5. — ~-wā *a rain of flowers* B 70^{a}.9. — ~-thokā *a cluster of flowers* CW 6.11. — ~-thvākā *id.* AH 27^{a}. — ~-dhul *the pollen of flowers* CW 6.12. — ~-na *the smell of flowers* Ś 162^{a}.5. — ~-pāsar *a bunch of flowers* Vi 70.20. — ~-bo *flowers* (*syn. comp.*) N 21^{a}.3. — ~-mā *a flowering plant* M 32^{a}.5; ~-mā-bo *a field fit for rice* (śālyudbhava) AH 53^{b}. — ~-māl(ā) *a wreath or garland of flowers* Bh 162^{a}.7. — ~-ras *the nectar of flowers* AH 27^{b}. — *ifc.* **ajil-**, **aswoy-**, **kaleho-**, **kuyi-**, **kule-**, **koyil-**, **khāco-**, **ghiwo-**, **cawo-**, **cawol-**, **campak-**, **cupwo-**, **chupiri-**, **jithi-**, **jilī-**, **tuk-**, **tel-**, **tvāk-**, **dugu-**, **dudhal-**, **dhali-**, **dhāli-**, **dhuk-**, **dhau-**, **dhwok-**, **palë-**, **mari-**, **lugajuli-**, **lugati-**, **sithi-**, **hari-**.

svāmi [*S.* svāmin], *s. a lord, master* M 20^{a}.6, *a husband* V^{1} 65^{a}.4.

svāya (-t), *v. t. to fix, to attach* B 38^{a}.11.

svāyakë (*caus. of* svāya), *see* **tihiṁ**.

svārth [*S. one's own affair, own property*], ch-g thawota ~ yāya *to appropriate, to make one's own* H^{2} 60^{b}.4.

śvās [*S. respiration*], ~ taya *to sigh* H^{8} 77^{b}.1.

svāhāne, *s. a stair-case, stairs* Ś 152^{a}.2.

h.

ha = he^{1} Bh 50^{b}.3.

haṁs [*S.*], *s. a gander, swan* H^{2} 80^{a}.4. hāku ~ *a sort of goose* (dhārtarāṣṭra) AH 35^{b}.

haṁsapār, *s. a medicinal plant* Vd 32^{b}.9.

haṁhaṁnaṁ, *adv.*: ~ jhāsukāl taya *to sob vehemently* B 48^{a}.11*.

hak, ~ biya *to shout, to cry* H^{2} 66^{b}.5*.

hakanaṁ, *adv. again, further* B 10^{b}.3.

hakapāl, ~ biya *to challenge, to defy* Bh 62^{a}.3. — haku° *id.* 3^{a}.4.

hakë^{1} (*caus. of* haya) = *simpl.* B 4^{a}.8.

hakë^{2}, *v. t.* = hatakë B 33^{b}.3.

hak-jili, *s. Asa fœtida* Vd 3^{a}.1.

hacakë, *v. t.* = hatakë H^{1} 37^{b}.3.

hajurī [*H.* ḥujrah *a cell, closet, from Arab.*], *s. a room, closet* Ś 149^{b}.1.

hat^{1} [*S.* haṭṭa], *s. a shop, market* V^{1} 20^{b}.1. — *ifc.* **cab-**.

hat^{2} = hathī B 53^{b}.1.

hatakë, *v. t. to say, to speak* H^{3} 33^{b}.1, *to shout, to cry* Vi 158.19; hatakāwo choya *to send word* B 13^{b}.3; hatakal choya *id.* 33^{a}.11.

hatāl, *s. a war, battle* B 36^{a}.7; ~ kaya *to wage war* (ch-hm-yāke *upon*...) 58^{a}.10; ~ phaya *to be superior in war* 13^{a}.11; ~ hṅyāya *to go to war* Bh 159^{b}.4.

hatās [*S.* hatāśa *whose hopes are destroyed, desperate*], *s. fear, apprehension* Ś 166^{a}.1. hatāsanaṃ *suddenly, in a hurry* Bh 84^{a}.1; hatā ~ *in a great hurry* M 20^{b}.2. — ~ cāya *to be agitated, to be alarmed* H^{3} 49^{b}.10; *to be eager, to be impatient* M 20^{a}.8.

hati, *cl-w.* kha cha ~ *a word* Ś 151^{a}.6.

hatyā [*S.*], *s. murder* V^{1} 85^{a}.2; ~ biya *to charge with murder* Bh 108^{a}.6.

hatyār [*cf. Mr. weapon*], ~ jwoṅ *a warrior* AH 51ᵃ.

hatyāhār, *s.* = hatyār H² 88ᵇ.2.

hathī, *adj. obstinate*(?) Ś 155ᵃ.1; ~ yāya *to insist on* B 11ᵃ.2 (haṭh).

hathyā, *s.* = hatyā B 58ᵃ.50.

haḍibihaḍi [*M.* haṛabaṛī *confusion*], ~·n *from carelessness* N 14ᵇ.4*.

han¹, *s. a carpenter's chisel* AH 61ᵇ.

han², ~ tenë *to think, to believe (erroneously)* N 17ᵇ.8.

hanaṁ, *adv.* = hanwoṃ V² 35ᵇ.1; ~ ma-khu *id.* Vi 64.7. athabā ~ *moreover* 134.28. — hanakaṃ = hanaṃ B 5ᵇ.3; hanakanaṃ *id.* Ns 36ᵇ.2.

hanalapë [*S.* han-], *v. t. to hurt, to injure* N 10ᵇ.6, *to slay* Bh 83ᵇ.4.

hani, *s. evening* Vi 44.24; ~ bahani *id.* B 40ᵃ.8.

hanë, *v. t. to carry, to wear* C¹ 151; kāl ~ *to pass, to spend the time* H¹ 11ᵃ.2. — hanë *forms periphrastic verbal forms without any marked change of meaning:* bo dasëṃ hanasāṃ = bo datasāṃ *even if it be extinguished* H² 39ᵃ.2.

hanwoṁ, *adv. again, further* H¹ 80ᵇ.3; meba ~ *another* Ś 163ᵇ.4. — hanwokaṃ *id.* Bh 34ᵃ.2.

hanyā-pu, *adj.*, ~-hma hmyāca *a favorite daughter* B 66ᵃ.1.

hanyā svān, *s. a wreath* CW 8.89.

haya (-l¹), *v. t. to bring* Bh 133ᵇ.4; *to fetch* B 54ᵇ.10; *to carry along* V¹ 59ᵃ.2. — hasëṃ biya *to leave (as one's share)* N 52ᵃ.4. — *In connection with other verbs (mostly in the 9th or 10th form or the conv. in* ·āwo) haya *denotes mainly a motion in general or toward the subject:* chosëṃ haya *to send along or out* H¹ 87ᵃ.1; sal-taṃ ~ *to call hither* V¹ 95ᵇ.1. — cosëṃ haya *to commit to writing* C¹ 270; śāsti yāṅāwo ~ *to inflict punishment upon* Vi 147.28.

hayaṁ, *s. a gander, swan* (haṃsa) AH 35ᵃ.

hayakë, *caus. of* haya V¹ 38ᵇ.6.

hayi, *s. a centipede* AH 34ᵇ.

hal¹, *s. a leaf (of a plant)* M 5ᵃ.7. — *ifc.* **cetak-**, **palë-**, **siṁ-**.

har² [*S. adj.* (*ifc.*) *bearing, bringing*], ch-g-yāta ~ yāya *to contribute to...* M 10ᵃ.4.

hal³, *s. Terminalia Chebula* AH 29ᵃ.

haraḍi [*M.* haradi], *s. turmeric* Vd 34ᵇ.4. — *ifc.* **kaṁci-**, **be-**, **mā-**, **mi-**.

haraṇ [*S. s. taking away*], ~ yāya *to take away, to carry away, to remove, to abduct* H² 88ᵃ.8. ~ juya *to be taken away* Vi 36.11.

halalapë [*S.* har- *to take (away)*], *v. t. to carry away* V¹ 75ᵃ.3, *to transport, to enrapture* Bh 47ᵇ.7.

hali (*s. spit?*), ṅā ~ tiyā *a fish put on a spit* N 45ᵇ.7*.

haritāl [*Tirh.*], *s. yellow arsenic, orpiment* Vd 32ᵃ.2.

hariṇ [*S.*], *s. a gazelle* V¹ 118ᵇ.3. — hariṇī [*S.*], *s. a female gazelle ib.* 1.

halu, *s. turmeric* Md 14ᵇ.1.

hal-than, *s. Zizyphos Jujuba* CW 6.13.

harṣ [*S. joy*], ~ yāya *to be glad* H² 90ᵃ.8.

harṣamān [*S. being glad, rejoicing*], ~ yāya *to be glad, to rejoice* V¹ 15ᵃ.2. ~·anaṃ *adv. joyfully* B 6ᵃ.8.

has [*S. laughter*], ~ kāya *to mock* H² 66ᵇ.6.

hast [*S.*], *s. a hand* H¹ 15ᵃ.3.

hasti [*S.* hastin], *s. an elephant* H¹ 19ᵃ.4. — hastinī [*S.*], *s. a female elephant* V¹ 117ᵇ.4.

hā¹, *s. a root* Vi 58.28. — *ifc.* **atili-**, **ateli-**, **abir-**, **abhil-**, **uphal-**, **usal-**, **uśra-**, **kaṁthagirī-**, **kutal-**, **kokhato-**, **cit-**, **cetak-**, **dugu-svān-**, **palë-**, **badiyār-**, **be-**, **byāl-**, **bhāgi-**.

hā² = ha, he¹: won dhāyā ~ ma siya *not know what to say* V¹ 95ᵇ.5.

hāk, ~ tinë *to throw away* H² 42ᵇ.10; ~ tiṅāwo (*or* tiṅaṃ) choya *id.* 40ᵇ.5;

~ tiṅāwo biya *to throw to* B 54ª.10. — hākā = hāk V¹ 10ª.6.

hākanaṁ, *adv.* = hakanaṃ Pg 2ᵇ.8.

hāku¹, *adj. black* P 12ᵇ.5. — ~ kwolot *a plant* (jhiṇṭī) CW 6.23. ~ jhwol *the apple of the eye* Ns 13ª.4. ~ jili *Asa foetida* Vd 32ᵇ.3.

hāku² = hāk H² 105ᵇ.2.

hāko, *adv. into the bargain, to boot* N 51ª.7.

hācakë (*caus. of* hāya¹), *to send word, to give notice* H¹ 84ª.3.

hāchi-tu, *s. a kind of plant* (chikkikā) Md 18ᵇ.2.

hā-che-kār, *s. catarrh* Vd 1ᵇ.5.

hā-jalapë = hā-jwolapë Bh 23ª.4.

hāji [*cf. Mr.* hājimā *a tumultuous jostling or thronging*], ~-hājiṃ sanë *to shake* (*violently*) B 59ᵇ.9*.

hā-jwolapë [hā = hāt; jwolapë = jojalapë?], lā-hāt ~ *to clasp the hands* M 17ᵇ.4.

hāt, *s.* = hāth V² 27ª.4.

hātakë [= hācakë], *to cause to play* (*a musical instrument*) Ś 169ᵇ.2.

hā-tapaṁ, *adv. completely* ("*with the root*") C¹ 241.

hāth [*M.*], *s. a hand* V¹ 41ᵇ.1.

hān, *s. a herd, flock; only ifc.* **sa-**, **sā-**.

hānaṁ, *adv.* = hanaṃ P 61ª.5.

hānë, *v. t.* = hanë V² 68ª.4.

hān-tapaṁ, *adv.* = hā-° H³ 36ª.8.

hān-thaṁ, *adv. completely* ("*with the root*") C² 117. — hān-tha-pu *id.* M 34ᵇ.4.

hāpu, *s. porridge* (odana) AH 55ᵇ.

hābu-svān-siṁ, *s. Butea frondosa* Md 38ª.2.

hāmal¹, *s. Sesamum* Vd 49ᵇ.3. — ~-cekan *the oil of S°* 29ᵇ.4. — ~-bo *a field grown with S°* AH 53ᵇ (hámabo).

hāmal² [*H.* ḥāmil *from Arab.*?], ~ taya *to carry*(?) H² 11ª.2.

hāya¹ (-t), *v. t. to say* (ch-hm *to*...) V² 64ᵇ.5; *to invite, to challenge* H¹ 62ª.1; *to call:* saṃsār hāṅā *called Samsāra* 70ᵇ.3. — hāṅāwo tayakë *to deliver, to hand over* (sam-arpaya-) H¹ 85ᵇ.2. — hāk *amounting to* B 4ª.11.

hāya² (-l¹), *v. i. to flow* (*water*) Vi 98.12, *to be carried about* (*by the wind*) 116.16.

hāya³ (-l¹), *v. i. to fall off or out* (*teeth, nail, hair*) H¹ 16ª.3.

hāya⁴, *v. i.* = hoya H¹ 67ª.3*.

hāyakë, *caus. of* hāya² M 20ª.1; mikhān khobi ~ *to shed tears* 20ª.1. suya-ni ku dhu ~ *to make* (*it*) *thirty two cubits long* B 4ª.3.

hār¹ [*S. adj. bearing, carrying*], ~ juya *to be taken away* M 15ª.3.

hāl-² [*H.* hāṛ *a skeleton*], — ~ kaṅkāl *bones, a skeleton* H² 104ᵇ.3. — ~-kanth *id.* H³ 56ª.5. — ~-kwos *id.* 30ᵇ.3.

hālakë, *caus. of* hālë Bh 24ª.6.

hāre- [*S.* hāra *a string of pearls*], ~-māl *a rosary* Vi 160.15.

hālë (hāwo Vi 61.27), *v. i. to call* (*out*), *to shout* H¹ 48ᵇ.2, *to cry, to scream* Bh 11ᵇ.6; *to buzz, to hum* H² 32ᵇ.7.

hāl-sal, *s. a cry* CW 1.62; *a sound* 1.61. — *ifc.* **sala-**.

hāsā, *s. a winnowing fan* AH 54.

hāsy [*S. laughter*], ~ yāya *to laugh* V¹ 23ᵇ.6.

hāhā [*S.* hā *an exclamation of pai[n] anger etc.*], ~ yāya *to shout* (*with ange[r]*) Bh 103ª.2. — hāhākār taya *to lamen[t]* H² 47ᵇ.4. — hāhātkār *cries of fear* Bh 166ᵇ.3.

hi¹, *s. blood* H¹ 45ª.1; ~ woyakë *to shed blood* B 23ª.1. — *ifc.* **māsik-**.

hi², *ipr. of* haya V¹ 43ª.1. — hiwo *id.* B 31ᵇ.10.

hi³, ch-g ~ thanë *to live on*... Vi 134.1*.

hi-⁴ (-n *or* -t?, *only:* hinaṃ, hiṅāwo *and ipr.* hiwo(!)), *v. i. to be fastened* (ch-g-s *to*...) H¹ 74ª.5.

hik = hāk Bh 62ᵃ.6.

hiku, *s. hickup* Vd 8ᵃ.5.

hi-khi, *s. bloody faeces* Vd 48ᵇ.5.

higuli, *s.* = heguli Md 34ᵃ.5.

hiṅ, *Asa foetida* Vd 11ᵇ.5.

hicu, mikhā ~ *a disease of the eye* Vd 1ᵇ.2.

hit [*S. good*], *adj. good* H¹ 25ᵃ.1. *s. a friend* H³ 39ᵃ.4. — ~-guli *adj. good, advantageous* 36ᵇ.3. — ~ yāya *to do good* H¹ 24ᵇ.5; thawoke hitan hlāya *to speak according to one's interest* H¹ 46ᵇ.2.

hiti, *s. a channel* Vi 98.15. — ~-dhāl *id.* Bh 33ᵃ.4. — ~-makar *a kind of sea-monster* H³ 96ᵇ.1. — ~-magal *id.* (makara) CW 2.7.

hitu, *forming an intens. with* hilē¹ M 27ᵇ.1.

hitu-hi, *s.*, laṃkha-~ *a whirlpool* AH 20ᵃ.

hi-dhāl, *s. streams of blood* M 14ᵃ.6.

hi-nal, *s. a blood-vessel* CW 8.52.

hi-nuli, *s. blood* M 12ᵇ.7.

hindu [*H.* hindū], *s. a Hindu* Ś 147ᵇ.5.

hi-pul, *s. bile* Vd 48ᵃ.3.

hi-phuti, *s. a drop of blood* H³ 33ᵃ.6.

hi-bāl, *s. a jet of blood* Vi 33ᵇ.4.

hiya¹ (-l¹) [= hilē¹?], *v. t. to churn* C¹ 290.

hiya² (-t), *see* **la.**

hil [hilē²], *ifc.* **til-**.

hilakē¹ (*caus. of* **hilē¹**), *to make revolve* B 53ᵃ.5.

hilakē², *caus. of* hiya¹ C² 290ᵃ.

hilā-bolā, *s. a barter, change* (id maya) AH 56ᵇ.

hilē¹, *v. t. to change* B 17ᵃ.9, *to exchange* 66ᵇ.12, *to barter* V 6.32; deśāntar ~ *to roam about from land to land* 94.28; mol ~ *to wring one's neck* Ś 143ᵇ.5. — *v. i. to revolve (wheel)* C¹ 147, *to change* H² 78ᵇ.4.

hilē², *v. t. to equip, to adorn* V¹ 3ᵃ.8*.

hihi, ~ lanē *to sob*(?) M 20ᵃ.7; ~ lanakē *caus.* Vi 43.18*.

hu¹, *s. cause, reason* V¹ 69ᵇ.4; ch-g-yā hun *owing to…, for the reason of…* V¹ 119ᵃ.4; thwo hun *therefore* V² 35ᵃ.6.

hu² [= huni], *go!* H² 51ᵇ.1; *forming imperatives* B 67ᵃ.11.

huwo = hune Vi 44.27.

huṁ = hune M 21ᵇ.1.

huṁ-huṁ, *pr. indef. some, the one or the other* B 49ᵃ.12. — ~-kan *adv. somewhere* 26ᵇ.5.

hukam [*M. from Arab.* ḥukm], *s. an order, command* B 21ᵃ.8.

hūti [*S. calling, invocation*], *cl-w.* (*for* kha, bacan ..) Vi 21.10.

huḍakalapē [*cf. Mr.* huḍakaṇeṃ], *v. t. to search* N 42ᵃ.1*.

hun = hune V¹ 21ᵃ.6.

huni¹, *s.* = hu¹: thateyā hunin *for this reason, owing to this* V² 48ᵃ.3.

huni² = hune V² 28ᵃ.3.

hunununaṁ, *adv.*, ~ khwoya *to weep violently* B 14ᵃ.2.

hune, *ipr. go!* B 11ᵇ.6 (huni). — *forming imperatives:* ka-hune *tell!* H¹ 57ᵇ.4, bisē-huni *run away!* B 53ᵇ.3, ñen-huni (*come to*) *hear!* 14ᵇ.2, swowo-hūṃ *look!* M 25ᵇ.5, jwoṅāwo-huni *take!* 9ᵃ.5. — con hune *I shall come to sit* Vi 45.1.

hunē [hu¹], thate-hunē *for this reason, owing to this* V² 45ᵃ.2*.

huṁtā, *s. a kind of bird* B 65ᵃ.9*.

hundāl [*M.* huṁṛār], *s. a wolf* CW 7.3.

hundhā, *s.* = hundāl Bh 168ᵇ.5*.

huya¹ (-l¹), *v. i., only:* pyākhun ~ *to dance* H³ 44ᵃ.4.

huya², *v. i. to be pleasant* H² 70ᵇ.1.

huyakē (*caus. of* huya¹), *to wipe away* (*tears*) Bh 46ᵃ.6; huyakaṃ yanē (*of a horse*) *to carry away in gallop* B 59ᵇ.1.

huyo = hune Vi 68.4.

huḷi, s., *only ifc.* **la-, laṁkha-, lā-**.

hṛday [S.], s. *the heart* H¹ 84ª.5.

he¹, wo yāya ~ ma siya *not know what to do* V² 21ᵇ.1; aṇ woṇë ~ ma siya *not know where to go* B 20ª.6.

he² [S.], *a vocative particle* H² 74ª.4.

he³, *impr. of* haya H¹ 90ª.1.

he-guli¹, s. *a good advice* H² 68ª.5 (= hit-guḷi H³ 36ᵇ.3).

heguli² [= heguli³?], *adj. red, fierce*(?) M 21ª.6*.

heguli³ [S. hiṅgura], s. *vermilion* Vd 33ª.1*

heṁ-gvāl, s. = hë-° H¹ 62ª.3.

heti [*for* su-heti], s. *a friend* H¹ 46ᵇ.2. *adj. friendly-minded, loving* H³ 7ª.3, ~-hına *id.* C¹ 169. — ~-pane s. *friendship* H³ 37ᵇ.10 = ~-pune H² 70ª.4.

hetik, s. = heti H³ 6ᵇ.7*.

hetu [S. *cause*], s. 1) *cause, reason* H¹ 80ᵇ.2; ch-g-yā hetun *owing to*… 19ª.2, yāyayā hetus *in order to make* H³ 49ᵇ.8; chatā hetu juro *something is going on* B 48ª.6. — 2) *a wonder* Vi 17.23, *curiosity* 64.31; ~ juwo-guli *wonderful, amazing* 124.32; hetu cāya *to become curious, to be astonished* 85.24.

heḍ, kanthu ~ ~ miniwo *a kind of fever* (kaṇṭhakubja) Vd 6ª.3*.

hedalapë, v. t. *to fasten* B 68ᵇ.6*.

hen = he¹ Vi 92.34.

henakë, v. *see* **kwo**.

heyakë, v. t. *to deride, to mock, to trick* V¹ 82ª.2.

heyu, *adj. feverish* Vd 8ᵇ.3; heyawo *becoming feverish* 16ᵇ.4; heyayu *becomes feverish* 19ᵇ.4.

hel¹ [S. hira], s. *a jewel, precious stone* H¹ 38ᵇ.1. — ~-l¹ āni *the finding-place of jewels* B 55ª.10.

hel², s. = hal¹ V² 45ᵇ.4*.

hel³ [M. her *to look*], *adv.*, ch-g ~('an) *as for*…, *regarding*… N 8ᵇ.5.

helakë [= hilakë¹], *to cause to turn (back)* Ś 166ª.2*.

heladhāl, s. *yellow orpiment* (haritālaka) Vd 30ª.3.

helā [S.], s. *carelessness* N 22ª.5. ~ yāya *to act carelessly* V² 48ª.3; *trs.: to ill-use* M 29ª.5.

helë, v. i. *and* t. = hilë¹ H¹ 76ᵇ.3.

hes(?), ~ yāya *to treat with disrespect* H² 47ᵇ.7*.

hë-gvāl, s. *coal* N 26ᵇ.4.

hënë, v. t. *to make a present of, to present* N 48ª.1, 40ᵇ.1*.

hotu, *see* **holë**.

honakë (*caus. of* honë), v. t. *to unite, to let join* N 38ᵇ.8; ch-hm-wo nāp ~ *id.* Vi 108.18.

honë, v. i. *to unite, to be put together* H¹ 52ª.1; *to be married* N 33ª.2; ch-hm-wo ~ *to join*… 35ª.3.

hoya (-l¹), v. i. *to bud, to bloom* V¹ 9ª.3.

hoyakë, *caus. of* hoya Ś 162ª.4.

holë, v. t. *to strew* H¹ 13ª.5, *to spread* M 38ª.4, *to sprinkle, to splash* Bh 9ᵇ.4. hotu ~ *intens.* N 45ᵇ.1.

holo [*onomat.*], s. *a crash, crack*: cāya *to crash* Bh 62ª.2.

hwone, °**ni** = hune Vi 88.23.

hwoya (-l¹), v. i. *to pour down (rain)* Bh 9ª.6, *to flow (blood)* 163ᵇ.2*.